Travellers in Eighteenth Century Europe

The Sexes Abroad

Edited by Julie Peakman

PEN & SWORD
HISTORY

First published in Great Britain in 2024 by
Pen & Sword History
An imprint of Pen & Sword Books Limited
Yorkshire – Philadelphia

ISBN 978 1 39904 960 3

A CIP catalogue record for this book is available from the British Library

Typeset by Mac Style
Printed in the UK by CPI Group (UK) Ltd, Croydon, CR0 4YY.

FSC www.fsc.org MIX Paper | Supporting responsible forestry FSC® C013604

Pen & Sword Books Limited incorporates the imprints of After the Battle, Atlas, Archaeology, Aviation, Discovery, Family History, Fiction, History, Maritime, Military, Military Classics, Politics, Select, Transport, True Crime, Air World, Frontline Publishing, Leo Cooper, Remember When, Seaforth Publishing, The Praetorian Press, Wharncliffe Local History, Wharncliffe Transport, Wharncliffe True Crime and White Owl.

For a complete list of Pen & Sword titles please contact

PEN & SWORD BOOKS LIMITED
47 Church Street, Barnsley, South Yorkshire, S70 2AS, England
E-mail: enquiries@pen-and-sword.co.uk
Website: www.pen-and-sword.co.uk
or
PEN AND SWORD BOOKS
1950 Lawrence Rd, Havertown, PA 19083, USA
E-mail: uspen-and-sword@casematepublishers.com
Website: www.penandswordbooks.com

Contents

Acknowledgements

This book is dedicated to Mona and Peter Scheuermann as without them this book would never have been written. I came into contact with Peter after his wife, Mona, had died leaving her book unfinished. He had contacted the Women's Studies Group to see if there was anyone who might take a look at it and perhaps use any of her material. Having always had a fear of dying before my near-completed book had been sent to the publishers, I agreed to have a look at it and see if I could help. Unfortunately, Mona was still in the middle of her book and it was not a project that I felt I could take on – it was still too unfinished and her ideas did not always mesh with mine. I thought I might be able to salvage some chapters, and sorted out getting together other scholars to contribute chapters to a book on eighteenth-century travellers. However, without Mona's permission to finish, change and edit her own chapters, it was impossible to rewrite them, but I still had all these new, completely different chapters from eager scholars. So I began to pull together the idea for a different sort of travel book (the catalyst having been Mona's idea on looking at positive aspects of travellers writing about foreign countries), instead looking at gendered difference of travellers' experiences (but keeping the positive angle). Thank you Mona (in spirit) and Peter for being there for the start of this book.

I want to thank the Wellcome Collection and to Wiki Commons Media for making their images freely available. I am grateful to Lester Crook for asking me to edit the book for Pen & Sword, and taking it on. Other publishers I contacted were a bit sniffy about looking at travel from the historical perspective – they wanted the slant to be purely from the English literature angle, which I did not want to do. This book could not have been completed without all the lovely contributors (see below) who made this book what it is, many of them also from the Women's Studies Group, and I appreciate all their hard work. As usual, I could not have done without the support from my very own constant travel companion this last 40 years, with thanks, love and gratitude to Jad Adams, a real trooper.

Contributors

EDITOR: Julie Peakman is a historian and author with research interests in eighteenth-century culture and history of sexuality. She is Fellow of the Royal Historical Society and Honorary Fellow at Birkbeck College, University of London. She is a frequent contributor to journals, magazines and television documentaries including BBC, Channel 4, Sky and the Biography Channel. Her books include *Libertine London. Sex in the Eighteenth-Century Metropolis* (2024); *Licentious Worlds. Sex & Exploitation in Global Empires* (2019); *Amatory Pleasures, Exploration in Eighteenth-Century Sexual Culture* (2016); *The Pleasure's All Mine. A History of Perverse Sex* (2013); *Lascivious Bodies: A Sexual History of the Eighteenth Century* (2004); and *Mighty Lewd Books: The Development of Pornography in Eighteenth-Century England* (2003). She has also edited six Volumes of *A Cultural History of Sexuality* (2011); *Sexual Perversions 1670-1890* (2009); and eight Volumes of *Whores Biographies, 1700-1825* (2006-7). She is also biographer of *Peg Plunkett, Memoirs of a Whore* (2014) and *Emma Hamilton* (2005).

Miriam Al Jamil's research interests centre on eighteenth-century art history, classical sculpture and travel writing. She is Fine Arts editor for BSECS 'Criticks' online reviews, chairs the Burney Society UK, and is active on other committees including the Women's Studies Group, 1558-1837. She contributes reviews, essays and talks to academic journals and online platforms. She has a chapter in *Antiquity and Enlightenment Culture* (Brill, 2020), and a chapter in *Pockets, Pouches and Secret Drawers* (Brill, 2023).

Valentina Aparicio is a Lecturer in Romanticism at Queen Mary University of London. Her research explores Romantic British, Latin American and Caribbean literary exchanges through the lens of decolonial and critical whiteness studies. Her current research focuses on Scottish women travellers who visited South America, analysing their friendships with local women. She is also currently working towards the publication of her first monograph on Robert Southey's Latin American and Caribbean Works. Her work has recently been published in *European Romantic Review* and *Essays in Romanticism.*

Maria Grazia Dongu is an Associate Professor of English Literature at the University of Cagliari. She published extensively on Thomas Gray's works, devoting an entire book to his travels through France and Italy. Her main research interests are life writing and the relationship between history and literature. She has recently co-edited a collection of essays on Intertextuality (*Intertextuality: Intermixing Genres, Languages and Texts*, FrancoAngeli, 2021).

Louise Duckling is an independent scholar working on eighteenth-century women writers and their posthumous reputations. She has published articles on Joanna Baillie, Charlotte Smith, Helen Maria Williams, and female biographies in the Victorian era. As a member of the Women's Studies Group, 1558–1837, she has co-edited two essay collections: *Woman to Woman: Female Negotiations in the Long Eighteenth Century* (University of Delaware Press, 2010) and *Exploring the Lives of Women: 1558–1837* (Pen & Sword, 2018).

Sophie Dunn is a postdoctoral researcher with a focus on travel, social identity and mobility in the long eighteenth century. She obtained her PhD in History from the University of St Andrews, and she was an ESRC postdoctoral fellow at the University of Liverpool. She has published a study on servants' newspaper adverts, analysing servants' willingness to travel in their employment.

Emily Paterson-Morgan is an independent scholar and the Director of The Byron Society. In addition, she is on the editorial boards of *The Byron Journal* and the *Gender and Culture in the Romantic Era* series for Anthem Press. She is currently researching Byron's engagement with adultery discourses in English print culture. In her professional life, she is Chief Academic Officer for Knowledge E and Director and Co-Founder of the Forum for Open Research in MENA. She also sits on the Executive Committee of the British Association for Romantic Studies (BARS).

Teresa Rączka-Jeziorska is associate professor at the Unit for Romantic Literature of the Institute of Literary Research of the Polish Academy of Sciences. She is a researcher of Romantic literature, the Eastern borderland of the former Polish-Lithuanian Commonwealth and Polish-Baltic cultural associations. She is the author of monographs on '*Know the waters of thoughts through the waves'. On Romantic Representations of River in the Works of Adam Mickiewicz and Taras Shevchenko* (2011), *Polish-Livonian Romanticism. Persons, Texts, Archives* (2016), *The National Specificity of Various Social Groups' Descriptions. On the example of the language of Irina Saburova's novel "Ships of the Old City"* (2017) and *Livonian Pictures. Landowner's Manor Culture in Old Polish Livonia of the 19th Century*

(2018). She is co-author of *Atlas of Polish Romanticism. World-Europe-Poland* (2015) and *Unknown Autograph of Adam Mickiewicz. Two Pages of Pan Tadeusz Invocation* (2018).

Eleanor Reynolds recently completed her PhD, entitled *Incorruptible: the Female Body and the Wax Anatomical Models at La Specola*, with Cardiff Metropolitan University. She writes historical novels featuring female protagonists with a passion for science and seeks to normalise the presence of women in scientific fields of study by celebrating their contributions to different branches of knowledge. Eleanor is also part of the Bloody Women duo which examines femininity in slasher films.

Brianna E. Robertson-Kirkland is a Lecturer in Historical Musicology at The Royal Conservatoire of Scotland and was the Lead Research Associate for the AHRC-funded project 'The Edited Collection of Allan Ramsay' at the University of Glasgow. She has been a Visiting Fellow at Chawton House (2017) and the University of Sydney (2017 & 2019) with her most recent visit culminating in several practice-based, collaborative performances between Scotland's *Concerto Caledonia* and Melbourne's *Evergreen Ensemble*. Her research has fed into the historically led album *Curious Caledonians* (2020). Recent publications include *Venanzio Rauzzini and the Birth of a New Style in English Singing Scandalous Lessons* (2022) and *Allan Ramsay's The Tea Table Miscellany* co-edited with Professor Murray Pittock and published with Edinburgh University Press in 2023.

Shirley F. Tung is an Associate Professor of English Literature at Kansas State University, specializing in the literature and culture of the Restoration and long eighteenth century. Her research, which spans the genres of criminal biography, epic and occasional poetry, periodicals and print media, and travel writing, has been published in *The Age of Johnson*, *Eighteenth-Century Studies*, *European Romantic Review*, *Huntington Library Quarterly*, *Journal for Eighteenth-Century Studies*, *Restoration: Studies in Literary Culture, 1600–1700*, and *SEL Studies in English Literature, 1500–1900*. Tung was awarded the 2020–2021 Innovative Course Design prize by the American Society for Eighteenth-Century Studies; and was the recipient of the 2022 Bodleian-BSECS (British Society Eighteenth-Century Studies) Visiting Fellowship, a 2023 Clark Short-Term Fellowship at the UCLA William Andrews Clark Memorial Library, and a 2023 New York Public Library Short-Term Research Fellowship.

Mina Tsai-Yeh Wang received her PhD in history at the University of Birmingham, UK and is currently an associate professor at the Department of History, Fu-Jen Catholic University, Taipei, Taiwan. She has been working on British political thought and political culture during the French Revolution, and modern British women and gender history. Her publications including journal articles in Chinese, such as 'British Debate on the Liberty of the Press during the French Revolution,' 'Moral Reflections on the French Revolution: A Study of Wollstonecraft's Political Thinking,' 'The Establishment of Modern Citizenship during the French Revolution and the Identity Problem of British Radical Expatriates in France,' and articles in English, including 'Pushing Boundaries: Hannah More's Interpretation and Transformation of the Social Roles of Women (forthcoming),' 'Women in Trading: Gender, Public Space and Political Representation in the Late Eighteenth Century,' 'British Female Radical Travellers and the Revolution Controversy, 1789-1815'.

Jo Willet was a television drama producer for many years. She won a BAFTA, a Royal Television Society Award and an International Emmy. Her first biography, *The Pioneering Life of Mary Wortley Montagu*, was published in March 2021. She is currently on her second, on the life of the actress Sarah Siddons.

Picture Research by Julie Peakman.

List of Illustrations

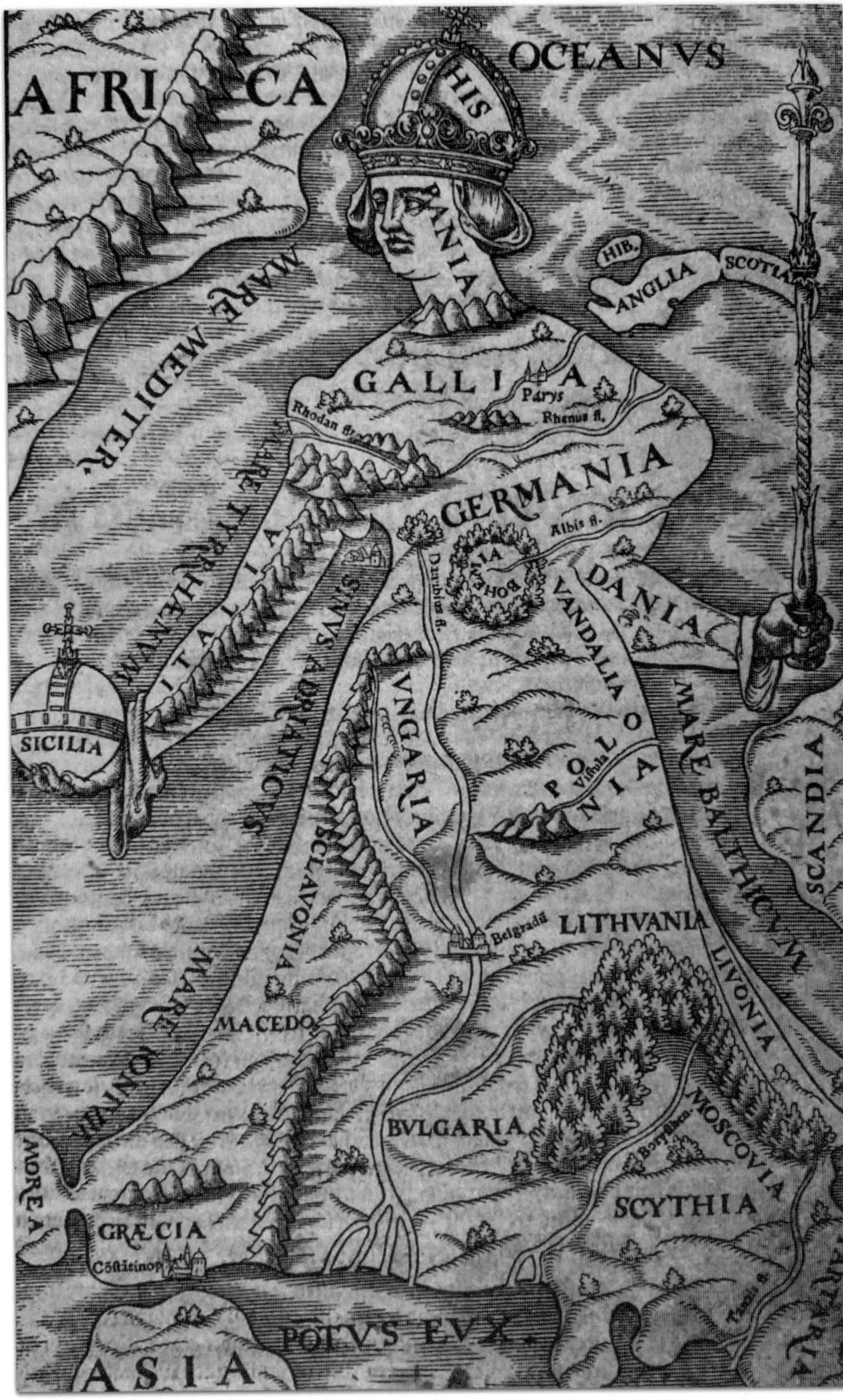

Sebastian Munster's Europa Regina.

Introduction

Julie Peakman

Travellers in Eighteenth-Century Europe is about the observations and reflections of men and women on what they saw when abroad. When I talk about the eighteenth century, I am referring to what historians call the *long* eighteenth century, which is taken roughly as around 1688-1830, beginning with the changes brought by the Glorious Revolution, and ending with the end of the Georgian period and the death of King George IV. The countries covered include some of Europe, namely France, Italy, Germany, Switzerland and Turkey – the latter, though not technically Europe nowadays, was part of the Ottoman Empire which included Greece, Albania, Bulgaria, Romania and was sometimes visited as part of the Grand Tour.

The world of travel was one in which men and women often had distinctly different travel experiences. These adventures were not only undertaken in a different manner (for example, men on the Grand Tour often travelled with a companion, women alone or with family or friends), but they often focused on different subject matter. Even when observing similar things, say viewing the same ruined site or sets of people, their perceptions would be different. More importantly, the subjects and objects each of them thought most worthy of their observation were often quite different; what was important to women was not always the same to that which was important to men. Gender is therefore crucial when reading men and women's travelogues, journals or letters. We can see what was important, what they found gripping, and what was disregarded.

We need to keep in mind not just the differences which become apparent in gender, but also in class. The aristocrat would more than likely have quite a different travel venture from a middle-class youth, since they had access to royalty and nobles in other countries and often had different aims and might be travelling for different reasons (as a diplomat or ambassador). Also pertinent in these considerations is our need to take into account to whom the letters were written or who the journals were aimed at - some letters such as Byron's to his friends and publisher in England were obviously written with the aim of boasting about his conquests and regaling his friends back home. Others, such as Lady Mary Wortley Montagu's letters, were written for her friends and family, possibly with the intention for publication, but definitely not in her lifetime. The intended recipient obviously affects the way of writing, and how travellers described what they saw and the kinds of things they saw. This invariably had an impact on domestic culture.[1]

Previous scholars writing about eighteenth-century travellers' books have examined travel writing from the perspective of English literature, examining language styles, such as the fact that writers used hyperbole, pretension or untruths.[2] In other words, travellers had the chance to construct their own particular personal narrative, which was often overblown and exaggerated or using a conventional style (a style which the poet Thomas Gray mocks in his Mock Guidebook examined in Chapter 3). Some have suggested that travellers often examined the sights before them as 'other' or foreign, placing themselves in opposition to the foreigner aligning themselves in the 'correct' normal version of life, as part of the British Empire. In this framework, nationalism was part of distancing the traveller from the exoticism of a place, or setting themselves apart from the locals. Travel writing played a role in the consolidation of British patriotism and, to a large extent, helped to influence the shape of Britain's sense of national identity.[3] 'Foreign' was classed as inferior while the familiar (read British) was seen as superior. When this happened, what surfaced was the apparent contempt in the traveller's voice on his/her observations,[4] what has been called a 'stoutly Anglocentric' attitude and 'patriotic chauvinism.'[5] Though this became a convention, this was not always so, as we will see in some of the observations made by travellers examined in this book. Obviously, there was no one type of travelogue or letter-sender and each added their own styles, interest, ideas, opinions and interpretations. Many of the men and women under examination here were happy to try and assimilate and often in praise of the countries they were visiting and the people they met.

Though the language of the actual travelogues is covered in part in this book, it is mainly focused on seeing the travellers from a historical perspective – what they felt and did, how they saw their experiences. These experiences, as we will show here, were not limited to description of travel and specific sights to be seen (tourism as a concept did not develop until the end of the century, and tours only really started with Thomas Cook's first tour in 1841), but also influenced singing, art and an understanding of history itself. As they stood in what they saw as times past, they used their imagination to understand how these buildings or artefacts impacted on people's lives, and how the processes of using things had evolved and why.

The Grand Tour was considered a part of every young gentleman's education, with visits to Italy via France, Switzerland, and Greece, often taking in Turkey, being on most itineraries. But female travellers were also taking extended trips abroad, having to be more intrepid in a man's world. Distinctions between how they discerned their experiences of other countries is important to our understanding of what they found positive or not; and how their interpretations of other countries influenced them. While the Grand Tour and the male traveller have been at the heart of many studies of the eighteenth century it is only relatively recently that female scholars (both from the English Literature and the History fields) have been uncovering female travellers and their stories. It is being recognised that the men who travelled on these trips were not necessarily all aristocratic men finishing their education; and that many women were also travelling and need to be included in an understanding of eighteenth-century travellers.

The early popular guides and travel reports were usually written by men. Antiquarians made close-up observations and took detailed drawings, taking these as empirical evidence – this is how collecting was going to assist them in bringing evidence home to Britain, a sort of embodied experience of the social and physical environment. But it was felt by men that women could not be trusted to define the landscape they saw as they were tied to the domestic sphere. Unlike their male counterparts, how could they be objective in their observations when they lacked the analytical skills? For a real understanding of the native culture, one had to have a mind capable of grasping the complexities of the natural world. However, as we see here, there was an understanding and fascination by women for subjects often overlooked by men, which made their contribution important in our understanding of eighteenth-century Europe and its people.

As a background, the book begins with an examination of the **Dilettanti** and the effects other countries had on these men, their recording of ruins and their collections of foreign objects. The subsequent chapters cover letters and/or journals of mainly British travellers: servant John MacDonald and James Boswell, both Scottish but from different classes; British poets Thomas Gray and Lord Byron, travelling with very different agendas and with very different effects; and Polish-Lithuanian Michał Jan Borch, who influenced German poet Goethe. Elite ladies such as Lady Mary Wortley Montagu and Lady Blessington are investigated to see what inspired them and how they assimilated (or not) the culture they were in. Artist Harriet Parry is examined to show different methods of recording her travels; writers Maria Graham and Mary Wollstonecraft to show the effects of the French Revolution on travelling; and British singers in Italy to show the effect of Italian operatic styles. The influences of Europe and the Orient seeped into the travellers' consciousness and most of them were keen to write down their feelings and experience; others to stay aloof and simply state what was in front of them.

Lady Mary Wortley Montagu sets the pace as one of the most well-known women to have had her account of her travels published (posthumously) and to give an insight into the real world of the women of Turkey. Mostly she is recognised as the person to bring back smallpox inoculation to England from Turkey, for although male travellers had heard of the process, none of them were brave enough to recommend or implement it. Montagu's understanding of women's position and all things Turkish was inevitably tied up with her own social, economic and political background, yet her writings about the Ottoman Empire would disrupt other writers' notions of orientalism which were circulating at the time. Most evident was Montagu's desire to appear to assimilate (as many male writers did not), but not *too* much (to keep in with 'Britishness' of the readers of her letters back home). To this extent her existence was a balance between being friendly to the local elite and gaining knowledge through social contact, while still retaining her Britishness. This can be seen in Lady Wortley Montagu's sociable attitude towards the women in the Hammam in Sofia, though she was acutely aware of the status of the women here and noted the difference between the elite women and their female slaves. She draws a thin line between being a spectator and a spectacle when undoing her riding habits at the Turkish baths for the women to inspect her stays. Whether her letters can be deemed titillating or even erotic has been debated; but Lady Charlotte Bury wrote in her journal 'they are deemed so naughty…one must keep up one's reputation for modesty and try to blush whenever they are mentioned'. [6]

Scholars of **Thomas Gray** have examined the possibility of his homosexuality. As early as 20 years ago, scholars were examining Gray's relationships with the companion on his Grand Tour and his friend from college Richard West through his letters and poetry. As has been pointed out by English scholar Raymond Bentman, Gray writes to Walpole romantic letters, full of expressions of endearment. Gray calls Walpole 'half of my soul'. He writes, 'I was in agonies for you'; 'I hope for a place in your heart'.[7] Bentman examines the poems which he sent to West suggesting Gray had difficulty with women and that in these suggestive lines, Gray is referring to classical men who loved other men. He focuses on the love he had for West, which had to be kept covert. The social and sexual climate at the time, one of persecution of homosexuals, would have made any sexual connection between these friends impossible without serious repercussions. But it was perhaps Gray's natural melancholy nature which also coloured his feelings about the sights he saw while travelling abroad. It cannot have been easy relying on his more exuberant friend's money either. But wealth was not necessarily needed in order to travel abroad; some men managed to travel with their work. **John MacDonald** was one of the few servants who managed to make a decent life for himself as he travelled abroad looking after his masters - and we are fortunate enough that he left us his memoirs. His account shows a very different life for the working man abroad, in a job where language skills and the ability to become quicky assimilated and knowledgeable about local manners and customs were an aid to employment. Being able to learn the local language wherever he had landed with his master allowed him to ensure he can supply his master's wishes, and gain esteem among his employers. He relates how many of the other servants preferred to indulge themselves drinking and whoring to the detriment of their careers.

James Boswell wrote extensively about his travels. His writings on Corsica highlight his ideas on its political situation and his notion of masculine ideals. These are given space in his portrayal of Filippo Antonio Pasquale de' Paoli, considered a 'General of the People' in the Corsican nationalist movement that rebelled against rule by the Republic of Genoa. Boswell gives his reader a great deal of precise information about the physical attributes of the island of Corsica itself as well as the history (back into the mists of antiquity) of its people and its politics. *The Journal of a Tour to That Island* is essentially a compilation of information that Boswell accumulates as he wanders around the island taking in new experiences and meeting various classes of people. Boswell's emphasis is on history, but the history of Corsica is not complete, nor even to be understood, without the physical realities of the island. In the *Journal*, Boswell is a chronicler of what he presents as an exotic new world in the island. Such a 'scientific' study, specifically the perspective of travel as science, is absolutely representative of Boswell's time.

For some of the travellers, science, travel and history overlapped. We only have to look at the Dilettanti to see how collecting and science had become wrapped up in elite men's careers and desires to better themselves. When Goethe first went to Italy and Sicily, he saw himself as a sort of anthropologist and general scientist and repeatedly refers to his work as 'scientific' in his *Italian Journey*. He saw his explorations of people in the same way he sees his explorations of flora and fauna, of geology and weather patterns. Such attitudes were taken up by **Michał Jan Borch**, whose extensive collections were admired by scientists. The chapter on Michał Jan Borch shows how such travellers could become obsessive in collecting objects and analysing them, classifying and categorising them as to better understand them and bring increased knowledge of science by contributing these skills. Like the members of the Dilettanti, men often used their travels as a means to be invited to join elite academies such as the Royal Academy or the Society of Antiquaries. Travelling abroad was sometimes undertaken with the intention of helping men and women with their careers, as seen in the chapters on Borch and British opera singers, but it did not always have the intended effect. Though Borch managed to develop his skills and finds in minerology, it did not necessarily find approval in his home country - his travels and research failed to gain him the recognition he wanted from his king in Poland; though male and female opera singers went abroad to master opera, they were not always appreciated when they came back home. The careers of **Michael Kelly, Anna Selina Storace and Elizabeth Billington** are explored in the chapter on British singers in Italy. While Italian singers came to Britain to sing and offer training to British opera singers, British opera singers also went to Italy for dedicated training. Importantly, Italian conservatoires were not open to women, making the gender gap immediately obvious.

The political climate had obvious effects on travellers, most notably the French Revolution. For the twenty-eight-year-old **Helen Maria Williams**, as she arrived in France in 1790 having already made a name for herself as a poet and novelist, she intended to witness and record the events of the revolution first-hand. By 1794 with the onset of the Great Terror, she was fleeing for her life. Though much has been made of her language in the many volumes of letters she published,[8] what really needs to be emphasised is her courage for having gone there alone in the first place in such turbulent times. This chapter shows how Williams used landscape metaphors to describe political situations but, more importantly, reveals Williams's mettle in the face of adversity. Rather than examine her time in France during the revolution, the chapter focuses on her reflections afterwards on her time in Switzerland. This must have been a difficult time for Williams as she saw her political ideals squashed in the face of the massacres that she had seen. Her support of the revolution (not uncritical) had become more ambivalent given her witnessing of all the violence, but her commitment to liberty held fast, her core remaining sympathetic to the disadvantaged and the poor. **Mary Wollstonecraft** is also known for her involvement in the French Revolution, her feminist polemic *Vindication of the Rights of Woman* (1792), and her attack on the exclusion of women in the Paine's *Rights of Man* was hailed by the French Revolutionaries. She situated herself in a similar spot to Williams in that she was middle-class and against an aristocracy that they both recognised as corrupt and exploitative. The two women knew each other in France as Williams hosted Wollstonecraft at her salons. Like Williams, Wollstonecraft was in favour of social justice and driven by the inequalities she saw. But it is her journey in Scandinavia that is analysed here, with her *Letters during a Short Residence in Sweden Norway and Denmark* offering deep personal exposés as well as her political revisions after the violence of France. Within all this, she was having to use her writing skills to remain financially independent and make a living to keep herself and her young daughter.

How women engaged with the lives of other women and the understanding of their labour was recognised by **Maria Graham** in her three months in the mountains of Rome. This chapter shows Graham exposing just how important female work was in the economics of both the family unit and the production process of the silk industry in rural Italy, thereby making an important contribution to women's labour history. Male travellers were less receptive to 'seeing' local foreign women in the same terms that a female traveller would. Graham's description sees the workers and their environs as stuck in the past, but recognises the women's work as making an essential contribution to the labour force. The chapter on **Harriet Parry** describes how she invented her own way of capturing her trip abroad, making a unique record using her own style of domestic art written and drawn in a scroll.

For some men, once in Italy things seem to become more sensuous and sexual. **Lord Byron**'s letters to his friends back home provide an entertaining account of the situation he found himself in Italy. No longer travelling so much, he had settled in Venice for a while and was obliged to follow the customs of *cicisbeism*, having to become the companion of a series of married women, not simply have sex with them – not Byron's usual style at all. Such wildly erotic accounts were rarely expressed in other men's accounts of their experiences abroad and not only make for lively reading, but provide an insight into the life of a *cicisbeiro*. Byron at once sets a racy amusing tone with the intent of making his readers laugh about his riotous sexual encounters with the ladies of Venice. While other writers may have commented on the custom, Byron was actually engaged in it full throttle. He managed to create a persona which was both wild and fey, a cultivated 'look' for his listening audience. **Lady Blessington** was only too eager to visit him while on her travels. Though she enjoyed her chats with Byron, and her visit to La Specula in Florence to see the naked wax models, she felt she had to modify her gaze in front of her male companions.

* * *

The effects travel had on men compared with women are profound. Men could more easily put their learning to better use in their careers, their advancement and knowledge was shared with various academies and societies. These (all-male) scientific societies disseminated their findings; women were not allowed to be part of these communities and rarely had access to spreading their findings further than their immediate family and friends. Many men published more broadly, women tended to share their adventures more closely to home, though some of them published their letters and journals. Men also had greater freedom when they travelled, being less vulnerable than women. They usually had more say in where they went and for how long they stayed abroad. Men openly desired local women they encountered though some, like Byron and Boswell, were decidedly too interested (Borch tried to restrain himself to mere observation). As we shall see, some women too took advantage of their relatively less restrained position compared to back home.

Dress is significant to these travellers, particularly in their attempts to define themselves as assimilating the culture. Lady Mary, as the ambassador's wife and more generally as an aristocrat, would have had most to lose in terms of reputation if she were seen to do something outrageous, yet clearly finds it not odd at all to be painted, more than once, in Turkish dress. Dashwood dressed in a Turkish outfit as a founder member of the Divan club and had other members painted in Turkish dress. Boswell, who came to be known as 'Corsica Boswell', wore his Corsican outfit often, always in the attempt to draw support for the Corsican cause that meant so much to him; and Byron had his portrait painted in Albanian dress.

This book will explore a group of travellers who were part of a group of curious and open-minded people willing to appreciate the culture of other countries, though they often compared things to 'back home'. In many cases, there was positivity on the part of the travellers' expectations and an overall cultural appreciation of the foreign places and peoples they encountered. While many other scholars have found the negative attitudes of travellers to be a prominent feature, in this book we can find travellers who often found the positive side to foreign countries; their curiosity piqued, they went out of their way to investigate things of interest and to make efforts to expose their opinions. This is a period in which generally cultural exploration was a joyous and reciprocal adventure (though difficult times for Gray and Wollstonecraft particularly); it was a period in which Western 'neighbours' explored each other's nature and customs as well as the 'Orient', and found their experiences important enough to them to leave for the record.

Chapter 1

Lascivious Travelling: Sex, Religion and Antiquarians in the Eighteenth Century

Julie Peakman

Women of Europe were often the subject of curiosity for both women and men travellers from Britain as we will see in chapters in this book. Indeed, in travelogues and map-making, there was a method of interpreting whole countries as incorporated as a female body. For example, Sebastian Munster's painting of *Europa Regina* in *Cosmographia* personified Europe as a woman. This perception was even taken up in erotic books such as *A New Description of Merryland* (1741) and *Merryland Display'd* (1741), showing how men had defined countries in terms of the female body:[1]

> Near the Fort is the Metropolis, called CLTRS [clitoris]; it is a pleasant Place, much delighted in by the Queens of MERRYLAND, and is their chief Palace, or rather *Pleasure Seat*; it was at first but small, but the Pleasure some of the Queens have found in it, has occasion'd their extending its Bounds considerably.[2]

Seeing continents or countries as feminine was nothing new, though in the eighteenth century, real women were very often more at the forefront of a young man's mind when he travelled abroad. Part of the experience (or at least his intentions) on his Grand Tour was sewing his wild oats, but often those abroad leaned into their opportunities a tad too much: Tales about Frances Calvert, the sixth Lord Baltimore, and his collection of women circulated through various gossip channels so much so that on his death in Naples in 1771, one wit declared he had left behind, 'a whole *seraglio* of white, black etc to provide for'.[3] A sexual ideal of the lascivious East circulated in Britain, with tales of scandalous harems and the sexualised Turkish women contained within. These were buttressed by translation of oriental erotica emerging in the West such as *One Thousand and One Nights* (later known as *Arabian Nights*) and more home-grown erotica based on Eastern themes such as *The Lustful Turk* (1828).

Those more intelligent travellers would have gleaned some information on the Turkish erotica available in the Ottoman Empire going back centuries which would, at some point, have influenced views about the East. As one scholar has pointed out, 'The Kitāb alflaylah wa laylah (*Book of the Thousand and One Nights*) was twice translated into Ottoman during the seventeenth century, and the translation by Musli b. Mehmed Beyânî (dated 1046/1636) contains significantly more erotic material than the Arabic original. The autograph manuscript of this translation....was taken to France by Antoine Galland (d. 1715), and probably provided the origin of some of the more sexually explicit stories in a number of western translations of the Nights'.[4]

Lord Baltimore's escapades put paid to the idea of Oriental eroticism as merely a flight of fancy emerging from the wild imagination of the traveller or erotic books. Notions of sexual intrigues in the harem were present in letters and journals and were the substance of pornographic books; in fact, Baltimore was living the dream: as one letter described, 'He lived a long time at Constantinople and wore the dress of the Country, kept his Seraglio of the finest Women and in short enjoyed the existence of a Turk.'[5] Baltimore fits the bill for many aristocratic travellers. Educated at Eton, he learnt Latin and Greek and came into a vast fortune after his father died in 1751, including inheriting shares in the Bank of England and succeeded him as Proprietary Governor of the Province of Maryland, a prosperous colony in America. Rumours circulated about his living in his own seraglio in Turkey. James Boswell, a known philanderer, had visions of following in Baltimore's footsteps – and he evidently did as, according to his own record, he went on to have countless sexual encounters with women abroad. While in Venice, Boswell told a friend, 'When I got to Venice I had still some small remains of disease [venereal disease], but strange gay ideas which I had formed of the Venetian Courtesans turned my head, and away I went to an Opera-Dancer, and took Lord Mounstuart with me. We both had her; and we both found ourselves taken in for the punishment which I had met with at Rome'.[6] He did not learn from Baltimore's experience but had obviously heard gossip about Baltimore's adventures in Constantinople as he wrote about him: 'He lived luxuriously and inflamed his blood, then he became melancholy and timorous, and was constantly taking medicines ... he is there leading a strange, wild, life, useless to his country, except when raised to a delirium, and must soon destroy his constitution.' People became further aware of Baltimore's position with the publication of *Memoirs of the Seraglio of the Bashaw of Merryland by a Discarded Sultana* (1768), the alleged memoirs of one of the women he kept in this seraglio. Apparently, he had envisioned continuing a similar arrangement back home and creating his own harem there.[7] He had hired a bawd to procure young girls, to bring them to his house and have sex with them, but the law caught up with him. He was arrested and went to trial for the abduction and rape of Sarah Woodcock in 1768; the book no doubt came out in response to the trial. While he was acquitted (as so many of these monied rapists were), the ensuing scandal provoked him to leave England. He died in Naples at the age of forty after years of ill health, most likely sexually diseased.[8] But Baltimore was by no means the first, nor would he be the last, to connect sexual licence and travel.

Groups of men who were defined by their love of sex and travel, and with their passion for antiquities, came together in somewhat lubricious societies. Sir Francis Dashwood and his friends had formed the Dilettanti club in 1732 and the Divan club in 1744 for friends who had travelled to Italy and Turkey respectively. The societies funded trips abroad to measure and draw ruined temples and buildings in order to map out parts of the ancient world but they also involved women of questionable reputation. Fanny Murray who became a famous courtesan was a member of the Divan club, at least Dashwood had her portrait painted dressed in Turkish costume, which hung alongside other similar paintings of the other Divan club members at his home in West Wycombe.[9]

The first meeting of the Dilettanti club took place at the Bedford Head in Covent Garden, but it moved over the years several times, and around 1757 it could be found at the Star and Garter Tavern in Pall Mall. Members' more serious intentions were to record archaeological findings with a decision to sponsor James Stuart and Nicholas Revett (1751–54) to tour Greece drawing and recording archaeological ruins, which were published in *The Antiquities of Athens* (1762). In 1755, they decided to found an Academy of the Arts which should

Sir Francis Dashwood in Turkish dress by Adrien Carpentiers, c. 1740s.

Fanny Murray in Turkish dress probably by Adrien Carpentiers, c. 1740s.

have a royal charter and that 'the President of the intended Royal Academy be allways and annually chosen from the Society of the Dilettanti … and … that all the Members of the Dilettanti society be members of the said Academy.'[10] Part of this Royal Academy would teach painting, but it would also collect art and antiquities which the Dilettanti would 'procure the first and best casts of the principal Statues, Busto's, & Bas Relievo's great or small'.[11] By the 1770s the club had become one of the forerunners in advocating classical art and archaeology in England. The members of the Dilettanti were not simply amateur ethnographists, explorers and collectors but took the business of antiquities seriously. As a result of his work, Dashwood was elected as Fellow of the Royal Society in June 1746, and a Fellow of the Society of Antiquaries of London in June 1769. His first Grand Tour took him through France and Germany in 1726 for nine months, and three years later he was away for a couple of years travelling to Italy to see the excavations at Herculaneum and visiting Florence, Rome and the Ottoman Empire.

The other side to Dashwood was more unrefined. Known for his 'hell-fire club' to which he invited prostitutes and gentlemen friends down to West Wycombe, he also liked to indulge his desire for sex and was one of the first exemplars of the elite gentlemen who effectively combined sex, travel and antiquaries in eighteenth-century Britain. His Dilettanti society would become one of the most fashionable clubs for educated elite men, some members giving lectures or sending reports on their findings to the Royal Society and the Antiquaries Society. Apart from collecting and uncovering ruins and cultivating client-patron relationships, the aims of the Society of Dilettanti were whoring and heavy drinking, as Walpole pointed out, 'The nominal qualification [for membership] is having been in Italy, and the real one, being drunk.'[12] Convivial masculinity also involved maintaining rituals of his select clubs – conducting ceremonies (often anti-Catholic ones), notably blasphemous sexualised parodies of the sacraments and specifically mocking Catholic practices – all part of the amusements

Sir Francis Dashwood by George Knapton, c.. 1742.

for members. While on his Grand Tour in 1740, Dashwood was signing his letters to friends as 'St. Francis,' and in a letter to Lord Boyne, suggested he wanted 'to make a party of Monks with you into the Country, remember that I am a Franciscan.'[13] This was most probably a reference to what they had witnessed on their earlier trip. Dashwood commissioned George Knapton to paint him as a Franciscan in 1742 worshipping the pudenda of the Venus de' Medici. Dressing up as monks and taking part in mock religious ceremonies at their meetings was to become one of the features of the 'Monks of Medmenham'.

Visitors abroad fed back anecdotes about corrupt Roman Catholic practices, reinforcing anti-Catholic feeling in England. Popish practices of worshipping relics, revelling in miracles, and giving indulgences instilled indignation in travellers. Latin services were seen as a contrivance to maintain control over their following, and to retain an air of mystery over their religion. Religious flagellation was viewed with particular contempt, one tourist remarking, 'One sees such processions, such penitents, and such nonsense, as is enough it gives one ye gripes.'[14] English travellers showed their aversion to these practices through their bad behaviour, one defecating on the steps of the altar and another allowing his dog to jump on the priest during mass and eat the host. While in Italy, on his visit to the Sistine Chapel, Sir Francis Dashwood was so disgusted at the spectacle of the penitents flogging themselves that he picked up a whip and commenced to whip them himself.[15] Reports of the lax morals of the Catholic clergy was another issue for another British traveller. As far back as his travels during 1675–1679, John Locke painted a lubricious picture of Cardinal Bonzi, the archbishop of Narbonne, who he saw at mass: 'He keeps a very fine mistress in the town, which some of the papists complain of, and hath some very fine boys in his train.' Anti-Catholic attacks were part of the rhetoric of many British travellers airing their view when abroad.[16]

Enough has been written on the activities of men abroad on the Grand Tour for us to know that many of their experiences were about sexual encounters. For some men like Bryon, this was not so much a rite of passage but a method of collecting conquests. He would boast to his publisher about his daily sex outings.[17] However, women were also becoming known for travelling abroad to either find a husband, follow a lover or take up with a new paramour. Lady Wortley Montagu would pursue her lover Francesco Algarotti (who incidentally, her friend Lord Hervey was also in love with). She set off on a trip abroad in 1739 allegedly for her health, but ended up in Venice living with Algarotti. Diarist Margaret Calderwood witnessed the cavalier sexual attitudes of women abroad on her trip to Brussels in 1756: 'There is a Mrs. Pope whose husband is an officer at Gibraltar, and she in the mean time traveled for her amusement, and has found a gallant here.... Miss Townsend, who run away with an officer who has a wife, was here for some time…'[18] However, women travelling alone would always be suspected of some indiscretions or other, whether true or not, for the very fact they were unescorted. Men were rarely subject to gossip for their sexual affairs abroad, rather it was expected of them.

Many young men saw the Grand Tour not merely as an opportunity to self-educate and gain knowledge of the classics, but as a chance to encounter sexual opportunities, a testimony to this being the concerns of worried fathers expressed about their wayward sons. Italy was known for its fully fledged prostitution and its beautiful courtesans, and a young man would not be regarded as manly if he had not at least gained a few sexual encounters on his travels, but this was not necessarily an activity of which a father might approve – or indeed, be willing to pay for. For others, the purpose was collecting artefacts, some of them related to sex. Ancient Rome was known for its admiration of the phallus with phallic artefacts, sculptures or paintings of copulating couples evident everywhere. Such objects occupied not only citizen's bedrooms, but were prominent in taverns, shops, temples and brothels, all articles to become the subject of fascination by the eighteenth century traveller and collector.

Lubricious Collecting

Early on, collectors, mainly elite gentlemen, had relied on an economy of gift exchange between learned men in possession of antiquities, but this changed mid-century. As the Grand Tour becoming more popular, travellers increasingly turned to local dealers for their collecting. Dealers like Ficoroni were expert in dealing with these collectors, who vied for medals, coins, manuscripts, statues and rings. This gave way to English and Scottish residents in Rome taking over as dealers, excavators and guides. The real competition began in 1750, when a couple of English artists, Thomas Jenkins and Richard Wilson, offered themselves as antiquaries-for-hire.[19] By the mid-eighteenth century Rome had already established itself as the centre of cultural activity, a hive of museums, art exhibitions and architectural wonders.

Much of the impact had come from the discoveries of Herculaneum (1738), Pompei (1748) and Stabiae (1749). Findings of erotic objects and frescos encouraged the desires of collectors to acquire Priapic objects and paintings – statuettes, vase paintings and other items were in such demand that local artists were making copies to be sold off as originals. These new discoveries near Naples took over as matters of interest from the well-trod and well-viewed monuments of Rome. While travellers were well-versed in the descriptions of Rome, Herculaneum and Pompei offered new wonders, and fresh insights. More exciting than the usual sites of Rome was the ancient city under volcanic dust, having lain dormant for centuries waiting for eyes to turn to it. The new

Members of the Dilettanti Society by Joshua Reynolds, c. 1777. Sir William Hamilton is in the middle.

city saw a shifting demographic of visitors as the old ideas of classical antiquity of the aristocratic gentleman on his Grand Tour succumbed to amateurs and ordinary people interested in everyday ancient artefacts – such as phallic lamps, erotic graffiti, kitchen utensils and everyday household items. There was a leap of interest from the heroic world of the classics to the movements of ordinary individuals of these ancient cities, which saw an empathy with the victims and a connection with everyday life.[20] Many of the collections of these objects would end up in the Museum of Naples in a section hidden from view, 'The Secret Room', not to be viewed unless by special permission until it was briefly opened in the 1960s, only to become properly viewable in 2000. Other artefacts would end up in the British Museum. An intimacy was seen in collections from the ancient Roman domestic sphere of Pompeii as opposed to the grandeur of the City of Rome. It made the observations of a city somehow more 'personal'. This new way of looking at the past would have its effect on which antiquaries were thought interesting. Among those were phallic objects and sexualised domestic items – and one of these collectors was Sir William Hamilton.

Sir William Hamilton

Sir William Hamilton arrived in Naples on 17 November 1764[9] with the official title of Envoy Extraordinary to the Kingdom of the Two Sicilies and would remain as ambassador to the court of King Ferdinand I and Queen Maria Carolina until 1800. As ambassador, Hamilton was expected to send reports back to the Secretary of State every ten days or so to promote Britain's commercial interests in Naples and to keep open house for English travellers to Naples. Any traveller worth his or her salt would aim to stop off to visit Sir William and Emma Hamilton to inspect his collection of antiquities and to view and admire Emma's 'Attitudes'.

Hamilton's position allowed him to make a concentrated effort in collecting. Within a year he had amassed several hundred vases, a grand collection which ended up at the British Museum in 1772. But it was not just vases which caught his eye, but all sorts of other artefacts, including gems, coins, statuettes and votive offerings for fertility. Hamilton was an avid collector of everything, as one historian has pointed out, 'from the date of his arrival in 1764 to his hasty departure with Emma thirty-five years later, nothing of interest, no curiosity of nature, no artist of any talent, no archaeological find, turned up in the vicinity of Naples without passing through, and sometimes remaining in, Sir William's hands, or at least his house, the Palazzo Sessa'.[21] He was also a dealer and a vulcanologist with an interest in Mount Vesuvius, which he could see from his palace in Naples. No doubt seeing the value in his vases, he entrusted Pierre François Hugues (self-styled as 'Baron' d'Hancarville) to publish a huge, lavishly illustrated book on them entitled *Collection of Etruscan, Greek and Roman Antiquaries* (1766–7). The Baron had tried to involved Johann Joachim Winckelmann (often considered the founder of archaeology and initiator of the discipline of art history), who went to Naples in 1769 to join them but he refused the proposal (later, he would be murdered in Trieste). As a result of his work, Hamilton was elected to the Dilettanti society in 1766 and wrote about his discoveries on Mount Vesuvius to the Royal Society. He would send much of his collection to his contacts in the British Museum along with some specimens of stones and rocks from the volcano arriving back to the British Museum in 1767–8. Unfortunately, one of the ships, HMS *Colossus*, sank off the Scilly Isles in a storm in 1798, taking with it a vast collection of Hamilton's vases, but much of his collecting landed safely in Britain.

An Account of the Worship of Priapus

Hamilton's collection of votive offerings is an example of the interest the Dilettanti and other collectors had in sex and religion. The offerings were of wax models of penises specifically designed for prayers for fertility. On first discovering these votive offerings, he wrote to Joseph Banks on 17 July 1781, 'I have actually discovered the Cult of Priapus in its full vigour, as in the days of the Greeks and Romans, at Isernia in Abruzzo.'[22] Banks was also a member of the Dilettanti, the Royal Society and the Society of Antiquaries. His avid interest in natural history was to see him on the trip on the *Endeavour* with Captain Cook to record their trip to Tahiti in the 1770s.[23] Hamilton sent Banks a letter containing an account of the festival of Cosmos and Damian along with a supporting letter from the governor of Isernia. He had gone in search of the Temple of Priapus near St Cosmos's shrine, but it would not be until 1878 that a Roman inscription would be found near Isernia with clear indications of the worship of the Roman god of fertility, Priapus.

Hamilton would write about the strange religious practices he came across in Isernia in his 'An Account of the Worship of Priapus' in 1786, relating the religious practice of the Neapolitan women who wanted to become pregnant. Hamilton had encountered an engineer, Andrea Piganati, working on a new road to Isernia, who told Hamilton about the fertility festival. There was an annual fair during which the celebration took place where relics of the saints were exposed at the church dedicated to Saints Cosmos and Damian (Hamilton's spelling of the saints' names varies), the festival lasting three days over 26–28th of September. All kinds of women followed according to Hamilton, 'Spinsters, Wives, Widows and Women of pleasure', as well as religious women from the Capuchins. On sale were various 'male members made of wax in different forms, and in all sizes along with votives for other body parts such as arms, legs and faces, but fewer of them. After paying for the votives, the worshippers then had to pay the two priests sitting nearby, to offer them up for prayers. These women had had difficulty in bearing children, or were simply wanting a child, and had taken votive offerings to the church.

Since the offerings were as a cure for infertility, it was mainly women who were involved in the festival. Each woman pressed the votive to her lips as she offered it up. Hamilton believed many of the women went home pregnant thanks to the work of the priests, the women having stayed over in the church with the priests, the male worshippers kept outside in the porch. It was Cosmo's big toe which was supposed to give rise to the miracles.[24] Hamilton described the votives:

> '*ex-voti* of wax, representing the male parts of generation, of various dimensions, some even of the length of the palm, are publickly offered to sale. There are also waxen vows, that represent other parts of the body mixed with them; but of these there are few in comparison of the number of the Priapi.'[25]

He had intended to attend the event of the Feast of St. Cosmo this year in February but it had been suspended due to 'the indecency of this ceremony'.[26] Presumably it had come to increased public notice because of the new road.

These votives were sold to the female worshippers from women with large baskets of them, then taken to the altar for a blessing, the priests paid for the prayers, which mounted up to a considerable sum, thus in effect the women worshippers paying twice: once for the votives, and again for the priests' prayers. Hamilton described the scene:

> On each table is a large bason for the reception of the different offerings. The Vows are chiefly presented by the female sex; and they are seldom such as represent legs, arms, &c., but most commonly the male parts of generation. The person who was at this fete in the year 1780, and who gave me this account (the authenticity of every article of which has since been fully confirmed to me by the Governor of Isernia), told me also, that he heard a woman say, at the time she presented a Vow.[27]

A further lucrative part of the process was told to Hamilton:

> The oil of St. Cosmo is in high repute for its invigorating quality, when the loins, and parts adjacent, are anointed with it. No less than 1400 flasks of that oil were either expended at the altar in unctions, or charitably distributed, during this fête in the year 1780; and as it is usual for every one, who either makes use of the oil at the altar, or carries off a flask of it, to leave an alms for St. Cosmo, the ceremony of the oil becomes likewise a very lucrative one to the canons of the church.[28]

Hamilton went on to collect the votive medals that he had observed Neapolitan women wearing, reporting, 'I had long ago discovered, that the women and children of the lower class, at Naples, and in its neighbourhood, frequently wore, as an ornament of dress, a sort of Amulet, (which they imagine to be a preservative from the *mal occhii*, *evil eyes*, or enchantment)', evidently relating to the Cult of Priapus. And thus his quest began: 'I made a collection of both the ancient and modern Amulets

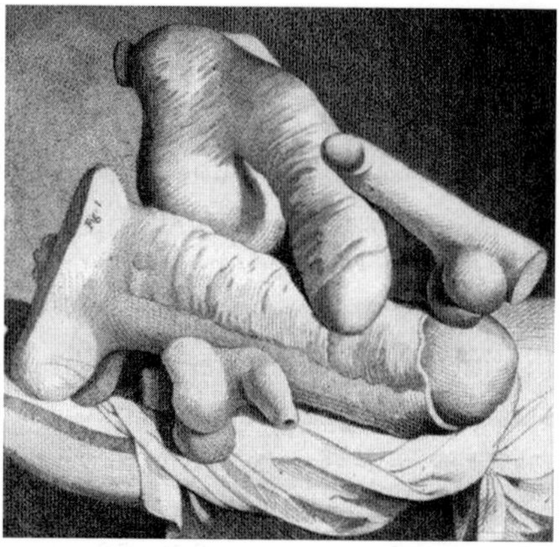

Frontispiece to *An Account of the Worship of Priapus*, 1786.

of this sort, and placed them together in the British Museum, where they remain'.[29] Too delicate to send through unattended, Hamilton took the Isernian simulacra himself and deposited them at the British Museum during his stay in London in 1783–4. In all, five cases of antiquities were handed over to P.H. Maty of the British Museum. Many of these broke and only fragments remain, kept in storage vaults hidden from public view.

Richard Payne Knight by Thomas Lawrence, 1794.

Hamilton's findings were to be explored in Richard Payne Knight's erotic book *The Worship of Priapus* (1786) with its spectacular rude etchings of Greek and Roman ruins in the guise of disembodied phalluses. The book was written for distribution to the members of the Dilettanti Society and sold for five guineas. The book was available in March 1787; 80 copies were privately printed for his fellow members of the Dilettanti Society. However, except for the most liberal-minded men of the day, many thought it too obscene to read. Thomas J Mathias wrote about the book in his *The Pursuits of Literature* (1794–7) that 'all the ordure and filth, all the antique pictures, and all the representations of the organs of generation, in their most odious and degrading protrusion, have been raked together and *copulated*…in a new species of blasphemy'.[30] He thought it a book written for sexually obsessed antiquarians, which may have had some truth in it, adding it was 'one of the most unbecoming and indecent treatises which ever disgraced the pen of man'.[31]

Knight, who would also become a member of the Dilettanti Society, published this account along with an exploration of pagan worship and other ancient religions. His intention was to explain Hamilton's account that made up the first part of the book, along with his own protracted essay on ancient religions in which he explains everything from the worship of the lingam in India to the stones of Stonehenge, taking in the religions of Egypt and the Greeks along the way. The frontispiece carries a bizarre engraving of the 'Great Toes' depicted as the phallic columns of a ruined ancient building. While Knight's essay tries to be an intellectual essay full of footnotes, it is in fact a meandering dull musing with much of the exploratory work lifted from Baron d'Hancarville's earlier writings. It sprawls into random topics and attempts to explain Hamilton's findings, when these had been more than adequately described by Hamilton himself. Knight wrote:

> The female organs of generation were revered as symbols of the generative powers of nature or matter, as the male were of the generative powers of God. They are usually represented emblematically, by the Shell, or *Concha Veneris*, which was therefore worn by devout persons of antiquity, as it still continues to be by pilgrims, and many of the common women of Italy. The union of both was expressed by the hand mentioned in Sir William Hamilton's letter.[32]

According to George Rousseau, who has examined the unpublished letters between Thomas Jenkins and Charles Townley, d'Hancarville was also a pornographer of the erotic in antiquity, publishing erotic illustrations.[33] D'Hancarville was arrested (this was either for publishing obscene material or to flee his creditors, depending on who you believe – possibly both). This may have been for his works '*Monuments of the secret cult of Roman Women*' and '*Venuses as they appear in antique gems*', probably published around 1779 but the dates are uncertain. Dutifully Hamilton, as a friend, travelled to Florence to rescue him from prison, but in 1779, d'Hancarville fled Naples. The 23 engravings of amorous poses illustrated in d'Hancarville's works appeared in 1793 entitled *L'oeuvre priapique.*

Knight had met Hamilton during his Grand Tour of 1772–73. He again set out for Naples on 12 April 1777, planning to visit Sicily, Paestum and the Lipari Islands. En route he kept a journal with the intention of noting down his observations and collecting images and quotations with a view to publishing it. Along for the journey were artist Jakob Philipp Hackert and his pupil Charles Gore, who were to make illustrations for the journal. Post-journey, Knight would also commission John Robert Cozens to add to the drawings that had been made *in situ* on the trip. Though this book was never published, it did serve the purpose of getting him elected to the Dilettanti Society in 1781. He later became a Trustee of the British Museum. While completing work on the *Discourse*, Knight began to collect ancient vases, gems, coins, and bronzes – later enlarging his collection dramatically by buying directly from Hamilton. Incidentally, Knight would also leave his own collection to the British Museum.

Emma Hamilton and Artistic Expressions

One of the attractions of visiting Naples for many travellers was to meet Emma Hamilton. Emma (formerly Lyon or Hart) had been the lover of Sir William

Hamilton's nephew, Charles Greville. Wanting to get his mistress off his hands so he could marry an heiress, the unscrupulous Greville persuaded his uncle to invite Emma to Naples on 'holiday' – or so Emma thought. Greville was quick to remind his old uncle how lucky he would be to find an obliging woman free from venereal disease: 'At your age a clean & comfortable woman is not superfluous, but I should rather purchase it than acquire it, unless in every respect a proper party offer'd'.[34] He even mentioned Emma's hygiene, confiding to Sir William, 'A cleaner, sweeter bedfellow does not exist.'[35] In essence, he was proffering Emma as a mistress. Arriving on her twenty-first birthday, she found herself to have been unceremoniously dumped. Once she realised her predicament, with nowhere else to go, she stayed with Hamilton and made the best of the situation, eventually making him proud enough of her to marry her. Emma was indeed to become a collector herself, not of items, but of poses. She had no doubt been influenced by sculptures (now in Naples Museum) found in the Villa of the Papyri, a luxury villa on the outskirts of Herculaneum (Ercolano) in 1754 and by the dancing maenads from the so-called Villa of Cicero, Pompeii, to form her 'attitudes'. William Hamilton had a lit frame made for her to perform her attitudes to best perfection. Goethe was impressed enough to give an account of their meeting and described Emma's performance in his *Italian Journey*: 'Sir William Hamilton, after many years of devotion to the arts and the study of nature, found the acme of these delights in the person of an English girl of twenty with a beautiful face and a perfect figure. He has had a Greek costume made for her which becomes her extremely. Dressed in this, she lets down her hair and, with a few shawls, gives so much variety to her poses, gestures expressions etc., that the spectator can hardly believe his eyes.'[36]

Emma frequently assimilated classical imagery for her own purposes, as did the artist who adored and painted her, including George Romney, Joshua Reynolds, Elizabeth Louise Vigée Lebrun, Angelika Kauffman and Hugh Douglas. These *tableaux*

Lady Emma Hamilton by Friedrich Rehberg and Tommaso Piroli, 1794.

vivants were figurative references to ancient finds, showing Emma's main purpose was to provide a new kind of performance, different from anything else. Various travellers captured Emma's poses in sketches of her Attitudes as she brought the ancient decorations to life. Pietro Antonio Novelli (1791), Friedrich Rehberg and Tommaso Piroli (1794) and William Artaud's *Sketchbook of Lady Hamilton's Attitudes* (1796) sketched her Attitudes, showing her use of everyday items such as shawls and vases as props.

As travellers were making drawings and paintings of Emma, others were building on their collection of sculptures and artefacts. Classifying collections was part of the occupations of artists and connoisseurs – and this connection between erotica and collecting would be prominent in the eighteenth century and continue for at least a century. It was to form part of the entertainment and hobbies of the eighteenth-century libertine gentleman collector to be reflected in a display that combined their erudition of the classics and their revelling in the rude or semi-pornographic world. An example of this influence can be seen in the work of Thomas Rowlandson, who focused on erotic paintings between about 1790 and 1810. Rowlandson made a series of cartoon paintings that mocked the connoisseurs for their interest in antiquities as seen in *The Sculptor's Shop*, (c.1785–90) and *The Connoisseurs* (1799). He portrayed the antiques dealer and sculpturer Joseph Nollekens, who had worked as a restorer and carved classical statues in Rome from 1760 or 1762, as a lecherous old pervert. The image suggests his interest in real naked women was more prevalent than his interest in sculpting nudes. Similar amusements were created by James Gillray, who made William and Emma the brunt of his jokes in *A Cognoscenti contemplating ye Beauties of ye Antique* (1801), in which he depicted Sir William leering over a bust of Emma as Lais. These works were not an attempt to meld the two aspects of erotic and nude sculptures to make it acceptable, but more likely these elements were simply within the sphere these men operated in. Rowlandson and Gillray were only too willing to mock the collectors, who would no doubt have appreciated the joke.

Chapter 2

'She set out with all the pleasure imaginable.'[1] Lady Mary Wortley Montagu's Turkish Travels

Jo Willett & Julie Peakman

Lady Mary Wortley Montagu. Stipple engraving by Caroline Watson, 1803.

Lady Mary Wortley Montagu (1689–1762) was an English aristocrat best known today for her introduction of inoculation against the smallpox to the West, for her stormy relationship with the poet Alexander Pope, and for her travel writing, specifically a collection known as *The Turkish Embassy Letters*. Montagu was brought up in England: her family were all supporters of the new Hanoverian monarchy, and involved with the Whig Party, favoured by George I. As Protestant free-thinkers, they were opposed to the Catholic Jacobite descendants of James II, who were at the time living in France and planning to re-conquer Britain. Montagu described herself as 'Whig to the teeth – Whigissima'. She eloped with the barrister and Whig Member of Parliament Edward Wortley Montagu in 1712 so as to avoid a forced marriage organised for her by her father, and the couple had one son, born in England, and one daughter, born in Turkey.

Montagu first travelled outside England when her husband accepted the post of His Majesty's Britannic Ambassador to the Turkish Ottoman Empire in 1716. The couple and their young son journeyed out overland by coach through a Europe where Turkey was at war with Venice and the Austrians had just entered the fray. Their journey took them to Turkey via Sofia, arriving in Adrianople (modern-day Edirne) in March 1717 and the family lived in Adrianople and Constantinople until July 1718, when Montagu's husband was recalled to London, travelling back first by ship and then overland through Italy and France. Montagu wrote a series of letters home throughout her time abroad and kept copies of the letters for herself for future use. Her *Turkish Embassy Letters* have been described as 'an Enlightenment travel treatise, but a relaxed and racy one,'[2] and 'the very first example of a secular work by a woman about the Muslim Orient'.[3] In fact, *Turkish Embassy Letters* is a misnomer, since more than half of the letters dealt with Montagu's travels to and from Turkey, through Christian Europe. When she returned home, Montagu was persuaded by her friend and mentor, the early feminist Mary Astell, to edit the copies of her letters into a volume describing her experiences. Her original letters and the copies she first made are not extant, but we can surmise that several of them were rewritten to improve the overall effect of reading the letters in the form of a travel narrative. Astell wrote a complimentary preface and her influence on the choice of letters is evident.

Montagu had already faced scandal when her *Town Eclogue* series of poems, co-written with Alexander Pope and John Gay, were published without the authors' permission, and so it was agreed between the two friends that the *Turkish Embassy Letters* would only be published posthumously. During Montagu's lifetime the letters were circulated amongst Montagu and Astell's friends and acquaintances, though Montagu wanted them published after her death. Horace Walpole reported that, as she lay dying, 'She expressed "great anxiety" that the two volumes of letters she had given the clergyman in Holland should be published, and her family were in terror lest they should be.'[4]

On her death Montagu's daughter and son-in-law, Lady and Lord Bute, sought to suppress publication – Montagu had always been a controversial figure and her family wanted to avoid a scandal. Despite their efforts, the letters found their way into print, appearing in the *London Chronicle* in 1763. By a lucky chance, the letters had been copied secretly and were finally published to great acclaim in May 1763. The volume instantly became a best-seller and inspired a whole vogue in Britain for all things Turkish.

Soon after the *Turkish Embassy Letters* were published, the *Monthly Review* praised them precisely because: 'There is no affectation of female delicatesse, there are no prettinesses, no ladyisms in these natural, easy familiar epistles.'[5] The reviewer praised Montagu for being atypical of her gender, and yet paradoxically it was Montagu's gender which was an important reason why the letters were seen as unusual enough to be published. They emphasised the fact that Montagu's gender allowed her access to material which other writers did not have. As Astell wrote: 'a lady has the skill to strike out a new path, and to embellish a worn-out subject, with variety of fresh and elegant entertainment.'[6] No doubt, Montagu's gender gave her an added impact compared with male travel writers, not least because she had access to secluded women in a way men did not.

While she recognised the traditional masculine qualities of rationality, accuracy and observational qualities evident in the travel writing of both Joseph Addison and of the Dilettanti Society (whose members included Horace Walpole, Joshua Reynolds and Sir Francis Dashwood), she saw how this stance was enhanced by women writers because of their gender, a fact which has made her work, as one historian said, 'a specifically gendered text which makes use of an emergent feminist discourse to resist the standard orientalist tropes about Eastern women found in many of the works of male travel writers such as Robert Withers, George Sandys, John Covel, Jean Dumont, and Aaron Hill'.[7] Indeed, Montagu saw in her own account an identification with Turkish women in a 'rhetoric of likeness' rather than a distance or dissimilarity. Throughout the letters, Montagu points out the errors of previous travel writers and claims for herself an authority based on her gender. She criticises Jean Dumont, stating that Dumont 'has writ with equal ignorance and confidence', and later adds that male authors 'never fail giving you an Account of the Women, which 'tis certain they never saw'.[8] Dumont's *A New Voyage to the Levant* (1696) reported on the Sultan's wives guarded by white and black eunuchs 'who never permit 'em to enjoy the least Shadow of liberty'[9] and declared there is 'no slavery equal to that of the Turkish Woman'.[10] His comments were countered by Montagu in her statement (below) that women never had so much freedom in England as the Turkish women. Only she, as a woman, can give a proper description of the Turkish women she describes.

Lady Mary Wortley Montagu. Stipple engraving by J. Hopwood, 1811, after Christian Frederick Zincke, 1738.

Another obvious point which has been made is that Montagu's class had an impact on her writings and her interaction with the people she met on her travels. Travelling as a diplomat's wife, she would have been treated with a certain amount of reverence according to her status. However, Anna Secor argues that, 'Montagu's letters reproduce dominant discourses which naturalize class inequality, even and especially in moments when they subvert Orientalist or gendered expectations.'[11] In this Montagu, as with other female texts, both supported and yet also undermined male-dominated language, discourses and attitudes and feminine convention. Her *Turkish Embassy Letters* are couched in a rhetoric of similarity. The upper classes of Ottoman society are presented as more similar to the British than to the lower classes, and class order in Ottoman Turkey is presented as parallel to that of eighteenth-century England. For all that has been said, her background involving her status, her intellectual circle, her position as a white elite Western woman and wife of an ambassador complicates any arguments to reduce Montagu to an eternal orientalist or a staunch feminist.

Montagu's letters differed from women's travel writing from the latter half of the century, not least because of her wit, liveliness and broad scope. Whereas most women's travel letters were small and domestic in scale and addressed to a close friend or relative, Montagu's examined the public and the political as well as addressing prominent figures. She wrote to Princess Caroline of Ansbach, a woman who had previously been offended by some of Montagu's *Town Eclogues*, praising Princess Caroline's son, Frederick Louis, by way of making amends. She rarely wrote about her personal affairs and her husband was largely absent from her narrative, as she preferred to try to take an objective standpoint, giving herself an air of authority.

Montagu's descriptions tended to be directly observational as shown in her interest in meeting new people, experiencing Turkish customs and seeing fresh landscapes, even if the process of travel itself was uncomfortable and frequently dangerous. She was alert to everything she encountered, but without outward judgement or criticism. In this, she was writing more in travelogue style, creating a narrative for an audience. She might write to her favourite sister about the Turkish costume she put on: 'The first piece of my dress is a pair of drawers, very full, that reach to my shoes and conceal the legs more modestly than your petticoats',[12] but she could also write to Pope about the experience of crossing the battlefield at Petrovardin, strewn with bodies, using a very different, more 'masculine' voice: 'I could not look without horror on such numbers of mangled human bodies, and reflect on the injustice of war, that makes murder not only necessary but meritorious.'[13]

This chapter will consider the influences of Montagu's status, education, and her opinions on what she came across in her travels. It will examine her exchange of ideas with Achmet-Beg and her Eastern experiences while considering her observational approach; and her viewpoint on the condition of the women in the Ottoman Empire.

Meeting Achmet-Beg

One of Montagu's experiences which would fundamentally shift her attitude towards the Eastern world before she arrived in Turkey, was her meeting with the Islamic writer and thinker Achmet-Beg. Along with her husband and son, she was to spend three weeks at his home after the ambassadorial party was detained at Belgrade until the Turkish official, the *bassa,* received word from Adrianople that the sultan was happy for them to continue their journey. Achmet-Beg (whose title, Montagu explained, 'is something like that of a count in Germany'),[14] she found cultured and informative; he found her charming. Her education of the East began with conversations between them; she wrote to Pope from Belgrade on 12 February 1717 that these were 'my only diversion.'[15] The two sat and ate a Turkish-style dinner of small dishes together every evening, conversing in their shared language of Italian. Much of Montagu's understanding of, and her thoughts on, the culture she was about to enter can be traced back to this time spent with Achmet-Beg. Her letters made no mention of her husband or son at the meals, but concentrated on her relationship and conversations with her host, whom she told Pope 'has been educated in the most polite Eastern learning, being perfectly skilled in the Arabic and Persian languages, and is an extraordinary scribe.'[16] These skills might have paved the way for 'the greatest preferments,'[17] but Achmet-Beg had wisely chosen a quieter life, enjoying poetry and drinking wine, despite his Islamic faith. According to him, Mohammed's edict on alcohol only applied to the common people, not those who knew how to drink in moderation.

One subject the two discussed in depth was religion. The Protestant Anglican Montagu explained to Achmet-Beg about the difference between the Church of England and Roman Catholicism, both agreeing on the folly of such Catholic practices as idolatry and trans-substantiation. Her anti-Catholicism remained firmly in place, reflecting the substance of the entire Hanoverian monarchy back in England which derived its authority from the fact it was not Catholic. She wrote to her friend, ex-priest Abbé Conti, that the two creeds of Islam and Christianity were remarkably similar and joked that the two English preachers they both knew, Dr Samuel Clarke and William Whiston, could probably convert the people in Belgrade to their views. Conti had already discussed religion with Montagu when they first became friends in London in 1715 after he himself realised that he could not continue to take confession as a Catholic priest, since he no longer believed in the concept of the Trinity; thereafter, he styled himself Abbé not Padré to signify his distance from the established church. The two became friends when Deist preachers, with their more generalized view on Christianity, were beginning to interest Montagu. She explained to Conti that Islam is broken into Muslim sects, much as Christianity is broken up into 'Catholic, Lutheran, Calvinist, etc.', adding, drily, that these sects 'are equally zealous against one another' as were their Christian equivalents.[18]

As someone who questioned Christianity in a culture where religion was part of the Establishment, but where religiosity was not seen as terribly important, Montagu could find much to agree with in what Achmet-Beg told her. Now she heard about the different Islamic sects, she recognised that there was a 'natural inclination of mankind to make mysteries and novelties,'[19] just as she had seen in churches in the West. Achmet-Beg was demystifying Islam for her and she approved of the fact that the Muslims were not, according to Achmet-Beg, really very religious at all – they were more like her Deist friends. She also noted that 'this is kept from the people, who are amused with a thousand different notions according to their preachers.'[20] Through their discussions, Montagu was convinced by her host that the Koran was an extremely powerful treatise, pointing out in her letter to Conti that the male travel writer Rycaut's conclusion that Turks were atheists had been mistaken. Achmet-Beg, she wrote, had told her the Koran, 'is so far from the nonsense we charge it with, 'tis the purest morality delivered in the very best language.'[21] Montagu did not go so far as to say that Islam was the source of Enlightenment, but she endorsed Achmet-Beg's beliefs as being of equal value to her own. Any misunderstanding of the purity of the Koran's message back in Britain she attributed to a failure in translation from copies obtained from Greek priests. The Koran was to be respected just as much as the Bible.

The two also discussed at length another of Montagu's favorite topics, 'the confinement of women,' and had frequent disputes about the subject.[22] Montagu was much taken with Achmet-Beg's joke that, when it came to the bad press over the way Muslim women were confined, 'there is nothing at all in it; only, says he, we have the advantage that when our wives cheat us, nobody knows it.'[23] Yet Montagu conveyed a somewhat blinkered view of women's position in Turkey, at least in her letters. She expressed a belief that women segregated in a harem had greater freedom than women had in the West. She would expand on this theme as she travelled further East, her eyes supposedly having been opened by Achmet-Beg to some of the advantages of this different way of doing things.

For Montagu, the chance to converse in depth with a Muslim man on the twin subjects of religion and the condition of women proved an invaluable one and helped her prepare herself for what she would encounter once she reached Turkey itself. It was a turning point from relative ignorance to a much greater understanding of her shifting worlds.

Montagu's Bath House Visit

Lady Mary Wortley Montagu in Turkish Dress. Lithograph by Villain after A. Devéria after C. F. Zincke.

Soon after staying with Achmet-Beg, and probably inspired by his discussion of Turkish baths or *hammams,* Montagu decided to visit one for herself in the city of Sophia. Her description of her trip, which she undertook alone, is one of the best-known anecdotes from the *Turkish Embassy Letters* and has received the most critical attention, ever since it was first read. She regarded Sophia itself as 'one of the most beautifull Towns in the Turkish Empire and famous for its Hot Baths that are resorted to both for diversion and health'.[24] She had also read accounts of George Sandys, who began his travels in the Ottoman empire in 1610 and whose work Montagu cites in her letters.[25] He viewed the *hammams* as the site of homoeroticism between women, declaring, 'Much unnaturall and filthy lust is said to be committed daily in the remote closets of these darksome Bannias,' continuing, 'yea, women with women; a thing incredible, if former times had not given thereunto both detection and punishment'.[26]

According to Montagu, the baths were luxurious with five domes attached to each other. There were no windows except in the roof, but the skylights gave plenty of light. The rooms which housed the actual baths were paved with marble, and around each room were two sets of raised marble 'sofas'. The ladies of aristocratic rank sat on the first row of sofas and cushions, while their slaves sat behind them, doing their mistresses' hair. Montagu emphasized the democratic nature of the arrangement, thanks in part to the nakedness of the women. All the women were 'without any distinction of rank by their dress, all being in the state of nature, that is in plain English, stark naked, without any beauty or defect concealed.'[27] However, somewhat contradictorily, as an aristocratic woman herself she noted the difference between the two groups: 'The first sofas were covered in cushions and rich carpets, on which sat the ladies, and on the second their slaves behind them'. None of the women bore any signs of the smallpox scarring which had disfigured Montagu herself and most Western women at the time, 'most of their skins shiningly white.'[28]

Montagu was inappropriately dressed in her riding habit at the time, but the women seemed unfazed by either her dress or the fact there was a stranger in their midst. The women were restrained, with perfectly good manners, who made no sign of anything untoward:

> [I must have] certainly appeared very extraordinary to them, yet there was not one of 'em that showed the least surprise or impertinent curiosity but received me with all the obliging civility possible. I know no European court where the ladies would have behaved themselves in so polite a manner to a stranger.[29]

There must have been two hundred women there, 'and yet none of those distainfull smiles or satyric whispers that never fail in our assemblys when anybody appears that is not dress'd exactly in fashion.'

Montagu deliberately drew on western cultural references to describe her reaction to the women so as best to align her British readers with her and to negate any suggestion of lewdness. First, she mentioned Milton's *Paradise Lost* and the bathers as having 'the same majestic grace which Milton describes of our general mother',[30] referring to Eve of the Old Testament. Such Christian references afforded the Muslim women bathers respect, without any guilt or shame applied to their nakedness. This was a deliberate ploy on Montagu's part to avoid any suggestions of obscenity connected to female nudity and provide levity to the scene. Additionally, she compared the bathers favourably to 'any goddess…drawn by the pencil of Guido or Titian',[31] thereby raising the tone of her assessment to the level of the aesthetics of the Italian Renaissance, so familiar to all the male participants in the Grand Tour at the time. As a female travel writer, Montagu stood outside the prevalent, male aesthetic discourse, but also was above their coarseness and salacious suggestiveness, simply admiring the beauty of the women, pointing to the literal qualities of Greek mythology, the women 'perfectly represent[ed as] the figures of the Graces'. This placing of Muslim women into a Western frame of reference was a deliberate attempt by Montagu to objectify them while levitating their significance to those beauties of classical mythology. Though as an aside, Montagu then confided in her readers, 'To tell you the truth, I had wickedness enough to wish secretly that Mr Gervase could have been there invisible. I fancy it would have much improved his art',[32] a reference to Charles Jervas, an Irish artist and friend of Pope's who had painted Montagu's own portrait.

Montagu recognized that the women had seized the opportunity to revel in an all-female space as they stayed for four or five hours at the bath, some talking, 'some working, others drinking coffee or sherbet… In short, 'tis the women's coffee house, where all the news of the town is told, scandal invented, etc.'[33] Here, the women could freely communicate without the interference of men. They also wanted to include her in their fun and in their rituals: 'The Lady that seem'd the most considerable amongst them entreated me to sit by her and would fain have undress'd me for the bath.' Part of this was curiosity and a need to know what she was wearing underneath her outer garments, but Montagu was not ready to jump naked into the party: 'I excus'd my selfe with some difficulty, they being all so earnest in perswading me.' To appease their inquisitiveness, she did at last comply a little: 'I was at last forc'd to open my skirt and shew them my stays, which satisfy'd 'em very well, for I saw they believ'd I was so lock'd up in that machine that it was not in my own power to open it, which contrivance they attributed to my Husband.' The Eastern women were convinced that 'the Husbands in England were much worse than in the East; for that they ty'd up their Wives in little Boxes, of the shape of their bodies,' Montagu explains.[34] Here, she was connecting herself to the women in a deliberately egalitarian gesture, in which western culture came out worst.

Early male travellers had been quick to sexualize the Ottoman women they saw. Montagu herself cites many of these writers and criticises them for their attitudes, as we saw with George Sandys's comments above. Describing the women as lustful and sexualised was a common trope from male travel writers and contemporaries would attack Montagu for emphasizing the beauty and dignity of the women she saw, rather than their 'otherness'.[35] Thomas Tyers, writing in 1782, thought that Montagu 'would deserve censure' from modest readers both in Britain and Turkey 'merely for the discovery'[36] of the bathers, despite the fact that male travellers had also sought out *hammams* and that there was nothing unusual at the time in the bathers being naked. Others saw a quite different sight of the women in the baths than Montagu had witnessed, such as Lady Craven, who described the hordes of naked females when she herself visited a Turkish bath in Athens as 'a disgusting sight.'

Eastern Leanings, Western Influences

The *Persian Tales* printed only a decade before no doubt influenced Montagu's romanticism of the East (she was known to have a copy). In Turkey, she was able to give full rein to this romanticism and sensuality in which she revelled. This was probably what led to her sometimes rosy-coloured view of her experiences in the Ottoman Empire.

Among one of the criticisms of Montagu's point of view has been that she was far more pro-East than she was pro-West, but this is an over-simplistic assertion not borne out in her writing. In fact, it was her enthusiastic approach to everything new, inspired by her immense curiosity, which led to her fascination with the different cultures she experienced as she and her husband crossed the English Channel and travelled Eastwards. Her enjoyment of mainland Western Europe did not mean she was blind to what she encountered there, and she was often critical of the cultures she came across in Europe, most notably of the trappings of the Catholic church, criticising its adoration of rotting relics, noting, 'I could not help murmuring in my heart at the profusion of pearls, diamonds and rubies, bestowed on the adornment of rotten teeth, dirty rags [relics]etc.'[37] Such anti-Catholic polemic was a common trait among British travel writers wanting to deride 'Popism' in order to ensure their Protestant Britishness or simply to assure of their detestation of religion altogether. Of course, they were writing for a captive audience who were primarily aristocratic, uniquely white, and nearly all British supporters of the Protestant Hanoverian monarchy, which partly defined itself as being non-Catholic. As Jeremy Black put it when writing about the Grand Tour, 'Cultural preferences were testaments of loyalty,'[38] and Montagu knew the code and edited her letters accordingly.

When Montagu arrived in Turkey, she was forcibly struck by the physical beauty of her new environment. She wrote to her friend, the poet Alexander Pope:

> The summer is already far advanced in this part of the world, and for some miles round Adrianople the whole ground is laid out in gardens, and the banks of the river set with rows of fruit trees, under which all the most considerable Turks divert themselves every evening; not with walking, that is not one of their pleasures, but a set party of them choose out a green spot where the shade is very thick, and there they spread a carpet on which they sit drinking their coffee.[39]

Ever interested in how societies functioned, she revelled in the beauty of her surroundings, but her interest inevitably turned to the people in the foreground. She quickly assimilated and threw herself into her new life; she learned to speak Turkish and adopted Turkish costume so she could move about incognito when travelling out to see the sights. She was the first Western woman to be invited to dine alone with Turkish officials' wives and presented herself as knowledgeable enough and personable enough to be admired and assimilated into intimate conversation with her hostesses. She was able to discuss with them their views on the terms of their marriages. Her overall impression was that Turkish women were well looked after by their husbands and 'are the only women in the world that lead a life of uninterrupted pleasure.'[40] She was, of course, meeting with the elite of Ottoman society. Since these visits would have had to be officially sanctioned both by Sultan Ahmed III, the autocratic ruler of Turkey at the time, and by her husband as the British ambassador, one can assume that she was a valued and trusted member of the elite community of Turkish nobles and British diplomats in which she found herself. However, Montagu's husband's ambassadorship was fraught with political problems. Now that the Austrians had entered the Turkish-Venetian war in support of Venice, the British were set on bringing hostilities to an end.

The previous British ambassador to Turkey, Sir Robert Sutton, and the British ambassador in Austria, Abraham Stanyan, sought to undermine the work Montagu's husband was doing and argued that the British should be more allied to the Austrian cause, and less to the Turkish. Stanyan wrote that Montagu herself was guilty of over-influencing her husband:

> they now begin to suspect the Grand Signor's favourite was the handsomer man and had got her over to the Turkish interest.[41]

Stanyan was probably ignorant of Montagu's meetings with the Turkish officials' wives, but if he had known of them, he would doubtless have disapproved. The French ambassador too noted that Montagu took an active part in her husband's diplomatic mission while his own wife had refused to participate in Montagu's incognito trips in Turkish dress to see the sights. It is obvious that as a wealthy, educated, aristocratic woman, she was a political player and was eager to be involved in discussions.

Montagu never forgot to whom she was writing back home and was careful to overtly express where her loyalties lay: In her letter to Princess Caroline of Ansbach dated 1 April 1716 she wrote:

> the perpetual spring they enjoy makes everything look gay and flourishing, but this climate, as happy as it seems, can never be preferred to England with all its snows and frosts, while we are blessed with an easy government under a king who makes his own happiness consist in the liberty of his people.[42]

Well aware of her position, she remained the attentive courtier and she was conscious that Turkey represented somewhere fundamentally different in the minds of the people from the western world. In these attempts to evoke Ottoman values, she used Western analogies to make her opinions and description clear to her readers. Writing to her friend, the poet Alexander Pope, in her description of her surroundings where she was staying, just outside Constantinople in a spa town where the family had gone to escape the heat, she playfully compared it to the Elysian Fields in classical writing: 'the beauty and dress of the women exactly resembling the ideas of the ancient nymphs as they are given us by the representations of the poets and painters.'[43] Drawing on her own (self-) education within the classical tradition, she explained her environs to Pope, knowing he would understand the references. Montagu went on to admit to Pope, however, that 'I am sometimes very weary of this singing and dancing and sunshine and wish for the smoke and impertinencies in which you toil,'[44] thereby implying a homesickness. Freed up from the national boundaries of their different settings, she used their shared knowledge of classical literature to reach across the miles that separated them. It was these comparisons with different worlds that fascinated her.

Various tropes, including anti-Catholicism, and casting the foreign as 'other', were important for travel writers in forging a national British identity. Joseph Addison expressed sadness at the decline of the classical world; Roman virtues, he argued, were allied with British ones. By contrast, he saw mainland Europe as subject to despotism. Montagu was aware of these outlooks – she knew Addison as her husband had accompanied him on his post-university Grand Tour and the two remained good friends. The *Turkish Embassy Letters* form part of this canon; as a white, English, educated aristocrat – albeit female – with the confidence she had had since birth of belonging to such an elite social circle, it was impossible for Montagu not to take up this point of view. For Montagu, it was part of her natural heritage.

Observational Approaches

Montagu knew of and had read the observational writing that male travelers were producing at the time. She wrote to an undisclosed recipient in June 1717: 'I see you have taken your ideas of Turkey from that worthy author Dumont', whom she dismisses as ignorant, despite his declared knowledge.[45] Jean Dumont's *A New Voyage to the Levant* had been published in 1696, soon followed by the English writer Aaron Hill in *A Full and Just Account of the Present State of the Ottoman Empire* in 1709. While Hill had been denied access to a Turkish *hammam*, with its female bathers, Dumont made it inside and he wrote that the women covered their 'distinguishing parts' when he arrived.[46] Montagu, by contrast, was made welcome by the women there, who saw no need to cover themselves. Her assertion in the subtitle to the *Turkish Embassy Letters,* 'drawn from Sources that have been inaccessible to other Travellers', was clearly justified. Montagu did indeed have unparalleled access to the women's spaces and an obvious communication with Turkish women that male travellers would not have. Yet, male accounts included descriptions of female domestic interiors that they could never have experienced.

Clearly, Montagu knew she had a distinct advantage over the male travel writers, investigating the world from a female perspective. Also, her status as the wife of the Britannic Ambassador, as a representative of the establishment, meeting the elite, was a position she exploited. In doing so, it was her detailed personal objective comments in her observations that gave her writing its value; she could write on a whole variety of subject matters from pre-nuptial baths to heated stoves, from slavery to childbirth, from face cream to whirling dervishes, from marriage possessions to a cure for smallpox. More than this, she was open to new ideas, interested in wrestling with details in her non-judgemental fashion. This shows up specifically in her intellectual inquisitiveness about the field of science. In Turkey, her curiosity led to inoculation against the smallpox, which would make her a champion of innovation once she returned. In a letter to her childhood friend Sarah Chiswell, 1 April 1718, she described in detail the methods used by Turks in inoculating as a protection against the deadly disease. Should she return to England, she wrote, she would have the courage to defy the doctors and introduce the practice to the West. Having herself narrowly escaped death from the smallpox in 1716 and see her only brother die from the disease the year before, she was aware of the considerable benefits this protection would have for the West. To her credit, she described the experiment with considerable care, knowing that it constituted valuable medical knowledge: 'the old woman comes with a nutshell full of the matter of the best sort of smallpox, and asked what veins you please to have open. She immediately rips open that you offer to her ...and puts into the vein as much venom as can lie upon the head of a needle...'.[47] To this end, she had sounded out the French Ambassador to the court as to how they viewed inoculation and only then declared herself 'very well satisfied of the safety of the experiment.'[48] So much so, that she had her young son innoculated. While male writers must have heard about smallpox inoculation, they had failed to suggest they should be tried in Britain. Montagu's bravery in trying out the practice for herself on her young daughter back in England constituted a vital step in the chain of events that would finally lead to the worldwide elimination of the disease in the 1980s.

Montagu was also much less gullible than some of her earlier male counterparts. They had been quick to believe the custom of the sultan signifying which wife he planned to sleep with that night by throwing his handkerchief at her. For example, Paul Rycaut in his *Present State of the Ottoman Empire* in 1668 wrote of the sultan: 'the damsels being ranged in order by the mother of the sultan, he throws his handkerchief to her, where his eye and fancy best directs, it being a token of her election to his bed.'[49] While another travel contemporary writer, Aaron Hill, had discounted the handkerchief story, and instead he described the story of the favoured wife creeping into the chamber and waiting for the sultan at the foot of the bed. Montagu simply asked the women themselves and found it to be untrue. Contradicting these accounts, she reported on what the sultan's wife had told her: 'She assured me that the story of the sultan's throwing a handkerchief is altogether fabulous…Neither is there any such thing as her creeping in at the bed's feet.'[50] Montagu's unique position as a woman writer had given her the opportunity to provide a more authentic record with the sultana's direct testimony adding veracity to her account.

The Condition Of Women

The big problem in her letters is why Montagu ignored the issue of misogyny of the Turkish men when she commented on misogyny of her own country and the stranglehold men had over British women. How could she hold such a differing view from male travellers' opinions? Though Montagu portrayed these women as discussing the issues of the day, she persistently refused to engage with the fact that they lived in a male-dominated society (as indeed, did she). Since women were so important a subject for her, her studied refusal to investigate more deeply the position of Eastern women in this letter, living as they did in such a significantly defined misogynist culture, seems a deliberate choice on her part, informed to some extent by her time spent with Achmet-Beg.

Once she arrived in Turkey itself, Montagu continued to be interested in and to write to her correspondents about the lives of the women she came across. Again, she appeared often to be struck by how good their lives were, compared to those of women back in Britain. Her apparent inability to distinguish between women's subordination at home and in the Ottoman Empire probably had more to do with the status of the women she met (as well as her own), rather than any willing ignorance of the poorer women. Though she was disappointed not to be allowed to visit the sultan's seraglio (which again would have been a more luxurious space), she believed that harems provided a valuable separate space for women and a secure unit for family life. She made a note to herself, 'Women not locked up.'[51] Montagu wrote to her sister, who herself had had a forced marriage, refuting the claims of polyamory in Turkey: "Tis true their law permits them four Wives, but there is no instance of a man of quality that makes use of this liberty, or of a woman of rank that would suffer it.'[52]

Contemporary male writers such as Aubry de La Mottraye in his *Travels through Europe, Asia, 1723–32,* and Joseph Addison corroborated the point that Turkish men rarely if ever took more than one wife. Moreover, Montagu explained to her readers that Turkish women had much more liberty than Western women. She described in detail the clothing which covered them completely: 'You may guess how effectually this disguises them, that there is no distinguishing the great lady from her slave, and… and no man dare either touch or follow a woman in the street.'[53] If women did have extra-marital relationships, there was no danger to their reputations because they seldom let their 'gallants' know who they were, she explained.[54] Rich women kept their own money in their own hands, so they did not need to fear their husbands because they were financially independent, she explained to her sister. Such fiscal information was pertinent to Montagu and her sister, since they both had personal wealth inherited from their father which neither was able to access: due to their marriages, their husbands had control.

Montagu went on to write that the women she met in Turkey had the right to divorce, and if they did, not only did they take all their own money with them, but their husbands had also to give them money. Again, Montagu's observations were corroborated by the contemporary male traveller Paul Rycaut, although another earlier French writer, Sieur du Lolé, writing in 1654, disagreed. Even in the case of a woman's husband being accused of a crime and executed, the men who came to take the husband could under no circumstances invade her sanctity: '[The] haram, (or women's apartment) which remains unsearched and entire to the widow. They are queens of their slaves, which the husband has no permission so much as to look upon.'[55]

Writing to her sister in 1717, her famous quote which so many have so far analysed in reference to Turkish ladies, she asserts, 'Tis very easy to see they have more Liberty than we have'.[56] Yet forty years later writing to her daughter she admitted, 'that Liberty is an Idea equally as chimerical, and has no real existence'.[57] The veil, which for centuries has been a symbol of repression for the West, Montagu turned into a protective garment, asserting that it acted as a 'disguise' which concealed what class a woman was. Thus the elite wife and the slave were indistinguishable outside the home, allowing women to move around to have extra-marital affairs. The liberty which Montagu alludes to here is the ability to become classless in order to evade the moral impositions placed on different women according to their status. It is based on the possibility of women to move unnoticed in the streets; but also their control over their own domain in the hareem and baths rather than their imprisonment in this space. She does not compare the limited physical mobility these women might have compared to herself.

In conclusion, it becomes clear that Montagu had an interest in some matters more than others, a focus which depended on both her gender and her class. Women's financial and social independence were clearly issues which engrossed Montagu's interest, yet the existence of slaves did not. A woman's financial independence was important to her, but slavery would have been commonplace to her as so many of the elite were reliant or involved in slavery, or at the least had copious servants. Montagu rejects the image of the cruel Turk: 'I know You'll expect that I should say something particular of [the market] of the Slaves, and you will Imagine me half a Turk when I don't speak of it with the same horror that other Christians have done before me, but I cannot forbear applauding the Humanity of the Turks to those Creatures. They are never ill us'd and their Slavery is in my Opinion no worse than Servitude all over the World.'[58] However, she did make some attempt to examine the darker sexual undercurrents which ran through life in Turkey when she recounted how she had come across a naked, blood-soaked, female corpse lying in the street, wrapped in a sheet. On closer observation, she could make out two knife wounds in the woman's body. While Montagu noted that the woman was surprisingly beautiful and that nearly all the male population of Pera went to look, she passed no value judgement on this behaviour. Montagu was acutely aware that the case would never be brought to justice: 'Murder is never pursued by the king's officers as with us. 'Tis the business of the next relations to revenge the dead person and if they like better to compound the matter with money (as they generally do) there is no more said of it.'[59] Montagu abstained from commenting on the implications of the murder and the disregard of a woman lying dead in the streets, deliberately skimming over the true position of this Turkish woman in society.

Here and elsewhere in her writing about women in Turkey, Montagu preferred not to dwell on female subjugation there. Instead, she positioned herself as

Fatima, the wife of the Kahya at Adrianopolis, rises to greet Lady Mary Wortley Montagu while her two daughters remain seated. Stipple engraving after T. Stothard, 1798.

someone who was doing her best to understand female life and to assimilate with the women she met. It seems she preferred to hold back from dwelling on unsavoury characteristics of the Ottoman Empire, finding it easier to show it in a positive light. Since Montagu was an intelligent woman, and only too well understood the suppression of women in her own country, she would have been making a deliberate choice not to mention the subjugation of Turkish women. Even when Montagu visited the Kayha's wife, Fatima, for a second time, having learned Turkish so the two could converse with each other, their interaction was kept deliberately light.

Montagu's letters written from mainland Europe during the years she lived in Italy, France, and Switzerland as an older woman were more direct. Where she was always acutely aware of keeping her British readership on her side in *The Turkish Embassy Letters,* in Italy she was less guarded. In January 1753, aged sixty-four, she wrote an essay to her daughter, Lady Bute, back in England, laying out her strong views about the education of her granddaughters. She clearly imagined that they would not be given dowries when they married and were likely to grow up to be 'lay nuns' for whom books and reading would be important.[60] She believed they should all read for several hours each day and advocated for women's study of Greek and Latin. While she recognized that beauty gave a woman agency – by implication, agency with powerful men – she argued that intelligence was of fundamental importance. If a woman could think for herself, she could fend for herself. For Montagu, education was the route to a woman holding her own in a man's world.

Montagu's travel letters provided a unique insight into the exchange of ideas between Protestant Georgian Britain, Islamic Turkey and Christian Europe and were genuinely multicultural, taking a clearly sociopolitical stance. The letters were imbued with confidence, her ideas elegantly laid out, and these alone, aside from all her other writing and her work on smallpox, gave Montagu her due place in the European Enlightenment.

Chapter 3

Thomas Gray on Tour: New Views on Much-Known Lands

Maria Grazia Dongu

Thomas Gray by John Giles Eccart, 1747/8.

Thomas Gray (1716–1771) is best known as a poet for his *Elegy Written in a Country Churchyard*, published in 1751. However, this chapter examines his letters in order to place him in the history of British travel literature. Although he wrote letters to his friends and parents on the Grand Tour with Horace Walpole in 1739–40, he never published them. In addition to his letters, he created an index for a planned travel book that parodied existing writing styles and cheerfully proposed a self-referential report in a letter to a friend. Here, he was tentatively exploring new ways to describe foreign countries by overriding the conventional styles of travel writing. It was still a long way off from Laurence Sterne's famous taxonomy of travel writers in his *Sentimental Journey* (1768), yet already Gray was expressing a need to write something new and different from the usual descriptive reports on France, Switzerland and Italy written by other travellers who had gone before him. He duly took notes on monuments and paintings, but erased any reference to them in his letters. Instead, he reproduced fragments of reality caught while travelling throughout the countryside or walking through cities and towns.

Gray's style is remarkable and unconventional. While he paid homage to the masterpieces of travel literature, he managed to find his own approach to this popular genre. As a poet, he was a master of visual metaphors and his letters are similarly structured by his sensitivity to shapes and colours, impressive views, and prospects. Struggling to find the unsaid and put it into words, he focused on the towns' streets and people he met. Although he chose to be the detached observer, his stance was never patronising. His acid commentaries were sometimes turned upon himself, especially when absorbed in the contemplation of nature and people seen in their proper setting. Gray's sublime description of the Alps is well-known, but equally impressive is his image of the locals, the picture of the lands loved by Horatius and his descriptions of his meeting with a famous Italian singer and encounters with friars. He portrayed foreigners through a poet's descriptive techniques and rhetorical strategies; these will be analysed in this chapter to highlight the balance of innovations and stereotypical conservative expressions that characterised his style.

Gray was young but highly educated in the classics, having been a student at Eton and Cambridge. He perfected his French, Italian and Latin in the two years spent on the continent and interspersed French and Italian words in his letters. Unlike his travel companion Horace Walpole, he did not go back to France or Italy again. However, his knowledge of both these cultures was impressive and the number of quotations in his poems, letters and essays testifies to this. Gray was trained to memorise quotes at Eton and Cambridge,[1] and he was constantly translating from other languages.[2] Therefore, his education in the classics had enabled him to think comparatively. His letters were never published in their original form, but William Mason, named by Gray as his executor, had the power to publish or destroy material not previously published, and Mason used a great deal of it. The letters he inserted in *The Poems of Mr Gray, to which are prefixed Memoirs of His Life and Writings* (1775) were the result of his cutting and pasting activities. For this reason, the best modern critical edition available is that edited by Paget Toynbee and Leonard Whibley published in 1935, but even they could not often achieve the difficult task of restoring the original text.

As the title claims, Mason's collection contains Gray's *Life* prefixed to Gray's poems. The biographer pretended to confine himself to the concise third-person narration to give room to Gray's autobiography in the form of his familiar letters. Juxtaposed biographical notes and autobiographic excerpts have been arranged into five sections. The longest one, Section II, is completely devoted to the Grand Tour and the one under examination here. In his introduction to it, Mason recommended the selected letters for their style, 'essentially different in their manner of description from any other that have either preceded or followed them.'[3] Samuel Johnson, who quoted many passages from Mason's work, praised Gray's letters as 'a very pleasing account of many parts of their journey'[4] and regrets Gray had not spent much of his time travelling. At the same time, Johnson recognised that Gray could not have written such fascinating reports had he not first been an armchair traveller himself. In Johnson's words, '[h]e that reads his epistolary narration wishes, that to travel, and to tell his travels, had been more of his employment; but it is by studying at home that we must obtain the ability of travelling with intelligence and improvement'.[5]

Notwithstanding his contemporaries' praise, Gray's travels in France and Italy have, up until now, had but cursory attention in modern scholarly literature. Most scholars have focused on Gray's description of the Alps[6] or on his later travel reports, such as the *Journal of his visit to the Lake District* (1769).[7] However, this chapter examines Gray's letters from France and Italy to demonstrate that these were rough material for a new travel report that foreshadowed Sterne's sentimental traveller. The collection of letters must also be considered an open work, with no narrative closure provided and with multiple plots. Gray and Walpole were abruptly interrupted in Reggio as they were planning to visit Venice. Whatever the matter for this sudden break of the report, we lack the final pages, the ending, which usually reverberates back its meaning on the entire story.[8] This chapter draws on this still scarce secondary literature highlighting Gray's stance as a new kind of traveller and the emergence of feelings of sympathy and empathy[9] in his letters.

As early as the first decades of the century, a new sensibility was developing among young people (self-)trained to analyse and describe themselves. Gray was part of that movement, writing letters at a time when British sociability was evolving.[10] Such letters were among the genres that influenced the rise of the novel, informing it to arouse social feelings and passions,[11] as the eighteenth century became increasingly involved in studying thought.[12] Evidence of this epistemological interest can be seen by analysing Gray's construction of his writing and his views based on his social and antisocial feelings, external visual stimuli, his self-knowledge, and mental images influenced by his classical background.

Thomas Gray and Horace Walpole: The Grand Tourists

Horace Walpole invited Thomas Gray to join him on the Grand Tour in 1738. The youngest son of Robert Walpole the Prime Minister, Horace had the social opportunities and financial support which his friend lacked. According to Walpole, their different milieus and fortunes led to an incurable disagreement, causing their sudden separation in Reggio. However, Mason puts the separation down to conflicting personalities; when commenting about Gray's correspondence being defective towards the end of his tour because he provided no description of Venice, Mason asserts, 'This defect was occasioned by an unfortunate disagreement between him and Mr Walpole, arising from the difference of their tempers.'[13] He was taking for granted Walpole's testimony, which reads: 'I reproached him with the difference between us, when he acted from conviction of knowing he was my superior; I often disregarded his wishes of seeing places, which I would not quit other amusements to visit.'[14] This divergence of personalities might have easily led to their disagreement, but the exchange of letters between the main protagonists and their friends hint at other motives. Allusions and truncated names might indicate either that Walpole had intercepted one of Gray's letters deprecating his friend's abusive manners or that Gray resented Walpole's preference for Cecco (Francesco) Suarez, a Florentine acquaintance of theirs, and their companion in Reggio.[15]

Horace Walpole after Joshua Reynolds, 1735.

It is believed that the two young men were gay, and that Gray was jealous of his brilliant friend. Some essayists have found traces of this relationship in Gray's letters to Walpole and their mutual friend from Eton, Richard West.[16] Their acquaintance with Horace Mann, a British diplomat, has also aroused suspicions; as historian Rictor Norton has pointed out, Hester Lynch Thrale Piozzi, 'who had an excellent eye for mollies, identified Walpole's long-time friend, Sir Horace Mann, as a sodomite.'[17] As his contemporaries wrote, Mann, as a long-time British resident of Florence, had been influenced by Italian effeminacy and had lost his British masculinity.[18] The fact that Walpole and Gray were welcome guests of Mann in Florence suggests Walpole's hold on Mann might have been sexual.[19]

The Grand Tour had a unique appeal to young men precisely because they could explore their sexuality unfettered while abroad, free from any social control over their lives and not cursed by the stigma attached to homoerotic love.[20] Eighteenth-century texts reveal that complaints and public condemnation against homosexuality were spread all over Britain by the 1720s, when Gray was still young.[21] In which case, Walpole, Gray and West had every interest in destroying any evidence of their involvement in same-sex relationships and none of the protagonists admitted to any bond other than mutual affection. While the language of Gray's letters might sound excessively effeminate to our modern ears, some scholars have contrasted them with others written by eighteenth-century writers to their male friends where there was no intimate involvement between them.[22] Gray's language may seem overtly erotic, but by enlarging the *corpus* of epistles examined, it has been demonstrated that 'the *epicoene* features in letters between predominantly heterosexual men suggest that, until later in the eighteenth century, there existed a public discourse which encouraged them to imagine their friendships with men in ways similar to their experience of affection for wives or female lovers'.[23] Not a line in Gray's extant letters from the Grand Tour hints at unrequited love, nor does he mention the sexual restlessness of Mann and his friends. Moreover, in his later years and replying to Mason's suggestion to downplay the quarrel between Gray and Walpole on their Grand Tour in his already mentioned *Memoirs of Gray*, Walpole blamed his pride due to his higher social station and Gray's sensitiveness for their quarrel in May 1741.[24] Mason also omitted many of Gray's letters from Italy, especially those addressed to Walpole and West, perhaps to shield Walpole, the only one of the three friends still alive in 1775.[25] Unfortunately, censorial editing has left us with little more than shadows and gossip regarding the past.

We certainly know that the two friends followed the usual paths of Grand Tourists in France and Italy, passing through Switzerland. In 1739, they left Dover and arrived at Calais. Then they visited Amiens, Boulogne, Abbeville, Clermont, and Paris, where they stayed for a few days, and then left for Rheims and Dijon, wishing to improve their French, which they believed easier in towns less sophisticated than the capital, and to meet friends who were coming from England. Changing their initial plan, they decided to cross the border to see Italy. They visited Turin, Genoa, Tortona, Piacenza, Parma, Reggio, Modena, Bologna, Florence, Rome, Tivoli and Naples. They then set out for the North-East and certainly visited Venice, but not together. There, Ambassador Smith[26] took pains to help Thomas Gray receive enough money to return to London.[27]

Their route was modelled on the traditional paths of eighteenth-century British travellers, as reported in their travelogues on the Grand Tour.[28] Their movements were altered by concerns regarding the international political context or the whims of Walpole, who loved to be the centre of the social scene in the cities they visited. Peers warmly welcomed the son of the powerful Robert Walpole, a brilliant conversationalist and extrovert, while the melancholic Gray was not at ease in those elitist circles, bent as he was to meditation and scholarly studies. Walpole was irritated by Gray's dependence on his notebook, which he considered useless.[29]

Like many British travellers on the continent, Gray's and Walpole's personalities were shaped on their Grand Tour. They perfected their French and Italian, sought picturesque views, watched public and religious ceremonies, visited monuments, and observed paintings, as well as becoming acquainted with the French and Italian intelligentsia.

Still in Italy, Gray had confessed to his friend Richard West his concerns regarding the future, as he recognised his own vocation for private life against public service.[30] On his return he would abandon his plan to enter law school in London and returned to Cambridge where he became Professor of Modern History doing what he loved the most: reading and writing. Almost reluctantly, he became the greatly admired poet of *Elegy written in a Country-Churchyard*, soon translated into many languages and which certainly struck a chord in Italy, inspiring Ugo Foscolo, who remoulded Gray's meditation into a vigorous call for an Italian uprising against the French invaders.[31] The circle was complete: the poet who had imitated and cited Dante, Petrarch, and Tasso had his works translated, alluded to, and quoted in Italian poems. Gray's vision of a poetic transfer from Rome to Britain seemed to have come true.

Gray's Grand Tour Letters as Travel Literature

There was a long tradition of travel literature in England, illustrated by the *Travels of John Mandeville*, which circulated in the fifteenth century, while Hakluyt's collections of reports (1589) described marvellous, unknown worlds. By the eighteenth century, the pragmatic approach to discoveries held by the Royal Society reshaped the travel report for a new age and new needs. Equipped with questionnaires to fill in, travellers visited exotic and unfamiliar lands and recorded what they saw: minerals, animals, plants, whatever traders and colonisers could exploit. Scientific realism became the focus of travellers within a culture of burgeoning imperialism.[32]

Gray had read various travelogues before his Grand Tour. In the thirties, Walpole wrote a lively parody of Addison's *Travels*, sent in letter form to Gray,[33] while the poet himself hints at Addison's work, interspersing his *Remarks* with quotations from Latin Literature.[34] Gray's own library included a rich array of travelogues, which had an influence on his understanding of the world. Among them were Jonathan Richardson's *Account of Some of the Statues, Bas-reliefs, Drawings, and Pictures in Italy* (1722)[35], which might have offered him a model for his *Notes on a Tour through France and Italy,* meticulously composed in 1739–1741.[36] In his later years, he would become acquainted with Sharp's *Letters from Italy* (1766);[37] he would praise James Boswell's *Account of Corsica* (1768) in his letters;[38] and would admire Sterne's *Tristram Shandy*,[39] which Walpole had suggested he read, declaring, 'Sterne's sentimental travels, which tho' often tiresome, are exceedingly good natured and picturesque'.[40] These cursory notes testify to Gray and his friends' appreciation of diverse travel-writing models all their lives. They were young when Addison's way of travelling and writing about the Grand Tour had lost its relevance and its hold on readers; older when

Sharp, Smollett and Sterne innovated the nearly exhausted genre by changing the items from simply seeing and describing to giving vent to their thoughts and inserting humorous comments and biting reactions to inhabitants and their way of life.

Gray's travel letters testify to the need for a new take on Addison's style, which was profoundly felt by Gray's *coterie*. He did not seek publishers for his letters from France and Italy. His rejection of the literary market prevented him from doing so;[41]perhaps he also considered his prose unworthy of the great national poet he aspired to be. However, he did write an amusing index to a travel book (see below), a book which he never actually wrote. When Mason published Gray's works in 1775, Gray's travel letters became entertaining reading material. The colloquial style enlivened by amusing puns, allusions, quotations, and the use of digressions endowed them with all the virtues eighteenth-century gentlemen appreciated in polite conversation.[42] Samuel Johnson appreciated Gray's letters from France and Italy in Mason's edition,[43] crediting Gray with two qualities apparently at odds – curiosity and reserve.[44] Commenting on Gray's journal of his visit to the Lake District, he especially praised Gray's curiosity, which 'extended to all the works of art, all the appearances of nature, and all the monuments of past events'.[45]

The Grand Tourist was principally a seeker of sights, demonstrating that he had seen and visited prominent places by reporting on them. The wealthy traveller bought paintings or sculptures to bring home to testify to his activity as an eyewitness and *connoisseur*.[46] He also wrote his report, tirelessly repeating words borrowed from other travelogues. Having been exposed to Latin literature and Italian paintings, Gray was not an innocent observer, but his visual archive was rich in real or mental images of museums, churches and monuments. Moreover, by selecting those images, his choice was being influenced by his knowledge of travel literature, history and art. He records what he sees with amusing self-consciousness while constantly distancing himself from the conventional travel writing of his times, parodying it, or simply focusing on different items, and 'people in the streets'.[47] Almost twenty years later, Sterne's Yorick would echo back to Gray's letters.

Writing Plan for a Mock Travel Book: The Index

The 12th of March 1740, when he was midway on his Grand Tour, Gray wrote a mock index to his friend Thomas Wharton,[48] which acted as a parody of travel writers who had gone before him. The letter starts with no usual greeting, but with the heading 'Proposals for printing by subscription, ... The Travels of T: G: gent:'.[49] The index reveals Gray's discriminating judgement on travel literature as he summarises the contents of his previous letters, arranging them in chapters and adopting the style typical of realistic, philosophical, or splenetic travelogues to provoke his reader's laughter. Assembling diverse modes of writing and using hyperbole, he ridicules features and rhetorical strategies used by Grand Tourists. The stylistic heterogeneity mirrors the variety of the letters that tried to meet his various receivers' expectations. The letter asks Wharton to indicate what contents 'to expatiate thereupon'[50] in his following letters. The diverse uses of personal pronouns mark the break between the two sections of the letter. Gray uses the first person when he directly addresses Wharton, and the third person or the common noun, 'the author', to define himself in the index. The lexical choice is indicative of the narrator's distance from his experience. At the same time, we perceive that he and his reactions are central to the narrative, as he shows his passions (and hate or contempt of others). The selection and description of objects and people result from his sentiments.

Gray's creation of a persona, the 'author' or narrator of the index, makes a mockery of previous travel writers. The 'author' is self-absorbed to the point that he reports minutely on his physical reactions to his voyage towards Calais; he wrote, 'the Author spews, a minute account of all the circumstances thereof'.[51] He dwells on trivialities that everyone knows about, but defamiliarises them in a contrived effort to construct their alterity: 'How they feed him with Soupe & what Soupe is. How he meets with a Capucin; & and what a Capucin is'.[52] He despises the Versailles building 'infinitely' and takes the opportunity to expand on taste,[53] yet in his letters, he declares that he adores the Versailles gardens; he dies 'of the Fright'[54] when visiting the Grand Chartreuse; feels 'mortal antipathy to a Presbyterian';[55] and despises a 'vile Italian comedy'.[56] Notwithstanding the author's egotistical attitude, the people he meets overwhelm him: 'they shut him up in a Post-Chaise & send him to Paris';[57] a French tailor 'covers him with Silk, & Fringe, & widens his figure with buckram a yard on each side';[58] and finally, he 'is devoured by a Wolf'.[59] His power and his authority lie in his ability to describe everything precisely, even the experience of being eaten by a wolf,[60] which, of course, cannot, in reality, be told.

Unsurprisingly, Gray provides sketches of the French and Italian Catholic population, especially nuns and priests. However, hyperbole and the zoomorphism of the clergy make them seem ridiculous, as was his intention. The animalisation of the Catholic cleric appears when the author promises to describe him in detail in a 'Description of the little Creature, called an Abbé, its parts, & their uses'. Additionally, the narrator vents suspicions about sexual promiscuity in nunneries, presenting them as an undeniably true universal fact: 'a Cut of the inside of a Nunnery; it's [*sic*] Structure, wonderfully adapted to the use of the animals that inhabit it; a short account of them, how they propagate without the help of a Male, & how they eat up their own young ones, like Cats, and Rabbets supposed to have both Sexes in themselves, like a Snail'.[61]

It was usual for British travellers to deplore the corrupt customs of Papist countries after the Reformation to distance themselves from 'foreigners' and align themselves with the Protestant faith of their birth. In so doing, they might avoid any accusation of religious contamination during their travels. Here, the young Gray is diminishing the status of the abbé and the nuns, turning them into animals and satirising their proliferation; his portrayals also mock the stereotypical descriptions given by other travellers about the devilish nature of the Catholics. To undermine these fabricated tales he uses overemphasis and personification of the vices attributed to southern European countries. Thus, when he 'enters into the Dominions of the Pope o' Rome, meets the Devil' and sees 'scandalous doings between the Vines & the Elm trees.'[62] Here, he is disdainful of the travel books with their scare-mongering of the rabid influence of the Catholic religion upon the innocent British youths on their Grand Tour.

Following the travel-writing tradition that had gone before him, the main concern of the 'author' or narrator is to accentuate the boundaries between England (pure and refined) and France and Italy (its opposites). Yet in doing so, he is satirising the older style of travel writing and how they conveyed their impressions. He wonders at the similarities, 'how there are Trees, & Houses, just as in England',[63] and accentuates the differences. For instance, he humorously explains that the French ear is 'entirely different' from the English one, so 'Sounds have a directly contrary effect upon one & the other'.[64] In doing so, Gray is advancing the travel-writing style by inserting his own personality in a parody of the old-style travel writing through exaggeration.

Sociability and Self

In the first letters from France, Gray enthusiastically explain the pleasures of discovery and his mingling with foreigners. The main passion driving him is pride in being Walpole's friend and curiosity towards the new environment. Initially, there was a strong bond of solidarity with Walpole as Gray participates in his friend's popularity in France and reacts positively to French sociability. It is then no surprise that Gray mostly uses the plural 'we' and refers to emotions, actions, and sights as being shared in the first letters from France. This was the beginning of his Grand Tour, and Gray's letters mirror Walpole's feelings, attitudes, and behaviour. In Rheims, the shy, reserved Gray fully met sociability requirements by playing cards and joining French hosts at a pleasant ball. They then 'paraded through all the principal streets of the city, and waked everybody in it. Mr Walpole had a mind to make a custom of the thing, but the women did not come into it; so I believe it will drop and they will return to their dull cards, and usual formalities'.[65] However, in expressing personal feelings in a letter to Ashton, he uses the singular 'I' while referring to his great sympathy towards people he loves: 'I am not so ignorant of Pain myself as to be able to hear of another's Sufferings, without any Sensibility to them, especially when they are those of One I ought more particularly to feel for.'[66] In this case, he uses sympathy in its common meaning, which is to feel sorry for someone's sorrows.[67] However, the definition can be extended to include sharing one's happiness.[68] Here, we can discern the two aspects of Gray's personality in his letter writing describing his sociability with Walpole and his more melancholy self.

Sociability was 'a long-term phenomenon' that defined capital élites in Paris. At its height, it led to a readjustment in aristocratic standards of behaviour and qualities: 'aristocratic prestige rested increasingly on the manners of the man of the world … and on the cultural practices of polite society, like theatre, music or poetry'.[69] England witnessed a similar remoulding of social practices in the late seventeenth century and earlier in the eighteenth century, with the flourishing of *coffee-houses*, which men could enter (women would be excluded except as maids[70]) if they exhibited proper manners and could join other people in rational and polite discussion.[71] There were also balls and theatrical, musical, and operatic performances, 'the efflorescence of commercialised leisure possibilities as well as shopping venues'.[72] Walpole and Gray participated in these activities and evaluated them with their refined taste.

Knowledge of the 'varied Drama of Society', as Mason puts his appraisal of Gray,[73] helped the author to be objective as well as sympathetic. Gray can criticise customary social entertainment in Rheims ('dull cards'), but also, he understands that a lack of dinners does not depend on 'any such aversion they have to pleasure, as out of a sort of formality they have contracted by not being much frequented by people who have lived at Paris'.[74] Gray discriminates between manners and customs, but without generalisations about others' qualities and virtues. On the contrary, he considers the situational context of the French province and people as the result of a closed and peripheral community. This analysis of diverse social environments reveals his lucid capacity to compare and discriminate between different kinds of sociability based on variable data. It has been argued that British eighteenth-century sociability mended breaches in the post-Restoration society by creating new social places where people could meet and search for sociable solutions for the challenge of living together, notwithstanding their opposite opinions.[75] Gray's tolerance testifies to this amiable disposition towards others. However, something changes within him in Rheims. A first rift occurs between the two friends, who increasingly appear as diverging entities in Gray's letters. Gray uses the pronoun 'we' less often, indicating a separation from Walpole, instead an aggressive 'pen' (Walpole) intrudes and changes Gray's narrative:

> The exceeding Slowness and Sterility of me, & this Place & the vast abundance of Mr Walpole & his Pen will sufficiently excuse to you the shortness of this little matter. He insists that it is not him, but his Pen that is so volubility & so I have borrowed it of [sic]him; but I find it is both of 'em that are so volubility, for tho I am writing as fast as I can drive, yet he is still chattering in vast abundance.[76]

His feelings of unease and insecurity transform Gray's attitude towards the surrounding landscape and people. Whenever Walpole's preference for meetings prevails, Gray proudly presents himself as the detached observer of the social performances,[77] egotistically focusing on his character, but denying the reader any description of the people dancing. When he can, he immerses himself in meditation, connecting himself to nature, to far-off friends in England, and even to visions of the past. It seems that in distancing himself from the way of the world, Gray finally finds himself, the self he can be proud of.

In Gray's letters from France and Italy, there is an evident shift from pride to humility. The objects he sees are the result of his gauging them against his perception of himself. The ghosts he evokes crossing the Alps or in excursions in the Roman Campagna connect him to his earlier classical education on Roman History and Latin Literature studies. The filter of his erudition appears overtly as fictionalised meetings with Hannibal[78] and Eloisa,[79] even mimicking other writers' styles.[80] Here and there, he quotes or imitates Latin poets.[81] In so doing, the disconsolate Gray, who cannot brighten up social meetings, found pride in his visionary power that crowded places with friendly people he had been long acquainted with thanks to his readings. He then bridges gaps between ages and cultures, sympathetically reaching out towards them. Intertextual references enact an intense dialogue with the past as Gray constructs himself and defines the foreign lands as cultural artifacts resounding with multiple echoes.

In Gray's Grand Tour letters, the uneasiness of the use of the personal pronoun manifests itself as the annihilation of the self. In the long journey, Gray has become tediously involved in the dull Florentine activities that – he foretells – will certainly turn him into 'nothingness'.

> I have struck a medal upon myself: the device is thus O, and the motto *Nihilissimo*, which I take in the most concise manner to contain a full account of my person, sentiments, occupations, and late glorious successes.

> If you choose to be annihilated too, you cannot do better than undertake this journey. Here you shall get up at twelve o'clock, breakfast till three, dine till five, sleep till six, drink cooling liquors till eight, go to bridge till ten, sup till two, and so sleep till twelve again. [...] We shall never come home again; a universal war is just upon the point of breaking out; all outlets will be shut up. I shall be secure in my nothingness, while you, that will be so absurd as to exist, will envy me.[82]

In the passage, Gray's self-pity dominates while the foreigners and Walpole's actions, in attuning himself to their social games, are questioned. It is a distorted echo of the previous description of the seemingly dull sociability in Rheims. The dejected Gray has lost his tolerant gaze on others and feels disconnected from the surrounding world. However, sympathy originates from self-pity. His personal experience fosters his connection with foreign and common people; being alienated from his English fellow-traveller, Gray feels sympathetic to other human beings in pain. He turns to West for comfort, the friend he is most in tune with. His feelings are as intense as ever, as the discord with Walpole increases. In a letter to West, he bitterly describes himself as shaped by his travel experience:

> As I am recommending myself to your love, methinks I ought to send you my picture (for I am no more what I was, some circumstances excepted, which I hope I need not particulize [*sic*] to you); you must add then, to your former idea, two years of age, reasonable quality of dullness, a great deal of silence, and something that rather resembles, than is, thinking; a confused notion of many strange and fine things that have swum before my eyes for some time, a want of love for general society, indeed an inability to it. On the good side you may add a sensibility for what others feel, and indulgence for their faults and weaknesses, a love of truth, and detestation of everything else. Then you are to deduct a little impertinence, a little laughter, a great deal of pride, and some spirits. These are the alterations I know of, you perhaps may find more. Think not that I have been obliged for this reformation of manners to reason or reflection, but to a severer schoolmistress, experience.[83]

Gray's self-portrait is illuminating. He describes himself as the sum of silence, imperfect thoughts, things seen, unsocial feelings, pride, counterbalanced by their opposites, sympathy, and indulgence for other people's faults. In other words, he understands that his emotional reactions to persons and objects have made him what he is. However, he is still incapable of fully articulating this change in thoughts and words. Objectivity has been erased, while subjectivity and the self have taken over. Throughout the travel letters Gray alternately focuses on himself as reacting to land and cityscape, and people around him. His emotions create 'otherness' as well as versions of self.

A Foreign, Yet Familiar Country

Gray, whatever his mood, saw the landscape as peppered with people slowly vanishing in the distance when travelling towards Paris by chaise:

> On every hillock is a wind-mill, a crucifix, or a Virgin Mary dressed in Flowers, and a sarcenet robe; one sees [not] many people or carriages on the road; now and then indeed you meet a strolling friar, a country-man with his great muff, or a woman riding astride on a little ass, with short petticoats, and a great headdress of blue wool.[84]

People are only strokes of colour, adding to the beauty of the depiction, like in a picturesque painting. Notwithstanding his young age, Gray was conversant with landscape pictures and in the construction of his picture in words, and he may have been influenced by the most important European landscape painters.[85] His refined taste and his studies had connected him to the continent since his days at Eton. He was aware of his dependence on his archive of images and words, as he clarifies by quoting Walpole, 'our memory sees more than our eyes in this country'.[86] Translating requires a degree of cerebral dexterity as well as travel writing: the author must constantly go from his own to the foreign cultural milieu and back again,[87] and in Gray's case, his classical education had provided him with the possibility of expressing himself in the language of the ancient poets. He was perfecting his art by reproducing images moulded by ancient writers in his imitations.[88] A clear instance of this talent can be seen in Gray's letter to Richard West (May 1740, Rome). The first part of the letter is a poem written in Latin, addressed to Favonius, West's code name among Eton's friends;[89] he then uses his classical references to portray a trip to the Campagna Romana in English:

> I am today just returned from Alba, a good deal fatigued, for you know the Appian is somewhat tiresome. We dined at Pompey's, indeed he was gone for a few days to his Tusculan, but, by the care of his Villicus, we made an admirable meal. We had the dugs of a pregnant sow, a peacock, a dish of thrushes, a noble scarus just fresh from the Thyrrene, and some conchylia of the Lake with garum sauce.[90]

In his *Memoirs*, Mason writes that he has inserted this particular letter to demonstrate that 'Mr Gray was extremely skilled in the customs of the ancient Romans.'[91] Gray's description nodded towards a lost world in maintaining the use of Latin for *conchylia*, *scarus* and *garum*, but one that sounded familiar thanks to the author fictitiously inhabiting it, and his use of the English language. Gray also moves from his own to French and Italian cultural references and any contemporary educated reader would recognise the code-mixing and the playful use of language in his sketches of the Italian or French people and his encounters. His use of different languages lightly shows off his erudition in a letter to Wharton:

> &, if you like my style, pray say so. this is à la Françoise; & if you think it a little too foolish, & impertinent; you shall be treated alla Toscana with a thousand Signoria Illustrissimas. In the mean time I have the honour to remain
>
> Your lofing Frind tell Deth [sic]. T: Gray
> Florence. March. 12. N:S: [1740].
>
> P:S: This à l'Angloise. I don't know where you are; if at Cambridge, pray let me know all how, & about it; and if my old friends Thompson, or Clark fall in your way, say I am extremely theirs. but if you are in town, I entreat you to make my best Compliments to Mrs Wharton. Adieu, Yours Sincerely a second time.[92]

His leave-taking leaves room for three 'impersonations' – of an affected Italian, of a French gentleman and, of course, his own learned English self. However, his letters always come back home to England and its more sober language. As has been pointed out by Clare Brant, '[l]etters disclose inner personations, in which history is one variable and temperament another. The process is not artifice but acculturation through form.'[93] In other words, Gray's impersonations reveal a process of cultural assimilation which does not cancel his own identity, but by moving to and from his cultural milieu, he embraces other etiquettes without condemning them. This enables Gray to switch between his own inner ideas and the world he sees on the Grand Tour. Exposed to new sights, languages and people, Gray tries to domesticate 'otherness' by relating it to his native country. For example, in Boulogne, Gray notes, 'it is a large, old, fortified town, with more English than French.'[94] A traveller like Gray moves from place to place, alternating between cultures to establish connections between the country he sees and his own country.[95]

Gray's descriptions have a visual quality that arises from the partial overlapping of native subjects and their foreign equivalent. When he describes the cathedral in Amiens, he writes that it 'is just what that of Canterbury must have been before the Reformation. It is about the same size, a huge Gothic building, beset on the outside with thousands of small statues, and within adorned with beautiful painted windows…etc.'[96] In doing so, he acknowledges the great divide in Christianity, which transformed brothers in faith into enemies, and similarities into differences. At the same time, he can mentally see English churches as they were before the iconoclastic attack on art and acknowledge the past of his nation. No contempt can be traced in Gray's travel letters, rather a serene self-identity stands untouched by the people and monuments he sees, much like what happens to travellers in a pleasant country.

The risk of contamination by the Catholic religion of innocent British youths on their Grand Tour was a trope often mentioned in travelogues; this is referred to in Gray's ironic passage 'we resorted to the Madonna delle Vigne to put up our little orisons, (I believe I forgot to tell you that we have been sometime converts to the holy Catholic Church)'.[97] Indeed, like many British travellers, Gray seems to be fascinated by the dramatic Catholic rites. In a letter to his mother, writing from Rome (April 15, 1740), Gray defines his visit to St Peter's as motivated by 'the adoration of three extraordinary reliques'.[98] He highlights the staged dramatic quality of the lights, 'disposed in the figure of a huge cross at the high altar, and seeming to hang alone in the air.'[99] Equally theatrical are the processions of religious brotherhoods, adding to the light spectacle, with their tapers coming and going to the altar where the relics are shown. The climax occurs when the flagellants whip themselves to purge themselves from sin, 'but really in earnest'.[100] His account is devoid of any moral disapprobation, merely observing the spectacle before him.

Gray excels at depicting crowds and rarely singles out figures, unless they are of a stately rank. He often paints comic pictures of the gatherings, notably of the worship of some figure by the masses, thereby lightly mocking the 'seers', when the Madonna dell' Impruneta was brought to Florence to 'avert the ill effects of a late great inundation.'

> […] in procession, attended by the Council of Regency, the Senate, the Nobility, and all the Religious Orders, on foot and bare-headed, and so carried to the great church, where it was frequented by an infinite concourse of people from all the country round. Among the rest I paid my devotions almost every day, and saw numbers of people possessed with the devil, who were brought to be exorcised. It was indeed in the evening, and the church-doors were always shut before the ceremonies were finished, so that I could not be eye-witness of the event; but that they were all cured is certain, for one never heard any more of them the next morning. I am to-night just

> returned from seeing our Lady make her exit with the same solemnities she entered. [...] The subject of all this devotion is supposed to be a large Tile with a rude figure in bas-relief upon it. I say supposed, because since the time it was found (for it was found in the earth in ploughing) only two people have seen it; the one was, by good luck, a saint; the other was struck blind for his presumption.[101]

Gray shows an interest in these historical public processions. As one with the crowd, he seems to temporarily suspend any disbelief, which resurfaces when he inserts the dubitative verb 'suppose'. Whenever no evidence is given, the tourist has only to infer and imagine. On his way to Naples, one of the privileged tourist destinations in the eighteenth century, Gray is seriously appreciative of the sights he sees and the history in which it is seeped, declaring, 'Our journey hither was through the most beautiful part of the finest country in the world; and every spot of it, on some account or other, famous for these three thousand years past.'[102]

In some ways, throughout his journey, Gray was incessantly searching for his own interiority within his letters. His naturally melancholic disposition, no doubt, gave him a less lively outlook than Walpole. However, he could still admire the people and sights around him. Understandably, he grew morose after his split from Walpole and turned to his friends for comfort. However, he finds his equilibrium, balancing his sincere curiosity for other human beings with his deep-rooted sense of belonging to his own nation: he can empathise with foreigners but does not disturb the scene.

Chapter 4

John MacDonald: A Travelling Servant's Life of Cultural Exchange

Sophie Dunn

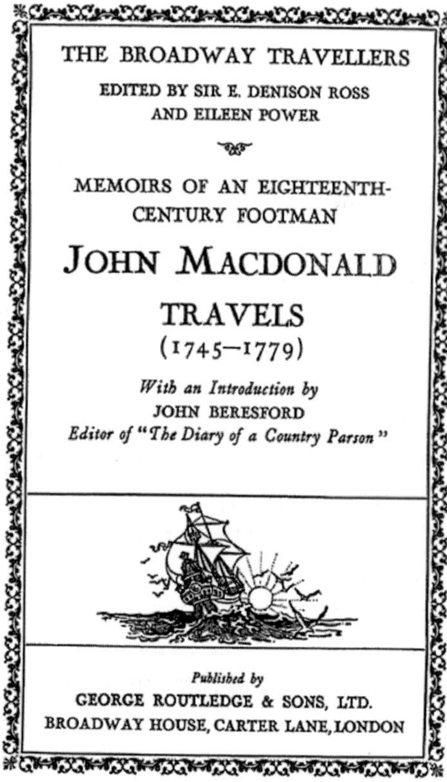
THE BROADWAY TRAVELLERS
EDITED BY SIR E. DENISON ROSS
AND EILEEN POWER

MEMOIRS OF AN EIGHTEENTH-CENTURY FOOTMAN
JOHN MACDONALD
TRAVELS
(1745–1779)
With an Introduction by
JOHN BERESFORD
Editor of "The Diary of a Country Parson"

Published by
GEORGE ROUTLEDGE & SONS, LTD.
BROADWAY HOUSE, CARTER LANE, LONDON

Between the 1750s and the late 1770s, John MacDonald (born 1741) travelled extensively as a servant to British travellers – MacDonald's life was one of constant mobility, first in Scotland, then wherever his masters wished to go. He saw most of the British Isles, large swathes of Europe, and even spent time in India. We know about these travels because MacDonald left a memoir published under the title *Travels, in various parts of Europe, Asia, and Africa, during a series of thirty years and upwards* in 1790.[1]

MacDonald's account is one of only a handful of published travel narratives written by servants, people who travelled in the service of other travellers. Servants' travel narratives provide a new perspective on elite British travel, and especially the Grand Tour. Travelling servants have long been regarded as inaccessible to the historian, but recent scholarship has presented new ways of engaging with source material created by servants and presenting their perspectives on travel.[2] While MacDonald's *Travels* contain a good deal of praise for his respective masters, the narrative is first and foremost about MacDonald himself, his sexual exploits, his linguistic or culinary achievements, and his clever ideas in tricky situations.

He does not engage in self-effacement as might be expected from a servant. Instead, he confidently portrays himself as perhaps the best thing that could happen to an elite traveller – to have MacDonald as his servant-companion.

This lack of subtlety at times opens a new perspective: MacDonald gives an account of not only his masters but also of other masters and servants he encounters abroad, therefore painting a vivid image of eighteenth-century European master-servant relationships. He has templates of a 'good master' and a 'good servant', and he judges those who fall short of his expectations, independently of their rank. His narrative, as curated as it might be, provides us with an idea of how a servant could subscribe to a society in which he had no chance of experiencing the luxurious travels he helped facilitate.

It is this confidence while knowing his place that turns MacDonald's *Travels* into a travel narrative set apart from the many narratives of the second half of the eighteenth century. Certainly, MacDonald does not reinvent the genre. His writings are not overly literary and occasionally it is difficult to discern the exact timeline or order of events from his somewhat breathless story-telling exercise. Like other British travel writings of the later eighteenth century, the *Travels* offer a mix of 'naïve empiricism, personal witness, and writing to the moment'.[3] He gives an account of places visited and people met, he sprinkles the text with remarks on foreign people's clothes and manners, he occasionally enjoys stereotyping and dislikes the French. But because of his background, writing as a servant rather than an educated elite traveller, his narrative attains a different quality: having little literary knowledge to fall back on, MacDonald keeps an open mind for his own impressions and judgments. More than once does he imply that he is better prepared (and perhaps better suited) for travelling abroad than his elite masters. His narrative is the counterpart to elite travel writing, it exposes elite writing as a hollow performance, and in his own self-aggrandisement he unmasks elite self-aggrandisement. In other words, MacDonald's travel narrative presents MacDonald as an active participant rather than a mere follower. The difference between elite travel and MacDonald's journeys lies in the emphasis, in the day-to-day tasks rather than in the personal quality of the traveller.

By nature of MacDonald's position in life and work, his narrative is focused on the more mundane aspects of travelling life. The geographical focus is on France, Spain, and Portugal, but MacDonald's interests do not change significantly with his own geographical location; instead he tends to discuss similar topics for different places. He was responsible for his master's (and by extension his own) physical well-being. The following analysis of his *Travels* will, therefore, pick some of the most common topics in his writing: servant's work, food and clothes and learning languages. From this, three interlinked key themes emerge: a servant's agency, the master-servant relationship, and instances of cultural exchange. The first section discusses foreign language skills as an instance of cultural exchange and how the knowledge or lack of foreign languages shaped both a servant's agency and the master-servant relationship. The second section will focus on MacDonald's opinions of the master-servant relationship and how it influenced the experience of travel. The last section explores how MacDonald actively participated in the act of cultural exchange while travelling.

Foreign Languages: Masters and Servants Abroad

Learning and speaking foreign languages is central to the master-servant relationship in MacDonald's *Travels*. Arturo Tosi has argued that lone travellers (invariably young men of some education who wished to economise) were most likely to know foreign languages, to mingle with locals on the Continent, and to write about it in their travel narratives.[4] Contrarily, Tosi implies that rich travellers of high social standing were less likely to know languages and he mentions servants as interlocutors between rich masters and locals: 'It was quite unlikely that those who chose to travel in such a grand style would become directly involved in the nitty-gritty negotiations and problem solving connected with the daily routine.'[5] Tosi's analysis demonstrates the centrality of foreign language knowledge for British travellers abroad: wherever they went, they had to contend with a myriad of accents and local dialects, let alone switching from one foreign language to another in a matter of a few miles in some parts of the European continent. Inns, passport offices, coaches – all necessities for travellers came with the necessity of communicating one's needs and wishes, or to react to the demands of an official.[6] But Tosi's focus is on those Grand Tourists who, quite literally, speak for themselves, in whatever language they possess. Servants are not part of his study, nor are there any other comprehensive studies that centre servants and their knowledge of languages.[7] MacDonald's account provides insights that can start to fill this gap. Writing from a servant's perspective he describes the necessity and benefits of learning foreign languages, and he provides not only his own example but that of other servants and elite travellers.

For MacDonald, learning languages is more than just prudent travel preparation. In his narrative, the act of learning foreign languages serves to set him apart from other servants as well as his elite employer. He learned this lesson through experience. In an early stint as a travelling servant on the Continent MacDonald found himself in Ypres, 'a city belonging to the Dutch. At this place his [MacDonald's employer's] coachman came with his chariot and horses, and stopped here one day to rest the horses.'[8] MacDonald offers insights into the very mechanics of eighteenth-century travel. Servants were drawn together by their employer from different places, with different tasks and responsibilities – and with different languages. 'The coachman could not speak French nor English, and I could speak no Dutch; but we spent the evening agreeably together. The landlord was interpreter between us.'[9] It is a relatively short episode, but it is representative of some of the challenges travelling servants met on the road – how does one communicate if one does not share a language with one another? How does one keep oneself entertained in a foreign place?

MacDonald's description evokes a quick camaraderie between servants – he did not know the coachman before that evening, they did not speak the same language, but they clearly managed to bond (if only for one evening). Of the same social status and serving the same employer, MacDonald and the coachman clearly had enough in common to socialise with and entertain each other. The servants drive the narrative – they bring the horses, rest the horses, and spend a pleasant evening together. The elite travelling employer does not appear, it is not mentioned how he spent the evening, nor whether he knew Dutch to communicate with his coachman. This focus makes MacDonald's narrative so intriguing – while his various employers receive much attention, there are many of these small moments to rebalance the score, to remind the reader whose travels we are following. It subtly changes the power relationship between servant and master, if not on the road, then at least in print.

Interactions like the evening in Ypres must have demonstrated to MacDonald that without the knowledge of foreign languages he had to rely on friendly strangers to interpret. Travelling on to Paris, his employer arranged for him to take French lessons: 'I lost no time to improve myself.'[10] But to his chagrin he found that even a second language was not enough to secure prolonged employment. On a subsequent journey MacDonald experienced the limitations of his skills: 'my master found he must go … to Italy for the air …; therefore I had warning given me, as he was obliged to have an Italian servant to take my place.'[11] Despite having travelled successfully together, MacDonald's employer replaced him with another servant. MacDonald is uncharacteristically coy about the reasons for his replacement (he openly admits to his failures that cost him jobs in other passages). But the placement in the narrative, shortly after the Ypres events, and the emphasis on the Italian servant for an Italian journey, suggest that MacDonald's lack of Italian language skills was the issue. Despite having done good work, MacDonald was not skilled enough for his master's needs, nor was he given a chance to make up for his lack of Italian knowledge. A servant's position was only ever as secure as the employer's needs matched the servant's skills.

The power dynamic between master and servant appears clear-cut in the question of hiring and firing. But MacDonald demonstrates that a servant could find ways to make subtle changes to this distribution of power. Through studying foreign languages, a travelling servant could gain more agency in the master-servant relationship. In Lisbon, Portugal, a few years after his evening in Ypres, the reader sees an evolved servant, one who had grown with years of service, one who had learned from past experiences and mistakes. It is one of the most evocative sections in his narrative, showing off both MacDonald's personality as well as his understanding of travel, and it is worth analysing it in steps.

First, while being in Portugal, MacDonald dismissed the Portuguese language:

> There was a great deal of company in the hotel, English, Irish, Scots, Welsh, gentlemen and servants. … The owner of the saddle-horses was an Englishman … As my master and I were going into Spain, at our departure from Lisbon, we both had a Spanish master. We did not mind the Portuguese language.[12]

His account evidences just how many British travellers could be found abroad at any given moment in the second half of the eighteenth century. Surrounded by so many English-speaking gentlemen and servants, MacDonald and his master clearly saw no need to study Portuguese. All their needs for communication, socialisation, and even transport were obtained speaking English. The next destination was Spain, therefore, all focus was on the Spanish language in anticipation, rather than on Portuguese in appreciation of one's surroundings. MacDonald does not provide details on who hired the Spanish master, but it seems likely that his employer paid for the lessons as he was supposed to benefit from them as well.

Second, beyond this aspect of practicalities, MacDonald did not pretend to education for education's sake. It sets him apart from the Grand Tourists with the finances and leisure to engage in learning without immediate purpose. MacDonald's intellectual efforts were tied to his employment in the moment:

> My master made not any improvement in the Spanish language, he was so much out. But I stopped at home, and got my lesson when the other servants went out amongst whores and after their own fun; and they laughed at me for staying at home; but, by and by, when their doctor's bills came in, I laughed at them. After eight weeks at Lisbon, when we were on the road, they were obliged to call me to interpret for them. When they left Lisbon their pleasure there was over, and I enjoyed my own satisfaction.[13]

While demonstrating MacDonald's wit and a good dose of smugness, this paragraph reveals his foresight. His master and other servants went out to enjoy life in Lisbon; MacDonald thought ahead towards the upcoming leg of the journey into Spain. His restraint in seeking out (sexual) pleasure literally paid off, as his newly gained language skills made him indispensable to his employer. In a final triumph, MacDonald notes: 'My master, though he could speak French and Latin as well as English, was obliged to ask me the names of things in Spanish because, when I was in Lisbon, I lost no time, but learned as much of the Spanish language as I could.'[14] MacDonald describes his employer here as the very image of the educated British gentleman who naturally learned French as part and parcel of his education befitting his rank.[15] And yet, this gentleman's disinclination to learning had put MacDonald at an advantage over his social and financial superior.

While MacDonald does not expressly say it, he had clearly learned from earlier experiences, particularly the experience of being fired over his lack of Italian. Instead of having to rely on others' availability and kindness to interpret, he himself became the interpreter. He learnt Spanish to keep his job, thereby displaying a degree of agency; he gained a bargaining chip in a situation in which he used to have none. MacDonald presents himself as someone with long-term thinking and a strategic approach to travel. He proved himself more adept at getting around in a foreign country than the man who hired him. He made himself invaluable as a servant by acquiring skills that others did not possess. Introducing a subtle change to the master-servant relationship, learning a foreign language also meant that MacDonald could engage much more with Spain and the Spanish than his master – a chance to understand more, linguistically and intellectually, of what he would encounter in foreign lands. Ultimately, he demonstrated that his individual approach was the most rewarding – independent of his social status as servant and his lack of riches. He set himself apart from both the group of servants and his elite master.

But MacDonald never left the realities of servant life too far behind. Despite this savvy approach to language learning, only a few pages later, MacDonald recounts a follow-up visit to Portugal – and his master hired a Portuguese interpreter.[16] While on this occasion MacDonald did not lose his job, the presence of another servant with a special skill must have been a reminder just how fragile his position was at all times. One moment a servant might be useful, the next another servant could step in and take over. MacDonald clearly believed in his skills, but his life story is evidence that even being as highly skilled a servant as MacDonald did not guarantee prolonged or permanent employment.

Master-Servant Relationships: A Servant's Opinions

MacDonald's narrative focused on his exploits and his experiences. But as the analysis of his language learning has highlighted, MacDonald was always caught in a web of interdependent relationships, between masters and servants and between servants and servants, which needed careful consideration and occasionally negotiation. These relationships cannot be reduced to master-servant power plays. Having to rely on or being fired in favour of another servant's skills forced MacDonald to consider the presence of other servants at all times.

Wherever MacDonald went, he explicitly noted the presence of other servants in his narrative – a feature that sets his account apart from elite travel writing. Elite narrators often either omitted their servants or mentioned them only when they had caused problems or as a narrative device.[17] MacDonald's matter-of-fact inclusions of servants populates the world he lives in beyond the selective exclusive realm of travelling elites. On the road to Cadiz, MacDonald and his master met 'two French gentlemen' who 'had a chaise and black servant.'[18] In Cadiz, he noticed a 'General [who] was an Irishman, and had a grand attendance, though not one British or Irish servant about him.'[19] In another house in Cadiz, he noted 'two Frenchmen and two Italians' as the only servants: 'there were no maidservants, it not being the custom for the single men in Cadiz.'[20] In fact, he elaborated, there was 'not so much demand for women-servants in Spain, as there are no fine places – only in the kitchen, and, as in Scotland, the cooks are mostly all male.'[21] What all these brief remarks have in common is MacDonald's habit to judge a situation by the way servants were involved.

An Irish General living in grand style without Irish servants in Spain might not have stood out to elite travellers. But to a British servant aspiring to be hired to go abroad, such a choice was significant. Likewise, his remark on the lack of female servants can be read as the observation of an expert: MacDonald's informed comparison is reminiscent of the comparative empiricism that was valued in elite travel narratives. The difference was, of course, that MacDonald applied his comparisons to the more mundane aspects of life – laundry, cooking and errands, whereas elite travel writers would focus on the aesthetics of landscapes or art and architecture.[22]

When MacDonald and his various employers stayed in the company of other travellers, he was often required to organise the workload with other servants: 'As Mr Coke's servant and I were British, we did the work one week, and the French servants another', he notes of a sojourn in Bagnères, France.[23] Servants of different masters had to communicate with each other and even created a form of rota. This arrangement highlights once more just how important foreign language skills were for travelling servants, even if they mostly worked with other

British servants. These relationships between servants presumably lasted only as long as their employers stayed in the same place, but for their duration they were of significance for MacDonald's daily life. And as his Spanish studies in Lisbon proved, occasionally, he had to set himself apart from everyone, including other servants, to achieve his goals.

MacDonald's perspective on other servants reveals his expectations of servant-servant relationships: practically minded and fleeting but also a reflection of the respective masters. His reports of elite activities were equally a portrayal of his expectations. He recorded how his social superiors lived, where and how they dined, whether they sat in carriages or rode horses, how they entertained themselves. His account blends travel narrative and a discussion of master-servant relationships. On Bagnères, he continued:

> They drink the water, ride out, some on horseback, others in carriages, meet to play cards, have balls, and there are fine walks round the town. … Sometimes the company dined in the wood or in a grove. When they came to the place, some walked about, others played cards till dinner-time, everyone speaking the French language.[24]

Similarly, of Lisbon he wrote: 'Some had carriages, others horses, while they remained at Lisbon; and they made a fine appearance when they went together an airing.'[25]

MacDonald evidently approved of their 'fine appearance' and whenever they engaged in gentlemanly activities. In both places, he lists these elite pursuits without further commentary, suggesting that he could not think of anything better to do for these gentlemen. He clearly respected their choices how to spend their time abroad, despite the stark differences between their leisure and his labour. In these passages, his account acquires not just the respect a servant has to pay his master, but the respect MacDonald had for someone who fulfilled the requirements of his social status. While rank is not mentioned once, it is implied in the idea of having horses and carriages at one's disposal, of engaging in walking without purpose, of making a fine, that is, genteel, appearance.

In fact, MacDonald had little patience with masters who failed to live up to their rank. His attitude to clothing represents this best. The following analysis juxtaposes two different masters who appear in MacDonald's account: the first one was a young man, incidentally the same who failed to learn Spanish in Lisbon while MacDonald did. At first, MacDonald seemed to have reason for pride in his employer: 'My master made the genteelest appearance of any gentleman in Lisbon.'[26] But this changed as soon as they entered Spain: 'I was mistaken, at the inns, for [my master]. I begged of my master to wear some of his gold-laced clothes, which he did all through Spain.'[27] Two points of interest are in this quote: one, MacDonald's master did not dress according to his rank and was therefore not recognised as the social superior by the Spanish locals. Two, MacDonald himself must have dressed well enough to make a better impression than his employer. Interestingly, it was the *servant* who took issue with this case of mistaken identity – and only after the servant implored the master, did the elite young man make an effort to live up to his rank.

Not so another of MacDonald's employers – described as a more mature man: 'As my master spoke the Spanish and French as well as Latin, and that, before he left Lisbon, he had a very rich Spanish dress made, trimmed with gold, every one took him for a Spaniard.'[28] MacDonald did not have to make up for his master's lack of language skills or cultural understanding. This man clearly understood what was necessary to uphold the clear distinctions of social status necessary for an orderly society. MacDonald did not have to beg him to wear gold lace, he could be proud of his master – and proud to be his servant.

Crucially, MacDonald did not equate grand living with happiness. Throughout his narrative, he seems happiest when he was abroad and the sole servant to a benevolent master. Living in Spain he writes: 'I cleaned my master's room and my own, and made our beds, and we were as happy as kings together.'[29] And about his last master (incidentally the man who knew how to dress) he writes: 'If ever there was an angel of a man, he was one. … He never did any thing without speaking to me for my advice…'[30] MacDonald's true happiness was to be taken seriously by those he served so faithfully.

This mutual appreciation between master and servant was not easily acquired. MacDonald presents it as the result of hard-won life experience. The perfect travelling servant was not born, he was made by the hierarchical society in which he served. As evidence, MacDonald presented his own biography: by 1760, at the age of nineteen, MacDonald had already accumulated plenty of life experience. He had served different, wealthy masters, had developed skills as a coachman and hairdresser, and fathered a child with a chambermaid. But experience alone meant nothing if one did not know how to understand it:

> I now set out on life, without conduct or this world's cunning. I was a greater plague to my master and benefactor than one would think. I did not know the value of good luck, nor of money. … My master knew what was good for me; but I had not the sense to take his advice. Gentlemen know the world better than we. I was put out of my latitude by contrary winds – I mean women.[31]

MacDonald assessed his youth self-critically. Writing thirty years later he chided himself for being naïve, unprepared, lacking forward-thinking and the good sense to know when someone else knew better. As a young man he clearly was not worried about money and, therefore, not prudent about it either.

Worse, MacDonald made himself unattractive as a servant to many potential employers, namely those with women in the household. After struggling to find employment due to his sexual reputation, he encountered a master who was willing to take him on – and his new master was under no illusions who he was about to hire:

> When I came, the Major said: 'I shall take you for my servant, for you must live with a single gentleman: no family will admit you into their house. I like a man that is given to women – that is gentleman-like – but to drink and swear is to be a blackguard.' I entered my service next day to the best of masters.[32]

Judging from MacDonald's account he took this advice to heart: his womanising habits continued, but, while he is mentioned drinking alcohol, MacDonald never describes himself as drunk after receiving this advice. On the contrary, he recounts incidents in which other servants' drunkenness served as a negative foil to his own moderation in drink.[33] He made sobriety part of his work ethic, even during interludes of unemployment: '[T]hat was my custom; when in place I was careful, and out of place I went genteel and was sober, and was ready in three hours to go anywhere in the world.'[34] From being unreliable and undesirable, he had turned into a skilled, reliable, and adaptive servant ready to drop anything at a moment's notice to travel.

MacDonald's individual conceptualisation of being a servant is framed within a generalised concept of social hierarchy: describing himself as a 'plague' to his master, the quote quickly turns from a personal clash between MacDonald and his employer in 1760 to a broader assessment of masters and servants. 'Gentlemen' did not just know better than himself – in using the plural 'we', he infers that servants as a group were less knowledgeable about the ways of the world than gentlemen. Coming so early in the narrative, this sentiment appears appropriate for a servant who knew his place, writing about a time in his life when he did not. It is only in comparison to the full account that this early assessment of status differences begins to grate: MacDonald frequently presents himself as better prepared and better suited than his masters to deal with the challenges of travelling abroad. He learned Spanish because his employer would not, he had to remind his master of status-appropriate clothes – these instances suggest that the servant understood being genteel better than the genteel master. MacDonald's growing confidence in his understandings and skills can be seen as a subtle redressing of the early rebuke: now, MacDonald knew the world just as well as gentlemen did.

What does this mean for his understanding of social status – his own and that of his masters? MacDonald was not a revolutionary. He did not question the status quo, nor did he show open disdain for his employers. In fact, he often praised them as particularly kind and generous to him and his writings confess his joy in serving them. But in slowly elevating himself throughout his book, in developing his skills and his character into a skilled, honest, loyal servant, MacDonald elevated his social value, too. While he deliberately showed no aspirations to climb the social ladder, he did emphasise his and his social stratum's importance. Without him and servants like him, his employers would not have been able to travel in style, to enjoy their genteel experience abroad. MacDonald made himself indispensable to the upper ranks of society and elevated elite travel through his service. His memoirs are ostensibly about himself and his individual experience, but they can also be read as a reminder of his value and what his work added to society.

'Seeing Me with my Umbrella': A Servant's-Eye View of Cultural Exchange

MacDonald's *Travels* do not dwell on concepts of social hierarchy and the individual value of its members. His philosophy can be found in his hands-on approach. MacDonald's use of food and cooking in his narrative connects the master-servant relationship with cultural exchange. Throughout his narrative, MacDonald employed references to food and drink as a personal form of refinement. He never overindulged; instead he emphasised that he – and by extension his masters – knew how to eat well. He listed dishes and judged how 'fine' they were, as if to determine whether they were suitable for a gentleman. In keeping with his matured approach to alcohol, his journeys made him somewhat of a connoisseur: 'In passing the Pyrenees, we had the best white wine I ever drank.'[35] His own cooking fulfils the same narrative function of sharing gentlemanly taste with gentlemen. MacDonald describes himself serving a variety of meals, from soups to game. He evidently took pride in his cooking and he travelled prepared: 'As for Cayenne pepper, I always had it with me.'[36] It seems unlikely that Cayenne pepper was part of a travelling servant's regular equipment. MacDonald's remark affirms his knowledge of fine dining and the tastes of gentlemen – as if he were one himself.

His cooking can be read as the practical application of all that he learned about elite living. According to the recorded reactions, the culinary results never failed to impress. In France, his English master 'desired me to dress some of the Queen of Scots soup' to be served to a French lady.[37] 'The lady liked the soup very much. She asked if I was the Cousinier?'[38] A few pages later, still in France, MacDonald cooked the same soup for an entire company: 'But I dressed the Queen of Scots soup to perfection; it pleased the company so well, both French and English, that my master next day gave me two louis d'ors.'[39] And some years later, in Spain, he repeated this feat: 'I made a fine dish of [Queen of Scots] soup, and [my master] invited the Frenchmen to sup with him. They liked the soup, and ate nothing else.'[40] The Queen of Scots soup was evidently MacDonald's signature dish, and he knew how to please gentlemanly taste buds. Moreover, these instances all include non-British partakers of the soup. Richard Ansell has identified both language and food as connectors between travellers abroad, transcending differences in origin or beliefs.[41] The favourable reception of MacDonald's cooking is such an instance of connection between foreign travellers as well as masters and servants who otherwise had perhaps little in common.

MacDonald engaged in cultural exchange in the most practical sense of the term: he introduced the fruit of his skills abroad, and he adapted whatever he found useful. Most strikingly, MacDonald credits himself as the man who introduced the English to umbrellas. Here is his description of this remarkable feat, on a sojourn in London in between two Continental journeys:

> At this time there were no umbrellas worn in London, except in noblemen and gentlemen's houses; where, there was a large one hung in the hall, to hold over a lady or gentleman if it rained, between the door and their carriage. … It rained, my sister had hold of my arm, and I had the umbrella over our heads. In Tavistock-street, we met so many young men, calling after us *Frenchman!* take care of your umbrella. *Frenchman*, why do not you get a coach, Monsieur? My sister was so much ashamed, that she quitted my arm, and ran on before, but I still took no notice but answered in French or Spanish that I did not understand what they said. I went on so for three months, till they took no further notice of me … After this, the foreigners seeing me with my umbrella, one after another used theirs, then the English. Now it is become a great trade in London, and a very useful branch of business.[42]

This story is remarkable in several instances: first, MacDonald claims he singlehandedly introduced the habit of carrying an umbrella to the English. Second, MacDonald assumed foreign habits, such as carrying an umbrella, and endured being taunted for it in public. Moreover, he played into it by pretending not to speak English at all. Third, MacDonald implies that foreigners in London were careful to hide the fact that they were foreign, lest they be mocked, too.

He credits himself with encouraging them through his persistent example to display their umbrellas, therefore magnifying the fashion and normalising the sight of umbrellas in London's streets. And, fourth, MacDonald points to the economic advantages created by his promotion of foreign accessories and fashions.

This extraordinary episode tells us as much about English attitudes to foreign influences as it does about MacDonald's personality and approach to travel. MacDonald being ridiculed for his French appearance resonates with the fear of travellers becoming 'Frenchified' or English young men's 'degeneration' into Macaronis, invariably seen as foppish, effeminate men who were in danger of losing their 'Englishness'.[43] On an individual level, the episode portrays MacDonald as someone who almost effortlessly picked and chose what he liked, no matter where he had found it. His travel experience was not unlike that of elite young men's experiences when they came back from abroad. Like them, he was not recognisable as truly English anymore. Unlike them, MacDonald did not translate his travels into societal currency, such as membership in exclusive clubs.[44] Crucially, MacDonald described here a time in his life when he was unemployed in London – he clearly had saved up enough money to support his lifestyle, but he was careful to keep his private and his working life separate. Around his employers he did not dress to impress.

Nor should the umbrella story suggest that MacDonald was free from all prejudice. He reminds his readers of the differences among Europeans: 'The Spaniards, like the Portuguese, are kind and civil; and have not the least idea of overcharging, like the French'.[45] Accusing the French of overcharging is par for the course in British travel writing, and MacDonald does not provide any evidence that this happened, let alone regularly. But overall, MacDonald tried to keep an open mind: 'I was surprised to see the people in Gascony: I thought I was in Scotland, for the people dress in the same manner, with short coats and blue bonnets, and there is not the least difference in their behaviour.'[46] The description of foreign people's dress is a common trope in eighteenth-century travel writing, and it is in these brief impressions and vignettes that the account is most similar to elite travel writing.

However, unlike many elite travellers, he did not use his foreign travels to show off his courage in the face of dangerous situations.[47] In fact, writing about Lisbon he was eager to dispel all prejudice: 'I must say of the country people, they are civil, innocent, and harmless; though it is said, a man's life is in danger, in Lisbon, if he be late out at night. That may be because the desperate, in all countries, flock to the capital.'[48] To avoid emphasising the element of danger abroad, he explained it with a common eighteenth-century phenomenon – people moving from rural areas to urban centres in search of better prospects.[49] The opportunity to deride Lisbon in favour of, for instance, London, was shunned;

instead, MacDonald generalised capital cities as focal points for people down on their luck.

Throughout, MacDonald tried to keep his account respectful of foreign people and places, and he even encouraged his employers to follow local customs, such as wearing gold-lace clothes. But perhaps MacDonald's greatest sign of respect for foreign cultures came in the form of religion: 'From the time I left Lisbon, [travelling through Spain] till I returned to England, I became, or travelled, as a Roman Catholick. I had seen many different religions, and found it was best to pay respect to the people, and conform to their religion.'[50] He illustrated this approach: 'At last I came to a cross road, where was the Virgin Mary, and Christ in her arms. I put off my hat, lowered it, and put it on again, and then crossed myself.'[51] He was immediately questioned by a French gentleman witnessing MacDonald's act of religious devotion: 'He said, Don't you belong to the Church of England? Yes, Sir. I thought you never paid any respect, in your worship, to the holy Virgin. In our worship we do not, but we esteem her.'[52] Many British travellers who wrote about their Continental travels included comments on religious sights and events in their accounts. Richard Bates and Richard Ansell note that anti-Catholic sentiment in theory did not necessarily translate into action abroad: travellers visited Catholic churches and cloisters as places of art and culture; Catholic processions were regarded as entertaining spectacles.[53] But few would have gone so far as to show signs of participation. Given the close ties between identity and anti-Catholicism in eighteenth-century Britain, MacDonald's stance is remarkable in that it not only observed Catholicism from a distance but actively engaged in outward representation.[54]

MacDonald's interpretation of 'travelling as a Roman Catholic' is limited to this outward representation; at no point does he suggest a change of his own beliefs. But he made a point of going 'to the church every place we came at' and therefore 'passed for a Roman Catholick.'[55] However, this method was not fool-proof – he got caught cooking meat for his master on a Friday: 'I told them, when my master was at St Lucar he went to see the High Priest, and desired to be permitted to eat meat as he was travelling through Spain for his health. The High Priest gave my master an indulgence to eat any sorts of birds while in Spain…'[56] MacDonald's account of his stay in St Lucar does not contain any reference to this interaction with a Catholic priest, let alone the acquisition of any form of dispensation.[57] We have to take MacDonald at his word here or we have to assume that MacDonald's respect for other religions included finding convenient loopholes and exploiting them when put on the spot. Nevertheless, MacDonald sufficiently respected the Spanish locals' beliefs to consider the effect of his words and deeds and employ this story, true or untrue, for emotional and spiritual comfort.

Much of MacDonald's approach to cultural exchange can be read as advice for travellers, especially travelling servants. He encourages openness and respect and a willingness to adapt to circumstances. These qualities were certainly of importance to travelling servants who were tasked with the legwork and therefore most likely to encounter and interact with foreigners – other servants, shopkeepers, or tavern keepers. But the most fundamental piece of advice MacDonald reserved for his employers, especially those inexperienced young gentlemen who went abroad as a form of education.

Near Briviesca in Northern Spain, MacDonald's employer pointed out a view, claiming he 'never saw a finer sight; such a fine country, and fine river.'[58] But MacDonald was having none of it: 'Sir, said I, there is a finer sight in Scotland ... from the castle of Stirling. If young noblemen and gentlemen would take notice of Great Britain and Ireland, before they went on their travels, it would make a good foundation for their remarks.'[59] Here, MacDonald is far removed from his own, earlier, assessment that gentlemen knew best – MacDonald knew best, he could tell gentlemen how to make the most out of their travels as well as their subsequent travel writings. In one sentence he delivers a damning critique of elite travel narratives, doubting their very foundation, implying that elite British judgment of foreign sights was ill-conceived as gentlemen did not draw the correct comparisons. If one had not seen the view from Stirling Castle, could one adequately evaluate the quality of views in France or Spain?

MacDonald's remark cannot be minimised to the mere expression of his Scottish pride. Having spent his formative years in Scotland, it often serves as a template for comparisons in his *Travels*, from dress to servants' work. The observation concerning Stirling Castle is to be understood in the same manner. What elevates the quality of this incident is the fact that MacDonald made not only the view from Stirling Castle but the whole of Britain and Ireland the ideal pre-requisite for British genteel education. He advocates for a home tour before the Grand Tour.[60] MacDonald's argument reflects the British discourse around the Grand Tour from the 1760s onwards. Increasingly, the Grand Tour was painted as 'unpatriotic' and the exposure to foreign, especially French, ways of life was seen as damaging to young aristocratic men. While the Grand Tour prevailed into the nineteenth century, its conceptualisation developed alongside new understandings of masculinity and foreign travel as a masculinity-building exercise.[61] MacDonald's account fits in neatly with other, elite, travel accounts of the time. Comparing foreign sights and all manners of experiences to British sights and experiences provided the cultural framework for these accounts, lest the traveller (or reader) strayed too far from the proper patriotic worldview.

But there is another dimension to his argument. Much earlier in his account, he chastises yet another English master for his lack of knowledge and perspective:

> I said, Sir, it would be of great service to young gentlemen, before they go abroad, to make the tour of Great Britain and Ireland, and there they would see the seats of heroes; and learn many things, particularly among the people of Scotland, Ireland, and Wales, whose disposition it is to respect former things, and learn their history without trouble. … But here [in France] you will hear of nothing but eating and dress, and plays, and operas. … The English often take up with men's wives, and when the same measure is returned to them, they don't like it … My master said, I would make a good Presbyterian parson.[62]

MacDonald's call to pay attention to history chimes with eighteenth-century interests in antiquarianism.[63] He was clearly well-informed on contemporary trends, in stark contrast to his elite employers who appear uninformed or disinterested. MacDonald criticised the English approach to travelling – the mindless consumption of entertainment and pleasures of all kinds, including sexual. Chastising his master for adultery appears ironic given MacDonald's own record, but it displays MacDonald's high standard for elite gentlemen. His master's apparent only response is to tease him for his moral stance – a reflection of MacDonald's good standing with his master as well as a sign of the master's condescension not to engage with a servant's opinion in a serious manner.

Moreover, without explicitly stating it, MacDonald draws a parallel between elite travel and his own travel biography: he himself first travelled extensively in Scotland, England, and Ireland before crossing over to the continent.[64] Indeed, MacDonald posits his own experience and education as the ideal way to approach travel. His understanding of gentility was carved out of a life of service, and he held himself to the same standards he applied to his masters. He considered his own introduction to travel – first in Britain and Ireland, then on the European continent – as the ideal order of events to appreciate the sights one saw. Unlike the patriotic and aesthetic discourse at the time he was not against the Grand Tour itself – after all, he built an entire career on it. MacDonald appears to see no difference between elite travel and servant travel anymore, the differences were entirely in the responsibilities and day-to-day activities, but not in the fundamental experience of travel itself.

The value of MacDonald's account lies, therefore, not only in the servant's perspective on the master-servant relationship during travel. It also gives us a new take on cultural encounters, adaptions, and exchanges. John MacDonald's account gives us the perspective of a servant traveller who showed respect to the foreign people and customs he encountered, who held both himself and his masters to high standards, and who adapted to any place across Europe as much as he could. This adaption process was partly out of genuine respect for the cultures and people he encountered but also due to the realisation that it made his life and travels easier. As a servant he bore the brunt of travelling's hardships – he met with the same dangers and inconveniences as his elite employers but, additionally, he had to contend with household chores, and the constant insecurity of his employment.

This elevates his travel narrative beyond the mere mirror of elite travel writing. John MacDonald ostensibly presents a travel account but also a narrative of personal growth – from the young troublemaker to the world-savvy traveller who wore clothes fine enough to impress the Spanish beyond his social status. But despite his obvious self-confidence and his occasional bouts of smugness, MacDonald never aspired to reach beyond his station in life. Instead, he held his elite employers accountable and tried to ensure that they lived up to their own station. In his youth he tried, and sometimes failed, to learn from his social betters, what made a gentleman, how to appreciate a good position in a worthy household. In his mature years, he presents himself as someone who had accomplished becoming the perfect travelling servant and was rewarded with angelic masters. As a seasoned traveller, he now had advice for young gentlemen setting out. Travel had given him a wider perspective than many of the educated gentlemen he travelled with possessed.

Chapter 5

'In the Character of a Corsican': Mediating Chieftain Masculinity in James Boswell's *Account of Corsica* (1768)

Shirley F. Tung

'BOSWELL, thy figure, thus display'd
In garb of Corsica array'd,
So warlike and so bold,
Seems like an herald from afar,
Come to proclaim a general war,
Of which so oft we're told.
But tell us, Boswell, why that crest,
That Moorish head upon thy breast,
So much expos'd to view?
Is it, that those, thy face who see,
May have a hot dispute, Which be
The blackest of the two?'

'Verses on Seeing the Print of James Boswell, Esq.
in the Corsican Dress'.[1]

'Corsica Boswell'

James Boswell (1740–1795) is primarily known as the biographer of the literary critic and lexicographer Samuel Johnson (1709–1784). While *The Life of Samuel Johnson, LL.D.* (1791) is notable for paving the way for modern biography by offering an unflinchingly frank account of its biographical subject, limiting Boswell's professional achievements to this one work would do him a disservice. In addition to being a practicing Advocate (i.e. Barrister) in the Scottish court of law, he was an active journalist, contributing over 600 items to journals and magazines, and anonymously publishing two periodical essay series, *The Hypochondriack* (1777–83) and *The Rampager* (1770–82).[2] Furthermore, during his lifetime, Boswell was famed, not as Johnson's biographer, but rather as 'Corsica Boswell,' named for his popular travel narrative, *An Account of Corsica, The Journal of a Tour to That Island, and Memoirs of Pascal Paoli* (1768).[3]

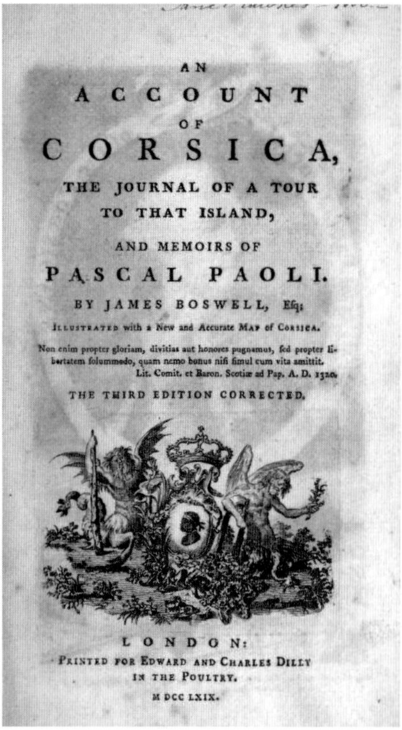

AN ACCOUNT OF CORSICA, THE JOURNAL OF A TOUR TO THAT ISLAND, AND MEMOIRS OF PASCAL PAOLI.

BY JAMES BOSWELL, Esq;

ILLUSTRATED with a New and Accurate MAP of CORSICA.

Non enim propter gloriam, divitias aut honores pugnamus, sed propter libertatem solummodo, quam nemo bonus nisi simul cum vita amittit.
Lit. Comit. et Baron. Scotiæ ad Pap. A. D. 1320.

THE THIRD EDITION CORRECTED.

LONDON:
PRINTED FOR EDWARD AND CHARLES DILLY IN THE POULTRY.
M DCC LXIX.

James Boswell's *Account of Corsica*, Title Page, 1769, 3rd edition

An Account of Corsica offered Britons insight into the short-lived Corsican Republic, which was established in 1755 by General Pasquale Paoli in direct defiance of the Genoese occupation.[4] With Genoese and French armed forces on the ground quelling the rebellion, travel to Corsica was restricted and extremely dangerous, but Boswell, who was in Italy as part of his Grand Tour in 1765, seized upon the rare opportunity to document the nation's ongoing struggle for sovereignty. Yet, *An Account of Corsica* is structured as a tripartite narrative that offers more than mere reportage; it divides into three parts – a history of Corsica, a travel journal, and the *Memoirs of Pascal Paoli*. A diarist and biographer at heart, Boswell balances an impartial historical overview of Corsica in the first part, with a first-person account of his experiences on the island, followed by his description of his time with Paoli – the latter of which he terms 'memoirs.' It was most likely the journal portion of the *An Account of Corsica*, rather than the history, that made it an unparalleled commercial success with the first edition in 1768 selling out within six weeks, followed by equally successful second and third editions and translations into numerous languages.[5]

This chapter will examine how Boswell's distinctive narrative style puts him as a traveller, front and centre, as the unspoken subject of *An Account of Corsica*. As a Post-Union Scot, who mourns the loss of Highland traditions and the fantasy of an independent Scotland following the Jacobite Rising of 1745, Boswell positions himself as a suitable narrator for the Corsican fight for liberty. I have argued elsewhere that Boswell's practices as both biographer and travel writer rely heavily upon recounting his own subjective impressions of people and places.[6] Boswell's focus on his mediational abilities is encapsulated by his self-description as 'an isthmus which joins two great continents' when he introduces Paoli to

Johnson in 1769 – just a year following the publication of *An Account of Corsica*.[7] Like this figurative isthmus that is instrumental in connecting the continents, Boswell goes beyond acting as a 'mere intermediary between Corsica and the reader.' Instead, he makes his narrative intervention integral to the text by providing both thematic continuity and emotional urgency, while simultaneously revealing the tensions and contradictions that arise from a first-person vantage point.[8]

James Boswell by Joshua Reynolds, 1785.

Boswell's vindication of the Corsican cause through its parallels to Anglo-Scottish history recasts, as well as temporally and geographically displaces, Paoli and his Corsican freedom fighters as the denizens of a medieval Scotland defended by Robert the Bruce. Also, Boswell connects the 1729 Corsican rebellion to the Jacobite Risings between 1688 and 1746 in a piece of fictional journalism. To advertise *An Account of Corsica* in January 1766, Boswell published an article in the *London Chronicle* regarding his 'motive in visiting Paoli ... to work out a scheme to have the Chevalier Charles Stuart (the Young Pretender) crowned king of Corsica.'[9] This elaborate fiction was meant to generate reader interest in the forthcoming travel narrative. Given that Boswell's aim for writing *An Account of Corsica* was to rally Britain's political and military support for Corsican independence, his choice of cultural comparison to the Scots is initially puzzling. While the impulse to save what he characterises as a Rousseauvian noble race from cultural extinction seems at odds with Boswell's praises of the British Empire, it also parallels his own self-characterisation as a Scottish laird of 'ancient blood,' who strives to assimilate English manners, ideas, and ambitions at the risk of erasing all traces of his Scottishness.[10] I will argue that in *An Account of Corsica*, Boswell attempts to unify the contradictions inherent in Post-Union Scottish identity by eliding the need for an allegiance to a nation, and instead, valorising an outmoded system of filial loyalty to a single figurehead. Thus, the travel account paints a compelling, though problematic, portrait of the 'violent and brave' Corsicans, who are fiercely devoted to their feudal chieftain, Paoli.[11] For Boswell as a writer, this kind of rugged masculinity embodies a heroic ideal that would operate sympathetically on the imaginations of the British reading public, and garner enthusiasm for the Corsican cause as well as acclaim for himself.

Boswell's 'Little Monument to Liberty'[12]

In the *Preface* to the reader, Boswell reveals that he altered his original plans for the travelogue:

> My first intention was to give only a view of the present state of Corsica, together with Memoirs of its illustrious General. But by the advice of some learned friends, whose judgement I respect, I enlarged my plan, and fixed on that of the execution of which the publick is now to judge.[13]

Boswell aspired to imitate the historiographical rigor and style of Joseph Addison's *Remarks on Several Parts of Italy* (1705), which 'compare[d] the Natural face of the County with Landskips [sic] that the Poets have given it' and set the precedent for eighteenth-century travel narratives.[14] Drawing from French natural history studies and political overviews of Corsica, *Histoire de l'Isle de Corse, par M.G.D.C.* (1749) and *Memoires Historiques &c. par M. Jaussin Ancien Apoticaire Major* (1758), Boswell initially intended to insert 'a large collection of remarks [written] while … in [*sic*] the island' and the memoirs of Paoli as his unique contributions.[15] These plans were altered, however, based on the urging of 'learned friends,' like Samuel Johnson, who cautioned him to keep his project manageable by focusing on his personal experience of Corsica: 'You cannot go to the bottom of the subject; but all that you tell us will be new to us. Give us as many anecdotes as you can.'[16]

Boswell heeded Johnson's advice only partially, adding his *Journal of a Tour to Corsica* as a textual isthmus that bridged the *Account of Corsica* – the aforementioned historiography that Boswell researched and composed in Scotland nearly a year after his journey – to the *Memoirs of Pascal Paoli*.[17] The travel narrative now took shape as a coming of age story that recounts a brave Corsican nation on the brink of independence, which is ungirded by a call for liberty patterned after Jean-Jacques Rousseau's political treatise on free civil society, *The Social Contract* (1762).[18] Further responding to Boswell's detailed publication plans in November 1766, Johnson admonishes him both for lacking originality in his perambulatory historical overview of Corsica and for interceding in political affairs:

> As to your *History of Corsica*, you have no materials which others have not, or may not have. You have, somehow or other, warmed your imagination.

> I wish there were some cure, like the lover's leap, for all heads of which some single idea has obtained an unreasonable and irregular possession. Mind your own affairs and leave the Corsicans to theirs.[19]

As if in direct defiance of Johnson's chastisement, Boswell makes Corsican liberation the organising principle behind *An Account of Corsica*. He introduces the travelogue with a preamble that expounds upon the importance of freedom to the human condition: 'LIBERTY is so natural, and so dear to mankind, whether as individuals, or as members of society, that it is indispensably necessary to our happiness. Every thing great and worthy ariseth from it.'[20] This introduction concludes by situating Boswell's account as an appeal from 'the first Briton who has had the curiosity to visit Corsica' to the 'Powers of Europe' to stop standing 'aloof' and to come to aid of the 'brave islanders, when their patriotick virtue is at its height.'[21]

Nevertheless, Johnson's critique anticipates the complications that arise when the travel writer, who serves as a conduit for the reader's experience, plays the role of political activist. Perhaps, Johnson was aware that much of the Corsican historiography portion of the travel narrative would be presented strategically to bolster Boswell's credibility and to justify his fanaticism. Indeed, Boswell adopts the initial posture of a knowledgeable and impartial travel writer to serve a propagandistic purpose.[22] The tripartite narrative structure enables Boswell to present his slow conversion from dispassionate observer to a champion of the Corsican rebellion against its Genoese overlords – a process that mirrors his narrative movement from an outsider to a member of Paoli's inner sanctum. To prime his readers for the first-person journal account that encompasses the second and third sections, Boswell sets the stage in his historiography by depicting the Corsicans in a number of rhetorical guises – a strategy that he practised as an avid diarist. In the private Grand Tour journals he composed from 1764 to 1766, which scholars have dubbed a 'Grand Tour of Selves,' Boswell pastiches fictional and historical characters to show 'himself in as many lights as possible.'[23] Boswell modifies this technique in *An Account of Corsica*, interweaving literary allusions, dramatic vignettes, and sociocultural comparisons to shed the best light on the Corsican populace and its leader Paoli.

The History of Corsica 'Adorned with Poetical Fables'

To the casual reader, the first part of Boswell's travel narrative appears like any other historical and political overview. It is divided into three chapters dedicated respectively to the 'Situation, Extent, Air, Soil, and Productions, of Corsica,' 'A concise View of the Revolutions which Corsica has undergone from the earliest times,' and 'The Present State of Corsica, with respect to Government, Religion, Arms, Commerce, Learning, the Genius and Character of its Inhabitants.'[24] Each part of this seemingly impartial historiography is crafted, however, to present Corsica as a heroic nation using illustrative examples that are legible to British readers and operate on their sensibility and imagination. Chapter one aligns Corsica with Ithaca from Homer's *Odyssey* to emphasise that the Corsicans are made hardy by their vertiginous environment. Boswell establishes the comparison of Corsica to Ithaca when describing the remote Corsican village of Nonza, which sits 'on a high rock, on the extreme pinnacle of which, some hundred fathoms above the gulf.'[25] Beginning with the claim that 'Nonza is literally what Cicero calls Ithaca [,] … "Stuck on the rudest cliffs like a little nest,"' Boswell quickly extends the comparison to Ithaca to the *entire* mountainous region of Corsica:[26]

> …the interiour parts of the island are in general mountainous… and inspire one with the genius of the place; with that undaunted and inflexible spirit, which will not bow to oppression. As Homer says of Ithaca: 'Strong are her sons, tho' rocky are her shores.'[27]

By the end of chapter one, Corsica is supplanted by its imagined literary predecessor, when Boswell 'conclude[s]… with Homer's description of Ithaca, which, in general, may be applied to Corsica.'[28] The final couplet of the passage that Boswell includes from *The Odyssey* indicates the import of this comparison: 'Ev'n to those shores is Ithaca renown'd/ Where Troy's majestick ruins strow the ground.'[29] No longer is Corsica just a landscape that fosters resilience and strength in 'her sons,' but rather, it looms large as a land of epic heroes as 'renown'd' as Troy itself.

Chapter two continues the narrative of Corsica belonging to the ancient world immortalised by classical literature. Boswell opens with a quotation from Livy, 'the origin of every nation is… Adorned with poetical fables', to indicate his method for recounting Corsica's past political and social upheavals.[30] Keeping to the spirit of 'poetical fables,' Boswell credits Herodotus with establishing that the Corsicans originate from the 'Phenicians' (i.e. Phoenicians) – an ancient civilisation famed for the Carthaginian queen Dido, chronicled in Virgil's *Aeneid*.[31] Boswell then recounts a long line of empires and countries that conquered the Corsicans, giving special credence to the 'Saracens [who] maintained the dominion there for a considerable time [and] first gave the title of kingdom to Corsica; and, to this day, the coat armorial of the island bears a Moor's head on its shield.'[32]

According to Boswell, this centuries-long history of conquest puts the need for Corsican liberty into relief:

> Let Corsica have been the property of the Phenicians, the Etruscans, the Carthaginians, the Romans, the Goths, the Saracens: let it have been a conquest of France; a gift from that kingdom to the pope; a gift again from the pope to the Pisans, and at length a conquest of Genoa; still we must have recourse to the plain and fundamental principle, that the Corsicans are men, and have a right to liberty; which, if usurped by any power whatever, they have at all times a just title to vindicate.[33]

Boswell argues that liberty is an inalienable right that the populace can enact, regardless of the duration they have been under another's yoke. To avoid veering into Republicanism, Boswell tempers this discourse by centering his attack on the unfitness of the Genoese government: 'The Genoese were the worst nation to whom Corsica could have fallen.'[34] Highlighting the mismatch between the Corsicans and their Genoese overlords, Boswell characterises the Corsicans as an 'impetuous, violent and brave' people that can only be 'governed ... by a state of which they stood somewhat in awe' – an awe that the Genoese are unable to inspire.[35] Unlike the previous line of illustrious conquerors, the Genoese did not claim Corsica through their 'cunning, and impotent attempts to seize upon the island,' but rather, were put in charge of the country by chance, through an 'unexpected course of events.'[36] Furthermore, Boswell stresses that these Genoese leaders share little in common with the imperial rulers that preceded them, because they are merely an opportunistic 'nation of republicans just in the neighbourhood,' who lack the power and stability to be competent rulers ('the Genoese ... were themselves in an unstable, and perilous condition, seeking the protection sometimes of one powerful state, and sometimes of another').[37]

Boswell's depiction of the Corsicans is of a noble but 'rude nation,' whose hard-won and tenuously held freedom from the Genoese requires the protection of a politically stronger and culturally enlightened imperial power, like Great Britain.[38] Boswell's sketch of Corsican governmental procedures emphasises the relative democratic process for electing governing officials (for example, the representatives in 'supreme council of state' are chosen 'by votes viva voce, if they are unanimous; and if not unanimous, by ballot'), suggesting a civil society in its nascence.[39] To delineate the Corsicans as a civilisation that requires the sovereignty afforded by British protection to flourish, Boswell also provides ethnographical accounts of their so-called 'rude' cultural practices, like how the 'Corsicans love much to lie round a fire [which is a] practice... peculiar to rude nations,' or the funerary custom of married women in the village, who 'beat and tear' a newly widowed woman 'in a most miserable manner.'[40] Ultimately, these comparisons to 'The Indians in north America [,] the ancient Germans,' and more pointedly, the 'Scots Highlanders,' are meant to operate upon the British Empire's enlightenment rhetoric for colonial expansion as reforming and advancing civilizations throughout the world.[41] Boswell directly solicits this civic-minded reader by invoking their shared moral sentiments and responsibility as Britons: 'When we thus view the Corsicans gloriously striving for the best rights of humanity … and forming a virtuous and happy nation, can we be indifferent to their success? Can we Britons forbear to admire their bravery, and their wisdom?'[42] As we will see, Boswell leverages his position as a Briton – and specifically as a bridge between cultures as an Anglo-Scot – to strike an emotional chord with his British reader.

The Scottish '*ambasciatore Inglese*'

In *An Account of Corsica, The Journal of a Tour to That Island, and Memoirs of Pascal Paoli* (1768) Boswell innovates upon existing narrative form. Despite the discrete categories signalled by the titles 'journal' and 'memoirs,' the life-writing portion of the travel account interweaves first-person recollections of the island with Boswell's record of Paoli's *bon mots* and his extended character sketch of the Corsican general. Here, Boswell appears to heed the advice that Johnson gave him in 1766, and supplies 'as many anecdotes as [he] can' by organising them in a journal format that prioritises his 'own experience and observation.'[43] As he reveals to the reader, Boswell aims to provide only curated details: 'In writing this Journal, I shall not tire my readers, with relating the occurrences of each particular day. It will be much more agreeable to them, to have a free and continued account of what I saw or heard, most worthy of observation.'[44] Likewise, the *Memoirs of…Paoli* follows a similar methodology:

> I wrote down every night what I had observed during the day…that I might afterwards make a selection at leisure. Of these particulars, the most valuable to my readers…must surely be the memoirs and remarkable sayings of Paoli, which I am proud to record.[45]

Boswell's reconstitution of these initial impressions – 'contracting parts, enlarging others, suppressing conversations, or introducing new material' – conveys the 'sense that he spent much longer than the bare week he had with Paoli.'[46] Not only does this reorganisation of memories enable him to manipulate narrative time, but Boswell can also reorder the chronology of his account to achieve a greater rhetorical effect than his historiography of Corsica.

The journal expounds upon the preceding historiographical depiction of Corsica as a semi-civilised nation on the brink of enlightenment, but contracts the scale of its examination. Boswell shifts from a temporally expansive, well-researched,

James Boswell by George Wilson, 1765.

sweeping overview of Corsican culture and politics to a prosaic, seemingly extempore, intimate portrait of his personal interactions with individual Corsicans. In the journal account the part is meant to stand in for the whole: either through villager anecdotes that are taken for fact, or synecdochally, as with Signor Luigi, the son of the Great Chancellor, whose 'ideas were entirely Corsican.'[47] These beginning pages of the journal prime the reader for Boswell's later encounter with Paoli – 'the father of a [Corsican] nation' – in whom he sees his 'highest idea realized.'[48] Additionally, this focus on Corsican exemplars mirrors Boswell's positioning of himself as someone who straddles both civilised and ancient worlds as an Anglo-Scot, and who is, therefore, able to act as the champion of and conduit for the Corsican cause.

Much like how the first section of the travel narrative expounds upon *The Social Contract*'s evocative claim that 'Man is born free, and he is everywhere in chains,' Boswell's second section follows in Rousseau's footsteps to support the 'little island [that one day] will astonish Europe.'[49] *The Journal of a Tour* begins with a visit to Rousseau in Switzerland to obtain a letter of introduction, since 'Rousseau had some correspondence with the Corsicans, and had been desired to assist them in forming their laws.'[50] Boswell's glorified depiction of the Corsicans 'fighting for liberty, and forming themselves from a poor inconsiderable oppressed nation, into a flourishing and independent state' is heavily informed by the Rousseauvian concept of the 'noble savage.'[51] Particularly, Boswell draws explicit 'parallel[s] between Paoli's insurgent Corsica and Robert Bruce's medieval Scotland' by comparing their patriotic courage, their landscape and livestock (e.g. Corsican horses are likened to 'shelties, which are found in the highlands and islands of Scotland'), and their social and physical similarities (e.g. 'The Corsicans are in general of small stature, and rather hard-favoured, much like the Scots Highlanders') to unite the two countries by a shared pastoral heritage.[52] These allusions to a medieval Scotland entrenched in the Wars of Independence, however, complicate Boswell's argument for Corsican sovereignty, as it suggests that this fight for liberty psychologically fulfills an unattainable fantasy of preserving a pastoral and independent Scotland. Moreover, while Boswell aims to convince his British readers that Corsica's 'spirit of liberty…can be found in the annals' of their shared history as a unified Britain, he configures this spirit in specifically Scottish terms – even resorting to dozens of Scotticisms that were edited out in the third edition of the *An Account of Corsica* in 1769.[53]

Although Boswell's travel account has been deemed as 'beneath the surface a text about Scotland,' the effect of his conflicted Post-Union Scottish identity on the narrative has yet to be explored fully.[54] Boswell portrays himself as a cultural chameleon to demonstrate how his duality as British envoy *and* liberty-loving Scottish nationalist gives him privileged access and insight into the Corsican cause. Instead of legitimising his role as a Corsican insider, however, Boswell's ambiguous identity, which is depicted as the subject of much speculation by the Corsicans, destabilises his ability to be both an imperialist and a revolutionary. He is alternately suspected of being a spy, mistaken for a recruiter for the Scottish regiment, treated as a foreign dignitary, and addressed by the honorary title *ambasciatore inglese*.[55] Boswell initially exploits this confusion by cultivating the belief that he represented British interests in order to elevate himself as a 'man of consequence.'[56] Also, it appears that Boswell refers to himself as English – used in *An Account of Corsica* as shorthand for British – and Scottish, interchangeably, to satisfy Corsican expectations. Upon arriving in Corsica, Boswell identifies himself as 'English' to the captain of the guard, who retorts, 'The English – they were once our friends, but they are so no more.'[57] In response to this negative reaction, Boswell is prompted by his 'feel[ings] for [his] country' to use his reputation among Corsicans to 'do everything in [his] power to make them fond of the British.'[58]

This performance of dual British and Scottish identities is evident when Boswell recounts entertaining Corsican peasants and soldiers by playing the German flute:

> I gave them one or two Italian airs, and then some of our beautiful old Scots tunes: *Gilderoy, The Lass of Patie's Mill*, "Corn rigs are bonny." The pathetic simplicity and the pastoral gaiety of the Scots music will always please those who have the genuine feeling of nature … My good friends insisted also to have an English song from me. I sung them "Hearts of oak are our ships, Hearts of oak our men" … I fancied myself to be a recruiting sea officer. I fancied all my chorus of Corsicans aboard the British fleet.[59]

Boswell transitions between national affiliations in response to his Corsican audience – first appealing to their 'genuine feeling[s] [for] nature' by using 'beautiful old Scots tunes' to highlight the pastoral aspects of Britain; he then shifts to 'an English song' to celebrate the martial prowess of the Royal Navy during the Seven Years' War. For the Corsicans, Boswell's nationality is also doubly inscribed. Their demand for a specifically 'English song' demonstrates that the Corsicans view the 'old Scots tunes' as foreign both to the English language and England itself, while still recognising Boswell's ability to comply with such a request.

Boswell thus indulges contradictory fantasies of a Pre-Union Scotland and a military alliance with Post-Union Britain when he shares Scottish and English tunes with his Corsican audience. The 'beautiful old Scots tunes' evoke a Scotland and Corsica united by idyllic 'simplicity and pastoral gaiety' and emphasise the importance of the preservation of tradition and cultural autonomy.[60] In contrast, the English song, 'Heart of Oak,' facilitates solidarity between Boswell and the Corsicans, but the tune situates their unity within the rhetoric of British maritime dominance. By imagining himself as a recruiting officer and the Corsicans as members aboard the British fleet, Boswell romanticises the same type of imperial power that endangers Corsican independence from Genoa and France. Boswell's juxtaposition of Bruce's medieval kingdom of Scotland against eighteenth-century Britain at the height of its colonial expansion highlights the tensions of a Scotland under British rule. This evokes an anachronistic parallel between the 1729 Corsican rebellion and the relatively recent Scottish and English military conflicts during the Jacobite Risings between 1688 and 1746. In this context, Boswell's call for Corsican independence is undermined by his complicity with the Union between Scotland and England and his adoption of a Post-Union British identity.

The 'Exalted … Character' of Paoli

Boswell's treatment of the biographical hero of his account of Paoli in the last section of the book is similarly complicated by his displacement of Pre-Union Scottish ideals within a Post-Union British model and disrupts the political tenor of *An Account of Corsica*. The memoir's preoccupation with 'that Plutarchan aim of communicating to the reader "what sort of man" Paoli was' takes precedence over showcasing Paoli as a suitable political ally for Great Britain.[61] Boswell initially idealises Paoli by expressing his growing anticipation over meeting the Corsican general as he nears Paoli's residence:

> When I at last came within sight of Sollacarò, where Paoli was, I could not help being under considerable anxiety. My ideas of him had been greatly heightened by the conversations I had held with all sorts of people in the island, they having represented him to me as something above humanity.

> I had the strongest desire to see so exalted a character; but I feared that I should be unable to give a proper account why I had presumed to trouble him with a visit, and that I should sink to nothing before him.[62]

Frontispiece portrait of Paoli, *Account of Corsica*, 1769, 3rd edition.

This simultaneous apprehension and curiosity to see the great Paoli is also felt by the reader, because, even though he does not appear until a third of the first-person account elapses, Paoli looms large in Boswell's imagination. When Paoli actually materialises upon Boswell's first sight of him ('I found him alone, and was struck with his appearance'), the *Journal* seamlessly gives way to the *Memoirs* without an obvious transition between the genres, as if the grand presence of the Corsican leader immediately grants him command over the narrative.[63] Once again, Boswell concomitantly deploys and corrects Rousseau's model of the 'noble savage,' admitting that he had expected Paoli to be a 'rude character, an Attila King of the Goths.'[64] Though Paoli defies these expectations, Boswell still delineates him in Rousseauvian terms, attributing his 'mark of a real great character' to a natural nobility found only in 'ancient noblemen.'[65] By defining Paoli's 'rule' as one based on an antiquated system of loyalties that mimic filial attachment ('They were men of power [who] could bring hundreds of followers into the field'), Boswell implicitly renders Paoli a Corsican Robert Bruce, possibly unfit for the demands of modern leadership.[66]

Despite his claim that Paoli's authentic nobility far exceeds 'modern nobility [who] are so anxious to preserve an *appearance* of dignity,' Boswell's memoir does not discuss Paoli's political significance, but instead, 'paint[s] [the General's] manner' to 'charm' readers into admiring Paoli for his character.[67] By capturing Paoli's great 'versatility of mind' in selected sayings over the course of a week, Boswell operates as a conduit through which he distills Paoli's 'exalted … character' for a British audience relatively familiar with the Corsican struggle for independence from Genoese rule but lacking firsthand insight into the people of the island and its leader.[68] Boswell attempts to foster in his genteel readership

Filippo Antonio Pasquale de' Paoli by Richard Cosway.

an affection for Paoli similar to the one expressed by the Corsican populace by couching his description of Paoli in the terms of polite society. In doing so, Boswell blurs the distinction between authenticity and affectation, praising his subject for possessing classical learning, a quickness of mind, and a knack for 'agreeable conversation,' which exceeds that of 'professed wits.'[69]

Rather than providing a detailed insight into the daily life, thoughts, and behavior of the Corsican patriot, Boswell's *Memoirs of Pascal Paoli* reads like an extended, glorified and glorifying character sketch, consisting of vague descriptions of Paoli coupled with the general's pithy 'philosophical speculations' ('I know the arguments for fate and free-will, for the materiality and immateriality of the soul [but] I always hold firm one object') and observations on the 'affairs of state' ('I am desirous that the Corsicans should be taught to walk of themselves. Therefore when they come to me to ask whom they should choose for their ... Magistrate, I tell them, You know better than I do, the able and honest men among your neighbours').[70] For example, though Boswell is 'struck with his appearance,' he does not detail Paoli's distinctive features, but rather, characterises him using imprecise terms: 'He is tall, strong, and well made; of a fair complexion, a sensible, free, and open countenance, and a manly and noble carriage.'[71] Similarly, Boswell labels Paoli a 'fine classical scholar [with a] mind ... enriched with a variety of knowledge,' and while he provides an assortment of Paoli's sayings, Boswell never presents the date, precise context, or 'a single conversational exchange between himself and the Corsican.'[72] As a result, Paoli may not be 'every moment of his life a hero' as Boswell purports, but *An Account of Corsica* certainly portrays its biographical subject as a hero in all the moments that Boswell shares with him.

This attempt to translate the natural marks of Paoli's ancient nobility into the affected attributes of a refined gentleman results in the puzzling *non sequitur* that concludes Boswell's memoirs of Paoli and *An Account of Corsica*. Before closing the travel narrative with William Pitt's comparison of Paoli to 'those men who are no longer to be found but in the *Lives* of Plutarch,' Boswell reproduces a letter from Paoli with a brief commentary valorising his subject's wit, specifically in comparing the Genoese government to highwaymen. Boswell's commentary concludes:[73]

> Can anything be more condescending and at the same time show more firmness of an heroic mind than this letter? With what a gallant pleasantry does the Corsican chief talk of his enemies! One would think that the queens of Genoa should become Rival Queens for Paoli. If they saw him, I am sure they would.[74]

This final appraisal raises a different, and arguably, antithetical idea of manliness to the one that Pitt evokes with the comparison to Plutarch's *Lives*. Boswell's reference to Nathaniel Lee's Restoration tragedy *Rival Queens* (1677) aligns Paoli with Alexander the Great, not in terms of his military ambition as in Plutarch's *Life of Alexander*, but as a love object at the center of two women's violent affections. This representation of Paoli as a dashing gallant capable of seducing Genoese royalty is based on a performative idea of masculinity influenced by Boswell's perception of himself as caught between states of *retenu* and *étourdi*, as well as his preoccupation with sexual conquest.[75] The comment comes at the end of Boswell's only recorded period of abstinence during his Grand Tour (Boswell heeds the warning that if he 'attempted to debauch any [Corsican] women, [he] might expect instant death') and may be the result of Boswell's projection of sexual frustration onto Paoli, whom Boswell notes is similarly abstemious.[76] Hence, the interjection plays upon the two contradictory meanings of gallant: one that upholds Boswell's earlier character sketch of Paoli as a 'calm...master of himself' – 'Fine; noble; spacious' – and the other belies a lack of sexual control and social propriety ('A whoremaster, who caresses women to debauch them').[77] Boswell mischievously insinuates that Paoli's 'heroic mind' and wit grant him access not just to women's hearts, but also their boudoirs.

While this reference to Genoese 'Rival Queens' initially appears to disrupt the sober character sketch of Paoli as Plutarchan hero, it reveals the literary turn that *An Account of Corsica* takes in the latter half – especially in the *Memoirs of Pascal Paoli*. Boswell's portrayal of the Corsican general as a gallant who captures the hearts and imaginations of his readers centers on a masculine ideal that combines the 'rugged, uncultured independence' of the Corsicans and the Highlanders with the erudition, wit, and 'intellectual relish' that is requisite of 'London life' and Boswell's Literary Club.[78] In a similar manner to the way that Boswell facilitates the 1769 meeting of Paoli and Johnson – thus uniting the 'father of a [Corsican] nation' with 'Monarch of English Letters' – this romanticisation of Paoli's 'heroic mind' at the end of the *Memoirs* melds 'political and military fantasies of heroism' with 'greatness of a ... literary kind.'[79] Consequently, instead of focusing on Paoli as a military leader, Boswell prioritises his cultural significance as a figure of ancient nobility – one that *An Account of Corsica* seeks to immortalise in textual form.

'An Account of the Armed Corsican Chief at the Masquerade'[80]

The rhetorical shift from the preservation of Corsican liberty to the preservation of cultural memory is indicated by an epigraph on the title page to *The Journal of a Tour to Corsica; and Memoirs of Pascal Paoli*: 'Olim meminisse juvabit.'[81] Roughly translated as 'Some day it will be a pleasure to recall,' the quotation is from book 1, line 203 of Virgil's *Aeneid* when Aeneas attempts to lift the spirits of his fellow Trojans after they have escaped their burning city.[82] While Boswell may be alluding to an imperial destiny for the Corsicans akin to the Trojans' eventual founding of Rome, the quotation also evokes a moment of great loss and the need for collective mourning through memorialisation. Whereas Boswell's historiography transfigures Corsica as Ithaca – the birthplace of another epic hero of the Trojan war, Odysseus – the epigraph to the *Journal* and *Memoirs* problematically aligns Corsica with ransacked Troy. Since this portion of travel account is dedicated solely to recollection, it appears that what would 'some day … be a pleasure to recall' is the 'idyllic pastoral existence, reminiscent of Horace' of an independent Corsica led by a charismatic, well-loved chieftain – an idyll that will be implicitly destroyed.[83] While at the time of the first printing of *An Account of Corsica* in February 1768, the Corsican Republic had yet to be quelled by Genoese and French forces, this call for remembrance signals a change in Boswell's role from a stalwart defender of Corsican freedom to a chronicler of liberated Corsica's last moments. Perhaps, like Aeneas, Boswell recognized the limits of his own performative oratory in saving what has been, or will be, lost.

This complete turn toward performativity in representing the Corsican cause is embodied by Boswell's masquerade as 'an armed Corsican chief' at the Shakespeare Jubilee of 1769.[84] A three-day festival from 6–8 September 1769 organized by the Drury Lane Theatre actor and manager, David Garrick, the Shakespeare Jubilee was held to fund a Shakespeare statue for the new town hall in Stratford-upon-Avon, but also, to rejuvenate the town's waning interest in its bard.[85] The highlight of the Jubilee was the masquerade ball held on the second night, which was attended by over 1,000 revelers, finely attired in costumes ranging from domino masks to 'characters from Shakespeare's plays, including the witches from Macbeth and Mistress Quickly from The Merry Wives of Windsor.'[86] Unlike the other revelers in attendance, Boswell was attired not in costume, but rather, an authentic 'Corsican dress' that was made for him during his travels, complete with Paoli's 'own pistols, made in the island, all of Corsican wood and iron, and of excellent workmanship,' which the General had gifted to him.[87]

Boswell poses as an anonymous contributor in the September 1769 issue of *The London Magazine* to provide a detailed description of this Corsican habit and his 'performance' in the 'character of a Corsican' at the Shakespeare Jubilee[88]:

James Boswell in dress of Corsican chief by John Sebastian Miller, 1769.

> He wore a short dark-coloured coat of coarse cloth, scarlet waistcoat and breeches, and black spatterdashes & his cap or bonnet was of black cloth; in the front of it was embroidered in gold letters, VIVA LA LIBERTA ... On the breast of his coat was a sewed a Moor's head, the crest of Corsica, surrounded with branches of laurel ... and on his life side a pistol was hung ... [He] wore no powder in his hair, but had it plaited at its full length, with a knot of blue ribbands at the end of it ... He wore no mask; saying that it was not proper for a *gallant* Corsican ... Mr. Boswell danced both a minuet and country dance with a very pretty Irish lady, Mrs. Sheldon, wife to Captain Sheldon of the 38th regiment of foot (Lord Blaney's): she was dressed in a genteel domino; and before she danced, threw off *her mask*.[89]

Rather than acting as a politicised and sober reminder of Corsica, which through the *Treaty of Versailles* between Genoa and France in May 1768 had succumbed to French rule, Boswell distinguishes himself as an object of spectacle.[90] Boswell's masquerade in Corsican dress operates as a form of wish fulfillment by allowing him to impersonate Paoli, and by extension, participate in the 'gallant pleasantry' that Boswell's *non sequitur* at the end of the *Memoirs* envisions. As with Paoli's Genoese 'Rival Queens,' Boswell's effectiveness as a gallant Corsican general is measured by his ersatz paramour, Mrs. Sheldon, who, inspired by Boswell's unmasked face, violates the conventions of the masquerade and exposes her own. This 'double exposure' highlights that Boswell's unmasked face is not part of his Corsican disguise, but rather, an attempt to draw attention to his identity as 'Corsica Boswell.'[91]

Boswell's masquerade in Corsican dress may also be read as a physical manifestation of his subject position as travel writer in *An Account of Corsica*. Just as he uses the Corsican dress to distinguish himself among the other maskers, Boswell's travel narrative is as much a 'monument to himself as a writer as it is to [Corsican] liberty.'[92] Certainly, Boswell's figurative role as an isthmus, or a conduit, for the reader's experience of the Corsican Republic illustrates the double nature of first-person travel accounts, which reveal more about their writer than their subject. This is illustrated by Johnson's praise for *An Account of Corsica* in 1769, which centers on Boswell's delivery of a moving, personal narrative:

> You express images which operated strongly upon yourself, and you have impressed them with great force upon your readers. I know not whether I could name any narrative by which curiosity is better excited, or better gratified.[93]

Whereas three years earlier Johnson had criticized Boswell for his 'warm[th] of imagination,' he now commends Boswell for enthralling the fancy of his readers.[94] Johnson's commentary, however, gestures to the limits of Boswell's narrative as political commentary. Boswell may have 'appeal[ed] to British sympathies,' but his travel narrative was ineffectual politically in convincing 'statesmen (like Pitt) ... of the possibility that Paoli ... might exert real power in a Mediterranean world of shifting spheres of influence.'[95]

Despite his failed attempt to sway British foreign policy, and the subsequent annexation of Corsica by France only months after the publication of *An Account of Corsica*, Boswell was still motivated to keep Corsica and Paoli in the press – even well over a decade following his fateful journey. In addition to supplying various periodicals with four separate pieces about his appearance in Corsican dress at the Shakespeare Jubilee, Boswell references Corsica in two issues – dated 1770 and 1777 respectively – of *The Rampager*, and publishes 'An Authentick Account of General Paoli's Tour to Scotland' in September 1771.[96] These publications indicate Boswell's movement from promoting Corsican liberty to promoting himself as an influential, celebrated author *vis-à-vis* the enduring legacy of Paoli and the Corsican Republic. In particular, Boswell constructs himself as a travel writer and memoirist up to the task of immortalising his 1773 trip with Johnson to the remote isles of Scotland in 1785.

Chapter 6

'A stranger in this country': British Singers, Travel, and Education

Brianna E. Robertson-Kirkland

Eighteenth-century London was a cultural hub, attracting the most renowned musicians and singers from across Europe to perform in concerts and operas. However, the popularity of Italian opera and the impact of foreign singers opting to establish long-term careers in Britain was that native singers increasingly found that they needed to travel to the continent to acquire the necessary vocal and musical skills to compete with their foreign colleagues. This chapter will consider how the experience of travelling and working in Europe impacted native British singers, including how they were received by British audiences once they returned from the continent. While travel was considered important in developing a British singer's professional career in the latter half of the eighteenth century, certain singers were heavily criticised, to the extent that they were deemed a foreigner in what was once their native land.

Nancy Storace by Pietro Bettelini, 1788.

British-born singers Michael Kelly (1762–1826), Anna Selina Storace (1765–1817), and Elizabeth Billington (1765–1818) all travelled to the continent in pursuit of further musical education and performance opportunities. Their travels often followed the same route as those on the Grand Tour and as such, these singers performed for, and were supported by, British Grand Tourists. Kelly's education and travels were published in 1826, and though scholars have criticised *The Reminiscences of Michael Kelly* for its inaccuracies and exaggeration,[1] it provides a detailed insight into the importance of travel, particularly when in pursuit of further education and how it could impact a singer's career.[2] Storace and Billington did not publish similar accounts of their travels, but both women made their intentions to travel for the purposes of education publicly known, thus providing a rare insight into what they deemed necessary and important in elevating their vocal careers. As will be discussed, once Storace returned to London, she styled herself as an Italian prima donna even though she was born and had received her initial vocal training in Britain. As such, she established a more direct link with her Italian heritage and showcased the many years she spent performing in Italian operas in Italy and Austria. Kelly also worked with Storace on the continent and, as such, *The Reminiscences* provide further insight into her journeys as well as his own. Kelly, Storace, and Billington later returned to Britain performing in concerts, operas, and oratorio. These singers were praised for pursuing further education abroad, but not all received the same praise once they returned from their travels. Indeed, critics commented that Kelly and Storace were so out of touch with British performance practice conventions that they were considered 'strangers' in their home country.

Many Italian musicians came to London to forge a musical career as Britain's music business offered migrants the opportunity to make a living, though this was seen as an opportunity rather than a certainty.[3] For many of these migrant musicians, there was no clear path to success; rather their careers more closely resembled that of a swinging pendulum, where they experienced years of hardship and years of prosperity. The castrato Venanzio Rauzzini (1746–1810) came to Britain to be the leading man at the King's Theatre, a position he held for three successive seasons. By 1782, just two years after he became the leader of the Bath Subscription Concert series, he landed himself for a short time in a debtor's prison in London.[4] After his release, Rauzzini was able to build a successful concert series, but there were periods of financial hardship when loyal subscribers would try to help by offering money or encouraging more subscribers to support the Bath concerts.[5] Fellow musician Domenico Corri (1746–1825) similarly came to Britain with a position already in hand. His wife, Francesca Corri (c.1750–1802), was invited to be a leading singer for the Edinburgh Musical Society, with Corri offered a position as an instrumentalist. After their arrival, Corri quickly became an impresario, a composer, a music master, and a publisher, who established publishing houses in both Edinburgh and London. Unfortunately, in 1799, Corri's London house, Corri, Dussek, and Co., was publicly declared bankrupt.[6] Though Corri worked to re-establish himself, including writing a popular singing treatise titled *The Singer's Preceptor* in 1810, he continued to experience periods of financial instability and ended up in a debtor's prison in 1807 and 1815.[7]

Despite the challenges of maintaining a lucrative career in Britain, the long-term impact these migrant musicians had on Britain's music industry is undeniable. Italian opera attracted audiences throughout the eighteenth century, with the King's Theatre, London known as the home of Italian opera well into the nineteenth century.[8] Italian singers were often lured to London to perform leading roles in concerts and in the opera, with theatre managers offering huge fees as an incentive. Such financial practices were regularly commented upon by Italian opera supporters and British nationalists who despised foreign musicians getting paid such high fees.[9] In 1794, John Payne noted: The 'genius' of the Italian language 'seems particularly adapted to poetry and music; for which the Italians are so famous; and hence the Italian singers are more admired and more liberally paid than those of any other nation.'[10] Singing treatises or training manuals promoting Italian singing methods were produced and published with increasing regularity throughout the eighteenth century, clear evidence that demand for Italian singing training among amateurs and aspiring professionals was also on the rise in Britain.[11] Many of the Italian singers who chose to remain in Britain established themselves as music masters, including Rauzzini, who trained some of England's most successful opera singers at the turn of the nineteenth century.[12]

Though there were several Italian music masters working in Britain, increasingly, aspiring professional, British-born singers opted to travel to the continent, particularly Italy, in search of further training and professional opportunities. Unlike Britain, Italy was famed for its music education, particularly the training provided by the music conservatories in Naples and Venice.

The popularity of the Grand Tour had cemented the idea that travel was an important form of liberal education, though such ventures were exclusive to the social elite. As such, aspiring professional singers were not the expected social demographic to engage in the Grand Tour; however, their journeys often followed a similar route through France, Italy, Austria, and Germany. Singers such as Kelly, Storace, and Billington performed for and were supported by Grand Tourists, who were keen to see and hear their vocal development since leaving Britain. The three singers spent many years living and working on the continent before returning to Britain to continue their vocal careers. Travel offered these singers the chance to train in Italy under the direction of some of the most proficient music masters, while also providing opportunities to experience the sights and sounds of Italian music and culture, which, as this chapter will discuss, directly influenced their singing.

Praising Home Musicians for Travelling in Pursuit of Education

According to James Buzard, 'The Grand Tour was, from start to finish, an ideological exercise. Its leading purpose was to round out the education of young men from the ruling classes by exposing them to the treasured artifacts and ennobling society of the Continent.'[13] Just like those members of the 'ruling classes', British singers who travelled to the continent were also in search of refining their music education as well as becoming known to the ennobling societies, though their reasons for doing so were practical rather than ideological. Italy offered training opportunities that were, simply put, unavailable in Britain. The Italian conservatories, institutions that offered dedicated musical training, had existed since the sixteenth century and gave aspiring professionals the chance to work with some of the finest masters and immerse themselves in their musical studies.

Musician and music historian Charles Burney (1726–1814) made a point of visiting many of these conservatories and documenting what he observed in *The Present State of Music in France and Italy*, published in London in 1771. The work provided a detailed account of the musical activities he experienced while embarking on the Grand Tour and, according to Philip Olleson, was so popular that it established Burney as 'a man of letters' granting him entry to the city's 'most fashionable literary society'.[14] Burney visited the Conservatorio di Sant'Onofrio a Capuana in Naples in 1770 and was surprised to see so many pupils packed into a room all playing different instruments and musical exercises.[15] While he doubted that such an environment produced refined performers, stating, 'in the midst of such jargon, and continued dissonance, it is wholly impossible to give any kind of polish or finishing to their performance', he clearly thought the Italian conservatory system was better than anything provided in Britain.[16] He proposed to establish a music conservatory in London similar in style to the Italian conservatories he visited. The proposal was initially unsuccessful, but it did lay the groundwork for the establishment of Britain's first music conservatoire, The Royal Academy of Music, which opened in 1822.

In 1778, the twelve-year-old Anna Storace announced her intention to travel to Italy, even though she had trained with Rauzzini and had been performing professionally in both opera and concerts since she was just seven years old. Her brother, Stephen Storace (1762–1796), had already been sent to Italy to study at the Conservatorio di Sant'Onofrio a Capuana, the same institution that Burney visited while on his Grand Tour. The Conservatorio di Sant'Onofrio exclusively trained boys and as such, Storace could not benefit from the same kind of immersive training as her brother, but she could still work with celebrated Italian masters and gain international recognition by performing in Italian theatres.

To fund her trip, Storace performed a benefit concert at the Music Room in Tottenham Street, London. The advertisement for this concert was written in Storace's voice, and it is possible she had composed it herself. What the advertisement makes clear is the importance of continental travel to facilitate education:

> MISS STORACE, encouraged by several Ladies of Distinction to have A BENEFIT CONCERT, Previous to her going to Italy for improvement, she has fixed on Thursday, the 9th April at the Music Room in Tottenham-street, near Charlotte-street, Rathbone-place; when she humbly hopes her Friends and Patrons will honour her with their company, to enable her to pursue her studies. Tickets 10s. 6. each to be had of Miss Storace, No. 3 Bentinck-street, by Berwick Street, Soho.[17]

The concert was not cheap with tickets costing the equivalent of five days' work for a skilled tradesman,[18] but Storace needed to generate enough funds to not only pay for the crossing but also for living costs for her and her parents once she arrived. Indeed, this is perhaps why Storace did not waste time in finding professional performance opportunities in Italy as soon as she arrived. One of her first engagements was singing in Giuseppe Francesco Bianchi's *Castore e Polluce* in Florence in 1779.[19]

Samuel Johnson (1709–1784), an English writer who penned one of the most influential dictionaries in the eighteenth century, gave five different definitions for improvement and four specifically align with Storace's motivations as outlined in the 1778 advert:

1. Melioration; advancement of any thing from good to better. Some virtues tend to the preservation of health, and others to the *improvement* and security of estates. *Tillotson.*
2. Act of improving. The parts of Sinon, Camilla, and some few others, are *improvements* on the Greek poet. *Addison's Spectator.*
3. Progress from good to better. There is a design of publishing the history of architecture, with its several *improvements* and decays. *Addison.*
4. Instruction; edification. I look upon your city as the best place of *improvement:* from the school we go to the university, but from the universities to London. *South.*[20]

The advertisement clearly aimed to emphasise just how important journeying to Italy was for the young singer. Such travels offered an opportunity for Storace to get better, not just through study, but also by being exposed to Italian musical culture, meeting composers, singers, and patrons, and engaging in performance opportunities in Naples, Florence, and Venice. There is no evidence that Storace was travelling to Italy to train with a specific tutor. Rather, the fact that she almost immediately started performing suggests that she opted to learn through experience rather than formal training. Such tactics paid off as by 1783 Emperor Joseph II recruited Storace for his new opera company in Vienna that specialised in Italian opera buffa.[21]

Rauzzini recommended that Michael Kelly travel to Italy in pursuit of further vocal training, with *The Reminiscences* quoting him as saying to Kelly's father:

> My dear Sir, depend upon it your son will never follow any profession but that of a musician; and as there is no person in this country who can give him the instruction he requires, you ought to send him to Italy. He is now at the time of life to imbibe true taste, and in Italy only is to be found. If you send him to Rome, let him study under Latilla; if to Naples (the better place of the two) send him to either of the Conservatorios; the headmaster at St. Onofrio is Monopoli, at the other, La Madona di Loretto, Finerolli is master. This celebrated Conservatorio produced Scarlatti, Duranti, Porpori, (at that time the greatest of all singing masters,) Pergolesi, Jomelli, Cimarosa, Paesiello, and a long list of celebrated men: let him go there, and depend up it he will one day repay you for it.[22]

Considering *The Reminiscences* was written decades after the conversation between Rauzzini and Kelly's father had taken place, it is unlikely that the above was directly from the singing master's lips.[23] Rauzzini had trained in Rome at the Accademia di Santa Cecilia, so while it is not unusual that he would recommend Kelly study in Italy, it seems unlikely that the singing master would belittle his own education by suggesting the conservatories in Naples were superior to the Accademia in Rome. Such a comment was tactical on Kelly's part since he eventually went to study at the Conservatorio di Santa Maria di Loreto in Naples with Fedele Fenaroli (1730–1818). Conveniently, the quote also highly praised Kelly's future music master.

Once Kelly arrived on the continent, he did not immediately begin his singing studies but was recommended by his patron, William Douglas Hamilton (1730–1803), to 'take a fortnight's pleasure' and see the sights of Naples.[24] Only after spending a period familiarising himself with popular tourist spots, such as Herculaneum, Mount Vesuvius, Baiae, Pausilippo, the Grotto del Cane, and other destinations, was Kelly finally introduced to his new master, Fenaroli, at the Conservatorio di Santa Maria di Loreto. In much the same manner as Burney had observed, Kelly was disturbed by the noise at the conservatory, describing it as a 'terrific Babel'.[25] Within a short period of time, Kelly moved to study with the celebrated castrato Giuseppe Aprile (1731–1813), who worked with him to settle and refine his singing while his voice changed from treble to tenor.[26] Indeed, Aprile was responsible for Kelly's professional début, where he performed a challenging motet composed by Genario Mano[27] in the Sicilian Festival di Santa Rosalie.[28] *The Reminiscences* claimed he was the first British singer to perform at the festival.[29] The performance clearly made a lasting impression on Kelly with *The Reminiscences* noting he had fully embraced Sicilian culture and dress. After leaving Sicily and travelling to Tuscany in search of further performance opportunities, he arrived wearing 'a Sicilian capote' with his long, fair hair flowing over it.[30] Upon seeing him step off the boat, Storace, whom Kelly had arranged to meet, commented, 'Look at that girl dressed in boy's clothes!'.[31] Kelly was seeking support from both Storace and her brother, Stephen, who had become great favourites in Livorno (or Leghorn as it was known by the British in the eighteenth century) and could provide access to a network of Italian and British nobility who supported musical performances in the city. Kelly was successful in his aims and found many performance opportunities stemming from his friendship with the Storaces, including mounting a successful concert in Pisa and making his operatic début in *Il Francese in Italia* in Florence.[32] Stephen Storace also arranged an offer of a five-year contract for Kelly to sing at the Theatre Royal, Drury Lane in London, though this offer was later rescinded.[33] Kelly's father clearly thought that returning to London would be detrimental to his son's progress, and as such had written to musical director Thomas Linley (1733–1795) stating if he did not rescind the offer, then he would take legal action against him.[34] Kelly would not return to London until 1787 after he was, once again, offered a position as the leading singer at Drury Lane.

Quite unlike Storace, whose education in Italy was very much a case of on-the-job training, Kelly had the opportunity to work with celebrated music masters to develop and refine his voice over time. However, where Storace and Kelly's education mirrored each other was in the opportunities to expose oneself to Italian customs and to network with those in positions of power. Indeed, Kelly evidently saw Storace as someone in such a position, with *The Reminiscences* acknowledging '*she* was at the time, though only fifteen, the prima donna of the Comic Opera at Leghorn' and was 'a very great favourite.'[35] Kelly might have had the credibility of a good education from known Italian masters such as Fenaroli and Aprile, but Storace had the ear of the audience.

Elizabeth Billington also travelled to the continent with the intention of improving her singing, but her public announcement in British newspapers made it very clear that she was going to study with a specific master. On 5 April 1786, the *Morning Chronicle and London Advertiser* announced: 'Sacchini who is at Paris is to have the sole direction of Mrs Billington in her further professional studies. The expense of the undertaking is to be her own.' The name Antonio Sacchini was already familiar to London audiences, as he had resided in Britain since 1772 and composed several operas that were staged at the King's Theatre. Popularity for his work eventually declined and he departed for Paris in 1782, where his work continued to be performed.

Michael Kelly by Adele Romany (between 1802 and 1814). (*Courtesy of the Garrick Club, London*)

Up until her decision to travel to Paris and train with Sacchini, Billington's professional profile had been steadily growing. She had initially made her operatic début at Smock Alley Theatre in Dublin, before making her London début as Clara in *Love in the Village* at the Theatre Royal, Covent Garden in 1786. While reviews mostly commended her performances, she was also criticised for sounding too Italian:

> Her deportment is easy and her air genteel. Her musical skill is considerable and though her voice is not powerful, it is possessed of sweet tones marked with variety and enriched by a very perfect shake. – Thus qualified, Mrs Billington could not fail of meeting approbation in a character like Rosetta, the airs on which are composed in an elegant stile. It will not be overrating the abilities of this young actress if we say that we never heard those airs more pleasingly executed; and where they admitted of comic effect it was introduced. It may be alleged that too much of the Italian manner characterises the singing of this performer: but that charge will be unfair as it is not the results of affectation, but teaching.[36]
>
> In her manner, the most refined sensibility went hand in hand with improved judgement; and though her borrowing from the Italian School, which she evidently does through all the airs, might at first be thought to take much from la naiveté of musical expression, yet we are cautious how we condemn what possibly gives an elegant finish to her manner. Upon the whole, her executions seemed universally felt and produced the loudest plaudits from all parts of the house.[37]

Adopting Italian-styled vocal expression into her singing was not the real issue at play; rather critics thought that the way she incorporated Italianisms was somewhat inauthentic. Indeed, both critics inferred that with better teaching, Billington may improve her understanding of Italian musical expression. Evidently, Billington took such criticisms seriously and in 1786, she publicly announced that she was going to train in Paris with Sacchini – a public declaration that she was committed to improving her voice through formal training with a credible master.[38]

Once she returned from her summer in Paris, reviews greatly praised her vocal ability and credited Sacchini for its improvement. On 10 October 1786, the *Morning Herald* stated, 'Of this accomplished singer we must observe that Sacchini's instructions appear to have been fully cultivated; her improvement is chiefly in the sustaining powers of her voice; the scientific phrase of which, is, the legato stile, – and in the cadence of which she is firm and distinct.' *The Public Ledger* similarly praised her improvement stating, 'Mrs Billington appeared for the first time this season in Clara in the Duenna and sang with so much taste, expression and power as confirmed the general opinion that she is beyond comparison the first singer on the English stage'.[39] Billington's additional training had raised her esteem both with audiences and critics, not just in Britain but also in Europe. *The Public Advertiser* in July 1792 stated that she had been offered '2000 sequins' or '1000 guineas' to sing at the Carnival in Venice the following year.[40] The costs stated by *The Public Advertiser* appear accurate and not exaggerated as Billington was negotiating similar fees for herself while working on the continent. In a letter to Emanuele Niecco in Venice written in 1798, Billington rejected an offer made to her to sing at the Carnival in Geneva, noting that she was 'surprised' by Niecco 'suggesting those prices'.[41] Instead, she asked for 2,000 zecchini or sequins and accommodation.[42] Such a letter not only demonstrates that Billington was a desirable commodity on the continent, but she also knew her value and position within the landscape of the European music industry, and as such, was able to negotiate her own fees.

Billington left Britain to embark on a tour of Italy in 1793, a trip that lasted just shy of a decade. Her husband, James, suddenly died in 1794, shortly after she made her début at the Teatro San Carlo in Bianchi's *Inez de Castro*.[43] His untimely passing is perhaps the reason she chose to remain in Europe, performing in Venice, Bergamo, Bologna, Milan, Florence, Leghorn, Padua, and Trieste between 1796 and 1799. Indeed, it seemed that Billington intended to make Italy her permanent home after she married a French commissary in 1799, and purchased an estate in Venice; however, in 1801, she returned to Britain with many suggesting that her cruel and greedy husband had driven her back to her native country.

Though Billington had issued no public statement prior to her going to Italy that highlighted her travels were for the purposes of further education or improvement, several authors stated that this had been her intention. In 1818, *The Quarterly Musical Magazine and Review* commented that 'Mrs Billington's education received its finish and fine polish in Italy', while in 1828, Richard Edgecomb commented, 'After performing at the theatre for several years, [Mrs Billington] went to Italy to improve her taste, and she returned from thence a finished singer'.[44] Her return in 1801 was greatly anticipated with handsome offers made for her to sing at both the Theatre Royals at Covent Garden and Drury Lane and audiences were not disappointed. *The Morning Post* stated she was 'one of the most perfect portraits of *Mandane*, which, as a whole, the history of the theatrical world perhaps has ever boasted.'[45] However, compared to her fellow colleagues, namely Storace and Kelly, the positive reaction Billington received from critics was rather unusual.

A Stranger At Home

Both Kelly and Storace returned to London in 1787 with the former engaged to sing at Drury Lane and the latter at the King's Theatre. Both singers were also recruited to perform at the esteemed Westminster Abbey Music Festival, which celebrated sacred music composed in England, and included large-scale performances of George Frederic Handel's oratorio works. Singing oratorio was a different beast compared to performing in the opera in England. Singers were expected to follow strict performance practice standards, particularly regarding stance, vocal expression, and added embellishments. Often such performance practices were unspoken until a singer had unwittingly broken with convention. Both Kelly and Storace received mixed reviews, with criticisms frequently suggesting neither had sufficient understanding of how oratorio repertoire was performed in England. *The Morning Chronicle* harshly criticised Kelly, stating:

> Mr. Kelly had the last song allotted to him in the piece "If God be for us." Whatever requisites this gentleman may have for the stage, he makes but a proper figure as an oratorio singer. What his excellencies are, we are yet to learn. His defects are evident and consist of a bad toned voice–no sostenuto– want of expression, neatness of execution, and even a tolerable shake. As he is a stranger in this country, we hint to him that if he were to take a book in his hand during the performance, instead of standing with his hands in his bosom, the change would not disgust an English audience.[46]

Though throughout *The Reminiscences* Kelly identified himself as a British native, *The Morning Chronicle* viewed him as a stranger who lacked the necessary knowledge and voice to perform English oratorio, and this was not the first time that Kelly had received such criticisms. His very first performance in England was singing the role of Lionel in *Lionel and Clarissa, or a School for Fathers,* a comedy written by Charles Dibdin (1745–1814). While *The Reminiscences* painted a rather positive view of Kelly's London début, remarking that he had worked on the dialogue with 'the eminent actor, King' and had introduced an Italian aria by Giuseppe Sarti (1729–1802), sung with English words written for him by Richard Tickell (1751–1793), in reality, reviews were mixed.[47] *The London Chronicle* made it clear that while Kelly was an accomplished singer, his style of singing was too Italian for the English stage:

> Last night Mr. Kelly, a vocal performer of character, made his first public appearance at this theatre, in Lionel, in *The School for Fathers.* Mr. Kelly does not belie the reputation he has acquired, as he may be pronounced to be a very capital singer [...] From his education in Italy however, he has imbibed the false and tasteless ornaments of Italian singing, of which we could wish he would divest himself as much as possible.[48]

Storace was similarly criticised for her performances given at the festival, with *The Morning Chronicle* stating: '[Storace's] performance of "Angels ever bright and fair," was such a reprehensible *caricature* of Handel as we never witnessed before, and we hope we never shall again. The Absence of Mrs. Billington was much regretted, and variously accounted for.'[49] While Storace's Italianisms were not explicitly mentioned, the review inferred that she had very little understanding of an appropriate Handelian performance style and did not measure up to Billington, who had long been considered an exceptional English singer. Unlike Storace, Billington until this point had spent much of her life living and working in England, and though she often incorporated Italianisms into her singing, she was still considered a daughter of England. Storace, on the other hand, had left England as a teenager, and clearly identified more with her Italian heritage than her English origins. Though early announcements that Storace was returning to England had mis-styled her as 'Madame Storace', advertisements announcing her participation in the music festival at Westminster Abbey made it clear that she intended to style herself in the Italian manner – 'Signora Storace'.[50] Furthermore, she used the Italian pronunciation of her name, with newspapers and periodicals occasionally misspelling it 'Storacci' or 'Storacce', presumably after hearing the name spoken.[51]

However, Joel Collver in *The English Lyceum* praised Storace's performance at the Westminster Abbey Music Festival and went out of his way to emphasise that she was a native of England and that her Italian training only enhanced her ability to perform English oratorio repertoire.[52] He argued:

> The fact was, that it was Storacce's [sic] excellence in the *comic opera* of the Italian stage, that pointed her out to the discerning Directors as a proper person to perform in a *sacred oratorio*; and they wisely concluded from the admirable manner in which she pronounced the words "*tuppe, tuppe, tuppe ta*" in the duett [sic] with Morelli, that her articulation was eminently calculated for the utterance of scriptive recitative, and in expressing the simple melodies of Handel – nor were they mistaken; for I will venture to assert, that there was not a person in the Abbey who had a book of the performance and could read, that did not understand almost every word she pronounced; and that she takes her *appoggiatura,* as easily – *as I take a pinch of snuff.*[53]

The fact that Collver felt it necessary to focus his comments on Storace's pronunciation of the English text is telling, as others thought her Italian training made it more difficult for the singer to clearly articulate the English language. The London periodical *Argus* printed a damning review of both Kelly and Storace, stating:

> Italianizing the English stage by the introductions of Storace is strong proof of the decay of British genius and the depravity of public taste. The manly tones of Bannister and Sedgewick and the sweet pipe of Mrs Crouch are better adapted to an English audience than the Italian touches of Kelly and the unintelligible articulation of Storace.[54]

Argus pointedly accused Storace's singing of being 'unintelligible', quite the opposite of Collver who praised her articulation of the English language. Even though Kelly and Storace were born and received their initial musical training in Britain, they had each spent eight years (in the case of Kelly) and nine years (in the case of Storace) living, studying, and working in Italy, leaving British critics and audiences to view the two singers as Italian.

As discussed above, Billington had similarly been accused of sounding too Italian, but that was before she left Britain to live and work on the continent for an extended period. In 1786, *The General Advertiser* published a comment on Billington's singing that neatly summarised her mixed position as an English woman, singing in English opera, but introducing Italian idioms in her singing:

> This Lady possesses indeed a most extraordinary voice, managed with the accuracy of science and touched with the graces of taste; and when her tones are somewhat released from the thraldom of Italian setters, she will justly be considered as the most distinguished of the vocal tribe that the English stage ever boasted.[55]

Other critics, such as John Bell's publication *British Theatre*, wished to emphasise her Britishness, stating 'Mrs. Billington [...] her *tone,* her *taste,* and musical *science,* are the pride of the British opera',[56] while the *World* gave Billington a rather backhanded compliment stating:

> A mawkish common wretch with a voice as little human as a bird organ and ignorance of all music like an organ grinder is the too frequent sufferance of the people which they are destined to endure an English singer. It is not so with Mrs Billington. Nature has gifted her with sweet and powerful tones; and she is skilful and modest in the use of them.[57]

Elizabeth Billington by Joshua Reynolds, 1803.

Billington's singing was unique in that she did not sound like other British singers, whom the *World* considered grotesque, but she was identified as British, singing in a style suited to the English stage.

Following her return to England in 1801 after eight years spent working on the continent, including singing in Italian theatres, newspapers acknowledged that Billington had greatly improved due to her studies and travel.[58] Unlike Kelly and Storace, these writers continuously emphasised Billington's Britishness, with *The Morning Chronicle* stating: '[...] the return of Mrs. Billington may be considered as an epoch in the English school. She is so peculiarly endowed with this new talent of execution that it is likely to influence the stile of the stage and to give a fashion to the art.'[59] As for her oratorio singing, Billington was similarly admired with *The Derby Mercury* stating, 'Her "*Angels ever bright,*" was in the best style of expressive simplicity.'[60] While Kelly and Storace were identified as Italian and criticised for it, Billington was celebrated for her travels, education and improvements, and hailed a trendsetter who would change singing fashions in Britain.

Elizabeth Billington by John James Masquerier, (before 1813).

It is important to note that Kelly and Storace returned to Britain in 1787 when English opera was considerably popular, and Billington was emerging as a celebrated English vocalist. Billington, on the other hand, returned to Britain in 1801 when fashionable trends had already shifted toward a blended Anglo-Italian singing style, a change that had slowly taken place throughout the latter half of the eighteenth century.[61] As such, Billington had returned to sing for audiences who had already embraced a blended Anglo-Italian style. Even so, her status as a British woman and esteemed opera singer, who through her travels had greatly improved her voice, made Billington the perfect candidate to solidify such a shift.

In conclusion, while all three singers benefitted from travelling, studying, and performing professionally on the continent, there are clear differences between Storace and Billington's experiences to that of Kelly. Both female singers had already been performing professionally on the English stage for a few years before publicly announcing their intentions to travel for the purposes of furthering their education abroad. The training opportunities open to Kelly were not open to Storace or Billington and, as such, they had to find other prospects. Billington was already an adult married woman who had been working for several years as a professional singer when she announced her intention to train with a particular music master in Paris. Had she been a young teenager, as Storace was, she might not have had the finances to travel and study. Storace required the support of patrons to fund her travels. Once in Italy, she quickly went to work as a singer and, alongside her brother, established an impressive reputation that made her a desirable person to know. By comparison, Kelly was able to train in illustrious institutions with noteworthy masters, taking time to refine and perfect his singing. However, such training did not mean that Kelly received better offers for professional opportunities, and he had to befriend Storace and her brother so he could tap into their network of patrons and musicians to improve his chances of finding lucrative professional performance opportunities.

Even though British newspapers, periodicals, and critics seemed to value the importance of travelling to the continent for further study, a singer was not always celebrated for it once they returned to Britain. In the case of Kelly and Storace, their travels and extended stay in Italy at such a young age appeared to transform them from British nationals to strangers in their native land. Indeed, Storace did not appear to want to identify as British after her return, instead emphasising her Italian name and heritage. After all, at the time she left England, Italian singers were among the most celebrated and highly paid in England, and so her decision to style herself as an Italian upon her return was perhaps a tactical one. Unfortunately, the result was that she and Kelly, who similarly left Britain for Italy as a boy, were frequently described and criticised as foreigners. Billington, whose extended stay on the continent was many years after she had been professionally performing in Britain as an adult singer, did not receive the negative or xenophobic comments experienced by her colleagues. She was celebrated as an English singer, who had significantly improved her taste and style of singing because of her travels. She was not considered a foreign stranger but was instead a familiar voice returning to sing in her homeland.[62]

Chapter 7

'Auch ich in Arkadien!' Michał Jan Borch's Travels to Italy

Teresa Rączka-Jeziorska

> On the whole, if each man is to be regarded as but a supplement of all others, and shows himself most serviceable and amiable, when he adjusts himself to such a relation, this must apply especially to the case of travels and travellers. Persons, purposes, relations of time, favourable and unfavourable conjunctures, these all dispose themselves differently with different travellers. Do I know a traveller's predecessors? I shall be able to draw both pleasure and profit from him, too, and shall, moreover, hail with interest his successor, even though meanwhile I should have been fortunate enough to survey the country described with my own eyes.[1]
>
> Johann, Wolfganag von Goethe, *Italian Travels*

These words quoted come from Johann Wolfgang Goethe (1749–1832), one of the greatest minds of enlightened Europe, whose works inspired generations that followed, especially the romantics. Not only were literature and art among the interests of this genius poet, politician, thinker, and philosopher, but he also possessed a passion for studying nature. Scientific fame was ensured not only by in-depth studies of plant, animal and human anatomy and development, but above all by publications in the field of mining geology.[2] He was also successful in the fields of meteorology, cartography and also geomorphology, including being the first to explain the role of granite in the structure of the Earth's crust.[3] Among these many passions, resulting from his combination of talent and diligence, were his fascination with mining and alchemy. The German scientist travelled quite a lot, both throughout his home country and abroad. However, while on his field trips, he shunned haste, striving to properly examine the abundance of nature. He believed that it was a 'living, misunderstood, but not incomprehensible' book.[4] From his tour around Italy in the years 1786–1788, he brought to Weimar one of the most magnificent scenographies, with which he discreetly filled his entire artistic legacy until almost the end of his days. His imagination was abundantly filled with previously unknown colours, smells and shapes. Looking with admiration at the beauty of Mediterranean lands and with ancient poems constantly at hand, he did not claim the right to compose more perfect verses. Study trips, in-depth observations of nature and the local landscape, contacts with the inhabitants of the places he visited, independent scientific experiments and, finally, the improvement of the art of drawing became more valuable than poetic laurels. On the pages of notes and letters spontaneously sent to his friends at that time, the German poet often shared an unusual experience that he suspected was felt by the mythical Antaeus: 'I feel as did Antaeus of old, who found himself endued with new strength, as often as he was brought into fresh contact with his mother earth': 'I felt at once the earth whereon I stand, through me, the sleeper, fresher spirit stealing, I rise refreshed, Antaeus in my feeling.'[5] His description of the journey three decades later (1816–1817) arranged his impressions into a compact literary form. It was then that he added the motto taken from baroque iconography: 'Auch ich in Arkadien!' (I too have reached Arcadia!),[6] as the time spent at the foot of the volcanoes seemed to him to be the happiest in his life. Despite his initial plans, Goethe did not make this journey alone. He was beyond the stage of making a 'rite of passage' having already reached maturity, and so he intended to make his scientific and cognitive trip into an expedition, just like numerous participants of the noble Grand Tour, so popular in the eighteenth century. Loneliness, when travelling in foreign countries, was not the loyal companion he desired. It was not only a painful longing for absent loved ones that troubled him but also the numerous difficulties and inconveniences of a long and less travelled route. That is why, when his postal ship arrived at various ports or when he crossed the most southern islands on horseback, he would gladly greet new friends who could teach him something new. He found such company among fellow travellers, the local intellectual elites, and German painters with whom he had surrounded himself because of his own artistic interests. In the second volume of the *Italian*

Michał Jan Borch by Ludwig Guttenbrunn, 1751.

Journey, first published in the fall of 1817, he included his notes from his stay in Naples and Sicily, describing a count named Borch, a man he came to greatly appreciate. He wrote,

> Count Borch has very diligently worked before us in the mineralogy of Sicily, and whoever of the same mind visits the island after him, must willingly acknowledge his obligations to him. I feel it a pleasure, no less than a duty, to celebrate the memory of my predecessor. And what am I more than a forerunner of others yet to be, both in my travels and life.[7]

Although it was often difficult for Goethe to pay compliments, especially to people who were not sensitive enough to appreciate knowledge and beauty in the way he himself did, he would praise Borch. The man he thanked for being a guide to the heavenly 'queen of the islands' must have been a rare and welcome gift as a companion.

Michał Jan Borch: Life, Research and The Grand Tour

Michał Jan Borch (1753–1810) was born in the Warklany estate in the so-called Polish Livonia (Livonian voivodeship) (present-day Latvia), which was a part of the Polish-Lithuanian state from the second half of the sixteenth century until 1772, only subsequently conquered by Russia. He was the son of Jan Jędrzej Borch (died in 1780), the Polish Crown's Deputy Chancellor (1767–1780), and, in the final months of his life, the Grand Chancellor of the Polish Crown, one of the most important officials of the Polish-Lithuanian Commonwealth. From childhood, Borch was surrounded by people of various languages, nations and religions. Polish Livonia (today Latgale, located within the borders of Latvia) lay on the cultural frontier and, from the Middle Ages on, was a place where the influences of Rome and Constantinople clashed. Apart from the indigenous Latgalian people, the area was populated by numerous newcomers from Belarus, Lithuania, Poland, and Russia, as well as Germans and Jews. In the eighteenth century, Latgale was dominated by Catholics, but there were also Orthodox Christians, especially Old Believers, Lutherans, followers of Judaism, and even hidden pagans (mainly among Latgalian peasants), cultivating the pre-Christian beliefs of their ancestors. The environment of young Borch was multilingual and multicultural, which should not be surprising since his family came from Westphalia, which never lost its German roots, despite deeply advanced Polonization and conversion from Lutheranism to Catholicism at the turn of the seventeenth and eighteenth centuries. The area was made up of a heterogeneous people of various languages and religions, allowing the Borch family to develop an attitude marked by tolerance, openness and acceptance of varying forms of otherness. The penetration of the Borch family into the circles of the Polish-Lithuanian magnates during the first half of the eighteenth century reinforced the development of these attitudes. All the more so as, after arriving in Vilnius or Warsaw, members of the Borch family themselves had to struggle with the label of 'stranger' pinned to them because of their origins. Like most children of the famous families of the Polish Crown and Lithuania growing up in the court of diligent and ambitious state officials who encouraged their children to become enlightened citizens, Michał Jan Borch was taught languages, history and the law of his motherland from an early age and was introduced to the military[8] and a social life of the gentility. His father, Jan Jędrzej Borch, managed both the family estates in Polish Livonia and their palace in Warsaw (at Miodowa Street), and consequently Borch spent a lot of time in the capital surrounded by the best teachers. He studied at the Collegium Nobilium founded there by the Piarists, where a strong emphasis was placed on civic education and natural sciences. He quickly gained distinction among the elites due to his competent and eloquent use of the French language, his literary writings earning praise from even Voltaire.[9] He learnt Italian, English, German, Russian, Latin and, of course, Polish, his mother tongue. He ascended the ranks of statecraft to finally become the voivode of Bełz (1787), as well as a Knight of Malta. He possessed an inborn curiosity about the world, a love of fine arts, a literary and artistic passion, and above all a great sensitivity displayed in his independent research, which attracted the attention of King Stanisław August Poniatowski. Once presented at court, Borch gained the patronage of the Polish monarch, who was himself a great aesthete, passionate about natural science and antiquity.[10] This inevitably had an impact on the count's further fate,[11] and his ensuing tour around Europe from 1774 to 1780.

The twenty-one-year-old Michał Jan Borch's journey was the usual complement to a young man's education[12] and was typical for many male youths of the Polish-Livonian aristocracy. For example, the Castellan of Livonia, Jan August Hylzen (1702–1767), sent his eldest son Józef Jerzy (1736–1786) on a tour of Germany, Austria, Belgium and Italy in the company of a Jesuit preceptor, priest Karol Wyrwicz, for two years in 1752.[13] Borch did not adhere to the guidelines imposed by his father despite the 'written and verbal' agreement he had made before he left. This brought a harsh reprimand as increasing demands for more money ensued. His father lamented:

> His [i.e. Michał Jan Borch] neglect in keeping to my guidelines dulled my desire to write, it's no use, I should not bother. I told him to avoid unnecessary expenses and not to spend anything on his own, he did everything to the contrary immediately after leaving the country. First,

> he used up the money he needed for the excursions, which he did not yet have, and he himself spent more than was necessary. My idea was to start the journey with the protection of expenses and focussed on learning, so that the younger age which is more suitable for studies would not be wasted for entertainment.[14]

Borch initially travelled in the company of clergy, including the priest Kopakowski,[15] and the Poznań Canon, Remigian (Remigiusz) Kossakowski (1730–1780),[16] but quickly parted ways with his recommended mentors, as well as extending the planned tour by several years. He had already formed a clear vision of wandering through the countries of southern Europe, as he saw fit. He was particularly interested in the fields of geology, mineralogy, botany, mining, metallurgy and the developing field of scientific chemistry and had clearly defined scientific motivations. Regardless of his father's sceptical voice, he stubbornly followed his heart conducting such independent practical research that was within his reach. For example, in 1774, he studied the phenomenon of solidification of the bonding mass, and also tried to obtain artificial millstones; a year later he studied the mechanism of copper casting furnaces, not realizing that some of the methods he was interested in had been used for some time in Sicily[17]. After leaving the borders of the Polish-Lithuanian Commonwealth, he not only journeyed geographically through Bohemia, Austria, Germany, Switzerland, France, and Italy, including its neighbouring islands, but, in parallel, journeyed intellectually, taking the route of the 'great journey for knowledge and experience'[18] of the future scientist he was to become. It is worth noting that the king's interest in the young Borch was present from the very beginning of this tour and had concrete motives, as can be seen in Borch's achievements in the following decade. The king was keenly interested in educating future specialists in countries where earth sciences were intensively developing and became involved in the launch of state mints using local aggregates (copper and silver),[19] carrying out intensive preparations for the appointment in 1782 of the Ore's Commission, focused on the extraction of minerals (metal ores, rock salt, coal).[20] Borch would later become a full member of several scientific societies, mainly Italian and French, including the academies in Lyon (1775), Siena and Dijon (1776) to name a few. At the end of May 1774, Count Borch set off for Kraków, as the surrounding area was specifically known for its rich natural deposits. Here, the young researcher gained a valuable opportunity to observe salt pits in the nearby Wieliczka and Bochnia, which would help him formulate conclusions on the methods of indicating minerals using plants.[21] Based on this research, Borch presented a talk at the Academy of Sciences in Dijon in 1776; and in 1780, hoping for their practical application in his country, handed his findings over to King Stanisław August Poniatowski.[22] Although his ideas did not gain approval at the king's court, his research turned out to be ground-breaking in the field of biochemistry.[23] He devoted his debut dissertation, titled *Sur le sel gemme et le salins de Pologne*, to the exploitation of rock salt and the Wieliczka mine, his work presented to the Academy in Lyon in January 1776.[24] It immediately aroused an enthusiastic response by the renowned Swiss naturalist and philosopher Charles Bonnet (1720–1793). After leaving Kraków, his work gained momentum. By June 1774, he had reached Olomouc and Vienna, and in the following month visited Haag am Hausruck, Salzburg, Munich, Augsburg and Ulm; and from September to October he stayed in Geneva. From there he moved to Lyon where he stayed for almost two years (November 1774 – September 1776). His stay in France and Switzerland strengthened the count's social position in fashionable cultural circles as more people came to hear about his achievements. He was admitted to the Académie de Lyon (1775) and became involved in the community of French Freemasons (*Les Amis de la vérité*),[25] whose members included leading representatives in the world of science. Here he gained acquaintance with François Rozier (1734–1793), the editor of the *Journal of Physics and Natural History* (*Journal de phisque et d'histoire naturelle*), who helped get Borch published;[26] and the botanist and archaeologist from Nîmes, Jean François Séguier (1703–1784), with whom he corresponded and exchanged samples for research.[27] The philosophy and ideals underpinning the 'Royal Art' (Freemasonry) had strongly influenced Count Borch's worldview, and this involvement became explicit in 1781, when he received a nomination as an outstanding speaker of the Grand Lodge in Warsaw;[28] their philosophy of 'friendship and brotherhood' broke national, religious and social barriers and through this, Borch blossomed during this time in Lyon. Masonic affiliation helped pave the way for Borch's further career, but also scientists and eminent personalities from Western Europe were impressed by his diligence and passion. Voltaire, whom he met in 1775 while visiting Ferney, was impressed by his proficiency in the French language, an aptitude rare among foreigners at the time. Voltaire saw him not so much a foreigner, but a talented literary 'scholar from Paris',[29] and introduced him to his friends, among them the future British politician and diplomat Philip Stanhope (the 5th Earl of Chesterfield, 1755–1815).[30] He became interested in Shakespeare's homeland (he even planned, with the consent of his parents, to travel there in 1778, but the visit did not come to pass).[31] It can be assumed that, thanks to the contacts made at that time, it was easier for him to go to other parts of western Europe (to Holland and England)[32] in 1790.

The Portrait of Michał Jan Borch (1753–1810)

The most famous image of the count, as seen above, was painted in Rome in 1778[33] by the Austrian painter Ludwig Guttenbrunn (1750–1819), who also painted portraits of Joseph Haydn and Marie Antoinette. His portrait of the count shows a young man with a dreamy look in his eyes, looking out from the painting in a French-style powdered wig, suggestively placing his left hand on a table covered with a colourful marble mosaic, on which, next to flowers, there are also books and a mineral sample. Just as significantly is that he is posed against a background of Mount Etna, the volcano that everyone on the Grand Tour wanted to explore. Was this young nobleman thinking about a new work or some important experiment? British diplomat and archaeologist Sir William Hamilton (1730–1803),[34] a collector of antiquaries, a vulcanologist and a self-taught archaeologist, was portrayed in a similar vein.[35] This style depicts the interests of the gentlemen collecting minerals and antiquities, a common trope in eighteenth-century portraits of the male elite. Hamilton was British Ambassador to the Kingdom of Naples and often showed keen young visitors on a tour of Mount Etna; he and Borch were connected, among others, by the exploration of Etna[36]. Undoubtedly, the painting by Guttenbrunn, currently in the collection of the Tretyakov Gallery in Moscow, aptly tells of Borch's extensive interests[37]. One can also easily guess that the main passion of the count was science. Borch's portrait captured by Guttenbrunn portrays a characteristic image of a person focused on scientific learning, with a manuscript page in his right hand, leaning on three learned books. Although Michał Jan Borch is depicted in the portrait wearing clothes of the Western fashion, he did not come from that part of Europe, but from the northernmost lands of the Polish-Lithuanian state.

William Hamilton by Joshua Reynolds, 1777.

The letters that the count regularly sent to his father confirm that from March to August 1778, he stayed exactly where the painting was created, the city of Rome. In the letters he consistently complained about the considerable expenses related not only to his extensive living costs, but also the financial strain from his scientific endeavours:[38]

> each month one hundred and twenty-five red zlotys it costs me, and I had other expenses, including printing a book dedicated to the Pope, I had to pay one hundred and fifty local thalers, which makes it 75 of our thalers. A penny after a penny is spent in foreign countries, and there are too many ways [to spend it]. Have mercy, my Beloved Father, help me, and by neglecting the necessary rescue, do not become an innocent cause of insults to your son and your own interests.[39]

The publication offered to Pius VI mentioned in the above correspondence (*Lythologie Sicilienne ou Catologue raissoné de toutes les pierres de la Sicile*, 1777) is one of his three books on Sicilian minerals. The first was published a year earlier in Naples, and the next, dedicated to the Prince of Parma, Ferdinand I,[40] a few years later in Turin (*Minéralogie Sicilienne docimastique et métallurgique*, 1780). Considering their dating, it can be assumed that on Guttenbrunn's canvas Borch was depicted with some handwritten fragment of these works, probably even before they were submitted for printing. These dissertations established his reputation within the scientific community, mainly due to their originality and innovation.[41] In *Lythologie Sicilienne*, he described the genetic relationship between minerals and the reasons for their formation, and in *Litographie Sicilienne*, he classified minerals in terms of hardness[42]. From the catalogue of Johann Wolfgang Goethe's library compiled by Hans Ruppert (1958), both volumes, together with the two-volume edition of the famous *Letters about Sicily and Malta* (*Lettres sur la Sicile et sur l'île de Malthe*, Turin 1782), quickly found their way into his book collection.[43] Goethe was keenly interested in geology and, like Borch, combined practice with science, focusing on systematic work and continuous development of research facilities. Goethe supported the idea of dividing minerals according to the order of their formation in a deposit, influenced from the belief that the various forces of nature interact with each other.[44] For this reason he respected the works of Borch and studied them closely. Goethe's handwritten annotations can be seen in his copies of Borch's works (signed with Goethe's own *ex libris*), with numerous references in his own works, notably his famous *Italienische Reise*, seen in Goethe's notes from his visit to Palermo on 13 April 1787:

> However, the industry of the Count [Borch] seems to me to have been greater than his knowledge. He appears to have gone to work with a certain reserve, which is altogether opposed to that stern earnestness with which grand objects should be treated.
>
> Nevertheless, his essay in quarto, which is exclusively devoted to the mineralogy of Sicily, has been of great use to me; and, prepared by it, I was

> able to profit by my visit to the Quarries which formerly, when it was the custom to case the churches and altars with marble and agate, were more busily worked, though even now they are not idle.[45]

As a philosopher and observer of the natural world, Goethe could not deny Borch's erudition and carefully followed Borch's achievements in their shared discipline. Besides, apart from almost identical interests and literary flair, Goethe had a lot in common with the young count. First of all, they used the same tools, focusing on individual perception and their own intuition. They were both attracted to eminent scientific societies and Freemasonry where they were able to develop intellectually and improve spiritually. Without a doubt, as their trips to Italy and the notes brought from it show, there were many more similarities. And although Goethe and Borch probably never met each other personally, thanks to this special love of knowledge, they actually spoke the same language, metaphorically speaking. Having inherited his father's extensive collection of specimens of stones and minerals in Weimar, Goethe followed his father's passion and added to his collection. The charts and classifications prepared by Goethe, based on the specimens and materials bequeathed to him by his late father, were, in his opinion, a reflection of the order of reality when reality was placed under scrutiny[46]. While Goethe examined Borch with a critical eye,[47] this did not diminish his high regard for Borch's achievements.[48] Perhaps Goethe's extensive connections throughout his contemporary Europe, both in the spheres of science and freemasonry, influenced his opinion of the young Count; the dispute between Michał Jan Borch and King Stanisław August Poniatowski was no secret and the king had prevented the count from promoting his publications in Poland, either by blocking them or, in the mid-1780s, by failing to subscribe to the 36-volume edition of Borch's collected works.[49] The king's sudden unfriendliness towards his subject, whom he had initially supported, possibly stemmed from political motives, or, it may simply have been the monarch's jealousy of Borch's achievements and European recognition. There was indeed much of which the monarch might well have been envious, primarily, the opportunity Borch realised in undertaking this fascinating trip into the cradle of European civilization. The king, an avid enthusiast of ancient architecture, sculpture and painting, never did visit Italy, although he wanted to go there all of his life.[50]

Borch's Italian Travels

Borch spent a total of four years in Italy, exploring in-depth such historic gems as: Turin (September – October 1776), Parma (October 1776), Rome (November

1776, October – November 1777, March – August 1778), Naples (November 1776, April – September 1777, December 1777 – February 1778), Siena (August 1778), Florence (September, November – December 1778, January 1779), and Lucca (September – October 1778),[51] which he visited twice. During the second visit to the Apennine Peninsula, after a few months' stay in Vienna,[52] Venice (May 1779) was added to the list of his southern sojourns. He re-visited Florence (June – August 1779) and finally Turin (September 1779 – September 1780).[53]

The route chosen by Borch took him on a similar path to many notable figures engaging with the foreign influences of European science, art and culture, including some of his own countrymen.[54] Borch, however, had his own travel methods, which included sailing round Sicily, Malta and Gozo (November 1776 – July 1777). His father remained unimpressed; having funded his son's continual expeditions in the expectation that this investment would result in the establishment of his son's reputation and standing, he saw little in the way of reward. The fact that his son had fallen out of favour with the king was even more upsetting. However, it became clear that Borch needed neither royal nor paternal approval to realise his scientific and intellectual ambitions but had enough insight to recognise at what cost:

> in privation and in the midst of thousands of griefs, I lose my time on the road, I strain my health with discomfort, and at the end, being enslaved to my last step, a second time I will go home, losing a lot of money, time not recovered; What is the benefit of [...] a successful journey? loss of money, sad four-month waiting, and the most unpleasant certainty of Parental oblivion towards the loving Son. Yesterday six years passed since I left my homeland.[55]

Despite having to face numerous adversities alone and without assistance during all these years of travelling following his departure from Poland, Borch's letters show that his efforts, despite all the obstacles and his own complaints, was by no means wasted. In addition to the previously mentioned publications on minerals, he wrote a number of studies in which he touched upon phenomena occurring in the natural world; his ode to electricity published in Italian and French (*Oda de signor conte Michaele di Borch tradotta dalla signora D. Anna Amalia Gentile* (Palermo, 1777) was a memorial on sea phosphorus (1778)[56] written in Italian and presented to academics of Siena. He also presented a treatise on Piedmontese truffles, *Lettres sur les truffes du Piémont*, presented in Milan in 1780.[57] It was, however, his account of a journey to the Mediterranean islands that earned Borch a significant degree of international attention, both within scientific circles and among a wider readership. His *Letters about Sicily and Malta*, (the first edition, Turin 1782) was quickly translated and published abroad, with two translations into German,[58] Dutch and Swedish.[59] This was a factual account (albeit in a literary form) of the count's challenging expedition from Livonia to the virgin lands of southern Italy, structured as an extensive series of correspondences preceded by a short table of contents, and illustrated with etchings by Cristofor Dall'Acqua (1734–1787), which was well received by English society.[60] The interests of the English readers were piqued when they read about Borch's harsh criticism of the famous Patrick Brydone (1736–1818), author of the two-volume book entitled *A Tour through Sicily and Malta* (London 1773–1774);[61] Brydone's work consisted of several dozen colourful letters, which had awakened in Borch the desire to see these unknown lands with his own eyes. The Scottish writer had ventured through these lands shortly before Borch in 1770 serving as a travelling teacher and preceptor to his companions. English readers might have been drawn to two illustrations presented in the first edition, *Passage du fleuve Platane* and *Église de Ste. Rosalie pré de Palermo*, which had been based on drawings by Henry Swinburne. Borch's report[62] documenting the seven-month journey between Naples and Sicily was illuminated by the picture entitled *Ruines du Temple de Junon Lucine à Agrigente* by Goethe's friend Jakob Philipp Hackert (1737–1807).[63] This German landscape painter had travelled around Sicily from April to June 1777 at a similar time as Borch,[64] and, just like him, climbed Mount Etna, so it is possible that their paths crossed during this period. Hackert was one of the few to have a licence to paint ancient excavations[65] and had hosted Goethe while in Italy and provided the German poet with drawing lessons. There were, of course, many more illustrations in the work of Michał Jan Borch, a total of 27 prints, and the author himself was mostly responsible for the graphic design, decorating his words with elaborate sketches depicting ancient monuments, contemporary buildings, plants, figures in regional costumes and genre scenes.[66] The book also includes three maps, among them one of the so-called 'New Sicily,' to facilitate the understanding of the text and, above all, to record the traces of the route travelled by Borch. But the critics of *The English Review* focused mainly on its cognitive qualities when discussing this work. They praised the mastery of the count's style and his remarkable ability to formulate unbiased, balanced judgments, especially in those parts of the letters that directly concerned the inhabitants of the south; their ethnic, demographic and social diversity, and, above all, their national character or characteristics. The *English Review* also applauded the 11-page dissertation on the medical and commercial use of exotic zabarra fibres, i.e. aloe (*Mémoire sur le fil de Zabarra ou d'Aloes*); Borch had presented this treatise to the scholars from the Academy of Lyons as early as 1777 and added to the book as a popularising appendix. Stylistically this work completely broke the epistolary convention, the *English Review* commented, 'The observations they contain seem pertinent and judicious: they appear to us to proceed from a mind active and capacious by nature, and stored with elegant and useful knowledge by education and industry'.[67]

It was impossible to level any accusations of sloppiness or lack of competence against Borch. Despite his young age, he had proceeded on his expedition with deep scientific intention and had undertaken thorough preparation of his journey. To circumvent Sicily, Malta and Gozo on his own, and to avoid the mistakes of others on the same routes, was a key feature of his 'private' Grand Tour.[68] It was full of unpredictable adventures and unplanned experiences, thereby escaping the conventions of his culture, and travelling beyond the impositions of both his father and his king.

Principles or Fantasies?

At the age of twenty-three, Borch had set off for Sicily from Naples on 23 November 1776, sated with that city's social entertainments, gushing with verve and motivation, but in many ways uncharacteristic of similar daredevils from the former Polish-Lithuanian Commonwealth.[69] He was driven by a curiosity to learn about a new part of the world, so very different in terms of nature, history and culture from the one in which he grew up. He intended to hire a Maltese speronara, a small fast rowing barge for six sailors, to sail first to Messina, then to Catania, then to Syracuse, and then to Malta and Gozo, just as Patrick Brydone had done before him. In addition to a large supply of provisions, he had taken a briefcase of letters of recommendation from 'good-natured' Italians, with whom he made friends in Campania. Contrary to the opinions of other foreigners who accuse the Neapolitans of a lack of courtesy towards strangers, he himself had absolutely no problems in being received. His new friends would help him, and his equipment would be supplemented with various tools, such as the London compass made in France, or a Fahrenheit thermometer[70] borrowed from the priest Giovanniego Maria Della Torre (1710–1782), all needed to carry out measurements on Etna. A planned trip to the exotic regions of the Italian Mezzogiorno would be truly challenging for Borch as the route was not a safe one. It was to be undertaken in the face of oncoming winter, a far more demanding season for sea navigation. The lack of properly organized transport, qualified guides, or elementary tourist infrastructure was also cause for concern.[71] Bandits awaiting a chance to steal, ransom-hungry pirates ready to kidnap and Saracen corsairs were a continuous threat, as was possible ailments related to the change in climate.[72] But Borch was not afraid to travel alone, including by mule during overland sections of his route, and was not deterred by his lack of sufficient financial resources. In the case of persistent hunger, he would settle for a meal of 'sea bullheads in oil'. He was well aware that he would not always be favoured by a propitious Sirocco wind, but was filled with enthusiasm. He poured his thoughts out on paper, entrusting them to a fictitious reader, known as 'Count N', who would, from now on, become the only proper addressee of all his letters. The aforementioned challenging journey ensured that he would rarely write to his father or his friends during this trip to the southern end of Europe. His new imaginary confidant was a silent witness to this excursion. In these overseas territories, Borch wanted to avoid following in the footsteps of his British predecessor, who had disregarded the hospitality and openness offered by the inhabitants of the islands too carelessly. The result in his depiction gave a rather superficial image of Sicily and Malta. According to Borch, Brydone's story was unreliable in that he believed negative 'second-hand' opinions about the inhabitants of the islands; Borch delighted in pointing out Brydone's mistakes. His own book, although fictitious, was based on his own real experiences. This approach brings its own advantages, as it allows for a new dimension to Borch's own excursion:

> My way of writing does not have the charm of the English description of the journey, but it has the advantage of offering, in its simplicity, flowers and fruit instead of a pleasant, though false, idea that I could bring to my reader amidst joke and laughter, it brings the truth to the fore.[73]

Borch was aware that he needed to keep his assumptions of another people in check. He was well aware of the superior air other travellers before him had taken, an attitude he wanted to avoid. Instead, he wanted to remain open and sensitive, maintaining a rational approach. Because of this, Borch refrains from any sarcasm or denigrations in his observations but remains objective. This is especially visible in the fragments that deal with an inherently controversial subject of national characteristics, usually arousing the greatest emotions among British readers:

> An Italian considers himself better than the inhabitants of northern countries and despises the vitality of the French, the zeal of the Germans, the taciturnity of the English, he considers himself the first nation in the world and looks loftily at Europe from the height of the Capitol. He only works as much as he expects to earn. If his needs for life were better met, soon self-love and the enjoyment of peaceful pleasures would completely choke the seeds of cognition in him. The Italians themselves agree that this is true. But if a foreigner is moved by the passivity prevailing in the cities,

> he will find the true philosophy in the countryside, in private homes, as in our country and in other countries. If Mr. Brydone had sought among these pleasant circles, he would not have said even half of the malice towards this nation, so otherwise famous and worthy of respect also in our time.[74]

However, for these kinds of insights, Borch uses a 'philosophy of friendship' characterized by his ability to establish a friendly dialogue with others. More specifically, in terms of civilization, his attitude could be interpreted as a commitment to oppose xenophobic views which were developing in some parts of the Old Continent, intertwined with the formation of new national identities. Borch's democratic and thoroughly positive views, which he expressed so boldly in subsequent letters, no doubt stemmed from the fact that he felt not so much a Polish Livonian, but a citizen of the world. Since he had been brought up in a multi-ethnic region of North-Eastern Europe, where there was no single language or religion, he was receptive to a similar type of multicultural periphery in other geographic locations. Although there were negative situations during this excursion, for example when meeting local peasants, where he acted with undue pride, he was far from perceiving people through reductive categorisation:

> it would be a disservice to the hospitality of the Sicilians to think that everyone there is so crude as to obstruct foreigners travelling in their country, mostly for reasons as childish as those mentioned by Mr Brydone. When you want to judge a nation, you cannot do it when some of the inhabitants you meet are either helpful or unfriendly towards you, or when you have a good or bad attitude towards them. In case of the Sicilians generosity and hospitality have always been the main traits of their character.[75]

His dislike of stereotypes cultivated by foreigners was also noticeable in his openness and affirmation of different behaviours. As a scientist, he held an objective view. He understood that one inhabitant's attitude did not sum up the whole nation's. He believed that a single unfavourable circumstance for the traveller, or an accidental error on the part of the people he encountered, should not in any way affect the overall assessment:

> for the nation is a whole, in which individual parts have thousands of shades. But every nation has, it must be said, its own flavour, its own virtues, its shortcomings which are commonly found in the blood of its citizens; the painter of the nation's character must carefully look for these, because they are its distinguishing mark. I make my comments on the basis of contacts not with individual members of the state, but as a result of constant contact with people of all states and of all ages.[76]

Besides, he had no reason to behave differently, as he repeatedly experienced various manifestations of kindness from the inhabitants of the province he was exploring. When the need arose, they often willingly provided him with a safe haven or shared with him the fruits of the fertile Mediterranean soil. In these places he felt as though he was amongst his relatives and friends. If we compare Borch's feelings on this level with Goethe's impressions about exactly the same areas, they have a lot in common in terms of cognition. However, this is undoubtedly a different perspective resulting from their places of origin: It can be assumed that Borch was a visitor with a subconscious inferiority complex as a result of the negative perception of his countrymen, a sentiment spread by travellers from Western Europe.[77] They saw Poland as being associated only with lawlessness, backwardness, dirt and poverty.[78] Up-and-coming and respected scientists such as Borch could hardly change these perceptions of others, but paradoxically thanks to his awareness of these other perceptions, when travelling, he saved himself from disparaging anything foreign of foreigners, as others had done before him. His remarks concerning regionally diverse communities are generally positive; he notices the religious zeal of the Syracusans manifested in the rich festive ceremonies; the persistent courage of the Maltese people allowing them to face the forces of unpredictable nature; and the diligence and frugality of the inhabitants of Gozo which in no way detracts from their sociability and hospitality. It is true that the characteristics of the people living on the mountainous coast of Calabria are presented as less positive:

> they look like bears rather than humans. Today's Calabrian people are characterized by barbaric speech, disgusting appearance, austere, repellent look, and hideous food.[79]

This description should be treated as a complement to his rich ethnographic portrayal of the islands and its people. Another aspect of this conspicuous attention to detail was in his recognition of various classes, while revealing a specific colouration of local customs. Borch generally treated the local peasants with respect (aside from minor disappointments and specific situations that sometimes force him to fairly obvious criticism). However, he focuses more on people of a demographic similar to his own, notably in Malta where he appreciated the daily life of future Hospitallers, filled with an exemplary knightly ethos; and the visit to the house of a certain clerk from Girgenti which, due to the old tradition, had to take place without the participation of women. Certainly, the pause taken in ancient Palermo also remained in the memory of Count Borch for a long time, as he arrived there by almost the same route as Patrick Brydone. The former cultural centre of the Kingdom of Sicily kindled his artistic soul with the beauty of ancient relics he saw. As Andrzej Abramowicz rightly noted, 'It is interesting that in this city Borch managed to see and evaluate the monuments of the past from the period that people of the Enlightenment usually considered barbaric, gothic and devoid of taste.'[80] Borch was helped by his extensive archaeological knowledge and his ability to measure buildings, examine the type of material from which they were made, and draw appropriate sketches.[81] Whenever he had the opportunity, he learned about the authenticity of the ancient coins and medals he had come across when meeting prominent collectors, with whom, like Goethe, he had made numerous contacts during his travels.[82] Also in Palermo, when visiting the houses of the local nobility, he did not shy away from the companionship of his own class; although he was a foreigner, they willingly invited him into their 'amusement circle' for a game of Faro or billiards. This seemed to him to be the custom of the so-called 'great conversation' that reminded him of the English Clubs. But what impressed Borch far more than the games was the fact that talented artists of all sorts, even deprecated castrati, could feast at a common table with the nobility.

The count's drawings from the places he visited on the islands depicted young girls in sensual poses and robes. These were used by Cristofor Dall'Acqua to prepare his own etchings, including several genre scenes[83], for Borch, who repeatedly rebuked local artists for not preserving the female beauty so masterfully sculpted by nature. In his letters, he courteously held accountable the abundance

'Danse des Paysanesse Siciliennes', Vol. 1, p. xvii in Michał Jan Borch, *Lettres sur la Sicile et sur l'Ile de Malthe: à M. le C. de N., écrites en 1777; pour servir de Supplément au Voyage en Sicile et à Malthe de Monsieur Brydonne; ornées de la carte de l'Etna, …, avec 27 estampes …* (Turin, 1782).

of the female form in the southern lands. Not shunning sophisticated rhetoric, he wrote about the female inhabitants of the Mediterranean as if they were works of art, noting in their slender figures the features of 'fine Greek drawing':

> Sicilian ladies are endowed by nature with exceptional qualities. They are very beautiful in general, Greek profile, lively eyes, soulful gaze, laidback walk, noble posture, small feet, refined wit, endearing politeness and rare honesty, proud behaviour, proper and courtly manners, such are their expressive features.[84]

'Jeune fille Lipparotte en habit de Nôces', Vol. 2, p. 112 in Michał Jan Borch, *Lettres sur la Sicile et sur l'Ile de Malthe: à M. le C. de N., écrites en 1777; pour servir de Supplément au Voyage en Sicile et à Malthe de Monsieur Brydonne; ornées de la carte de l'Etna, …, avec 27 estampes* (Turin, 1782).

His perception of sexuality through the prism of ancient canons of beauty went hand in hand with the ability to identify complementary internal features for the ideal woman. According to Borch, every well-mannered young lady should have certain attributes. Coming from a traditional Catholic home, where great importance was attached to impeccable etiquette and elegant appearance, he intuitively paid attention to it. As an aesthete who can appreciate the right proportions of elegance, he could not ignore the female body. This is shown in his discreet observations on the exceptional charm of girls in Malta, manifested by them in the choice of clothes and shoes, as they have a slim waist and 'the most beautiful legs in the world'; or the intimate rituals of girls in Sicily, who, as he saw himself, are not ashamed to bathe completely naked and afterwards play and sing together. While he tried to keep a distanced level of observation, he showed himself as a man of his time, admiring women of other countries, but discreetly. He controlled the erotic fantasies that could bring him to uncertain ground and escaped overtly sexual expressions of some of his counterparts, and instead, just like Johann Wolfgang Goethe, was able to modestly vent his romantic spiritual inclination:

> Oh Sicily, if my pen had not been as weak as my heart is tender I would create a praise worthy of your inhabitants and your happy climate, that

> would soon be on everyone's lips, to describe this stay as honoured with all the gifts of nature.[85]

The paths of these two travellers travelling the Italian Eden echoed one another one final time on the summit of Mount Etna. The volcano offered them a spectacular journey through various geological epochs among rare trees and flowers, aromatic herbs, and minerals not found anywhere else, as well as bizarre light-reflecting bodies embedded in the mountain. Already behind the walls of Catania and in its foothills, both men were astonished by the preserved lava deposits, which destroyed the city in 1669. For Borch, it was a true spectacle, in which all the elements participate, as he was attempting the climb in December, that is, in the middle of winter. He immediately began to conduct extravagant experiments, such as one with a piece of lava, heated over fire in an ordinary pot with a little water. Goethe inadvertently accused his predecessor of only reaching a certain height of Mount Etna,[86] as many others had before. Borch carried out detailed measurements using the barometric method, and then compared them with the readings from his thermometer; this he later discussed in detail in the *Letters*. The place connected them not only as seasoned travellers, but as collectors enjoying their multi-coloured fossils. Both experienced a sense of completion and achievement fulfilled. From the top of Mount Etna, they saw the paradisiacal islands of Sicily, Malta, and Lipari as well as the entire coast from Messina to Syracuse with all its bays and meanders, almost to the tip of Africa, in perfect miniature, as if on a perfectly drawn map of a completed route.

'Mehr Licht' [More Light][87]

Borch ended this journey with a sense of fulfilment, and above all with joy, mobilizing his personality, eager for new excitement and experiences. On the news of his father's death in 1780, he was forced to end his foreign travel and returned to Livonia. He did not abandon his research activity, but directed it to a more mature path. In his home town of Warklany, he found new ways to use his vital energy. His scientific successes failed to bring the expected applause or recognition, however, either in Warsaw or in St. Petersburg.[88] Despite the respect and fame that Borch gained in Europe, in 1781 the Russian Academy of Sciences were still unprepared to acknowledge his scientific achievement and refused to accept him as a peer among its fully fledged associates.[89] Only five years later, the count became a member of the Free Economic Association in St. Petersburg. He also became politically active, published in both the scientific and now literary fields, and finalized many projects undertaken in Italy, including the bringing of the relics of Saint Victor to Latgale.[90] The potential of talent and comprehensive erudition of Michał Jan Borch formed during these Mediterranean journeys was undoubtedly reflected in his later literary works, scientific dissertations and completed collections of books.[91] His presence was finally felt in Polish cultural activity radiating throughout Livonia, the continual reminder being his charming Warklany residence, surrounded by a sentimental garden in the English style.[92] It is not surprising then that the author of *Faust* saw him not only as a guide to the Italian islands but as a kindred spirit:

> And what am I more than a forerunner of others yet to be, both in my travels and life.[93]

Chapter 8

Through an Exile's Eyes: Touring Switzerland with Helen Maria Williams

Louise Duckling

> I have always loved liberty with a sincere love. I hope that I have proven that my principles (and the political principles of a woman always derive from her feelings) have always been on the side of the oppressed. I could not rest an indifferent spectator of the events happening in front of me.
>
> Helen Maria Williams, *Souvenirs*[1]

A good writer will take you on a voyage of discovery. In the act of reading, you will cross imaginary borders into new territory. The Nobel Laureate Wole Soyinka playfully explored this idea when he described the writer as 'a creature in a permanent state of exile', with their goal being to eradicate 'the barriers of reality'.[2] Soyinka's definition is informed by his own status as a writer in political exile and resonates powerfully today, when record numbers of people are being forcibly displaced worldwide. The experience of exile has become a central motif in our modern media and culture, but as a concept it can also offer creative possibilities for re-examining the past. Inspired by recent ideas and theories of migration, this chapter will tell the remarkable story of an eighteenth-century woman writer's journey into exile.[3] In 1798, Helen Maria Williams published *A Tour in Switzerland*, breathing radical new life into the Grand Tour narrative. Writing at a time of war and revolution in Europe, she invites her readers to observe a brutally oppressive world through an exile's eyes. Her ambitious narrative exposes the man-made borders and boundaries that foster inequality in Switzerland and beyond, but she fixes her gaze hopefully on the future. Williams's vision is transcendent and transgressive, intending not only to break new literary ground, but also to break down barriers between people. Inspired by her positive encounters with the individuals she meets on her travels and her sublime encounters with the natural world, Williams provides an awe-inspiring model for a brave new society. Crucially, Williams's status as a woman in exile helps her to imagine a world of such potential and possibility.

The Journey Begins

To better understand Williams's journey into exile, we first need to understand her incredible journey as a writer.[4] Her career began following her return to London in 1781.[5] After the death of her father, Williams had grown up in Northumberland in an affectionate, woman-centred household with her mother, her sister Cecilia, and her half-sister Persis. They were a strong family unit, bound together by an ethics of care and their Dissenting Presbyterian faith – qualities that played a fundamental role in shaping Williams's interests as a writer. Arriving back in London, the family's Dissenting connections brought them into contact with intellectual society. Notably, they received support from the prominent author and Presbyterian clergyman Andrew Kippis, who became a valuable mentor for Williams.

In this environment, Williams flourished. She achieved celebrity status as a poet in the 1780s during a period of female ascendancy in popular literature. In 1786, the *European Magazine* was tempted to declare her the brightest star in this luminary group of women, 'unrivalled by any of her sisters.'[6] Williams's fame and literary reputation were built upon a fashionable public image that celebrated sympathy and feeling. As a heroine of sensibility, she was emulated and adored in the first published poem by an adolescent William Wordsworth.[7] Williams also established a reputation for herself within an intellectual circle that included Elizabeth Montagu, the renowned 'Queen of the Bluestockings', and Dr Samuel Johnson, the distinguished man of letters. Johnson was sufficiently charmed by Williams's poetry to learn stanzas by heart so that he could recite them to her at dinner.[8] Yet what is fascinating about Williams's story is not so much her early positive reception and impressive fan base, but her extreme reversal of fortune. Intellectually marginalized from the British cultural scene that had once embraced her, she would ultimately experience a double exile: in France, and later in Switzerland.

Williams's fall from grace can primarily be attributed to her unswerving passion for political writing. As a member of London's Dissenting community, which had long campaigned for religious and civil liberties, she was sensitive to societal exclusion; from the outset she wrote about wide-ranging issues of social justice and reform.[9] In an age when politics was a precarious subject for a female author, she initially walked the tightrope well. Her early poetry included anti-war and anti-slavery themes with a universal humanitarian appeal,[10] and the 1,500 subscribers to her widely admired *Poems* (1786) covered a broad political spectrum.[11] The dramatic turning point for the young celebrity would be her decision to chronicle the French Revolution. In 1790, following a three-month tour of France, Williams published her eyewitness account in *Letters Written in*

France.[12] The book was a commercial success and widely read; fulfilling the role of foreign correspondent, Williams assisted in the circulation of knowledge to a mass audience. She returned to France accompanied by her mother and her sisters, established a highly successful Parisian salon, and became acquainted with many of the leading revolutionaries. Yet when the French Revolution collapsed into violence, British enthusiasm and optimism were largely replaced with disillusionment and fear. At a time of cultural and political instability, Williams's literary career was now set on a turbulent path: steadfast to the cause, she continued to publish pro-Revolutionary prose, producing eight volumes during the period from 1790 to 1796. Her decision to remain at the epicentre of a Revolution that was increasingly reviled in Britain – coupled with her long-term and widely publicised liaison with a married man, the radical John Hurford Stone – irrevocably tarnished her personal and literary reputation.[13]

In 1793, war broke out between Britain and Revolutionary France. Williams's avowed aim in her *Letters Written in France* had been to throw out 'a line of connection across the divided world', but her strategy was destined to failure.[14] In the years of war hysteria that were to follow, a deep gulf existed between the two nations. Williams was now alienated from her place of birth and in October 1793 she was briefly held in the Luxembourg prison with her family and other British expatriates. They were released after a successful intervention by a French businessman, Marie-Martin-Athanase Coquerel, who would soon marry Williams's sister Cecilia. The marriage was of great importance in providing the family with security at this time; they also benefited from the resourcefulness and financial support of John Hurford Stone, whose commercial dealings in France had been a success. However, in political terms, the situation had become increasingly precarious for Williams. She was now in very real danger in France – not only as an English citizen (and therefore a wartime enemy), but also as a well-known and outspoken associate of the moderate Girondin faction. Many of those whose political sympathies she shared had been imprisoned, and close friends had been sent to the guillotine.[15] As one of the first 'to deprecate, and to proclaim' his tyranny, it was no time for her to be in Robespierre's Paris.[16] Williams's mother urged her to leave. Stone offered a route to safety: exploiting his business acumen and contacts, he procured passports for travel. In June 1794, fearing for her safety during the excesses of the Jacobin Reign of Terror, Williams fled with him to Switzerland.[17]

Since childhood she had longed to visit the Swiss mountains and 'wander amidst those regions of mysterious sublimity',[18] but this would be no typical Grand Tour: terror, fatigue, and border politics would disrupt her six-month journey. Nor is her published account a conventional piece of travel writing. In her Preface, Williams confesses that she is aware 'the paths which I had delighted to tread had been trodden before'; a long tradition of writers had sketched Switzerland's sublime scenery, and so she aspired to create something new. Her originality lies in her observations on the moral situation in Switzerland, and her comparisons with France; unsurprisingly, Williams's political motivation has become the focus of modern critics, not least because the text was a timely intervention.[19] *A Tour in Switzerland* was not printed until 1798, when the Helvetic Revolution was underway, and it serves to justify the imminent French invasion led by Napoleon Bonaparte and the collapse of the Swiss Confederacy. What is perhaps most startling about Williams's account, however, is her unusual position as an exiled woman traversing multiple boundaries – of gender, genre, and geography – and witnessing an epochal moment in Europe: what can readers discover from such a journey?

Into Exile

The most visceral elements in *A Tour in Switzerland* revolve around Williams's accounts of tyranny in Robespierre's France and of oppression in the 'oligarchical' Cantons of Switzerland.[20] The mood is set in the opening pages as the author describes her journey into exile; in imminent danger, we witness her relief in being able to secure 'the privilege' of a passport for Switzerland.[21] Williams describes the Reign of Terror as being 'like some mighty pestilence' infecting and corrupting the cause of French liberty.[22] We can easily imagine the fate of less fortunate dissidents, those who are denied the privilege of travel: in the Republic, death and the grave are 'well-fed monsters'.[23] As testimony to the depravation in Parisian society, Williams describes a brief trend for 'strange, unhallowed orgies' by the name of *des bals à la victime*; conducted in 'a rage for pleasure', people could only attend these festive balls if their relations had been guillotined.[24] Williams's escape from this grotesque and terrifying world is both literal and psychological. She enters Switzerland 'to repose my wearied spirit on those sublime objects – to sooth my desponding heart with the hope that the moral disorder I have witnessed shall be rectified'.[25]

Williams travelled with hope.[26] Yet, as she tours through Switzerland in her exiled state, she necessarily reveals the constraints imposed upon her by borders and boundaries. Only certain routes can provide safe passage for all her party, others are closed to them altogether, and at various checkpoints and military posts they are required to present their permissions for travelling. At St Maurice, entrance to the Swiss Republic is locked and forbidden to 'those who shrink from examination', and at Bern, the party is questioned 'with stern severity' about the motives of their visit.[27] Williams makes a point of highlighting the arbitrary nature of these borders. They are sites of human conquest, which can define our status as subjects or slaves, and she describes the Swiss predilection for territorial boundaries as nothing short of a 'geographical religion'.[28] At the town of Solothurn there is a particularly long 'ceremonial of examination' – despite their passports being in perfect order – to ensure they bear 'no mischievous traces of intelligence with France'.[29]

In Solothurn (as in certain other towns) there is open hostility towards French emigrants, who are subject to insult and even danger. Williams has deep empathy for their plight, not least because her own situation remains delicate: she has been warned to 'conceal carefully' any relationship with France during her tour.[30] At Locarno, the population has been swelled by the French seeking refuge, 'whose prospects were then falling fast into the shade'. Williams has a particularly poignant encounter with an émigré vicar near St Barnardin, a virtuous and accomplished man of letters, with no hope of being permitted to revisit his country. He finds solace in his breviary, his Bible, and the works of the poet Ovid, who is described as 'an exiled fellow sufferer'.[31] Williams is devastated by the vicar's story and by the fact she has 'no power to extricate him from a situation which seemed almost insupportable'.[32] Exhausted and facing an uncertain future herself, Williams registers her trauma in descriptions of the landscape. Metaphors for exile appear in the text, as when trees 'whose roots have been riveted for ages to the soil' are 'torn from their base'.[33] Most strikingly, as Angela Keane has noted, the psychological pressures of her journey 'reveal themselves in the physical difficulties of ascending mountains or traversing rivers.'[34]

As a reflection of Williams's psycho-emotional state, travel is incredibly tough and often dangerous. The ascent to St Gotthard causes great fatigue and Williams suffers from the cold; it is an extreme but awe-inspiring landscape 'of savage wildness and terror'.[35] At the mountains of Kerenzen the enterprise becomes even more perilous, with narrow paths leading the party to the very edge of the precipice. The difficulties and 'sublime horrors' of the journey at times appear almost insurmountable.[36] The threat of avalanche is a recurring theme. Travellers owe their fate to the capriciousness of the weather: a storm on a lake transforms a sailing trip into another experience of 'terror', with everyone taking a turn at the oar to brave the tempest.[37] The hardships of travel are often compounded by the natural physical barriers that Williams encounters, echoing the political borders within which she is confined. Time and again, the mountains close upon her, and the rocks form a narrow channel, sometimes forbidding all possibility of passage – and yet, despite every obstruction, there is still hope. In her Preface, Williams vividly describes the 'electrical fire' of the Revolution flashing around the Swiss borders: 'Behold the subtle spark,' she says, 'which finds a conductor in the human heart, escaping beyond its prescribed limits'. For Williams, the 'spirit of freedom' is powerful and cannot be confined.[38] She invites her readers to escape with her into new territory beyond limits: an exiled space, a sublime new space, where change can occur.

Liminal Spaces: Breaking Down Borders

While exile is largely defined as a dysphoric and deprived state, critics such as Hamid Naficy have made a case for its 'euphoric possibilities' driven by 'a desire for liberation and freedom'.[39] An exile lives on the threshold between two cultures, in a state of 'in-betweenness'; in Williams's case, alienated from her place of birth (England), she is from neither here (Switzerland) nor there (France). Instead, she inhabits a more nuanced, deterritorialized space of vast potential. From this space, the exile is in a position 'not only to question, even subvert, much of their previous authenticities, authorities, identities, and cultural practices but also to forge new ones in their place.'[40] Liminality is therefore a powerful concept for those interested in the study of borders; it is associated with fluidity of identity and meaning; with transgression, subversion, or transcendence.[41] Taking these ideas into consideration, Homi Bhabha states that the liminal is the place from which 'the minority, the exilic, the marginal and the emergent' may speak.[42] In *A Tour in Switzerland*, Williams very deliberately draws attention to her sublime experiences in liminal spaces; in these transcendent moments, she finds a new and powerful voice to argue for political and social change.

The theme of liminality is pervasive not only in Williams's state of exile and the places/spaces she occupies, but also in the very nature of the text. It is worth pausing to consider the form of *A Tour in Switzerland*, as in itself it provides a canvas of possibility. Blurring the boundaries of genre and disrupting the typical Grand Tour narrative, Williams's travelogue encompasses memoir, political philosophy, nature writing, and history. Imposing no formal constraints, the alternation between multiple modes allows Williams to blur the boundaries between the private and the public, merge the topographical and political sublime, and move creatively between past and present. The layering of form and detailed observation lend an encyclopaedic quality to the text, bestowing an air of objectivity and authority to Williams's voice. To serve her narrative purpose, Williams is also prepared to disrupt the temporal sequence of her journey. In sweeping away distinctions of genre and chronology, Williams creates a universal, timeless platform from which she can challenge social injustice.

Moments of transcendence punctuate the text, sometimes coinciding with positive reflections on the heroic and sublime potential of mankind. One such moment can be found in the 'delicious serenity' of Williams's journey on Lake Uri. At the threshold between day and night, in the 'soft gradations of twilight', the party forget themselves in the grandeur of the landscape. They gaze in silence and 'rapt astonishment' at the 'shadowy greatness' of the sight, until the moon lights up 'the whole majestic scenery with glorious and chastened lustre'. The moonlit radiance serves as a metaphor for enlightenment: for Williams, it is fitting that William Tell, the Swiss folk hero who fought against tyranny, is commemorated by a chapel in this 'august and sublime' place.[43] Other threshold spaces provide moments of forgetting and illumination, as for example during Williams's ascent of the Alps of St Barnardin. During the challenging climb she is overcome by the effects of heat and altitude; arriving at the icy boundary of the glacier, delirious and breathless, she throws herself upon the grass to rest. While her travelling companions explore the world of ice above her, Williams remains alone at this border place.

Taking in the magnificent views of the surrounding mountains, hills, and glaciers, Williams immerses herself in hours of meditation, composing a devotional hymn in celebration of the awe-inspiring landscape, and losing herself in time.[44] She describes how, in the pure air of the mountains, meditation assumes a state that is

> something of tranquil rapture, remote from all that is selfish, or sensual. It seems as if, while raised above the haunts of men, we leave below all mean and earthly sentiments, and that, as we approach the etherial [sic] regions, the soul contracts something of their unchangeable purity. …we forget every thing, we forget ourselves, and have scarcely a consciousness of existence.[45]

Williams's ascent of the mountains is a form of sublime transcendence, in which she literally and spiritually rises above the ordinary and the everyday. It seems fitting that Williams uses this purifying moment to open her second volume of the tour; having elevated herself 'above the haunts of men', she now embarks on a lengthy criticism of men's earthly failures. Her mountain experience also serves to reinforce a key moment of epiphany that occurs in the first volume, reminding the reader of the immutable and universal nature of Williams's political philosophy. This first and most powerful moment of transcendence takes place at Europe's largest waterfall: the Rhine Falls at Schaffhausen. The trip to the Falls requires a good deal of effort: the direct route to Schaffhausen through Austrian territory 'was forbidden ground' for someone with a French passport, forcing a 'long circuitous route' via Zurich.[46] This indirect route of travel echoes Williams's circuitous narrative technique: she describes the episode out of sequence, jumping ahead in her itinerary and disrupting the chronological flow of the book. It is significant that Williams places this event so early, and so out of place, in the story of her journey; in its refusal to be constrained within a traditional story arc, the moment epitomises the transgressive tendencies of the text.

As Williams approaches the Rhine Falls, there is a sense that she is moving within a confining landscape towards something immense. She describes the 'half-seen chaos' of the mountains and we catch glimpses of things partially obscured. The Rhine itself is 'concealed for some time…from our view' until a vantage point is finally reached and the cataract bursts 'in all its overwhelming wonders on the astonished sight'.[47] Now Williams's language erupts with a long, breathless description that feeds all the senses:

> That stupendous cataract, rushing with wild impetuosity over those broken, unequal rocks, which, lifting up their sharp points amidst its sea of foam, disturb its headlong course, multiply its falls, and make the afflicted waters roar – that cadence of tumultuous sound, which had never till now struck upon my ear – those long feathery surges, giving the element a new aspect – that spray rising into clouds of vapour, and reflecting the prismatic colours, while it disperses itself over the hills – never, never can I forget the sensations of that moment! when with a sort of *annihilation of self*, with every past impression erased from my memory, I felt as if my heart were bursting with emotions too strong to be sustained.[48] (my emphasis)

The 'sensations of that moment' invoke touch ('sharp', 'feathery'), sound ('roar'), and sight ('prismatic colours') and promote an extreme bodily response in which the heart is 'bursting with emotions.' This passage can be interpreted on different levels; it serves as evidence of Williams's aesthetic sensibility and can also be viewed as an emotional release following the trauma she has experienced. The sublime moment also generates a spiritual response, representing a kind of purification in the face of nature. Williams describes this experience of transcendence as 'a sort of annihilation of self'. In this powerful moment, the 'expanded spirit' seems too confined; we are taken out of time, and the mind is called 'from all its little cares and vanities, to higher destinies and regions'.[49] Moving beyond a state of subjectivity, Williams is elevated to an objective place of intellectual power. Her transformation calls to mind an idea explored by the feminist and philosopher Julia Kristeva in *Strangers to Ourselves* (1991), a book which explores the notion of the foreigner, the outsider, in a country and society that is not their own. Kristeva confesses that if she can be objectively aware of her own difference, then 'I lose my boundaries, I no longer have a container'. This process leads to a '*destructuration* [disintegration] *of the self*' which can serve as 'an *opening* toward the new' (original emphasis).[50] In essence, Williams enters this kind of transformative space as she experiences 'a sort of annihilation' at the

Falls. Breaking down the borders of her own self, Williams seizes the opportunity to speak of the world and its inequalities from a liberating new perspective.

On the Side of the Oppressed

Williams is now ready to deconstruct political boundaries. As she passes through each destination on her tour, she draws attention to the oppressive barriers of law, government, and social convention. As an informed outsider, Williams speaks with a tone of moral and intellectual authority for those who do not have a voice. Her authority is amplified in part through her citation of numerous sources, weaving a rich cultural tapestry that includes Milton, Shakespeare, and Rousseau. Previous works by men that have applauded the natural beauty and political liberty of Switzerland are referenced and subjected to a 'feminizing scrutiny': in a process of 'radical excursus', Williams 'swims against the idealization of Helvetica.'[51] She challenges the 'fault of former travellers' in celebrating the notion that Switzerland is a 'land of freedom',[52] by recounting tales of avarice, despotism, ignorance, and injustice from the past and from the present. The effect is diffuse and cumulative: as she travels from place to place, she adds layer upon layer of evidence to support her political case. Moving beyond the single perspective of her own story, she adopts the multiple perspectives of a non-linear history, across many generations and territories.

Williams observes that during her tour she scarcely passed over a territory which had not been the scene of an uprising. The history of the region is one of resistance followed by submission, involving complex political alliances and power struggles over border territories. In telling this history, Williams harnesses the exemplary power of stories, and we can trace many parallels and patterns among them. In fourteenth-century Glarus, heroic men roll stones from the mountain to crush an invading Austrian army in the valley beneath them; around the same time in the region of Basel, a brutal tyrant throws men to their death from the mountain if they offend him. Insurrection is an inevitable outcome of the despotic structures of government. In the Levantina Valley, the inhabitants have revolted twice in the eighteenth century, 'stung into disobedience by some act of proconsular tyranny'.[53] The government of Zurich is corrupt with vices, and power is invested in a tiny minority of men; it is 'nothing but a mere oligarchy, incompatible with every idea of a free political institution'.[54] In Lugano, the power of the bailiff is almost unlimited in all civil and criminal matters, with no clear and '*just* bounds' to provide an effective regulatory mechanism.[55] In the Grisons, there is a 'democratic' government but (as Williams tartly points out) this is 'a Swiss democracy, where, under the name of liberty, the greatest outrages are committed against the principle'.[56]

Moral and political vices are rife in this region, involving avarice, bribery, and corruption. During recent turbulence in Geneva, revolutionaries have been condemned to death. In the Pays de Vaud, which is subject to arbitrary rule by Bern, celebrations marking the French Revolution are brutally repressed. As Williams makes explicitly clear in her discussion of the absolute power of the council of Bern, their faults amount to a 'long list of transgressions against the privileges of equal freedom'.[57]

Williams adopts the city of Basel as her home base during the tour and uses it to provide a case study of inequality in Switzerland. Of the 40,000 inhabitants, more than 30,000 people 'enjoy no privileges'.[58] All political and commercial rights are held by about 7,000 burghers, while the disenfranchised majority are forced to pay heavy taxes from which the burgher class is exempt. This exploitative model is upheld by just 300 self-elected burghers who wield the power of government for life. Williams describes the workers as a migrant class living in 'a state of complete degradation'. They are considered 'merely as strangers', regardless of whether they are first- or second-generation immigrants (or even if they have been living in the city for 'several successive' generations).[59] Unable to exercise in trade directly, they are bound to work for their governors, with many employed making cottons and ribbons. Williams exposes the unfair practices at the heart of this system of commerce:

> Over the manufacturers of these articles, the governors find it advantageous to manifest some portion of their right of sovereignty; for in vain the father of a family may cultivate his field of flax, and prepare it for use; in vain his wife may spin, his infants turn the wheel which winds the thread, and he himself weave the woof; the web when woven is not at his disposition – he has no right over the produce of his labour, no power to dispose of what he has acquired by the sweat of his brow and the toil of his hands; he must carry his little stock to the capital of his Canton, and there, and only there, is permitted to sell it; while the burgher of the town, who is the purchaser, has previously arranged the price at which it shall be sold.[60]

This passage provides a good example of the relentless and impassioned rhythm of Williams's prose when she describes a vexatious law or despotic action. Here, the family toils 'in vain…in vain' with 'no right…no power'. When discussing the same exploitative practices in Zurich, she is equally enraged on behalf of the ordinary worker: 'To labour for the profit of the Burgher is the occupation of his life, and the end of his existence; to murmur is treason, to resist is death'.[61]

These repressive tendencies are also visible in the Swiss treatment of religious minorities.[62] In Protestant Basel, no Catholic rites are allowed, and Jews are treated with abhorrence. The Genevans expel Catholics and there is a 'narrow spirit of bigotry' among the lower classes.[63] In France, by contrast, Jews, Muslims and Protestants are all recognised. The source of the problem, in Williams's estimation, is that the Swiss population is largely uncultivated and has not yet learned the divine lesson of toleration. Culture and learning serve as a barometer for a decent and civilised society; prejudice belongs to the unenlightened. In the Grisons, 'ignorance holds its leaden sceptre',[64] while in Lucerne there is not a single bookseller. In Basel, she discerns 'neither the love of arts, of literature, of liberty, or of any earthly good, but money'.[65] Once the centre of science and the home of the great philosopher Erasmus, Williams laments the poor state of learning in the city, where colleges are empty of students and professorships are merely sinecures. To force her point, Williams declares that in Basel 'genius is treated like other strangers', with the cultivated few appearing 'as a solitary flower on a desart [*sic*] heath'.[66] This sad fact is reflected in salon life. Female societies involve everyday gossip and people watching. While such activities are unedifying, they could at least be fun; instead, they are a joyless means of 'murdering time'.[67] The male 'clubbists' are especially uncultured, although this feature is not peculiar to Basel: here, as in London, Williams points out how men who attend such clubs are destined to become unfit for all other society.

Men's behaviour in public life is often ridiculous and, in her attacks on the male establishment, Williams demonstrates her capacity for humour. There are moments in *A Tour in Switzerland* when she brilliantly deploys sarcasm, irony and an acid wit for satirical and political effect. At a ceremony in Lugano, she witnesses a 'tribe of poets' – including professors, doctors, bankers, trustees, and attorneys – offering panegyric odes and sonnets in praise of a former bailiff.[68] Williams wryly explains that she was unable to discover what distinguished acts this God-like man had in fact performed. At Bellinzona, there is another opportunity to witness a civic ceremony celebrating a former bailiff. Here the praises are even more 'sublimely tuneful' than in Lugano, elevated into 'more than Virgilian rapture'.[69] The tributes are so ridiculous they are funny, but Williams reminds us they are not from the pen of 'some comic rhymester', but the actions of cynical and sycophantic men. Should we be more aggrieved, she asks, by 'this vile adulation, or the miserable vanity that stoops to receive it'?[70]

The male obsession with power, adulation and vanity is not confined to Swiss civic society. Williams also satirises the Romantic notion of the English Lord on a Grand Tour by presenting two examples of men travelling for glory and adventure. The first of these so-called 'travelling philosophers' ordered his carriage to be dragged to the top of the mountain so 'that he might have the fame of crossing St Gothard [*sic*] in a vehicle with wheels'.[71] Who would attempt such an arrogant and ridiculous adventure, Williams asks, but the Emperor, the burgher master of Bern, or an Englishman? The second case is of a young English nobleman who, despite repeated warnings of the dangers, attempts to swim down the cataracts of the Rhine and is dashed to pieces on the rocks below. The examples given are Grand Tours of self-aggrandisement and foolishness, disconnected from the reality of lived experience in Switzerland. Always on the side of the oppressed, Williams follows a radically different path.

Finding Her Own Territory

Helen Maria Williams. Artist unknown, nd.

Williams is deadly serious about the principle of equality, but she introduces a note of levity when discussing her own experience as a traveller. There is no affectation or grandiosity on her female tour; instead, moments of bathos punctuate the text. Williams confesses to many travel mishaps. For example, near Bellinzona she enters an inn with her travelling party and enjoys a rest, a meal, and a lively discussion with the other guests. After a delightful two hours, the bill is requested, and only then does she discover they are not in an inn after all but have stepped into the local magistrate's house. While this was a pleasant mistake, there are problems on the tour with real innkeepers, whose prices increase in line with the volume of celebrity guests they have hosted. At Bellinzona, Williams's party pays a premium 'in consequence of the magnificent ideas of expence [*sic*] which our landlord had acquired by conducting the charming Duchess of Devonshire over St Gothard [*sic*]'; the high cost is ill-suited to their 'plebeian purses'.[72] Williams also has a propensity for getting lost – in her own thoughts, and on mountains. When descending the Alps, she cannot find her mule at the spot where he was left; with darkness approaching, while she has been forgetting herself in meditation on the mountain, the mule had rather soundly 'formed a better judgment of the fit hour of retreat'.[73] A makeshift chair is made to carry Williams down the mountain, unceremoniously, while the sensible mule is caught marching home.

The effect of these anecdotes is to lend a tone of authenticity and modesty to Williams's voice. She is confident to admit her mistakes. She also admits when she is unqualified to discuss a subject, which lends greater credence to her argument when she does pass judgement. This reflective strategy strengthens Williams's intellectual authority, whether she is discussing the cruel barriers in society or the positive means to overcome them. Never self-absorbed, she remains intellectually open to the scenery and the people she encounters. Williams retains this objective self-awareness throughout the journey and is always receptive to new possibilities. As an antidote to the oppressive accounts of French and Swiss tyranny, we therefore discover myriad examples of happiness, good sense, tolerance, and respect. There is a more hopeful path to liberty and Williams claims it for her territory.

Williams highlights many life-affirming and positive moments on her journey that convey her vision for a happier world. There is a joyful and surprising encounter with drunken Italian priests singing 'amorous love-songs, and chanting bacchanalian glees'.[74] A day spent on the lake at Lugano, on the holy day of St Lawrence, culminates in a striking experience when a 'sacred song' is heard, 'proceeding from female voices, flinging its sweet full cadence upon the breeze, and dying along the waters'.[75] In a magical moment of harmony and community, the oarsmen slacken their oars and join the chorus. Williams also describes meetings with individuals in which she acknowledges their capacity for simple kindness and harmonious living. These include a visit with the theologian and physiognomist Johann Kaspar Lavater. Williams admires Lavater's simple eloquence, and the fact that his sense of right and wrong are based on applying principles, rather than the constraints of religious doctrine. Near Basel, a farmer impresses her with his 'plain, honest, sensible' demeanour.[76] Elsewhere she remarks upon how touched she is to observe the care, and even tenderness, shown to animals in Switzerland.

For Williams, education is of paramount importance in building and sustaining a fair and just society. In this respect, Revolutionary France (despite its many other problems) is provided as a model of excellence. Museums, libraries, and botanic gardens have been opened throughout France to enable the 'dissemination of instruction'. Paris is now a centre of the arts. Williams raises ethical concerns about the French looting of art objects from Italy, as spoils of war, but she praises the fact that admission to cultural establishments is accessible to all: 'both learned and unlearned'. The National Library is open to the public every day, with equal access given to men and women who work alongside each other in silent study. Institutions such as the newly opened Louvre Museum are celebrated as 'receptacles of knowledge'. Williams exults in the idea of 'so many fellow creatures rescued from vice and slavery; for such are the necessary effects of ignorance; since if knowledge, as Bacon observed, be power, it is also virtue, freedom, and happiness'.[77] Williams invokes the famous quote, coined by the English philosopher Francis Bacon in 1597, but expands the maxim to reflect her own political ideals of liberty. She is convinced that knowledge can lead Switzerland to a freedom 'unsullied by anarchy or violence'.[78] Unsurprisingly, therefore, she celebrates learning wherever she encounters it on her tour.

In Lucerne, she is delighted to discover that the ladies enhance their natural beauty by 'cultivating the graces of the mind'.[79] In Zurich too, despite the political and economic corruption, there is a more cultivated society. Williams acknowledges the many municipal regulations in the city that provide relief and instruction for the poor, which include an orphanage, an institution offering apprenticeships to poor children, and hospitals for invalids of every religion and background. Public education is also provided by the State. Williams encounters a wonderful scene in a church in Zurich where a large group of children is receiving religious instruction. For Williams, this is one of the most pleasing moments she experiences in Switzerland, since they are being taught 'habits of virtue and piety which shed a cheering and steady light over the intricate mazes of a turbulent world'.[80] This harmonious effect of faith combined with learning is evident when Williams visits the abbey of Engelberg (whose literal meaning is, fittingly, 'mountain of angels'). The benevolent abbot is described as a man of good sense and literature, as well as piety, and he cherishes equality. Here, there are no divisive boundaries: 'every wanderer has…his claims to protection allowed, and every visitor finds a welcome'.[81] This abbot has given asylum to two emigrant nuns, who avoid idleness and poverty by exercising their talent for making artificial flowers and other elegant items. Williams is sorry to leave this mountain of angels and the healing space created by this venerable abbot.

Williams's description of the nuns is one of many references to French women in the text. While she derides the mercenary opportunism and vanity of the rapidly enriched Parisian 'belles' in post-Revolutionary France,[82] she conveys a deep and tender admiration for those who have experienced anguish. Williams declares 'that the noblest examples of fortitude and resignation under sufferings were, during revolutionary government, displayed by women'.[83] On a domestic level, in France and in exile, skills once employed as an amusement are now the means of economic survival, as noblewomen support their families by selling ornamental needlework and drawings. In *A Tour of Switzerland*, one of these noblewomen takes centre stage in a long, embedded story that serves as a revolutionary morality tale. Here, Williams provides a woman-centred perspective to explore the traumatic effects of male power structures, and to offer a new model for society. The sequence opens near Bellinzona, where Williams finds herself separated from her travelling party and takes a wrong path down the mountains. This is known to be dangerous territory: a traveller has recently been murdered nearby, and Williams has witnessed 'the hideous spectacle' of two men hung in gibbets.[84] Echoing the violence in France, we are reminded that Williams is travelling from danger; she is displaced, scared and alone. In this moment, she will come face to face with another woman in exile, and experience a moment of connection and belonging.

As Williams sits in fear at the base of the mountain, she is rescued by a French émigré. This noblewoman is Madame de C – with whom Williams strikes up a cherished friendship. They walk together in a solitary region of the valley that the Frenchwoman has come to regard 'as *her own territory*' (my emphasis).[85] In this feminized space, Madame de C – confides in Williams, sharing her powerful story. Following the Revolution, she had been left alone in France to care for her husband's property, while he had emigrated to safety. Losing communication with her husband, and in fear of the scaffold, she secures a means of escape. As in Williams's case, 'life was then included in the gift of a passport'.[86] She attempts to join her husband in Switzerland, but upon her arrival discovers that her 'eternal exile' will not be softened by his presence: he has abandoned her for a mistress.[87] Madame de C – experiences an overwhelming sense of misery and powerlessness, but she manages to find the means and motivation to support her family. She takes delight in honest work by selling her embroidery, turning her accomplishments to good purpose in 'an effort of virtue'.[88] In this respect, as an autonomous worker, her tale serves as a counter-narrative to the poor exploited families living under the burghers' rule in Basel and Zurich. The affair of Monsieur C –, meanwhile, soon comes to a pitiful end: he has been seduced by a woman known for her tyranny over men and she leaves him as soon as his money runs out. Seized with remorse, he returns to his wife as a sick, humbled, and broken man. Portrayed as a foolish victim, he is forgiven, and returns to live under the care of Madame de C – in her charming cottage. Overcoming the trauma of exile, Madame de C – finds happiness within a transformed family home.

Williams provides a myriad of stories in *A Tour of Switzerland*, many of which only occupy one or two sentences, and so it is noteworthy that she dedicates such a large amount of space to Madame de C –'s tale. The 'History of an Emigrant Family' is given a dedicated chapter that occupies one-seventh of the first volume, condensing within its narrative the key themes of the text: exile and belonging, oppression and liberation, and the transgression of traditional boundaries. In this tale, women hold the key to a brave new future. Here, change is not to be found by overturning male power with female tyranny, as in the case of Monsieur C –'s resourceful seducer who establishes 'dominion' over her male 'captives'.[89] Instead, the enterprising Madame de C – triumphs over her dissolute peer, reforms her wayward husband, and redefines the gendered boundaries and modes of power within her home. In a matriarchal world of dignity and compassion, Williams finds the new territory she is seeking.

The Journey's End

At the end of her tour, Williams can safely return to Paris. In an unpredictable narrative that defies conventional boundaries, she has traversed perilous mountains and beautiful valleys, provided a philosophical history of Switzerland, and imagined a kinder future. In this multi-layered text, Williams has made a compelling case for her revolutionary principles, as universal values that 'know no geographical boundaries'.[90] A principal idea at the heart of her philosophy is that compassion must be shown for those in need. Inviting her readers to see the world through an exile's eyes, she argues that 'affording an asylum to the unfortunate is a debt which both governments and individuals owe to humanity'.[91] Williams stands with those who struggle for equality and liberty, and harnesses the power of storytelling to break down social and political barriers. In the closing pages of the book, Williams uses a travelling metaphor – reverberating with echoes of her own tour – to describe the journey of the mind. Like the traveller who struggles for months, climbing mountains, ascending in heat and ice, the human mind can reach 'at once, with an incredible effort, the highest probable attainments of political discovery'.[92] On the road to enlightenment, she has travelled with anger and rage, but also with humour, humility, and humanity. For Williams, the process has been transformative. 'Switzerland has opened to me a new world of ideas', she exclaims,[93] and she has taken her readers with her on this sublime journey of discovery.

Chapter 9

'I cannot yet give up the hope': Mary Wollstonecraft and Observations on European Travel

Mina Tsai-Yeh Wang

Mary Wollstonecraft (1759–1797) was a leading British radical thinker of the eighteenth century. Compared with the substantial body of research on the subject of gender and feminism in Wollstonecraft's work, her political reflections and self-reflections of womanhood and motherhood during her travel after the end of 1792 have received relatively little attention. As Wollstonecraft remarked, the art of travelling, 'is [an] … art of thinking'.[1] There were two personas speaking in the texts written during her travels: one spoke for 'the human race' with observations on the political movement and problems that occurred during the fulfilment of the French Revolution or other relevant political actions;[2] the other one used the first person to talk of herself,[3] that is, her role as a woman and mother living abroad during this extreme time.

Mary Wollstonecraft, Portrait by John Opie, engraving by James Heath, 1797.

This chapter intends to explore how Wollstonecraft considered the political conflicts she witnessed in Paris and how she explained the reasons the outcome of Enlightenment ideals turned out to be political terror. It will examine her understanding of the future possibility of the French Revolution during her stay in France and her subsequent journey to Scandinavia. Her first-hand observations were one of the few British travel accounts responding to the problems of the revolutionary age. A traveller like Wollstonecraft was not only seeking to witness her readings of the world and to confirm and correct what she had learned, but to ask herself why she was travelling and how her life should be conducted. During her travel to France and Scandinavia, while suffering from severe depression, she wanted to pursue improvement of all kinds and to prove that she deserved liberty and independence. Furthermore, this chapter will demonstrate that Wollstonecraft was more than a sentimental woman traveller afield alone as Godwin had described;[4] she was an anxious mother too. Her writing revealed her happiness with the growth of her child, her exhaustion as a single mother, and her worry about her daughter's future within a patriarchal society.

Travel During the French Revolution

After the fall of the Bastille in July 1789, travel to France became bound up with politics. Surprising numbers of Britons continued to visit France and to experience at first hand the revolutionary events and the consequences of them. Due to the unstable relations between Britain and France, even before this, travelling occurred in waves in accordance with the state of relations between these two countries.[5] Generally speaking, in the second half of the eighteenth century, especially after the end of the Seven Years' War, as Linda Colley points out, the British gained self-confidence following the reduction in the French threat,[6] and as a result many people made up their minds to visit Europe at this relatively quiet time. French culture and fashion had always been a major attraction for British people who wanted to travel to the Continent. After the outbreak of the French Revolution in July 1789, despite the chaos it brought, voyaging across the Channel was still possible. People with republican enthusiasms, such as Helen Maria Williams (1759–1827) and Mary Wollstonecraft, ventured to France at this particular moment in order to witness such dramatic events and write down their reflections and observations as journalists. When the Revolution developed into the Terror, however, few people risked travelling to Paris. Those who journeyed to Europe found a detour and avoided France altogether.

In 1793, Britain had joined the First Coalition and waged war against France and the political environment in France rapidly became hostile to foreigners. On 9 October 1793, according to Michael Rapport, the Convention 'decreed the arrest of British and Hanoverian subjects and the seizure of their property in France' and it 'wanted no exceptions to the law'.[7] A few days later, those British radicals who were previously protected by their political stance were now put in prison. Thus, many Britons who remained in France after the end of 1793 were to become prisoners. Helen Maria Williams, Charlotte West (d. 1821) and Grace Dalrymple Elliott (1754–1823), among others, were sent to prison.[8] Wollstonecraft escaped the police sweep, because she had moved to Neuilly-sur-Seine on the Western outskirts of Paris in June 1793,[9] and obtained American citizenship by registering as the wife of her American lover, Gilbert Imlay (1754–1828), at the American Embassy.[10]

Wollstonecraft turned out to be one of the few British radicals who lived through the Terror in France, and witnessed the violent turn of the Revolution. Later on, she travelled to Scandinavia in the summer of 1796, which area, far from being a popular travel spot, was beyond the boundary of the western society. This special and somewhat mysterious experience made her reflect on the process and frustrations, not only of her own life, but western civilization and Scandinavian society. Generally speaking, British radicals such as Joseph Priestley (1733–1804), Richard Price (1723–1791) and Helen Maria Williams neither explained the relationship between the enlightenment ideals and political chaos of the Revolution, nor talked much about the future development of the Revolution. Most of them blamed the violence on the long oppression and despotism of the *ancien régime*, which caused the French people's revenge and lack of civic virtue. Living in London before setting off on her trip to Paris, like many Britons who were sympathetic to the Revolution, Wollstonecraft wanted to go to France and to observe how the revolutionary changes might bring benefits to people. All she witnessed was, however, a disordered and bloodstained society. Thus, she began to wonder how and why the Revolution had gone wrong. Should she carry on having confidence in it? Was there another way to fulfil Revolutionary ideals in human society? She had been trying to find answers in her journeys. Her subsequent works, *An Historical and Moral View of the Origin and Progress of the French Revolution; and the Effect It Has Produced in Europe* (1794) and *Letters Written during a Short Residence in Sweden, Norway, and Denmark* (1796), written during the journey, reveal her abiding concern with the impact of the political changes upon European society.

Wollstonecraft's Political Reflections in Revolutionary France

By midsummer 1792, many of Wollstonecraft's radical friends, such as William Priestley (1771–1838, the second son of Dr Joseph Priestley), James Watt (1769–1838, son of the inventor), Thomas Cooper (1759–1839), Thomas Christie (1761–1796), Thomas Holcroft (1745–1809), William Wordsworth (1770–1850) and Samuel Rogers (1763–1855) had already visited Revolutionary France and tasted the revolutionary way of life. It was at this time Wollstonecraft agreed to make a trip to Paris together with bookseller and publisher Joseph

Johnson (1738–1808) and the Swiss painter Henry Fuseli (1741–1825).[11] Yet, when the party arrived at Dover in September 1792, there was news of upheavals taking place in France. Visiting France at this time could bring them into danger. Wollstonecraft's two companions decided to return to London, and thus, on 13 September their trip ended.[12] The Jacobins, led by Maximilien Robespierre (1758–1794) and Jean-Paul Marat (1743–1793), among others, had overwhelmed the Girondins by the middle of 1792, and they conducted a violent campaign against all moderates, constitutionalists and former monarchists, with the help of the Paris *sans-culottes*. The news of the September Massacres in Paris produced doubts and revulsion among many British sympathizers'. Yet, Wollstonecraft wrote to her friend, William Roscoe (1753–1831):

> Mean time let me beg you not to mix with the shallow herd who throw an odium on immutable principles, because some of the mere instrument of the revolution were too sharp. – Children of any growth will do mischief when they meddle with edged tools. It is to be lamented that *as yet* the billows of public opinion are only to be moved forward by the strong wind, the squally gusts of passion.[13]

A general aversion to the Revolution had spread throughout Britain after the fall of the monarchy in France in August 1792 and the following September Massacres. Wollstonecraft, however, remained optimistic about the Revolution and she determined to set out for Paris alone. She explained that the radical inequality that prevailed in France and the corruptions of the *ancien régime* were the main reasons for the excesses of the Revolution and the subsequent Terror. The result was gloomy and lamentable, yet predictable.

Thus, she left for Paris on 8 December 1792 with the aim of writing an account of the Revolution for British readers. As soon as she arrived, she found that Paris was very different from what she had expected. Commenting in London, she had tried to rationalize the chaos brought about by the Revolution, sympathized with the grievances of the French people while commending the principles of the Revolution against the *ancien régime* and believed that the Revolution was implementing the political philosophy of the Enlightenment. Nonetheless, in her letter to Joseph Johnson, on 26 December 1792, the account of her Paris experience was filled with horror at the turbulence and bloodshed:

> I have been alone ever since; and, though my mind is calm, I cannot dismiss the lively images that have filled my imagination all the day. – Nay, do not smile, but pity me; for, once or twice, lifting my eyes from the paper, I have seen eyes glare through a glass-door opposite my chair, and bloody hands

> shook at me. Not the distant sound of a footstep can I hear. My apartments are remote from those of the servants, the only persons who sleep with me in an immense hotel… – I wish I had even kept the cat with me! – I want to see something alive; death in so many frightful shapes has taken hold of my fancy. – I am going to bed – and, for the first time in my life, I cannot put out the candle.[14]

Now, as a witness to events in Paris, she could no longer dismiss the violence of the Jacobins and the *sans-culottes*. She felt horror and had nightmarish visions in her mind. She saw Louis XVI pass down the street to attend his trial 'with more dignity than I expected from his character, in a hackney coach going to meet death'.[15] Admitting the cruelty and selfishness of the Jacobins' campaign and the ignorant populace, she predicted the death of the king.

During the time she was staying in Paris, the political environment in France was hostile to foreigners and suspicious of any political enemy.[16] As a result, Wollstonecraft avoided political issues in public from 1793 to 1795. As she explained to her sister Eliza, letters crossing the English Channel during this period were very likely to be inspected by the French government; she wrote on 13 June 1793, 'I write with *reserve* because all the letters are opened.… I shall soon have an opportunity to write you by the same conveyance, mean time this will assure you that I am alive'.[17] Again she wrote on 24 June 1793: 'I feel quite lonely here now the communication is shut' with a postscript at the end of this letter: 'Do not touch on politics -'.[18] After 9 October 1793, all the Britons who were not resident in France before 1789 were to be held by the Convention as hostages; even simply using or wearing British products could lead to the possessor being considered a suspect.[19] Days later the decree made no exception for foreign radicals who were previously protected by their political stance.[20] On 10 March 1794 she wrote to her sister Everina:

> It is impossible for you to have any idea of the impression the sad scenes I have been a witness to have left on my mind. The climate of France is uncommonly fine, the country pleasant, and there is a degree of ease, and even simplicity, in the manners of the common people, which attaches me to them – Still death and misery, in every shape of terrour, haunts this devoted country – I certainly am glad that I came to France, because I never could have had else a just opinion of the most extraordinary event that has ever been recorded.… If any, of the many letters I have written, have come to your hands or Eliza's, you know that I am safe, through the protection of an American.[21]

In July 1794, she wrote:

> Of the state of things here, and the decree against the English I will not speak – The French will carry all before them – but, my God, how many victims fall beneath the sword and the Guillotine! My blood runs cold, and I sicken at thoughts of a Revolution which costs so much blood and bitter tears.[22]

Thus her 'Letter on the Present Character of the French Nation', written in February 1793, in which she exposed the chaos of the Revolution, was not published during her lifetime. In the summer of 1793, in the midst of the Reign of Terror, she began to write *An Historical and Moral View* discussing the morality and development of the Revolution. Though she did not mention specific political events after 1790, readers can clearly feel the atmosphere of terror and author's criticism of terror. The book was not published in London until 1794, after the end of the Reign of Terror. Jane Rendall suggests that Wollstonecraft pointed out two major problems in France in this book. One is that wealth led to luxury, corruption and selfishness of the nobles, and merchants were addicted to 'mercantile speculation', while the bourgeois spirit of independence and reason was neglected. The second is that the revolutionary leaders were not educated in political philosophy and their minds were corrupted by French feudal customs.[23] Wollstonecraft had indicated the cause of these two problems: the negligence of benevolence and the prevalence of selfishness. Residing in Paris, she not only criticized the lack of morality in the development of western civilization, but also pointed out that the revolutionaries and the public were trapped in their enthusiasm for self-interest. The society was full of false patriotism and thus false civilization, so the Revolution produced by this selfish society entered into a state of violence and disorder.

Edmund Burke (1729–1797) had denounced the democratic equality of the French Revolution in his famous *Reflections on the Revolution in France* (1790) and post-*Reflections* writings. He viewed this egalitarian Revolution and the advent of political democracy as a process leading to the decline of civilization into savagery. The anarchic political reality of France in the 1790s had proved his prophecies correct. Wollstonecraft agreed with Burke that equality and liberty were the main principles, yet she refuted Burke's argument in her first political pamphlet, *A Vindication of the Rights of Men* (1790), and in her subsequent work, *An Historical and Moral View*. She argued that the Terror was a predicable consequence of the injustice and inequality of the *ancien régime*. 'The character of the French', Wollstonecraft argued, had been 'so depraved by the inveterate despotism of ages, that even amidst the heroism which distinguished the taking of the Bastille, we are forced to see that suspicious temper, and that vain ambition of dazzling, which have generated all the succeeding follies and crimes.'[24] She did not judge violence and chaos as fatal consequences of the Revolution; instead, she thought these were necessary phenomena. She revealed her faith in democracy, in rationalism and in historical progress: more democracy, with 'the harbinger of reason',[25] was the only path to a just and liberal society and would lead the Revolution to a positive end in the long term.

In addition, she ascribed an 'effeminate' character to the French due to the same political causes. The effeminacy, vanity, and frivolity of the French people were common claims in eighteenth-century Britain. Following her arguments of *A Vindication of the Rights of Woman* (1792) that women's morality was seriously influenced by long-established inequalities, most of the French, too, were accustomed to polite customs, and thought only of 'how to please and be pleased'.[26] She agreed with Burke that Marie Antoinette represented the manners of the *ancien régime*. Burke described the queen as a civilized lady and tender mother.[27] In contrast, the manners of Marie Antoinette, for Wollstonecraft, were artificial, insincere and selfish, and had permeated the French national character.[28] In addition, the system of the *ancien régime* led to the pervasively theatrical character of the majority of people in all aspects of life: 'Their national character is, perhaps, more formed by their theatrical amusements, than is generally imagined: they are in reality the schools of vanity. And, after this kind of education, is it surprising, that almost every thing is said and done for stage effect?'[29] Lacking the proper cultivation of minds and feelings, Wollstonecraft continued, the French character exhibited insincerity and self-interest, which was fatal to the Revolution.

Revolutionary violence also proved that the French character had been malformed under the influence of the *ancien régime*. Wollstonecraft wondered, 'How, in fact, can we expect to see men live together like brothers, when we only see master and servant in society?'[30] The overthrow of the monarchy was the right direction towards civilization, but it was not suited to the state of the French people's self-knowledge. She ascribed the failure of the Revolution to internal moral and social causes. 'From implicitly obeying their sovereigns', as Wollstonecraft explained, 'the [F]rench became suddenly all sovereigns'.[31] 'The depravity of the higher class, and the ignorance of the lower respecting practical political science', rendered them both incapable of achieving the great objects of the Revolution.[32]

Wollstonecraft's concepts of freedom and virtue are interdependent. Only when people have freedom can they be independent, and only if they are independent can they use reason, develop sensibility and intelligence, and cultivate their moral judgment, and only thereby can they possess virtue. This was the result of her thinking on power relationships and gender roles in the family, which influenced her way of observing civil and political society. She loathed patriarchal authority and violence, and disagreed with women who were emotionally and economically weak and had to depend on men. Those who are accustomed to being under authority only develop a habit of servility and irrationality. Neither master nor slave/woman understood the essence of freedom. Wollstonecraft carefully observed the problems of family and slavery in various places in the later travels. When she was in France, she criticized oppressive and selfish 'love', such as parents' treatment of children, and the ruler's treatment of the subjects, which were irrational and unjust, and through which the oppressed could not develop rational judgment. While in northern Europe, Wollstonecraft continued to be concerned with the problems of despotism and liberty in family and society. In her view, when any individual grew up in an unjust environment, he/she who was a victim of tyranny might become a perpetrator.[33]

During the writing of this book, many Girondists who were Wollstonecraft's friends were executed at the end of 1793, and Paris from 1793 to 1795 was full of police persecutions.[34] Most of the British rational dissenters such as Price (died 1791), Priestley, Williams, and John Hurford Stone (1763–1818) firmly kept their faith in millennialism, believing that a rational God would lead the world to a perfect state. Even though the current international wars and the Reign of Terror in France revealed that God's providence would not be fulfilled quickly and simply, they still maintained their faith that God's plan was perfect and unquestionable, and that the French Revolution was the message of the coming millennium through which the happiness of all mankind would gradually be realized. Compared with these British dissenters, although Wollstonecraft supported the idea of the Revolution, she could not agree with the millennialist way of explaining the course of the Revolution. Instead, she questioned whether 'revolution' was the best way to promote the future perfectibility of mankind.

For her, a democratic government was only for 'a people in the highest stage of civilization',[35] and everyone must be highly rational. France had not yet reached that state, however. *An Historical and Moral View* revealed Wollstonecraft's criticism of selfish patriotism and patriots. In her preface she denounced the 'fatal mock patriotism' that had long enslaved the people with all its 'folly, selfishness, madness, treachery'.[36] The highly sophisticated and elegant manners developed in monarchical Europe still showed the characteristics of self-interest and injustice. Despots or the upper class showed 'a narrow love of themselves' without universal benevolence and rationality.[37] The oppressed were gradually indifferent to their lost natural rights. They lived like animals and become tools for the tyrants.[38] In her view, human history had always praised this kind of vanity and violence, which were covered in the name of heroism and patriotism.

Such a society had not yet cultivated its reason, thus there was only limited moral judgment.[39] Hence, narrow patriotism should be transformed into a more equal and tolerant love for all mankind under a more enlightened government, so that true civilization could develop.[40]

On the other hand, Wollstonecraft saw the gradual development of reason.[41] She did not believe in original sin, and regarded religious anecdotes related to original sin as nonsense, which had been used by the Christian church to establish despotic and oppressive systems in Europe.[42] Still, she acknowledged the changes wrought by chivalry. The system of chivalry decreased the brutality of the European nobles, and gradually established 'the *point d'honneur*' and 'the character of a gentleman'. Although such chivalry still exhibited the characteristics of a privileged society and was not entirely based on the idea of reason, 'this kind of bastard morality' at least improved society.[43] Historian Daniel O'Neil points out that in the eyes of the Scottish Enlightenment thinkers, the progress of chivalry formed a sense of responsibility to others and a higher level of human civilization, which was no longer a self-interested one.[44] Wollstonecraft, however, did not fully embrace the idea. She criticized that no matter how good European chivalry was, it was only a false and one-sided display of virtue without rational basis.[45] The constitution of European countries still ignored the natural rights of people.

Relatively few scholars have paid attention to her later political reflections, and some mistakenly believe that she gave up the ideal of the Revolution. Moira Ferguson and Janet Todd indicate that 'Letter on the Present Character of the French Nation' revealed pessimistic thinking on the fulfilment of Enlightenment ideas in reality. They argue that, after residing in Paris, Wollstonecraft was disappointed with the French Revolution and the republic, which would not improve people's virtue, but destroy virtue and civilization.[46] According to them, Wollstonecraft's radical political thought changed dramatically. In fact, however, Wollstonecraft did not completely deny the possibility of the Revolution in her article. Her experience in Paris made her understand that it would be a long-term process to educate everyone into a rational person, yet she still looked to the future: 'I cannot yet give up the hope, that a fairer day is dawning on Europe' despite her worry.[47] Moreover, as evident in her works written after 1794, Wollstonecraft disclosed her republican ideas and her belief in the future perfectibility of mankind and human society again.

For Wollstonecraft, 'The progress of reason' was gradual and so it was advisable for France to 'advance the simplification of [its] political system, in a manner best adapted to the state of improvement of the understanding of the nation.'[48] Wollstonecraft maintained that 'the sudden change which had happened in France, from the most fettering tyranny to an unbridled liberty', made it 'morally impossible' to expect anything could be managed peacefully and with the wisdom of experience.[49] She still emphasized, in spite of all obstructions, that democratization was synonymous with the civilizing process itself,[50] and that such a Revolution, on the basis of democracy, would bring about a gradual and beneficial change in the people's education and in their character in the long term, and 'the fruit of their liberty' that would ripen gradually.[51]

Wollstonecraft's Political Reflections in Scandinavia

Taking along her surviving hopes for the Revolution, Mary Wollstonecraft went to Scandinavia in the summer of 1795. In her *A Short Residence*, a travelogue mixed with emotional outbursts and political observations, as we have seen above, she revealed her abiding concern with the impact of the political changes upon the entire society.

Although Wollstonecraft became disappointed with Revolutionary practices in France, her experience in Scandinavia reawakened her optimism about the improvement and progress of humankind. In Sweden, she found that the French Revolution had not only made royalty more cautious, but had so 'decreased every where a respect for nobility', and the peasantry 'have not only lost their blind reverence for their seigniors, but complain, in a manly style, of oppressions which before they did not think of denominating such, because they were taught to consider themselves as a different order of beings'.[52] Norway, a country subject to Denmark, instead of an enslaved province, seemed to her the freest community she had ever observed. Their landed property was distributed in small farms, which had produced a degree of equality; the wealthy merchants divided their personal fortune among their children; local governments were responsive to democratic forces, and thus '[t]hey have not time to learn to be tyrants', said a gentleman she met on her trip. She was told that the previous year a man, who abused his power, was 'cashiered'.[53] In another district of Norway, the small villages provoked in her the idea of 'the golden age': yeomen with small farms, with simple honest characters, revealed the quality of 'independence and virtue; affluence without vice; cultivation of mind, without depravity of heart; with "ever smiling liberty", the nymph of the mountain.'[54] In her journeys, therefore, she saw that Revolutionary theories had begun to reveal positive potential for the development of civilization in other European countries. Although there were many imperfections, she believed that, with proper education and the development of civilization, the cultivation of arts and science would follow,[55] and people and governments would grow to maturity according to the natural pace of each particular nation.

Wollstonecraft wrote in the Appendix to *A Short Residence* that it was because of these evils that reformers wanted a hurried reform or violent revolution in order to destroy the evils quickly. Such actions were, however, mistaken. She wrote:

> An ardent affection for the human race makes enthusiastic characters eager to produce alterations in laws and governments prematurely. To render them useful and permanent, they must be the growth of each particular soil, and the gradual fruit of the ripening understanding of the nation, matured by time, not forced by an unnatural fermentation. And, to convince me that such a change is gaining ground, with accelerating pace, the view I have had of society, during my northern journey, would have been sufficient.[56]

Wollstonecraft achieved a new level of consciousness regarding the impact of the French Revolution on enlightened civil society. She acknowledged that revolutionary change accelerated human progress at an 'unnatural' pace, which forced new governments and laws onto an inadequately prepared society. It was therefore more effective to carry out progressive reforms that were suited to the particular soil of each nation; then the fruits of social reform would ripen gradually.

Her criticism of the effects of commerce and industry shows her ambivalent feelings towards modernization. Basically, she agreed that commerce could encourage independence and equality, because the wages that men earned emancipated them from slavish dependence on a feudal lord or the servile receipt of alms from the rich. In Norway, she also insisted that, when all men and women were employed with fair mercantile profits which were sufficient to reward their industry, 'whilst none are so great as to permit the possessor to remain idle', a state of independence and virtue could be expected.[57] Otherwise, the 'want of proportion between profit and labour' debased men into a dependent state which was detrimental to the improvement of civilization.[58] Yet, Chris Jones stresses that Wollstonecraft condemned the system of commerce and industry and maintained that the system turned men into 'unthinking, unprogressive automatons to make fortunes for individuals'.[59] In her last work on the French Revolution she worried about the rising new ruling class, the bourgeoisie. She thought the Terror had been created in the hands of these ambitious, selfish and cold-blooded men. Now, what distressed Wollstonecraft during the course of her Scandinavian tour was that she perceived that the bourgeoisie was also emerging in northern Europe. The 'tyranny of wealth', in the words of Wollstonecraft, exploited the common people and was even less merciful than the aristocracy.[60] As we can see, she appeared to have foreseen the harm caused by capitalism and stressed not only political and gender equality, but also social equality. She pointed out the problem, but she did not find a good solution.

In the mid-1790s, nationalism was on the rise in various European countries, and the hostility between Britain and France increased. Even though Wollstonecraft was registered as an American citizen's wife, that is to say she would not violate the 'Law of Suspects' of the National Convention or any other anti-British decrees during the Reign of Terror, she revealed her uncomfortable feeling towards such strict laws to suppress freedom of movement and freedom of speech and the press, and was dissatisfied with international tension and incessant war. As always had been her stance, she regarded the exclusive love of one's own country and exclusive local sentiment as a manifestation of narrow mindedness and unfreedom.[61] In the port cities along the Norwegian shore, she observed that most people in the region were patriotic, but lacked public spirit in that patriotism. She explained that public spirit expressed 'the grand virtues' of human nature, caring for public welfare, and requiring higher intelligence in order to achieve this highest virtue.[62] This, on the one hand, reflected the republicanism of Jean-Jacques Rousseau (1712–1778), but on the other hand, it revealed that Wollstonecraft's political ideas were a blend of Rousseau's general will and her belief in universal benevolence. As she observed, only a small number of men of letters, church men or medical doctors in Norway cared about political topics arising from the French Revolution. Most people, such as shopkeepers, ship owners and farmers, cared only about their families, how to earn money and get rich. This led people to be narrow-minded and not to care about national and international affairs.[63] She reflected that the men of letters in this area were not yet fully morally and politically enlightened. She believed that through the dissemination of knowledge via publication and reading, the people of Scandinavia would discuss the French Revolution and its politics, and thus enlighten their mind gradually. Then a public spirit would emerge in the society of the Northern countries in the future.[64]

Furthermore, Wollstonecraft thought about the pros and cons of agricultural and commercial society repeatedly during her journey: was the Rousseauan republican agricultural society the golden age for human beings? Were people better remaining in the state of nature? Did commerce create new tyrants of wealth? Didn't commerce give birth to liberty[65] and disseminate knowledge? Wollstonecraft spent her whole life exploring the way people reached happiness. Does human happiness remain in Rousseau's state of nature where people maintain 'unconscious ignorance'? Or is it in 'the high-wrought mind'? She wrote on her Scandinavian trip:

> You will ask, perhaps, why I wished to go further northward. Why, not only because the country, from all I can gather, is most romantic, abounding in forests and lakes, and the air pure, but I have heard much of the intelligence of the inhabitants, substantial farmers, who have none of that cunning to contaminate their simplicity, which displeased me so much in the conduct of the people on the sea coast.... The description I received of them carried me back to the fables of the golden age: independence and virtue; affluence without vice; cultivation of mind, without depravity of heart; with 'ever smiling liberty', the nymph of the mountain. I want faith! My imagination hurries me forward to seek an asylum in such a retreat from all, the disappointments I am threatened with; but reason drags me back, whispering that the world is still the world, and man the same compound of weakness and folly, who must occasionally excite love and disgust, admiration and contempt.[66]

Wollstonecraft disliked the lack of freedom in the process of European civilization. But after she exiled herself to the underdeveloped north of Europe, she realized that although there had been many drawbacks in virtue in the civilized society of Western Europe, it was still better than staying in the savage and ignorant state of nature. For her, in a low-level society without moral and intellectual development, it was like being imprisoned in the Bastille from birth, and any opportunities for a person's enlightenment had been deprived. How could it be possible for ignorant people to realize the necessity of the French Revolution? Therefore, she wrote in Risør, Norway: 'Talk not of bastilles! To be born here, was to be bastilled by nature – shut out from all that opens the understanding, or enlarges the heart.'[67] Hence, Wollstonecraft further affirmed the importance of environment on every person's mind and virtue. As she stressed,

> I am more and more convinced that the same energy of character, which renders a man a daring villain, would have rendered him useful to society, had that society been well organized. When a strong mind is not disciplined by cultivation, it is a sense of injustice that renders it unjust.[68]

In other words, an individual's injustice was not solely his fault; when the whole society treated him unjustly, or when the society did not tolerate him, this person had been driven step by step to the path of injustice. It was wrong education and unjust environment that made him a villain. Therefore, any strong man might be benevolent, but living in a society without rationality and virtue, or in a society that was oppressive, the power of a strong man was likely to turn to a bloody and violent revenge tool. Wollstonecraft believed that all people had various potential for improvement, but she no longer had an affirmative answer to whether the person could make use of reason and intelligence and become benevolent. There were many possibilities in the process of change.

Similarly, any action motivated by charity required a rational society. When she was in Paris, 'Freedom is a solid good, that requires to be treated with reverence and respect.'[69] In the summer of 1795, Wollstonecraft once again reflected on why the French Revolution from its good intentions turned out to be evil. She knew very clearly that British radicals were used to blaming the failure of the Revolution and the corruption of the French character on the long-accumulated wrongs of the *ancien régime*. She was increasingly questioning this view. In the past two years of the Terror, the French revolutionaries seemed to be virtuous and enthusiastic to establish a republic of virtue. Yet there were no less evil and oppressive political policies in practices. She thus emphasized in *An Historical and Moral View* that, because most French people were irrational and selfish, the French Revolution, intending to carry out public interest and common good, had to be deemed to have failed and degenerated into bloody violence in the short term.

Self-reflections As A Woman and Mother During Her Travels

Wollstonecraft was far from a cold, unsentimental traveller. From the perspective of her books and the letters written during her travels, some deep reflections on women's life-journey and motherhood were provided. Wollstonecraft, who had not yet experienced love, motherhood, and marriage when writing her two *Vindications*, firmly believed that rationality should suppress passion, that human society had been progressive, and that society in progress would inevitably drive the improvement of all human beings. Wollstonecraft often protected her mother from the violent treatment of her father when she was young. From the beginning of 1784 to 1786 she founded a boarding school for girls in Newington Green, London. Yet serious financial problems forced her to close the school. In 1785, despite the opposition from her other friends, she insisted on going to Lisbon, Portugal, to accompany her best friend Fanny Blood who was in the critical status of dystocia and finally died; she then sailed to Ireland as a governess for a period of one year. In 1787, returning to London, Wollstonecraft decided to become a professional writer and one of 'a new genus' of women who refused to follow the old track.[70]

Wollstonecraft had been a social and political critic in the 1780s employed by Joseph Johnson, criticizing political corruption and social injustice in the hierarchical world, and finding faults with any abuse of power and any form of slavery. After she went to Paris at the end of 1792, however, she experienced heartbroken fatal love with Gilbert Imlay in a foreign country and became a depressive single mother trying to bring up her daughter during and after the Terror. What she witnessed could not have helped her state of mind. While she was determined to be an independent and strong woman, the experience of residing abroad made her understand that there were things or emotions beyond her power to control or change. The private letters Wollstonecraft wrote during her travels show her vulnerabilities since she had few resources either in France or in the chilly and desolate areas of Scandinavia.

Imlay was the American entrepreneur whom she met in Paris in the early 1793 and fell in love with. By the end of the summer of 1793 she was pregnant. We learn a lot about Imlay from Wollstonecraft's point of view thanks to her preservation of her correspondence to him. Yet there are no surviving letters from Imlay to Wollstonecraft. According to her, Imlay was an intelligent, sound and rational man, 'a most natural, unaffected creature'. He criticized the corruption of old Europe and revealed his zeal for life in the American wilderness with his own farmhouse and family.[71] Her letters written during this love affair displayed her efforts to maintain her judgment based on reason, but her melancholy and worry for her future and Imlay's absence won over her again and again. Their daughter Fanny Imlay (1794–1816) was born in Le Havre on 14 May 1794. Soon after, Imlay left Wollstonecraft and the child for his business affairs and was absent for long periods at a time. In the daytime, Wollstonecraft's daughter and her writing of *An Historical and Moral View* absorbed her time. Her infant daughter gave her some happiness when residing alone in a suburban area of Paris during the Terror.

Though endeavouring to be independent, Wollstonecraft sometimes felt fatigued at the effort of nurturing and raising her daughter alone in the extremely cold winter of 1794–1795 and with limited means.[72] She struggled to live without Imlay's financial assistance:

> I am determined to try to earn some money here myself, in order to convince you that, if you chuse to run about the world to get a fortune, it is for yourself – for the little girl and I will live without your assistance, unless you are with us. I may be termed proud – Be it so – but I will never abandon certain principles of action.[73]

This is the real Wollstonecraft during her travels: a melancholic and frustrated woman yet energetic and powerful mother abroad with her daughter; and this was a time when it was uncommon for a woman to be travelling alone with a baby in the eighteenth century, not to mention during the unstable 1790s in France and Scandinavia. She finally returned to London in April 1795 and there swallowed an overdose of laudanum, but survived. At this time, Imlay's shipping business in Norway had run into difficulties in 1795 and he wanted to distract her attention from their relationship and thus persuaded her to travel to Norway as his agent to sort out business affairs for him.[74] For a woman who had just recovered from a suicide attempt, accompanied by little Fanny, this task was demanding, not to mention how tough it would be to journey to remote and unfamiliar destinations in the cold North-Eastern winds: 'I am extremely fatigued with the child, who would not rest quiet with any body but me, during the night – and now we are here in a comfortless, damp room, in a sort of tomb-like house', she wrote to Imlay at the beginning of this trip.[75] '[I]n spite of all my efforts, the child – every thing – fatigues me, in which I seek for solace or amusement.'[76] We might think that Wollstonecraft was emotionally dependent on Imlay because she followed his suggestion and took on his mission immediately, but she also revealed her courage and strong will in accomplishing such a tough job, at the same time being the mother of a little daughter. During her trip, she wrote a successful piece of travel literature, *A Short Residence*, in which, despite her bitter personal experience with Imlay, her self-representation trembled in the balance between unquenched hope for the future and sound observation of the northerly countries.

Although it was a business trip requested by Imlay, she did not mention any details of such a purpose in *A Short Residence*. As Mary A. Favret indicates, Wollstonecraft rewrote her travel as a form of escape from all the constraints of the world, wandering freely to the wild and remote north, and in a melancholy tone owing to her hopeless love.[77] In the process of exploring new territory, Wollstonecraft not only enjoyed strange landscapes, but disclosed a more intimate self than in her previous works: she did not speak on behalf of the human race like her two *Vindications*;[78] instead, she used 'the first person' to talk of herself.[79] As she put it, 'A person has a right, I have sometimes thought, when amused by a witty or interesting egoist, to talk of himself when he can win on [*sic*] our attention by acquiring our affection.'[80] This Scandinavian journey let her breathe fresh air and pulled her out of depression. Once she was liberated and sent ashore, the narrator demonstrated her free movement physically and mentally with a new expectation of happiness as well as for the progress of human civilization.[81]

Reaching a cascade near Fredrikstad, the roaring of the falls made her feel that her life was like the impetuous dashing of the rebounding torrent from the dark cavities. She asked herself, 'why I was chained to life and its misery?' '…it seemed as impossible to stop the current of my thoughts', yet, the narrator re-claimed her soul's dignity in powerful tones: 'I stretched out my hand to eternity, bounding over the dark speck of life to come.'[82] Her intense emotion was heightened by the physical landscapes which she saw. Surrounded by such breathtakingly beautiful scenery, she confessed, '[for] years I have endeavoured to calm an impetuous tide – labouring to make my feelings take an orderly course. – It was striving against the stream. – I must love and admire with warmth, or I sink into sadness.'[83] Though she suffered from frequent depression, she refused to be nobody or to cease to exist as though simply a passing dust.[84]

She had been in a series of deep depressions. A trip that began with an anticipation of being emancipated from constraints and which stirred such romantic responses, became in the later part of the journey a dread of her solitary existence and her totally free spirit: 'I was destined to wander alone'.[85] Towards the end of her Scandinavian travels, depression and sorrow finally wore down Wollstonecraft once more. After returning to London in October 1795, she tried to commit suicide, and was rescued again. Most readers of Godwin's *Memoirs* of Wollstonecraft might think she attempted suicide solely due to her fatal affection for Imlay. Yet Wollstonecraft knew very much about her nature – 'strange compound of weakness and resolution'[86] – even before she had met Imlay. In addition, as her private letters or published journals written in France and Scandinavia displayed, she had painfully constructed a self-identity of a courageous independent professional writer in public despite her severe depression. Most important of all, Godwin intended to represent Wollstonecraft as a lonely 'female Werter [*sic*]' who travelled further north with an expectation to meet her lover once again. Godwin somehow neglected her actual role as a mother with a little girl, which was an important experience for Wollstonecraft after 1794.[87]

Wollstonecraft's travel experience made her understand that any seemingly good political idea might turn out to have negative consequences in the process of realization. As long as it was a work involving the mind of human beings there would be many variables. Influenced by her sights in Paris, she came to understand that political and social change was far more complex than she had learned from both books and her radical friends and that radical political change was not the best way to future perfection. Before her visit to Paris, Wollstonecraft's support for the Revolution revealed her ideas about the ways of social and political progress, not her understanding of the real policies and laws made by the revolutionaries in Paris. Like most British radicals in the 1790s, she failed to consider the nature and reality of the new France. Her self-reflections of being a woman and mother somehow softened her as well during her wandering afield in various parts of Scandinavia. She rethought her views on the topics of gender, family and motherhood, the boundary between desire and self-discipline, passion and reason, and the questions of power relationship between men and women within family and in public again and again. For

Wollstonecraft, unlike some other travellers of the time, she did not merely describe what she saw, but took time to reflect on her personal feelings and political thoughts as the incidents and countries she saw affected her.

Although Wollstonecraft was still dissatisfied with hierarchical society and 'things as they are',[88] and she still held faith in republicanism and future perfectibility, she gradually derived different reflections on the political systems and on herself. She condemned violence and tyrants of all kinds, explored the reasons for repeated setbacks in the process of the Revolution, and pointed out that the selfishness and vanity of the revolutionaries had hindered the better results of the Revolution. Compared with British radicals who had proposed and insisted on a set of plans for political reform, the most fascinating element of Wollstonecraft's thought was that, based on her republicanism and virtue of universal benevolence, she made corrections and reflections in different periods of time due to her travel experience, and thought about the problems that would arise in the process of political reform. Thus, she no longer supported radical revolution; she turned to a gradual and pragmatic reform method, starting from the education of the public and the dissemination of knowledge.

As she wrote in one of her last letters, 'We ought not to be too anxious respecting the opinion of others. – I am not fond of vindications. – Those who know me will suppose that I acted from principles. Nay … I am at ease with regard to the opinions of the *best* part of mankind. – I *rest* on my own.'[89] She did not stick to a set of methods or principles, but relied on her own independent judgment, and was willing to adjust her thoughts as the situations around her changed and through what she observed on her travels. However, in the end, vulnerability and melancholy were part of her nature, which could not be abated by rationality.

Chapter 10

Women's Labour in Maria Graham's *Three Months Passed in The Mountains East of Rome* (1820)

Valentina Aparicio

Maria Graham painted by her husband Augustus Wall Callcott. Date unknown.

In 1818, having lived now for some years in rural Dundee, Maria Graham (1785–1842) was bored. Graham was an intellectual woman with a deep interest in foreign cultures and histories, who had published her diaries of life in India, and had travelled to Africa in her youth. Now, she claimed in her letters, she could spend months before seeing a face outside the family. Between 1816 and 1818 she wrote repeatedly to her personal friend and publisher John Murray in London about her isolated domestic life in Scotland, and how much she missed being part of London's artistic circles.[1] At the time, she was also dissatisfied with her marriage and with the little intellectual interests shown by her husband Captain Thomas Graham.[2] For these reasons, in 1819, when the couple decided to travel to Italy for leisure, Graham lost no time in planning her next publication. The couple travelled with the painter Charles Eastlake and, after failing to engage and befriend Lord Byron,[3] Graham dedicated her time to writing her short narrative *Three Months Passed in The Mountains East of Rome* (1820). When Maria Graham set out to write about the Roman Campagna, however, she was treading literary territory previously travelled by many authors before. Traveling to Italy in the tradition of the 'Grand Tour' was part of the basic constitution of British male elite education and already had established roots by the seventeenth century.[4] Although initially the Grand Tour had been a masculine and aristocratic voyage, by the eighteenth century and with the betterment of travel conditions and the rise in British households' disposable income, British women travellers of the Grand Tour were commonplace too.[5] Still, Graham expected her voyage to offer her not only the intellectual excitement she so deeply desired, but also an opportunity to distinguish herself from other writers. She aimed at writing a narrative that presented something new to the public, rather than adding to the already countless accounts of Roman antiquities.

While her Italian travelogue was not as successful as her Indian and later South American diaries, this chapter will argue that Graham did successfully present something innovative to her audiences, although she might have not been aware of it. Clothed in a rhetoric of Orientalism and deeply determined by the generic conventions of travel writing at the time, Graham's *Three Months Passed in The Mountains East of Rome* inadvertently offered one of the first detailed accounts of the centrality of Italian rural women's labour in the process of industrialisation of Italy. The first section of this chapter will focus on Graham's relationship with the traditions of the Grand Tour narrative and Oriental travelogues, arguing that both are reshaped and combined in her description of Italy. The second section focuses specifically on her recognition of rural women's labour in the silk industry, something unusual for the period. This labour, however, is not presented as something new but as part of the traditional structure of the Campagna. The chapter closes by assessing why this might have been the case in Graham's writing, detailing possible discourses and conventions that limited Graham's ability to present women's participation in the silk industry as a new proto-industrial phenomenon.

Representing the 'East' of Rome: Reshaping Grand Tour Narrative Conventions

As Regina Akel's biography of Graham suggests, throughout her life Maria had a strong desire to distinguish herself not only from men, but also from other women. She considered certain topics, ideas, and forms of behaviour often associated with femininity as below her, so that standing out was not only essential to her survival in the book market, but also to her self-perception as exceptional among women.[6] Although women's participation in the Grand Tour was commonplace by the time Graham visited Italy, their experiences and the way they represented them were still limited by gender conventions. As has been noted, when writing about Italy,

> women had to tread a line between the display of too much antiquarian learning, which would have been deemed unfeminine, and sufficient knowledge of ancient history and literature to allow them legitimately to lay claim to the legacy of taste and the promised land of Rome itself.[7]

Graham's text was no exception to these conventions. She travelled without a *ciceroni* or Italian antiquarian guide, which gave her the opportunity to show her personal mastery of the history of antiquity. Graham also wrote the text in a gender-neutral manner. As Claudia Georgi has remarked, she refers to herself with the gender-neutral 'the writer' throughout the book, avoiding attracting attention to her femininity.[8] She also mentions her husband only a handful of times throughout the text, downplaying her role as a wife and presenting herself as the central traveller figure that displays a vast knowledge of both the region and its history. This authoritative voice, while intending to escape the limitations set to women writers, often falls into a critical British perspective of Southern Europe, positioning itself as able to judge what it sees and assuming what seems a masculine 'objective' tone. For Georgi, in this text Graham's 'narrative persona … emerges overall as a well-read and rational but occasionally condescending or dismissive traveller'.[9] She supplements this voice with accompanying documentation in annexes to substantiate her claims, another practice that was common for women writers.[10] Graham's text includes in her annexes a papal edict, the contents of the *Santa Croce* (a text that young children in Italy had to study), and a historical account of the destruction of Monte Fortino by Pope Paul IV. To these more traditional social and political documents is also added a collection of popular poems translated from Italian into English by Graham. These appendixes reveal precisely the elements that seem to interest Graham the most in her travels: political history, folklore, and the life of the lower classes.

While travelling women used different techniques to secure legitimacy for their own written accounts, they also focused on particular themes related to those aspects of life that generally played a bigger role in women's lives. This was especially the case with social relations and sociability rituals, which had more importance in the lives of women than in those of men. Thus, women normally tended to record 'details of sociability and the spaces in which it took place'.[11] Female writers were also often more interested in customs than men and 'consistently singled out representations of women in their observations when viewing antiquities'.[12] Maria Graham's *Three Months Passed in The Mountains East of Rome* followed this trend, and most of these traits can be found in her narrative. Her attention to women in Italy, in particular, stems from this generic practice. However, she also innovates significantly, which leads her to inadvertently discover and represent aspects of Italian life that had been ignored by other authors, both Italian and British. Firstly, Graham innovated in terms of location. The author, who spent a year in Rome, decided not to write about the city that was the focus of most Grand Tour narratives. Rather, she focused on a location that was less studied: the Roman Campagna in the Lazio region. She also innovated in terms of temporality. Her focus was on present-day inhabitants, although she had to validate her knowledge with references to antiquity. Graham's work is still a narrative of the Grand Tour as the itinerary is set by the clear intention of the travellers to see the marvels of antiquity in the Roman Campagna. Nonetheless, Graham offers at least an equal focus on present-day social and economic practices.

Three Months Passed in the Mountains East of Rome begins by outlining a clear preoccupation with time and temporality. She explains in the 'Preface' that 'the visitors of the 'eternal city' seem to have forgotten that there are still living men to till the ground, and to dress the vineyards that surround it'.[13] Graham was right, as most travellers did not describe the inhabitants at all and, if they did, they focused on the elites rather than on the lower classes.[14] This would not have been completely outside of the norm for women's writing since, as Rosemary Sweet suggests, it was more usual for women to remark on current life in Italy and people's customs.[15] While highlighting how many of her contemporaries focused mostly on the past, Graham uses her focus on the present as a way of both offering new information and revealing her knowledge of the history of antiquity. She writes that she will:

> describe the present state of the near neighbours of Rome; to show the peasants of the hills as they are, and as they probably have been, with little change, since "Rome was at her height;" to give such an account of their moral and political condition.[16]

Throughout the text, Graham aimed to establish connections between Roman antiquity and the practices of rural communities in Lazio, essentially presenting them as a picture of the past. For Graham, this is directly related to the landscape itself, and the historical knowledge that she has acquired in her education. Throughout the travels, Graham remarks on the present and past location of several ruins related to antiquity. She suggests that 'the wall of ruin that surrounds everything that is new and fresh in Rome, force the thoughts back upon the past, and veil the present, as the future, from our eyes'.[17] Graham's text intends to peer through this veil of the past by intending to describe the present. However, Graham was not interested in the *conversazioni* of the higher-class ladies. Instead, she is strongly interested in rural women. Looking away from the surroundings that were too determined by the ruins of antiquity, she looked to the Roman Campagna and its inhabitants for inspiration. This was extremely unusual: guidebooks about Rome did not, as was usual for other locations, have sections on customs and manners.[18] According to Timothy Webb, Rome as well as Italy more generally, were often described as depopulated spaces in the Romantic period, where a traveller could engage with the spirit of the history of the place without dealing with contemporary developments. Thus, writers of the period saw Rome as a 'City of the Dead' and 'tended to eliminate or marginalize contemporary Romans'.[19] This is a view that Graham innovatively challenged, and which makes her stand out amongst her contemporaries, male and female.

However, to succeed in this, Graham had to deploy other discourses typical of narratives that did not belong to the Grand Tour. By way of avoiding some of the conventions of the Grand Tour, she became determined by the conventions of the type of travelogue she had published before: the Asian travel narrative. As can be seen in the previous quotes, one of the ways in which Graham circumvents the difficulty of talking about the present in a landscape necessarily marked by the past is by referring to discourses that made the past and the present indistinguishable. This is done by turning to eighteenth-century ways of understanding the development of history that Graham would have been familiar with through the Scottish Enlightenment. Graham grew up visiting her family in Edinburgh and participating and listening to the discussions on history taking place in the city. Scottish Enlightenment texts, which mediated the French early works of philosophical history, were partly adaptations of Montesquieu's theory of savagery and barbarism in *The Spirt of the Laws* (1784). These eighteenth-century texts proposed a theory often called 'stadial history' that identified four stages of development of all human societies: savagery based on hunting, barbarism based on herding, early civilisation based on agriculture, and proper civilisation relying on commerce, and of which the final stage was capitalist commerce. Societies were supposed to develop through these stages through time, which equated types of economic systems with historical 'development,' although some regions of the world could be more 'advanced' than others at any point in time, making the past and the present overlap wherever a less 'advanced' society could be found. These views, which can be found in texts like Adam Smith's *Theory of Moral Sentiments* (1759) and Adam Ferguson's *Essay on the History of Civil Society* (1767), were extremely influential in European understandings of non-European life. Thanks to this, Graham could see the agricultural communities in the Campagna, within this framework, as pictures of the past, making the rural territories pictures of antiquity. But the use of this view of history was also exceptionally common in narratives of the East and other non-European territories. As a consequence, I argue, Graham goes a step further by linking stadial history and narratives of non-European travel together in her Italian travelogue.

In the preface to *Three Months Passed in The Mountains East of Rome*, Graham suggests that the lives of the peasants she observes are a picture of the past, which readers might not 'easily imagine to be consistent with the civilized state of Europe'.[20] Graham observed the lives in the countryside, therefore, through what Johannes Fabian called a proto-anthropological perspective, determined by a 'denial of coevalness.' Fabian defined a denial of coevalness as 'a persistent and systematic tendency to place the referent(s) of anthropology in a Time other than the present of the producer of anthropological discourse'.[21] This was already established by the time Graham was writing as an essential feature of the genre of travel writing when looking at 'non-civilized' or non-European peoples. For instance, Joseph-Marie Degérando's assertion that 'the philosophical traveller sailing to the ends of the earth, is in fact travelling in time, he is exploring the past; every step he makes is the passage of an age'[22] reveals the sentiment underlying the period in relation to travel away from the centre of the world and the location of the present, which in Graham's case is London. Graham takes this structure and uses it to represent rural Italians, portraying them as literally living in the past.

Despite her desire to break free from the conventions of the Grand Tour, therefore, Graham found it difficult to break free from some of the larger ideological views of stadial history that underpinned travel writing more generally. Her object of interest – people from the Campagna who lived mainly off agriculture – still seemed to be inevitably tied to the past, either in its economy or in its culture and customs. Deploying the main tropes of stadial history, Graham sees communities based on agriculture as pictures, themselves, of the past. She also suggests that antiquity is continually present in the lives of the rural communities in other ways, even in their legends and mythology. She writes, for instance:

> Horace is looked upon by the people in this neighbourhood, as at least as great a necromancer as Virgil was by half Europe in the tenth century; and when they have no other name at hand to give to an ancient ruin, it is always, "Perhaps it may have been built by the poet Horace".[23]

This passage captures the spirit of many others that can be found in Graham's Italian narrative. It suggests not only a link with antiquity, but also the superiority of the observer to judge the reality of an assertion about a land she had never visited before. While Graham admires the relationship between present-day Italians and ancient Romans, she also presents them as lesser and ignorant.

They present a mixture of characteristics including some from antiquity, others from medieval Europe, as well as a 'primitive' naivety. Through this rhetorical movement Graham achieves two things. On the one hand, she gets away with writing about the present by disguising it as the past, a subject more traditional for the region she is describing. On the other hand, Graham is also setting a direct relation between the present and the past of rural Italians in a way that was commonly used for non-Europeans.

Italians of the East of Rome appear, as a consequence, repeatedly Orientalised in Graham's narrative. When arriving at the village of Poli, where she would spend most of her time, Graham describes the village as in a decaying state.[24] Graham compares the villagers to Asian nomadic groups described in Edward Gibbon's *The History of the Decline and Fall of the Roman Empire* (1776–1789). She writes: 'the observation of Gibbon, quoted above, though it concerns the wandering Tartars, is equally applicable to the shepherds of the Appenines, between whom and the wandering tribes of northern Asia there are some points of resemblance'.[25] Nineteenth-century Lazio appears as an almost Gothic Oriental landscape with a climate riddled with illness, and so hot as to be almost inhabitable for a British person.[26] The inhabitants meanwhile adhere to a Catholic religion that resembles pagan festivals,[27] participating in idolatrous rites,[28] while the women, some of 'the ugliest' in Italy,[29] act as 'fortune-tellers'.[30]

Graham's own travelling party, on the other hand, presents itself as a group of travellers from the future. She describes herself as a discoverer of a new land, very similarly to what would have been done in non-European territories. When visiting the shrine of Mentorella, for instance, Graham declares: 'we were the first English that had ever been seen in these mountains'.[31] Moreover, she sees her group as emissaries of future cosmopolitan development from the world of commerce. The clearest expression of that comes from the traces of Imperial mobility in Graham's own party. While her gender and her travel companions remain almost invisible throughout the text, Graham does describe that they were accompanied by:

> our servant, a Caffre, from the Mozambique channel, who insisted on marching first with a long gun and whose appearance, the peasants observed, would most probably frighten any robbers we might meet, a black man being so rare here that something almost supernatural is attached to his appearance.[32]

The representation of the Campagna as a 'racially' homogeneous place highlights its isolation and disconnection with imperial commerce. While Graham and her readers would have lived in locations like London and encountered ethnic diversity throughout their life in the centre of the Empire, the Campagna is placed as completely different. The latter region is presented as a place where a black man's presence is seen with superstition, 'the mothers bringing such tribes of children to him to be kissed, as a charm against certain infantile diseases' that he could not walk in peace.[33] In these instances, Graham presents her group and its composition – a woman explorer, a painter, a black servant, and a navy captain – as a collection of explorers from the present who have come to survey and record the practices of a land of the past.

Underlying this narrative, however, is a contradiction to Scottish Enlightenment thought: Graham's idealised past of the Campagna is disrupted in the narrative by the interference of the growth of the silk industry, which shaped the life of rural communities at the time. In what follows I will argue that Graham's work, while denying coevalness and orientalising rural workers, also unknowingly presents an early recognition of the economic role of Italian women in the proto-industrial development of the region. Graham accidentally showcases not, as she believes, women whose 'habits and manners savour of an older world',[34] but rather the very process of incorporation into the modern workforce that gradually took place in the area at the time of her travels. In this way, Graham's text, which intended to cast into the past the lives of these rural women, accidentally gives the reader a glimpse into the future.

Women's Labour in the Campagna: Graham's Glimpse into the Future

Graham's attention to present-day inhabitants of the Campagna was strongly focused on women. Rosemary Sweet has argued that women writers of the Grand Tour tended to pay attention to elements that were typical of women's roles in their own society, looking for example at 'household management, noting the washing, the markets selling household provisions, the dirt or, indeed, cleanliness'.[35] Graham herself did this, but also remarked with surprise on the participation of women in agricultural work, highlighting how she saw 'men, women, and children going out to harvest-work, or to gather figs or plums from the neighbouring vineyards'.[36] She also represented Campagna women as working constantly:

> The coarse clothing is chiefly made by the women, who, with the distaff and the spindle, spin their wool and flax in the winter, weave it in the spring at looms let out at a cheap rate, and dye or bleach it before midsummer, when first the harvest, and then the vintage, call them to harder labour.[37]

Graham's view of women's central role in almost all economic activity in the region was not an inaccurate representation. Historical records show this to be true. In the region,

> [women] worked on everything except for the digging and the ploughing of the fields, although they also did it in cases when it was absolutely necessary to work with a plough or with the pickaxe. Moreover, the weeding out or the harvesting of the corn or wheat, were exclusively women's work as well as the vine harvesting or the olive picking.[38]

Graham's attention to women's roles is remarkable, since in the region women were discriminated against in terms of labour, as Polly Thanailaki argues. According to this author, in the centre and south of Italy, the birth of a boy was considered more advantageous and was therefore celebrated, as 'the social prejudices dictated that the male members in a household were thought of as more useful for the family's economy because they were considered to be stronger helping hands in the farming labour'.[39] In reality, however, women often worked very hard both at home and in the fields, and a lot of the labour relied on them, although it was normally invisible or taken for granted.[40] In this sense, the observations of Graham reveal an empathy and an attention to women's roles that was unusual for the period and an ability to identify the social and economic contributions of women more clearly than it was common, possibly thanks to being a woman traveller observing the social structure from the outside.

However, Graham went even further. Even though, as previously shown, she suggests that the economy of the Campagna was mostly agricultural and 'ancient,' there are several glimpses into the present that her narrative offers. Graham not only describes women's participation in agriculture but also in the process of proto-industrialisation of Italy. Proto-industrialisation was 'the production of goods (mainly textiles) in cottage workshops by a cheap labour force supplying national and international markets',[41] a process in which women played in fact an exceptional role across Europe. She describes how the lives of women in the Campagna were dictated by the silk industry, detailing the difficult year-long process of home silk-cocoon production:

> The trees are planted by the sides of the little rivulets, and kept always as pollards, the twigs being allowed to go for three years, that method producing the greatest quantity of leaves for the silk-worms, to which insects the women of Poli assign more than one-half of their house-room, from the time the grub leaves the egg in April till July, when the cocoons are fully spun. The greatest cleanliness is, of course, necessary in the feeding

> and attending to the silk-worms; but still the smell they emit, and the heat which it is necessary to maintain for them, must make them unwholesome inmates. The Polese do not manufacture the silk, but carry the cocoons to Palestrina or Tivoli to market.[42]

This long and hard process of production of cocoons was essential for the production of silk in industrial urban centres, and it relied mostly on women's labour. While described as a traditional process, in fact this process was related directly to the move from an agricultural to an industrial economy in the region, a process of which the protagonists were women, although often ignored, and that Graham's short narrative helps to recover.

The job of production of silk cocoons was laborious, time-consuming, and essential to provide money before the harvest:

> It was they [women] who had 'to put the seed of the worms to the warmth of their breasts, until the time that they were ready to hatch.' Theirs was the tiring and unrewarding task, in which they were aided by their children, of providing a constant supply of mulberry leaves to satisfy the voracious appetite of the worms, and to clean up their droppings.[43]

This proto-industrial silk-cocoon production seeps inadvertently into Graham's text, showing how it actually reflected modern developments, even as they were not explicitly described as different from the ones Graham described as 'ancient.' According to Simonetta Ortaggi Cammarosano, silk production was 'not only the most widespread of rural industries; it was also the most important ... Italy produced more raw silk than any other country in Europe, and in the world it was second only to China'.[44] This proto-industrial work, however, was carried out at home on a seasonal basis by women, as a form of supplementing income. According to Cammarosano, there was a traditional gap between the work women did and how much it was recognised in central Italy that came directly from the *ancien régime* social structures and that was passed on to perceptions about the work in the silk industry.[45] Women worked in the silk trade in the afternoons, by spinning and weaving during their rest hours often with rented looms. This work was not only unrecognised but also naturalised, as women had traditionally worked extensively even in the heaviest and most physically taxing jobs in agriculture, so that the proto-industrial work in the production of silk became invisible and integrated as a complement to the other seasonal labour.[46] This lack of recognition has also affected the ways historiography and records have been used, even today. There is a clear lack of data related to the number of women who worked at home in the production of materials used in the silk industry[47] however, as we can see clearly from Graham's account this was widespread and formed a large part of the household income at least in Poli. While data is scarce, Cammarosano suggests that it is likely the majority of the women's workforce was engaged in textile production in Italy, and that as early as the seventeenth century this was wage labour.[48] In Italy, overall, the role of women in the state's economic growth during the nineteenth century cannot be overstated, both in urban and rural areas, through work in factories and in silk production at home.[49]

The production of silk cocoons was not, like that of agriculture, for family use. The women used the cocoons, already by Graham's time, to feed industrial production elsewhere:

> In the Napoleonic era, many of the looms in the Tuscan countryside which were used for flax, wool, and hemp belonged to women who no longer worked for themselves, but for urban merchants and manufacturers … On the other hand, there were the increased controls being exercised by the 'manufacturers,' with looms sometimes being physically concentrated in one place.[50]

While this description refers to Tuscany, we can see from Graham's previous description of the production of textiles in Poli that the model was not dissimilar. In her narrative, the reader is told the looms are in fact 'let out at a cheap rate' and are all located in the centre of the village.[51] Graham also records the hardship that women had to face, and the difficulties and poverty related to selling silk cocoons to urban centres. Graham writes, for instance, about:

> a young girl, as she returned from Palestrina, whither she had been to sell her silk; for her mother had promised her a new skirt, and a silk boddice, from the profits of her worms. But, alas! This year, the cocoons will hardly buy an apron.[52]

The process described here, where children and women were engaged in the production for urban buyers, shows the direct link between what Graham was observing and the process of industrialisation. Given the poverty of the countryside and the growth of the silk industry, the participation of women in silk production was only going to grow further throughout the century.[53] Graham's attention to the constant labouring of women is accurately reflective of the lives women led at the time. By the 1840s these women would move to huge silk mills in urban centres, where they would be given crammed and poorly ventilated lodgings, and would work year-round on silk.[54] While Graham was able to identify this work, the lack of recognition of women's labour for textile industries that was carried out at home would only worsen over time. The difficulties in counting the industrial labour of women heightened later in the century when in 1881 records changed the way in which they recorded women's unspecified employment to the label 'housewives,' subsuming all the seasonal or discontinuous work they did from home, which would remain uncounted.[55] This makes Graham's early recognition and description of this work an even more valuable account.

Finally, it is worth mentioning that Graham identifies activities related to the silk production directly to class in Poli. The village is presented as impoverished, but not all inhabitants are poor. There are, for instance,

> a few of the better sort of women, and there are eight or ten who have left off their country costume and adopted the French style of dress, [who] make parties into the country and walk together in the evening, and sometimes play at cards. These, instead of spinning, or knitting, embroider flounces and frills; but books never enter into their amusement or occupations; and even music is only cultivated by the priests.[56]

Graham's description of these women is condescending and relates directly to her perspective of these 'richer' women as not truly sophisticated, but rather imitating the higher classes. Nonetheless, it is evident that Poli then did present a structure in which there was a number of richer families amongst the rest of the village's population. There was also a school mistress for girls, funded through the charity of a woman of the Conti family, who would 'teach the girls to read, to sew, to spin, and to knit'.[57] This part of her book shows how, as part of the richer women's charity, girls were taught economic activities that were essential to become part of the workforce for the production of silk. These were not the activities in which the richer women engaged, however, and the production of silk and weaving is contrasted by Graham with embroidery, as two sides of the different classes found in the Campagna.

As we can see from this, Graham showed an attention to working-class women and girls that was unusual for the period. In this sense, while Graham's representation is an orientalising one, as explained above, her travelogue also made a contribution in recording women's labour and their central economic role during the period. As Nicola Verdon has suggested, most scholars have until today 'concentrate[d] on the male experience of labour in the formal economy of paid work outside the home',[58] leaving studies on rural women as very scarce and revealing an underlying bias in the way in which labour has been understood through gender lines. Graham's description presents an interesting approach to this issue by revealing the importance of women's work in the process of industrialisation. However, although she identifies these series of proto-industrial and urban-related activities that women in the countryside engage with, Graham goes through great pains to insist that this is a society stuck in time and mostly reliant on agriculture. Why then does Graham not recognise that this is a new phenomenon? The following section will offer a brief detail of probable causes of this limitation.

Rural Life and the Internal Orient

Claudia Georgi suggests that while 'Graham's Italian travelogue features no imperial ambition', it still 'suggests British cultural superiority when pondering on the ruins of the fallen Roman Empire',[59] particularly compared with the present 'decadent' state of Lazio.[60] This is done, as explained above, by adhering to a rhetoric that suggest the Italian Campagna can be seen as an image of the past, mainly because of it being in an 'agricultural' stage of development in stadial history categories. This forced Graham to suggest that the region's system relied almost exclusively on agriculture, although it could be devised from the text that the silk industry was beginning to play a large role in its economy. While Graham spends a lot of time describing the silk industry in the Campagna, she makes sure to suggest that ultimately the system in the region is based on subsistence farming of a 'primitive' or 'ancient' kind. Graham's intention to describe the present condition of what she sees as an agricultural society drives her to rely on tropes used in oriental travelogues. Graham writes of the Campagna, for instance, that 'no man here thinks of cultivating the most he can of what his soil is fittest for, till he has planted enough of everything else for the yearly supply of his family'.[61] Rather, Graham argues, 'their riches consist in the yearly produce of their labour … They have no habit of laying up store for the future'.[62] According to Graham, not only do they depend directly on agriculture, but the people of the region are presented as not interested in or inclined to commerce, although the reader knows the silk cocoons are produced throughout the year and sold in town to supplement the household's farming income. These assertions, at odds with what Graham herself described, go to the root of her orientalist representation of Italy. The section seems to suggest that the people in the Campagna do not really think of the long term or try to produce extra money. If they have any extra profits, Graham says, they are spent in decorating themselves and on useless trinkets: they are naïve and simple people. Their disinclination to store for the future is explained because 'their happy climate permits them to depend [on it] with more certainty than in the northern parts of Europe'.[63] The weather also induces in them a 'moral lethargy' that only leaves them when they need to defend themselves from the banditti.[64]

These representations echo Jean-Jacques Rousseau's famous view of the 'noble savage' as an 'ancient' stage of human development where man's 'imagination portrays nothing; his heart yearns for nothing. … His soul, perturbed by nothing, is concerned with no idea of the future'.[65] These views came from even earlier examples, such as that of the imagined Caribbean native described by Jean-Baptiste du Tertre in the *Histoire Generale des Antilles Habitées par les François* (1667–1671), who sells his blanket in the morning without realising he will need it by night. This type of view fed directly into Scottish Enlightenment stadial history and had gained immense popularity in the context of describing why 'primitive' peoples were stuck outside of the more advanced system of British commercialism. In line with Montesquieu's climatic determinism too, Graham argues that good weather induces laziness, the land being too fertile to encourage the inhabitants to work harder, one of the most common tropes used to describe non-Europeans particularly in relation to Africa, the Americas, and Southeast Asia. The descriptions of mainly agricultural work and general laziness, however, are clearly contradicted by the description of women's constant work given by Graham herself.

There are multiple reasons Graham might have done this. On the one hand, it is clear Graham might have subscribed to stadial history and orientalist views and was rehearsing them, even as they clearly flew in the face of what she was seeing. Referencing these widely accepted historical views might have also been a way for her to secure a place in the book market. According to Indira Ghose, for women orientalist discourses were a part of a larger set of strategies for legitimating the content of their travelogues. For Ghose, 'women travellers sought access to Orientalism as a strategy to negotiate a form of gender power and to contest male dominance in scientific and scholarly modes of writing'.[66] This is clearly seen in the case of Graham, who offers a quasi-anthropological view of Italian life, and deploys a male-dominated scientific and historical rhetoric to validate herself as an observer. By adhering to these discourses, she can validate her assertions in the context of the male-dominated travel writing industry, sacrificing the image of the women she observed in the process.

Orientalising and casting the observed object into the past seem to be part of the European travel writing genre itself at the time. The denial of coevalness that Fabian identifies, and its link to non-European territories and peoples in travel writing, which is highlighted in the first section above, was ubiquitous in the Romantic period. One question that immediately emerges, nonetheless, is why Graham would deploy this series of tropes onto a European population, and on people who belonged to a region that was seen as the origin of European civilization. I would like to suggest that this was related to another process taking place at the time: Occidentalism. Saree Makdisi has described this process, through which Western Europe slowly began building an image of itself as the Occident:

> The unevenness of the racial designations of the common people during the Romantic period in England is precisely an indication of the uneven incompleteness of the process of inclusion that was still taking place at home, as savage or Orientalized domestic populations were slowly being transformed into Occidentals, "whites" like "us."[67]

The local European 'savages' were precisely rural populations which were described, as Makdisi reveals, as oriental while they were slowly being reclaimed and occidentalised in Romantic writing. Makdisi shows how, during the Romantic period, 'north and south, metropolis and periphery, white and native, to use Said's terms, were so much in flux that it was quite impossible to cleanly demarcate the line where one "enclosure" ends and its opposite begins'.[68] Thus, as Makdisi explains, 'it was quite normal for "polite" observers to deploy the discourse of barbarism and savagery with respect to the common people well into the nineteenth century'.[69] In fact, according to Makdisi, the orientalising of rural workers in Italy very much persisted into the twentieth century.[70] The denial of coevalness described by Fabian, therefore, was applied in Italy so long as the process of occidentalising these regions remained incomplete. During the Romantic period when Graham was writing, these logics of time were being used to describe people and territories that were seen as not sufficiently European. This is precisely what Graham does when describing, in the 'East' of Rome, the '*internal* non-Western, or, more precisely, Orientalized, populations and spaces that were seen to be undesirably out of synch with the temporal requirements of modernity'.[71] In Graham's text we see this process developing, so that while she is able to see what she could have described as a proto-industrial development, she is unable to describe it without an orientalising lens.

This process was also aided by the geographical location of Italy. As Maria Todorova suggests, 'the conventional division of Europe into East and West is a comparatively late invention of eighteenth-century philosophes'.[72] This division, Todorova argues, was at the source of a phenomenon similar to Orientalism that arose in the nineteenth century regarding the Balkans. Thanks to this division:

> the geographic east of Europe and the world situated to the east was [seen as] lagging behind Europe primarily in economic performance, East came to be identified more often, and often exclusively, with industrial

> backwardness, lack of advanced social relations and institutions typical for the developed capitalist West, irrational and superstitious cultures unmarked by Western Enlightenment. This added an additional vector in the relationship between East and West: time, where the movement from past to future was not merely motion but evolution from simple to complex, backward to developed, primitive to cultivated.[73]

This same process, which I have described here as at least orientalising, and which overlaps with Makdisi's own description of the orientalising of English peasants, is at play in Graham's Italy. The overlap between 'Easterness' – in this case the mountains to the East of Rome – 'ancient' economic systems and 'primitive' religious superstitions is all present in Graham's 'Eastern' Italy. They are a sign of the region lagging in history. This compound effect of the three aspects of location (Eastern Italy), genre (travel writing), and class (rural workers) explains why Graham describes a social process that is recent, namely rural women's participation in providing for the growing silk industry, as ancient and not economically significant.

In a final appraisal of the value of Graham's representation, recovery, and the highlighting of women's labour in her narrative, it can be seen that while her representation of Italy falls into these orientalist descriptions, her description also simultaneously and often contradictorily reveals the important role played by women in the economy of the Campagna, even as it is often downplayed by the author herself. Particularly, Graham's descriptions offer details on the role of rural women in Italy's industrialisation, and constitute a source for the recognition of women's labour. Thus, Graham's narrative contributes unknowingly to the recognition of women's history, despite being mediated by a problematic orientalist discourse, by the requirements of women's travel writing at the time, by larger generic conventions, and by an underlying Eurocentric discourse on the nature of history. As the work of economic historians like Katrina Honeyman, Maxine Berg, Pat Hudson and William Robert Lee have revealed, the contribution of women to industrialization through labour both at home and outside the home has been ignored and underrecognized well into the twentieth century. In this sense, Graham's account provides a compelling example of the obstacles and the ambivalent ways British women could look at other women through a traveller's eyes.

Chapter 11

Travels through post-Napoleonic Europe: Harriet Elizabeth Parry's trip to France, Switzerland and Italy, 1819

Miriam Al Jamil

During the summer of 1819, Harriet Elizabeth Parry (1785–1861) from Speen Hill near Newbury in Berkshire made a tour of France, Switzerland and Italy. She recorded her impressions on a five-metre-long roll of linen-backed paper which, along with a later manuscript charting a tour to Scotland in the form of a linear map, she preserved in a fabric-covered handmade container. The British library bought this at a sale in 1984, with no previous provenance extant.[1] This chapter examines Parry's journal of her tour in Europe which defies the usual categorisation of travel writing both in form and content. The manuscript is not recorded alongside published work by other female travellers and despite the many small watercolours included, Parry is not known as an amateur artist.[2] The aim is to uncover her assumptions and priorities as one of the new travellers flocking to post-Napoleonic Europe, to

Harriet Parry's scroll.

examine the journal for evidence of gendered, class or national partiality and to suggest ways it surprises or confirms our expectations and contributes to current scholarship on women's travel writing. Comparisons with some contemporary published accounts give useful contexts in which to locate Parry's account.

The Parry family

Harriet Elizabeth Parry was from a middle-class provincial family and her journals form the only extant testimony of her life. She was born in the village of Speen near Newbury in Berkshire in 1785. Her father, Charles Henry Parry (1755–1788), was the vicar of the parish church of St Mary from 1780 until he died in 1788 at the age of thirty-three.[3] Her mother was Mary Parry (1751–1836), daughter of the previous vicar, Thomas Shepherd (1716–1796), who then became vicar again, 'when in compassion to the young widow and her children, the Bishop re-appointed her father, with whom she continued to reside in her old home.'[4] Parry had two sisters, Anna Maria (1782–1872) and Catherine Louisa (1788–1832), and a brother, Francis Charles Parry (1780–1878). There may have been an older brother, 'my eldest son' of her father's will who was buried in March 1793, a year that saw many child burials in the parish.[5] We know nothing about Parry's education but the evidence from her first travel account points to a conservative Anglican upbringing and a conventional focus on female practical skills in needlework as well as music, history, languages and literature.

More information is available about Parry's brother Francis, and through his work, she could have developed a measure of social and political awareness which coloured her experiences of travel. Francis was educated at Winchester and University College, Oxford. He then lived in London and was admitted to the Middle Temple on 22 June 1803 and called to the bar three years later. He was a Commissioner of Bankrupts and Deputy Registrar of the Bankruptcy Court from 1810 to 1832 and his last record at Middle Temple is dated 1844.[6] He married Marian Hawker in 1814 and had two children, all of whom predeceased him.[7] He wrote two books, the first published just before Parry's trip to the Continent. This was *An Account of the Charitable Donations to Places within the County of Berks* (London, 1818). The second, published much later, focussed on the debate about dissenters and education.[8]

Francis Parry, like his sister, maintained his connection to his home county and through him, we glimpse something of Parry's childhood in the small village of Speen. She recorded her personal attachment by naming it on her travel accounts.[9] Francis Parry demonstrated a keen legal interest in the documented evidence of County financial mismanagement or inefficiency. His first book drew on his work as an appointed commissioner to investigate cases of corruption and the misuse of donations intended to found schools or aid the poor. He was 'praised for his zeal, his integrity, and the industry with which he had applied to the subject'.[10] Without official powers, he could only invite those charged with maladministration to account for their actions. His own father's parish was not spared his rigour, as witnessed by a statement from John Nelson, the curate there in 1818, '…the parish of Speen contains about two thousand inhabitants, and […] many of the children belonging to the parish are sent by subscribers to the National School at Newbury. We are desirous of establishing a parochial school; but the want of sufficient means has hitherto prevented the accomplishment of our wishes.'[11] The parish registers reveal that militia were stationed in the area and soldiers from the East Suffolk regiment and the 15th Regiment of Light Dragoons married in the church and were buried in the churchyard from the 1790s, alongside inmates of the two workhouses, some unnamed. Foundlings sent from London to nurse in the area and the children of itinerant labourers from Ireland were also baptised and buried there.[12] Parry and her family would therefore have witnessed the local distress and hardship which accompanied the Napoleonic war years. Her journal account reflects her eagerness to experience the Europe which the wars had denied her during that time.[13]

Parry's Journal, 1819

Parry's 1819 travel account combines written descriptions, thumbnail watercolours, detailed measurements and practical facts about her progress. She signed the inner flap of the container she made for her two journals with her name, address and the date, January 6th 1829. This marked the object with personal value and enabled Harriet to assert it as her property in the event of sharing and lending it within her circle. Such labelling generally features in collections of printed books but also relates to Barbara Burman and Ariane Fennetaux's discussion about the routine 'Marking and Reckoning' necessary for household linen and other textiles within the domestic feminine realm, to record ownership.[14]

The textile-covered and hand-made container for the documents is a signifier of a woman's account, though the content of Parry's journal rarely fulfils the widely held gendered expectation that women's travel writing concentrates on 'personal feeling and social observation' rather than on the historical and political discussion reserved for male-authored accounts.[15] There are few entries which necessarily indicate female authorship. She elected to record details which would be useful for other travellers to know. Her most likely audience would be a network of family connections, some of whom might have contemplated a trip abroad. Close examination of her illustrations and a reading of the text could be enjoyed during a sociable gathering with the manuscript spread out on a table, carefully rolled out as it had been during her trip, contributing to the sociability of shared reading discussed by Abigail Williams.[16] Parry's travel experiences could gain her an authoritative voice for her writing within the family.[17] As Emma Gleadhill notes, 'Women sought to find spaces in which they could create and control their own travel narratives and produce their own understandings of taste, virtue and connoisseurship'.[18] Although Gleadhill's examples are drawn from elite women, I suggest the same impulse to claim recognition shaped Parry's narrative and subsequent management of her account.

The roll-format account, though different from the published travel guides which proliferated in the early nineteenth century, nevertheless draws on many of their techniques, appropriating elements of the format as the most suitable for her account. She drew columns down the right side to record the regions and towns through which she passed, alongside the staging posts and mileage, and flanked her observations with dates down the left side. Typical of published itineraries which she may have consulted before her journey was Reichard's 1816 *An Itinerary of France and Belgium, or, An Account of the Post and Cross Roads, Rivers, Canals*...etc., translated from the French and published by Samuel Leigh, who specialized in travel writing. The Advertisement states, 'The translator flatters himself that the present volume, uniting all the advantages of a Gazetteer, a Book of Roads, and a History of France and Belgium, &c. will be found an interesting and useful companion to the British tourist.'[19] It includes lists of posts and costs, exchange values, packet sailings and alternative routes presented in table form. Such comparative lists of facts gave Parry a means to order and organise her own experiences, to give them structure and status with many resemblances to book-keeping columns, another method of recording which was likely to be familiar to her from domestic household accounts.

Commercially produced and widely available pocketbooks were a means of documenting daily experience, often incorporating miniature scenic prints which may have inspired Parry for her own watercolour sketches of views and sights measuring a few centimetres and bordered in black ink.[20] Pocketbooks were a useful means of recording many peripatetic forms of writing.'[21] Parry's use of an accounting style of organisation, combined with her personalised container expressive of other forms of female skill, are further evidence of the creative adaptations made by women in their records and albums, including collaging and fabric samples which are the subject of new scholarly attention.[22]

Parry never mentions those who accompanied her on her trip but it is unlikely that she went alone and her intended family audience would have known the plans and preparations she had made. In the same year, Scottish engineer and political economist William Playfair (1759–1823) noted that 'two years ago, excepting the officers of the army or navy, few of the present race under the age of forty-five, had ever been out of England; but such has been the rage for seeing France, that now there are few of any age who have not been over for a longer or shorter period.'[23] Parry and her party would have been among the despised new 'crowds' of non-elite travellers to the Continent described in an 1826 review. This contrasts 'the insignificance and frivolity of a modern excursion' with the grandeur of the earlier Grand Tour, the 'glory' of which is now 'trampled underfoot by crowds of pedestrians, equestrian, and vehicular vagabonds, making their way by means of a guide-book and a vocabulary.'[24]

Travels in France

From 1815, new opportunities for travel enabled British travellers to the Continent to visit sites of the recent conflict, particularly the Waterloo battlefield. Eventually it became 'one of the standard destinations' for middle-class visitors throughout the nineteenth century.'[25] Parry's itinerary did not include sites of recent conflict, but her account unavoidably reflects the post-Waterloo political landscape of Europe. The legacy of the recently exiled Emperor is present throughout. By the time she travelled to France, the withdrawal after three years of the post-Waterloo Allied army of occupation had been facilitated by the speedy arrangement of reparations and the final peace settlement at the Congress of Aix-La-Chapelle in September 1818.[26] Eugene White notes, 'The effects of reparations may have been cloaked by the bad harvests, but there is good reason to believe that they were a significant drag on the economy [which went through] a prolonged period of distress' into the 1820s.[27] Travel-writer Mariana Starke (1762–1838), on her return visit to France in 1817, observed that Parisians' former *gaieté de coeur* had been replaced with 'thoughtfulness, reserve, and discontent.'[28] There was widespread dissatisfaction with the restored Bourbons. Playfair believed that many Parisians were uncomfortable, thinking the king had not forgiven them for the Revolution.[29] He identified the causes of 'a rooted discontent' and suggested that 'the cries in favour of Buonaparte are not so much from good-will towards him, as they are intended for showing a dislike to the present government, with which the people are highly dissatisfied [and] because their vanity and self-love are mortified to be under a family that they treated so ill, and swore never again to obey.'[30] His detailed lists of French debts, taxes and shortages reveal more fundamental causes for the resentment.

Sudhir Hazareesingh notes the 'sheer scale' of the Napoleon cult which developed after 1815.[31] Richard Whately's 1819 mock-sceptical pamphlet *Historic Doubts Relative to Napoleon Buonaparte* questions the reason for 'the persevering attachment and blind devotedness' of the French to this man, given the manifest disasters inflicted on the people, and frames Napoleon's career as an improbable fiction.[32] At the same time, associated with the growing cult, there were persistent rumours that the Emperor would again return. The years 1819–20 were among those during which a particular intensity of unrest associated with the rumours was recorded by local officials across France They reported the ongoing circulation of small portraits, busts, medals and engravings depicting his image, a circulation which Napoleon had encouraged during his reign and which traveller Katherine Wilmot noticed in Paris in 1801–1803.[33] During the summer of 1819, while Parry was journeying through France, police uncovered a large hoard of portraits in Cambrai, and their suspicions fell on 'a group of English travellers'.[34] In November that year, a street trader in Paris admitted that he had sold 8,000 busts over four days.[35] The strength of the complex and enduring legend of Napoleon as the glorious embodiment of the spirit of the Revolution, even though he had betrayed its spirit when he became Emperor, was one of the contributory factors in the eventual downfall of the Bourbons.[36] Napoleon was transformed into a victim by many in France but also in Britain after his final exile was decided without a trial or consultation with Parliament.[37]

Katherine Turner notes that Napoleon had become a popular theme of women's travel writing from the 1820s.[38] Parry's observations reflect an ambivalence in her opinion of Napoleon but show her susceptibility to romanticising his legacy. They are short and selective and do not offer direct commentary but reveal that she was well informed about current events. Starke's account includes far more about Napoleon's civic projects, particularly in Paris: 'The improvements this city owes to Napoleon are innumerable.'[39] Many visitors mention works begun but not finished, with observations similar to Playfair's note that 'Everything in France is incomplete, either from want of time, or through length of time.'[40] The sense these impressions convey of a curtailed and unfulfilled material heritage is shared by Parry and revealed through the objects she mentions. We glimpse the recent past through her details of Napoleon's personal and domestic life: 'Maria Louisa's bed of most beautiful Lyons silk [and her] curious bath with the top & sides of plate glass' (22nd June) at Compiegne where Napoleon first met Maria Louisa in 1810, and the 'Fountain of Lions built by Bonaparte on ye birth of his son' in the Boulevard Italien in Paris (26th June). These observations contrast with Parry's less enthusiastic report on the restored royal family, seen on their way to the Royal Chapel in the Tuileries: 'Louis 18, of immense size, & supporting himself with 2 sticks'. On the return from mass, they 'shew themselves on a balcony facing the gardens' (27th June). Playfair characterises these daily displays and ceremonies as part of a performance by a puppet king 'tormented by the preservation of forms and customs that have absolutely no meaning whatever.'[41]

Parry offers vignettes of political events through her notes on the tombs and graves of heroic military men. There is a sense of pathos in her examples. The two monuments in the Hôtel des Invalides which draw her attention are those to the Viscount of Turenne (1611–1675) and the Marquis de Vauban (1633–1707), both celebrated Marshalls of France during the *ancien regime*. Parry notes that 'The Presence Chamber is magnificent. A throne with a canopy of purple velvet covered with gold fleurs de lis and a gold chair', and mentions the art shown at the 'Palace of the Luxembourg'. Following such unexceptional observations, she adds simply that 'Marshal Ney was shot in the garden' (25th June). Ney, as a Grand Armée commander under Napoleon who called him the 'bravest of the brave' made the fatal decision to support Napoleon on his return from Elba, resulting in his controversial execution in December 1815.[42] Parry's 'fleurs de lis' reference indicates the culpable authority for this act, as a synecdoche for the restored monarchy. The Duke of Wellington and the Emperor of Russia were also implicated by their refusal to offer protection under the 12th Article of the Capitulation of Paris. Parry mentions Ney's grave and that of another executed General, Charles de la Bédoyère at Père Lachaise cemetery, both 'in an obscure corner' (27th June). The only other tomb she names is that of 'Abelard & Eloisa', under a 'sort of Gothic Pyramid,' only just transferred there from the Jardin Élysée in 1817. She responds to the romance of the location, an ambience planned from its first burials in 1804, with its 'garlands of fresh flowers' and Cypress trees.

At Fontainebleau, Parry admires the furniture and tapestries but adds, 'In an anti room to the State room is a common little round mahogany table on which Bonaparte signed his abdication' (29th June). She continues to describe the other 'beautiful tables', and the 'china vases & ornamented clocks'. The iconic pedestal table, depicted in many paintings of the 1814 event, remains a feature of the Salon of Abdication.[43] For Parry it is 'common', disappointingly unexceptional, and as a result, diminishes the Emperor. In contrast, Lord and Lady Holland, 'the most consistent of Napoleon's British admirers', visited Fontainebleau in 1814 and the 'fatal room' where the table brought back personal memories.[44] Lady Elizabeth wrote to her sister, 'Alas! Alas! Why did he go to Russia and why was he so headstrong?'[45] Her 'uncritical Bonapartism', and devotion to 'the greatest man of our times' is here expressed in terms almost of maternal regret about the wilful actions of misguided youth.[46]

Parry is selective about the historical facts she includes in her account. She notes that the chateau at Chantilly was 'nearly destroyed at the Revolution' (22nd June). Repairs were only begun by Louis Henri II, Duke of Condé from 1818 and the Grand Chateau itself was not rebuilt until the 1870s. She mentions the 'good stuffed dogs and wild beasts in the entrance' which point to a questionable and makeshift use of the space in the absence of an overall decorative scheme, though her enthusiasm for the stuffed animals at the Jardin des Plantes suggests she enjoyed these displays. Some details point to the likelihood that she learned her facts from a local guide who still supports Napoleon. We learn at Notre Dame that 'the candlesticks were given by Bonaparte' (27th June). Her information is not always accurate. She credits the castle she later viewed and sketched as 'built by the Romans' (9th July), though the ruin at Martigny dates from the thirteenth century.[47] In some cases, current conditions are ignored. For example, she describes the cathedral at Amiens as 'very fine', and 'covered with statues and ornaments, inside and out' (21st June). She does not mention that extensive restoration work was in progress, following destruction of much of the sculpture during the revolution and the subsequent use of the building for storage. Replacement of many of the sculptures was not begun until 1821, so she would have seen the damage for herself. She also chooses to include her own comparisons, drawing on her own experience. On the road to Fontainebleau, she describes the 'high grey rocks' through the forest as 'like those at Tonbridge Wells' (29th June). Later, as she approaches the Jura mountains beyond Champagnole, she notes that 'the road winds backwards and forwards like the Malvern terraces' (2nd July). These remarks point to her previous visits to English spa towns for health or fashionable social life. Her continental journey expands her horizons, but her points of reference are still English, as was the case in many published English travel accounts. Lucy Morrison suggests that 'All the authors are careful to situate themselves as proud of their English nation in contrast with the foreign landscapes they are presenting to readers.'[48]

Through the Mountains

Before she leaves Paris, Parry sees a panorama on display at the Palais Royal, a 'representation of the Simplon Road' (28th June). This is a road she soon sees for herself. She is naturally preoccupied with the conveniences or otherwise of the roads she travels and is observant of the changing topography throughout her account. She includes meticulous notes on the countryside and terrain, and we encounter cascades and waterfalls, birches, beeches and firs, cornfields and vineyards. She notes the house where the prolific and popular writer Madame de Genlis (1746–1830) lived, 'with a bocage by the side of it', and adds a quick sketch (1st July). She also mentions Voltaire's home at Ferney (3rd July). She is aware of literary landmarks though we cannot infer her reading preferences from this. The ordered prosperity of Geneva, its English Chapel, promenade and rowing boats on the lake suit her mentality. She visits shops under a covered archway, mentioning the premises 'where the celebrated musical watches etc. are sold' (5th July). We are conscious of the superlative adjectives she uses and her reaction to sublime scenery, the steep climbs and 'stupendous' descents, and her evocations of dramatic tableaux, for example 'on a sudden turn of the road there is a magnificent view of Mt. Blanc' (3rd July). Turner has discussed how the Romantic poets' delineation of sublime landscapes provided expressive possibilities for tourists' travel narratives after 1815.[49] Parry's precise and economic descriptions belie the effort and exertions she makes, particularly in the mountains. Her nine-hour expedition on the Glacier Montanvert across the Mer de Glace involves 'several avalanches on return' and later a hazardous 'path for a mule & hardly wide enough for that with the mountain on one side & a precipice on ye other' (9th July). She has already mentioned the 'cross erected to mark the spot where a traveller who fell down a precipice was preserved from harm' (7th July). She shares that traveller's lucky escape. One senses her delight at her own bravery and anticipation of retelling her adventure later.

Parry's frequent observations about the evidence of Napoleon's uncompleted projects, where the objects remained though the lineage was overthrown, become more frequent as she passes over the Simplon and conjure the poetic associations explored by contemporary Romantic poets. For example, Shelley published his poem *Ozymandias* about the fall of kings not long before Parry's journey and it may have been familiar to her.[50] Diderot had recommended to artists that 'a strong image of transience' would make their paintings of ruins more effective, to show how 'the powerful men of the earth who believed they built for the ages [are reduced so that] nothing remains of their work' but debris.[51] Napoleon's military projects were dramatically evident for travellers crossing the mountains on their way to Milan. For military purposes he completed the first carriage road over the Simplon Pass in 1807, described by Starke in a later edition of her journal as the eighth wonder of the world.[52] Travellers also mention that Napoleon endowed mountain convents and 'constructed several houses termed "refuges", at different distances, for the shelter of passengers in the dangerous months', though his 'caravansera, on the top of the "Simplon", has been left half finished.'[53] Parry includes the refuges and galleries forged through the rock in her brief descriptions and agrees with Starke that the single-arch bridge built over the Saltine river is 'the finest work of art' (10th July). Napoleon's presence increasingly intrudes into Parry's account. She notices 'Nap:Imp: inscribed on the rock after coming out of the Gallery' and just before the bridge at Iselle, 'on ye left of the road side is a fine marble column flung down, one of 6 made by Bonaparte for one of the gates of Milan' (12th July). When she reaches Milan, she notes the 'beautiful gates' which were 'begun by Bonaparte but not finished' (14th July). Her journey traces the emperor's engineering achievements, his arrested plans and the evidence of his ambition as King of Italy. Milan seems to lay bare the extent of his vision.[54]

Art and Culture

In spite of the frenetic pace of Parry's journey, she finds time to enjoy the cultural life of the cities, and she proves to be both an appreciative and a critical observer. In addition to descriptions of the route and features of her tour, an important element of Parry's account is the references to the plays she sees in Paris and the operas in Italy, suggesting she regularly enjoyed such events. Guidebooks on Paris and many contemporary visitors' descriptions outline the plays, opera and other entertainments on offer there. For example, Major W. E. Frye's (1784–1858) journal for 1815–19 is enthusiastic and praises many individual performers. Unfortunately, the 1908 editor of his published journal notes in the preface that 'it has been thought advisable to leave out a certain number of pages devoted to theatricals [...] the interest of which to modern readers does not correspond to the space occupied by them'.[55] Lady Sydney Morgan (1781–1859) was more disparaging about French theatre: 'The French actors, though they are generally graceful, do not tread the stage with the same ease and freedom as the English', and she uses Kemble's declamatory style for comparison.[56]

Parry spends five days in Paris from 23rd to 28th June 1819 at around the same time as Major Frye and together, their accounts document a range of performances on the Parisian stage. Parry's choices suggest that she preferred popular spectacles and romantic plotlines. On 23th June, she sees 'Aristophane' and the ballet of 'Acis and Galatea'. The first may refer to *Les Comices d'Athènes, ou Les Femmes Orateurs* 'translated from the Greek of Aristophane' by Eugène Scribe (1791–1861) and Antoine-François Varner (1789–1854). It was a comédie-vaudeville in one act which premiered in Paris at the Théâtre du Vaudeville on November 7th, 1817 and was published the same year.[57] Based on Aristophanes' *Ecclesiazusae*, the plot centres on the chaotic government which would result if women were in charge, a satirical piece of light entertainment which incorporates songs and many parts for women.[58] The ballet which completes the evening's event may have been based on a ballet d'action, *Acis et Galathée* (1773), originally created by the celebrated ballet master Jean-George Noverre (1727–1810). Parry is very impressed with the principal dancer.

The following evening, she visits the Théâtre de la Gaité to see a new play which had premiered in March that year. It was a historic melodrama, *La Fille de l'Exilé, ou Huit Mois en Deux Heures*, an adaptation by the director and playwright René-Charles Guilbert de Pixerécour of Mme. Sophie Cottin's (1770–1807) *Elizabeth, or, The Exiles of Siberia* (1806).[59] Parry describes it as 'The Exiles of Siberia', the name of the book rather than the play. On 25th June, she attends a play, '*La Fenetre Secrette*', and a ballet, '*La Rendez vous Bourgeois*', at the 'Theatre Francois' or Théâtre Feydeau, which was the home of the Opéra-Comique.[60]

We do not know the extent of her language skills but melodrama and action would require less fluency and afford more entertainment. Lady Morgan's descriptions of Parry's preferred theatres contrast them with the serious drama at other venues. The Théâtre du Vaudeville 'is rich in parodies, which follow rapidly upon every new piece given at the opera,' and the Théâtre de la Gaité offers 'dramas, melo-dramas, pantomime, dancing, and petites piéces of every description [...] the audience, generally speaking appeared to me to be extremely coarse', an adjective unlikely to have pleased Parry.[61]

On 14th July, Parry visits La Scala Opera House in Milan. She describes the Opera House: 'An immense house- 6 tier high – the opera Henry 8th – no music & poor acting – Anne Bullen a miserable little thing – & Cath of Aragon a fat vulgar woman. A curious illuminated clock over the stage (the hands illuminated).' The opera is probably *Enrico VIII, ossia Anna Bolena* (1816) by Ippolito Pindemonte (1753–1828), based on a translation of *Henri VII* (1791) by Marie-Joseph de Chénier and *Anna Bolena* (1788) by Alessandro Pepoli.[62] The libretto was by the popular Italian librettist Felice Giuseppe Romani (1788–1865), 'writer of the second rank' who later worked with Gaetano Donizetti (1797–1848) on his version of *Anna Bolena* of 1830, which became a celebrated production.[63] Parry is scathing about this less well-known opera and its performers and more interested in the clock which features in a contemporary print of the interior.[64] In Turin she patronises the Teatro Regio, which offers 'all recitative not much worth hearing only one man & one woman who sang pretty well' (20th July). Her judgement is based on the appearance of the female singers in Milan and on the vocal style of performers in Turin. She is attuned to various types of singing and particularly opinionated about church congregations, probably due to her family background. She attends a service at the village of Simplon where the 'mass and sermon [are] in German: an organ & all ye people singing to it in the highest key possible – screaming (11th July)'. Her awed reactions to the magnificent interiors of the great cathedrals and the description of gold and gems adorning the body and tomb of St Charles in Milan contrast with her less enthusiastic observations about Catholic citizens and peasants as they express their faith. However, it is difficult to discern her opinion of the market traders in Novi when she writes that early in the morning 'most of them set down their baskets & knelt down on the steps of ye church to say their prayers' (16th July). We might detect respect for this simple ritual, the interruption of the commercial business of the day to prioritise religious obligations.

In addition to an interest in performance, Parry's account demonstrates her appreciation of fine art. She lists some of the paintings by 'modern artists' in the Palais du Luxembourg in Paris, a gallery space given to contemporary salon artists in April 1818, mainly featuring narrative paintings of classical or national historical subjects. She mentions *La Convalescence de Bayard* (1816–17) by Pierre Revoil (1776–1842) and the *Judgement of Brutus* (1799) by Heinrich Friedrich Fuger (1781–1818). At the 'Galerie des beaux arts' (Pinacoteca di Brera) in Milan she sees 'a great many original paintings' (14th July) by Nicolas Poussin, Salvator Rosa and Annibale Carracci, as well as statues, prints and original works by Canova. She notices the 'damp walls' on which Leonardo's fresco could be seen in the Convent of Santa Maria delle Grazie.

Parry's sixteen miniature sketches throughout the account are not as polished as those made by Marianne Colston, who had them reproduced as engravings for her travel diary. Parry is content to border her drawings in ink to illustrate the views she describes. They are fairly accurate observations, easily compared with other artists' renditions. For example, her drawing of the Bridge of Ganther closely matches a print from Ackermann's Repository of Art in its composition and viewpoint.[65] She draws from scenic stopping points on the road and from boats taken across lakes. She records the number of windows in palaces and the proportions of towers and arches in churches with an understanding of perspective. She uses pencil and washes of blue and grey skilfully adapted to different landscapes and features with occasional yellow to indicate a golden dome. Her journey through the Alpine region inspires the most complex and detailed representations of 'sublime' scenery. Her view of the Village of Simplon is the largest drawing at approximately 3.5 x 6cm (11th July). It is depicted from a high point on the road as a collection of buildings against a mountainous and wooded backdrop, with a small cart turning a corner. People do not feature in Parry's illustrations, even as convenient indications of scale, but there is an engaging immediacy and honesty in her work which allows us access to her personal impressions of the tour.

Return Home

Parry returns to Southampton on the Chesterfield packet on 3 August 1819, the same ship which travel writer Marianne Colston boarded three months later on her wedding day, 1st November, for her trip to France but which other travellers did not always find a reliable service.[66] By this time, Harriet's writing is hasty and her observations cursory. She has given up her drawings and lost patience with the hotels. On 27th July, having left Lyons, she writes, 'Nothing in ye country or towns very observable.' Both Honfleur and Le Havre are described as 'a disagreeable sea port,' and her few positive remarks simply note 'nice' or 'pretty' houses or churches. The pace of her travel and the ground covered in a few weeks suggest that it was a tiring tour. She particularly mentions the flagstones and unpaved roads and the uncomfortable movement of the coach, so her journey entails visceral experiences of the inconsistent terrain. She is relieved to return home.

Six years after her return, Harriet undertook a second journey, this time a tour through England and Scotland. Her account takes the form of a linear map illustrated by increasingly detailed vignettes of towns and houses which often include the names of owners, tenants and incumbents of church livings, the latter a clear personal interest for her. It is oriented from south to north to suit the direction of the journey and uses the mapping style which was popular from the seventeenth century onwards, such as John Cary's map of 1814 with its marked areas of woodland or lakes.[67]

Harriet's mother and sisters moved to Clifton, Bristol some time after the death of her grandfather in 1796. Her mother and younger sister Catherine Louisa died there.[68] But Harriet's life took a different turn. In 1832, at the age of forty-six, she married Andrew Allen, a fifty-six-year-old widower of Westminster, London. His brother officiated at the ceremony in Speen church.[69] The Allen family connected Harriet with an important American dynasty which opposed Independence. Facts about the family's history would have given her the opportunity to engage with international events, and political and moral issues beyond her previous experience. We can only guess at her opinions and views. Allen's father had been the Attorney-General of Pennsylvania in 1766 before moving to England where he died in 1825.[70] His grandfather William Allen had held many public offices, served as Provincial Grand Master of the Pennsylvania Freemasons, and founded what became the University of Pennsylvania. He supported the artist Benjamin West in his career and retired to England because of his opposition to Independence. He later added a codicil to his will to free the enslaved people he owned.[71] Harriet and her husband moved to Clifton where they worshipped at St Andrew's Church, rented a pew and where Andrew was buried in 1850.[72] Her sister Anna Maria married sixty-one-year-old widower Thomas Newman there at the age of fifty-eight. Many of the Church records which would have given more details were unfortunately destroyed, along with the church, during the bombing of the Second World War.

By 1851, the two widowed sisters were living together in Speen and memorials in the church honoured them as 'two Christian ladies, benefactors of this and the adjoining parishes.'[73] This suggests that they spent their remaining years undertaking charitable work. Harriet Parry/Allen died in 1861 at the age of seventy-five and was buried in the churchyard at Speen. Her travel accounts give us a picture of a conventional, religious approach to life, a middle-class upbringing and dedication to family and community, but we also glimpse the lively mind engaging with new experiences, observing and recording for her own satisfaction as well as in anticipation of companionable discussion at home. Her accounts are unmediated by considerations of a general reading public, so they represent a valuable additional resource for the study of women travel writers.

Chapter 12

'She won't give up her unlawful love (myself)': Byron's tales of Italian adultery

Emily Paterson Morgan

So altered since last year his pen is –
I think he's lost his wits at Venice –
Or drained his brains away as Stallion
To some dark-eyed and warm Italian

Lord Byron in a letter to John Murray[1]

Lord Byron (1788–1824) was one of the more well-travelled members of his generation. Born in London, he was raised in Aberdeen until he unexpectedly inherited a dilapidated estate in Nottinghamshire in 1798. He finished university and immediately set off on a two-year journey across Europe on his Grand Tour in 1809. Transforming his experiences into a wildly popular poem, *Childe Harold's Pilgrimage* Cantos I and II (1812), Byron became an international celebrity. However, when his wife left him (causing widespread speculation and a swirl of sordid rumours), a defiant Byron left England – never to return. After travelling through Belgium, Germany and Switzerland during the summer of 1816, Byron arrived in Italy and – after a month of exploring – settled in Venice in November. From here he

Lord Byron by Thomas Phillips, 1813.

wrote hundreds of frank, witty, and vibrantly detailed letters to friends, family, and business associates.

Few readers would ever say of Lord Byron's correspondence what fellow poet William Wordsworth sheepishly admits of his own, 'This is a wretchedly dull letter'.[2] This is especially true of the lively letters written from Italy; covering everything from politics to prostitutes, these animated accounts make for riotous reading. Flitting from lubricous accounts of sexual excess to plaintive appeals for hair loss remedies and toothpowders – and even announcing he is breaking off writing to make love to his mistress (recommencing the letter with an account of her skill) – Byron's letters are laced with humorous anecdotes and shrewd sociocultural observations on Italian life and customs. Small wonder, then, that Byron's Italian correspondence was highly regarded amongst his friends and contemporaries. Indeed in 1863, long after the poet's death, noted author Charles Lamb wrote to publisher John Blackwood regarding the commissioning of a journalistic piece on 'Life in Italian Cities', and admiringly stated 'there is nothing so graphic about Italy as the sketches in Byron's letters [...] Perhaps it was the very blending of Dirt and Levity in himself which led him to the exact appreciation'.[3]

Lamb's phrase 'exact appreciation' is striking, suggesting both precise comprehension and esteem. This is noteworthy in a period where travellers' accounts were more likely to be characterised by derision than admiration. For it is a striking paradox of British travel writing from the late eighteenth and early nineteenth centuries that descriptions of Continental marvels are almost universally tarnished by a patina of discontented yearning for British shores and customs as foreign travel prompted jingoistic pride in British travellers. This nationalistic fervour is particularly evident in traveller responses to Italy which were, as historian Jeremy Black highlights, typically marked by 'contempt, indifference, or neglect'.[4] (There is perhaps a hint of this underlying Lamb's disdainful reference to 'Dirt', conveying an impression of sordid sexual undertones lurking beneath the superficial grime of eons). Such scornful attitudes were often coupled with an underlying smugness – the conviction that Britain was infinitely superior in every imaginable way. Black provides the example of British traveller Henry Carr on whom the glories of ancient Rome were utterly lost, leading him to complacently claim in 1739 that not one building in the imperial city 'strikes the eye [...] like Grosvenor or St James Square'.[5] The British might embrace recreational and educational foreign travel, but they rarely doubted the superiority of their native shores.

In stark contrast, Byron's correspondence paints a highly appealing portrait of Italy, favourably contrasting his pleasant existence with England's 'cloudy Climate' and 'chilly Women'. '[I]t is very agreeable for Gentlemen of desultory habits – women – wine – and wassail all being extremely fair & reasonable', he writes, urging friends to come and visit 'the garden of the world'.[6] He even claims to be abandoning English for the 'beautiful' Italian language, deeming it a fitter poetic medium than the 'harsh northern whistling grunting gutteral',[7] and demands to be buried in Venice rather than 'an English grave'.[8] 'No other English writer threw himself so completely into the physical and imaginative enjoyment of Italy', observes historian Kenneth Churchill,[9] a claim substantiated by the contrast between Byron's laudatory descriptions and those of his contemporaries. For example, whereas novelist Lady Morgan's travelogue *Italy* (1821) offers a gloomy description of Venice as 'forlorn and demolished', with a dwindling population, rotting foundations, and houses 'falling into the canals',[10] Byron enthuses about the luminous fragility of Venetian mists. Indeed, his adulatory accounts of the majestic grandeur of Venice in *Childe Harold's Pilgrimage* helped to transform the 'fairy city' into a popular destination for British travellers, while his ardent descriptions of Italy, 'the throne and grave of empires', ensured Byron a starring role in John Murray's 1836 *Handbooks for Travellers*.

Venice's main attraction for Byron was not the crumbling architecture wreathed in translucent fog but rather the potential for 'promiscuous concubinage'. Deliberately catering to the British perception of Italy as a seething hotbed of sexual sin – a view largely based on the popular accounts of debauched dissipation produced by eighteenth-century noblemen on the Grand Tour – Byron boasts of fornicating with some two hundred women in a matter of months as he 'drained his brains away as a Stallion / To some dark-eyed & warm Italian':[11]

> [T]he Tarruscelli – the Da Mosti – the Spineda – the Lotti – the Rizzatto – the Eleanora – the Carlotta – the Guilietta – the Alvisi – the Zambieri – the Eleanora da Bezi (who was the King of Naple's Gioaschino's mistress – at least one of them) – the Theresina of Mazzurati – the Glettenheimer – Gioaschino & her Sister – the Luigia & her mother – the Fornaretta – the Santa – the Caligari – the Portiera – the Bolognese figurante – the Tentore and her sister – cum multis aliis? some of them are Countesses – & some of them Cobblers wives – some noble – some middling – some low – & all whores.[12]

'I have had them all & thrice as many to boot since 1817', he concludes with brazen glee. As Roberto Bizzocchi observes, travellers' accounts 'usually tell us more about the traveller's own culture and outlook than the reality' of the country they visit.[13] Byron's letters, with their entertaining descriptions of the 'incontinent Continental system',[14] suggest he admires the louche epicurean hedonism of the great rakes of the previous century, reinvigorating their *topos* of Italian immorality and breathing new life into it for the amusement of his friends back in London.

Yet Byron, writing letters as 'a foreigner, far from my own country',[15] also provides valuable insights into 'the present state of Italian morals' and those he wittily dubs 'the continental incontinent'.[16] His letters contain detailed descriptions of the specifics of this 'Meridian morality', where '*polygamy* is all on the female side'.[17] 'Their moral is not your moral', he informs his publisher John Murray, 'their life is not your life – you would not understand it [...] the Coventual Education – the Cavalier Servitude – the habits of thought and living are so entirely different I know not how to make you comprehend a people – who are at once temperate and profligate.'[18] Byron, however, has an 'exact appreciation' of these practices, to appropriate Charles Lamb's apt phrase, and his letters offer unique insights for his readers (both contemporary and current).

'The Laudable Practise of Love Making' – Italian Sociosexual Ethics

Whereas other travelogue accounts of Italy were often inspired by religious, political or philosophical convictions, Byron writes from the vantage of 'a foreigner who loves an Italian woman' – or rather, many Italian women, all of whom are apparently 'about five feet ten inches high, with great black eyes and fine figure[s] – fit to breed gladiators from'.[19] And Venice, which Byron pungently describes as a 'sea-Sodom', was a rich source of amusements for a famous and rather dashing young nobleman. He told jocular stories of *amicazia* (the adulterous liaison) and *cicisbeismo* (the wife's selection of a formally recognized *cavalier servente*). The term '*cicisbeism*' refers to the practice of an unmarried young man of good family (usually a younger son) attaching himself to a married woman and serving as her formally acknowledged escort and companion. This man, as historian Roberto Bizzocchi explains, 'had the public and declared task of living side by side with another man's wife, as part of an arranged and desirable triangle'.[20] He would spend much of the day with her, walking in gardens, visiting friends, and attending parties where he hovered in subservient devotion behind her chair attending to her every need and whim. Although Bizzochi suggests that the openness of the relationship ensured *cicisbeism* was 'a social institution' rather than an 'erotic practise', Byron's letters show liaisons undoubtedly occurred and – at least in Ravenna – were an accepted and even expected part of matrimonial life.[21] Indeed, according to Byron, wifely infidelity was so common that, when faced with a 'Sodomite', the women of the region simply shrug and 'express their hopes that he may yet be converted to Adultery'.[22] Byron's accounts of *cicisbeism* form a striking contrast to the quivering indignation displayed by other English visitors. For example, in her travelogue *Italy*, Lady Morgan

Lord Byron in Albanian Dress by Thomas Phillips, 1813.

praises the country's former imperial glories but unequivocally denounces female adultery as a public calamity which had plunged a formerly virile nation into degenerate effeminacy and 'annihilated national morality'. 'The morals of Italy fell with her beauties', she writes sententiously.[23] Contrastingly, Byron, never one to miss a sexual opportunity (one travelling companion recalls how, on arriving at a Belgian inn, the poet 'fell like a thunderbolt upon the chambermaid'),[24] was swift to take advantage of such 'amatory habits'. Thus, although Lady Morgan is relieved to find there were 'no *cecisbeo*' in Genoa,[25] he is delighted to discover the custom was still active in Venice. Shortly after his arrival in the winter of 1816, the self-exiled poet makes the happy discovery that 'most of the women in Venice' are 'dissolute'.[26]

Characterised by the same lightly ironic touch and burlesque register we find in his amatory epic *Don Juan*, Byron's spirited correspondence describes his erotic pursuits in detail and his correspondence is imbued with a wonderful sense of immediacy and the feeling that we are involved in an intimate *entre-nous* exchange with a close friend. In a merry letter to old school friend and notorious womaniser James Wedderburn Webster (whom Byron had cuckolded in 1813), the poet paints an alluring picture of female promiscuity:

> Young and old – pretty & ugly – high and low – are all employed in the laudable practise of Love making – and though most Beauty is found amongst the middling & lower classes – this of course only renders their amatory habits more generally diffused.[27]

A more detailed explanation is sent to his publisher John Murray. A 'woman', Byron observes, 'is virtuous (according to the code) who limits herself to her husband and one lover – those who have two or three more are a little *wild*; – but it is only those who are indiscriminately diffuse – and form a low connection [...] who are considered as overstepping the modesty of marriage'. Indeed, the custom of infidelity is so firmly entrenched that there 'is no convincing a woman here – that she is in the smallest degree deviating from the rule of right or the fitness of things – in having an "Amoroso".'[28] In fact, Byron concludes dryly, the 'greatest sin seems to lie in concealing it – or in having more than one – that is – unless such an extension of the prerogative is understood & approved by the prior claimant'.[29]

While spousal fidelity was of little consequence, loyalty to one's lover is of paramount importance. Byron was shocked at the 'awful notions of constancy' demanded in Italy. 'I have seen some ancient figures of eighty pointed out as Amorosi of forty, fifty, and sixty years standing', he exclaims, appalled at the idea of an adulterous liaison with all the rigid and intractable permanence of marriage.[30] Caught straying himself, Byron discovered that male lovers are deemed 'perfidious' if they 'look at anybody's wife except [their] Neighbours'.[31] Errant women likewise faced censure, as he illustrates in a note to friend and fellow poet Thomas Moore describing a 'row the other night' when a woman was exposed for infidelity – not to her husband but to her *cavalier servente*. 'Great scandal', Byron writes with relish, 'planted by her lover – *to be* thrashed by her husband for inconstancy to her regular Servente [...] all the women furious against her'.[32]

Correspondents were left in no doubt that Byron infinitely preferred the Italian sociosexual customs (and the Italian women) to those of 'that tight little island' he had left behind.[33] 'All this will appear strange to you who do not understand the Meridian morality – nor our way of life in such respects', Byron writes to Murray in 1819.[34] The calculated use of 'our' highlights his own adoption of local sociosexual mores, carnal customs which he learnt from (and practiced with) adulterous women of every class from 'the fisherman's wife – up to the Nobil Donna'.[35] The following sections will look at the three most significant affairs which Byron had whilst in Italy: that with Marianna Segati, the wife of his Venetian landlord (a merchant draper); the more casual liaison with Margarita Cogni, a rural baker's wife; and finally the 'unlawful union' with Teresa Guiccioli, a 'Romagnuala Countess'.[36]

'La Bel Sangre' – *Marianna Segati*

When Byron first arrived in Venice in November 1816, he took lodgings in Calla de Piscina 1673, close to the magnificent Piazza San Marco. 'I have got some extremely good apartments in the house of a "Merchant of Venice",' he informs Thomas Moore.[37] This 'Merchant' was a draper, Pietro Segati, 'who is a good deal occupied with business, and has a wife in her twenty-second year'. This is the first extant mention of Marianna Segati, whom Byron elsewhere describes as 'by far the prettiest woman I have seen here'.[38] He concludes his letter with the exciting information that 'I have fallen in love, which, next to falling into the canal (which would be of no use, as I can swim), is the best or the worst thing I could do'.[39]

A week later, and the enraptured Byron is waxing even more lyrical to John Murray – Marianna is his 'Goddess' and he is 'in love – fathomless love'.[40] 'Our little arrangement is completed', he writes smugly, 'the usual oaths have been taken – and everything fulfilled according to the "understood relations" of such liaisons'.[41] In a subsequent letter, he gleefully tells Murray that he manages to have sex with her every day, under her husband's nose, 'receiving from one to three (and occasionally an extra or so) pretty unequivocal proofs of mutual good contentment'.[42]

Describing his 'proper liaison' with Marianna to his friend and factotum Douglas Kinnaird, Byron explains that because she 'is married' their 'arrangement was formed according to the incontinent Continental system'.[43] In another letter he offers further details of this 'system', explaining that 'a *relazione* or *amicizia* seems to be a regular affair from five to fifteen years – at which point if there occurs a widowhood – it finishes by a *sposalizio*' (wedding).[44] 'The Italian ethics are the most singular ever met with', he muses:

> It is not that they do not consider the thing itself [adultery] wrong, but *love* (the *sentiment* of love) is not merely an excuse for it but makes it an *actual virtue*, provided it is disinterested and not a *caprice*, and is confined to one object.[45]

Certainly, Marianna was happy to become his 'Donna' or mistress, and her husband appears to have been remarkably indifferent to what was occurring under his own roof, suggesting that such practices were – if not expected, then certainly commonplace. Byron reinforces this impression, writing that although 'Segati [...] must have known that I made love to Marianna', his friends should not to be 'alarmed' because 'jealousy is not the order of the day in Venice, and daggers are out of fashion, while duels, on love matters, are unknown – at least, with the husbands'.[46]

Yet Byron, despite his display of urbanity, was not quite as suave as he pretended. He was deeply mortified when the cuckolded Segatti burst into Byron's room one night to find Marianna 'fainting upon a sofa' surrounded by 'all the apparatus of confusion, dishevelled hair, hats, [and] handkerchiefs [...] and the lady as pale as ashes' following a violent lovers' quarrel.[47] The cause of this quarrel, Byron admits ruefully to Thomas Moore, was an illicit meeting with Marianna's sister-in-law, 'a well-looking [...] girl of about nineteen'. She had snuck into Byron's apartments that morning and they were just getting to know each other:

> when, lo! in a very few minutes in marches, to my very great astonishment, Marianna S * *, in propriâ personâ, and, after making a most polite curtsy to her sister-in-law and to me, without a single word seizes her said sister-in-law by the hair, and bestows upon her some sixteen slaps, which would have made your ear ache only to hear their echo. I need not describe the screaming which ensued. The luckless visitor took flight.[48]

Byron 'seized Marianna', who 'fairly went into fits in [his] arms and, in spite of reasoning, eau de Cologne, vinegar, half a pint of water, and God knows what other waters beside, continued so till past midnight'.[49] At this point her husband arrives and a discomfited Byron is forced to awkwardly dissemble.

This farcical scene, reminiscent of a Restoration cuckolding comedy, draws attention to a crucial feature of the 'proper liaison' or '*amicizia*' in which Byron was currently involved – namely that while the affair might not be permanent, there was an expectation that it be 'confined to one object' for its duration. Marianna had seen her sister-in-law's gondola nearby and, jealously protective of her 'amoroso', had stealthily returned 'to perpetrate this piece of pugilism'.[50] In his descriptions of Marianna's keen-eyed suspicion and furious response, Byron conveys the impression that Italian women are fiercely protective of their sexual property, shielding it from depredations by other women. This possessiveness is also visible in the fervid undercurrent of violence which pervades their protestations of passion; Byron frequently displays a sort of perplexed admiration at the intensity of his mistresses' emotions, their 'excessive attachment' visible in phrases such as 'I would go for you into the midst of a hundred *knives*' and 'I wish you well even to killing'.[51]

Yet Byron, despite 'swearing innocence, eternal constancy, &c. &c.', was almost constitutionally incapable of fidelity and unable to resist a pretty woman.[52] He gleefully writes to Murray of how one of his other paramours came face to face 'with la Signora Segati – who was silly enough one evening [...] to threaten her'. However, Margarita Cogni, a fiercer opponent than Marianna's easily vanquished sister-in-law, was uncowed:

> Margarite threw back her veil (*fazzilo*) and replied in very explicit Venetian – '*You* are *not* his *wife* – and *I* am *not* his *wife* – *you* are his Donna – and *I* am his *donna* – *your* husband is a cuckold – and mine is another; – for the rest, what *right* have you *to* reproach me? If he prefers what is mine, to what is yours – is it my fault? If you wish to secure him – tie him to your

> petticoat string – but do not think to speak to me without a reply because you happen to be richer than I am.[53]

Byron was amused by this 'pretty piece of eloquence' from the woman he called 'La Fornarina', and seems rather flattered by the idea of two women fighting over him before an entranced crowd.

This incident reiterates Marianna's possessiveness and expectation that her lover would be faithful to her for the duration of their affair. It also emphasises her perception of other women as a threat to her sexual property and her willingness to confront those she viewed as trespassers upon her carnal preserve. Margarita seems to share this conceptualisation of the female rights of sexual conquest. 'If you wish to secure him – tie him to your petticoat string', she shouts at her rival, casting Byron as a passive object in a purely female conflict. The casual, gossipy style of the letter makes it easy to envisage the bourgeois Marianna, confronted by an Amazonian virago exposing her matrimonial indiscretions to a packed marketplace, retreating in embarrassed confusion.

'Wild as a Witch' – *Margarita Cogni*

Margarita Cogni, taken from author's own 1st edition of *Finden's Byron Beauties; or, the Principal Female Characters in Lord Byron's Poems* (1835).

Byron first met Margarita, the wife of a rural baker, in August 1817. He and a visiting university friend, John Cam Hobhouse, had retreated to the rural village of La Mira to escape the fetid Venetian summer. In a letter to John Murray, Byron recounts how they were 'sauntering on horseback along the Brenta one evening' when they caught sight of two pretty women.[54] Though his mistress Marianna was also staying nearby, Byron was unable to resist the charms of this 'very tall and formidable Girl of three and twenty – with the large black eyes and handsome face of a pretty fiend'.[55] He and Hobhouse propositioned the two women and Margarita responded 'that she had no objection to make love with me – as she was married – and all married women did it'. Unfortunately for Hobhouse, however, her unmarried companion 'took fright [...] at not being married – for here no woman will do anything under except adultery'.[56] The affair lasted a few weeks and then Byron resumed his travels around Italy, leaving the baker's wife behind.

Byron returned to Marianna and his lodgings in the Segati household in the autumn, when the cooler weather ensured Venice's canals ran clean once more and the city was less noisome. By early 1818 he had tired of both his bourgeois mistress and his humble lodgings, and decided to move into a rather grander abode – taking apartments in the Palazzo Mocenigo overlooking the Grand Canal. Margarita soon followed because, Byron explains, once 'she found herself out to be a favourite she came [to Venice] pretty often'.[57] Occasionally, when she arrived to find another woman *in situ* (Byron 'being at that time somewhat promiscuous'), there would be a scene of 'great confusion – and demolition of head dresses and kerchiefs' as rivals were ousted.[58] Unlike Marianna, she paid no attention to her lover's exploits in her absence. For 'two years – in the course of which I had more women than I can count or recount – she was the only one who preserved over me an ascendency', Byron boasts to Murray, 'as she used to say publicly – "it don't matter – he may have five hundred – but he will always come back to me"'.[59]

However, while less jealous than the bourgeois Marianna, Margarita was equally prone to the violent displays of fierce passion which the poet presents as characteristic of Italian women. He describes her as 'wild as a witch – and fierce as a demon', possessing an animalistic intensity he found extremely attractive.[60] One night, when he was caught in a storm out on the lagoon, he returned to find her standing in the rain awaiting his return and looking 'like Medea alighted from her chariot' with 'lightning flashing round her' and 'waves rolling at her feet'. 'Her joy at seeing me again was moderately mixed with ferocity, and gave me the idea of a tigress', he writes flippantly, though her welcome was disconcertingly tempered with insults. 'Can' della Madonna', she shouted at him angrily, 'Dog of the Virgin'.[61] Margarita's fervid intensity was intoxicating and much more erotic than the pallid frigidity of Byron's former English lovers. 'I like this kind of animal', he writes ruminatively, 'and I am sure I should have preferred Medea to any woman that ever breathed'.[62] Though undoubtedly alluring, however, such ferocity was also slightly unnerving. Byron confesses to Thomas Moore that he is more than half convinced that if he 'put a poniard into' Margarita's hand, 'she would plunge it where I told her – and into *me* if I offended her'.[63]

One day, Margarita decided to leave her husband and move into the Palazzo Mocenigo on a permanent basis. Byron writes ruefully in one letter that he is 'a little embarrassed with [his] unexpected acquisition' and explains how it came about:

> The chaste wife of a baker – having quarrelled with her tyrannical husband – has run away *to* me – (God knows without being invited) & resists all the tears & penitence & beg-pardons of her disconsolate Lord – and the threats of the police – and priest of the parish besides & swears she wont give up her unlawful love (myself) for anybody – or anything – I assure you I have begged her in all possible ways to go back to her husband – promising her all kinds of eternal fidelity into the bargain but she only flies into a fury [...] As the morals of the place are very lax – all the women commend her & say she has done right.[64]

Here again the poet suggests that such behaviour was normal in Italian society. However, in stark contrast to the censorious condemnation of writers such as Lady Morgan, Byron's tone is one of appreciative amusement, presenting this 'lax' morality as an endless source of humorous anecdotes as well as sexual gratification.

Indeed, Margarita is the inspiration for some of Byron's funniest letters, from his laudatory description of her unspoilt figure ('a great desideration in a hot climate where they grow relaxed and doughy and *flumpity*'),[65] to the accounts of her vain insistence on peacocking about in the 'hat and feathers' of a fine noblewoman rather than the *fazziolo* veil worn by 'the lower orders'. Byron 'put the first in the fire' but 'got tired of burning them before she did of buying them'.[66] One of his most provocative anecdotes concerns her extreme religiousity; 'I forgot to mention that she was very devout', he informs John Murray slyly, 'and would cross herself if she heard prayer-time strike', even during lovemaking 'when the ceremony did not appear to be much in unison with what she was then about'.[67]

Eventually, Margarita's histrionics palled, particularly as she became more jealous, beating Byron's other women and stealing his letters (even though she could not read) because she suspected they came from potential rivals. When Byron issues her congé, she responds with a typically 'devilish spirit', 'threatening knives and revenge', breaking into the Palazzo, and even throwing 'herself into the Canal' in a highly melodramatic suicide attempt which, as Byron points out dryly, was a somewhat meaningless gesture in a city where she and every other inhabitant swam extremely well.[68]

'Strictest Adultery' – *Teresa Guiccioli*

Shortly after dispensing with Margarita's leonine charms, Byron embarks on the longest and most significant of his Italian liaisons. He first met the newly married Countess Teresa Guiccioli in January 1818, but it was not until April 1819 when they met again that he fully appreciated her appeal. 'I have fallen in love with a

Teresa Guicolli, taken from author's own 1st edition of *Finden's Byron Beauties; or, the Principal Female Characters in Lord Byron's Poems* (1835).

Romagnuala Countess from Ravenna who is nineteen years old and has a count of fifty', he tells Hobhouse.[69] In a surprisingly temperate letter from a man in the grip of passion, he describes her as 'very pretty' but also 'a great Coquette – extremely vain – excessively affected – clever enough – without the smallest principle – with a good deal of imagination and some passion'.[70]

Byron and Teresa enjoyed a heady fling of just ten days, and Byon sends Hobhouse titillating details of how he 'consummated' this 'unlawful union with all the proper rites' in a gondola.[71] However, Teresa's inexperience in 'the laudable practice of lovemaking' saw her make so many indiscrete comments that her husband eventually swept her back to their estates in Ravenna. Byron, seemingly indifferent, immediately resumed relations with his old bedmates that same day (though he continued to send ardent love letters to Teresa). Their dalliance would probably have ended there if not for the fact that in Ravenna, as Byron subsequently discovered, 'the good old Italian custom' of *cicisbeism* was still widely practised.[72]

Thus, when Teresa fell ill and begged for Byron, her husband dutifully sends for him. Although Byron sets off to Ravenna immediately, this apparent display of devotion is undermined by the fretful letter he sends Lord Kinnaird (Douglas's rakish older brother). 'What the deuce should I do without the possibility [...] of seeing her to any purpose in her present state', he writes pettishly, frustrated by the enforced celibacy resulting from Teresa's miscarriage.[73] Following her recovery, he returned to Venice. However, Teresa immediately fell ill again and Byron was recalled to Ravenna once more; on this occasion, as he coyly informs Lord Kinnaird, her sickness did not prevent them having sex immediately upon his arrival.

Byron was soon installed in the Guiccioli palazzo as Teresa's formally recognised *cicisbeo*, with, to his profound surprise, her husband Alessandro's grudging permission. He clearly found this dynamic rather unsettling, perplexed both by the fact that Teresa's family 'naturally considered [him] as her relation' and by the fact that Alessandro not only tolerated his presence but actively sought it, inviting him on carriage rides and condoning his move into the conjugal home.[74] More confusing still was Teresa's insistence on openly flaunting Byron in Ravenna society. 'The G's object appeared to be to parade her foreign lover as much as possible – and faith – if she seemed to glory in the Scandal – it is not for me to be ashamed of it', Byron writes, bemused that 'nobody seems surprised – all the women on the contrary were as it were delighted with the excellent example'.[75] This cultural acceptance of adultery is illustrated by Teresa's response when Byron gave her a beautiful diamond broach. Rather than cherishing it secretly as a precious token of illicit (and illegal) love, she returns it to him with *her own hair* in it (I shall *not* say *which part* but *that* is an Italian custom), he tells Kinnaird with suggestive coyness.[76] This was not the first time Byron had received a lover's pubic hair (Lady Caroline Lamb's can still be found in the John Murray collection at Albemarle Street in London, blood stained from where she had cut too close to the skin), but to receive it encased in 'a broach of brilliants' was something new.

He writes to Teresa shortly after arriving in Ravenna, begging her to 'instruct' him in how 'to behave in these circumstances' because he is 'not clear as to what it is best to do'.[77] A quick learner, Byron's letters are soon full of information and anecdotes, as he regales his correspondents back in London with salacious gossip about high society life in a city which 'preserves perhaps more of the old Italian manners than any city in Italy' and all the women 'make love a good deal'.[78] However, he notes warningly in another letter, this amatory 'system has its rules – and its fitnesses – and decorums – so as to be reduced to a kind of discipline – or game at hearts – which admits few deviations unless you wish to lose it'.[79]

For example, married women 'always wait a year' before selecting a *cicisbeo*,[80] and are typically only allowed one lover (anyone who 'has more than the usual Staff establishment of Aides de *Cons*' is considered 'somewhat *capricious*', Byron writes knowledgably).[81] Equally, a wife without a lover is something of a novelty; Byron writes to Hobhouse with news of 'a Sposa Fiorentina – a pretty Girl yet in abeyance – but no one can yet decide who is to be her Servente – most of the men being already adultered – and she is showing no preferences to any who are not'.[82] This anecdote presents female infidelity as less a social nicety and more a social necessity, and there is an impression of communal concern regarding the selection of a new wife's *cicisbeo*. Thus, when urged to abandon her English lover, Teresa allegedly responds, 'It is hard that I should be the only woman in Romagna who is not to have her *Amico*'.[83]

Byron ascribes this standardised promiscuity to the marriages arranged between very young women and much older men. 'The reason is that they marry for their parents and love for themselves. – They exact fidelity from a lover as a debt of honour – while they pay the husband as a tradesman'. So common was the practice that when Teresa's husband Alessandro became jealous and sought an annulment, everyone was apparently shocked by his behaviour – so out of keeping with regional practices. In a letter to Murray, Byron smugly recounts how everyone is 'furious *against him* [Alessandro] – for his conduct – & his not wishing to be cuckold at *three score* – when every [one] else is at *one*'.[84]

'That Amatory Appendage' – The Cicisbeo

In his 1818 poem *Beppo*, written while living in Venice, Byron coyly alludes to the practice of *cicisbeism*. The titular hero of the poem, following a long absence during which he was kidnapped and enslaved in Turkey, returns to Venice to find his lovely wife Laura (believing him dead) had fallen in love with another man. Husband, wife, and the 'vice-husband' (also described as a 'supernumerary slave') live in amiable harmony thereafter. Byron's phrase 'supernumerary slave' is apt for, while not arduous, the duties of the *cavalier servente* were undoubtedly tediously subservient, whiling away the hours with fawning flattery and minor acts of submissive devotion, 'a flatter of fiddlers and a fan-carrier' as Byron phrases it.[85]

He was initially amused to learn that, as Teresa's *cicisbeo*, he was expected to escort her to *conversazione* and balls, where he should take care of her shawl and stand respectfully behind her chair until she chose to leave – at which point he was supposed to lovingly dispose the shawl about her shoulders; 'I am drilling very hard to learn how to double a Shawl, and should succeed to admiration – if I did not always double it the wrong side out – and then I sometimes confuse and bring away two – so as to put all the Serventi out – besides keeping their *Servite* in the cold', he writes on one occasion.[86] He announces on another that 'I double a shawl with considerable alacrity – but have not yet arrived at the perfection of putting it on the right way – and I hand in and out and know my post in a *Conversazione*'.[87]

Although Byron undoubtedly relished the comedic nature of this inherently ambiguous position, and despite his eager adoption of Italian customs (and the sexual perks they facilitated), he also viewed the *cicisbeism* tradition as undignified and emasculating. These sentiments are reflected in the increasingly bitter tenor of his letters. He writes a lengthy complaint to Hobhouse in which he admits that, while 'not tired of Italy', he is wearied by his position; 'a man must be a Cicisbeo and a singer in duets and a Connoisseur of operas – or nothing here – I have made some progress in all these accomplishments – but I cant say I don't feel the degradation'. 'I like women', he continues unnecessarily (Hobhouse being well aware of his friend's amorous propensities), 'but the more their system here develops upon me – the worse it seems'.[88]

He paints a picture of his mistress as fervidly jealous – even of her own maidservants and the series of nursery maids hired to care for Byron's illegitimate daughter Allegra (insisting each one is 'uglier than the other').[89] That being said, Teresa's suspicions were not unfounded; just two months after his arrival, Byron dispatches a 'precious epistle of Gossip' to John Cam Hobhouse describing two young women he had his eye on, both friends of his mistress: Gertrude Vicain ('a very pretty woman') and 'Ursula – Something – one of the prettiest creatures I ever saw'.[90] Detected 'in an illicit squeezing of hands', however, 'the friend was whisked off' and Byron soundly scolded.[91]

Following this, his letters to England become increasingly full of complaints about Teresa's expectations of 'incontinent fidelity',[92] and he repeatedly complains that Italian women:

> are extremely tenacious – and jealous as furies – not permitting their Lovers even to marry if they can help it – and keeping them always close to them in public as in private whenever they can. – In short they transfer marriage to adultery – and strike the *not* out of that commandment.[93]

Of course, Byron being Byron, even when in the grip of indignation he displays a ready appreciation of the ridiculous, regaling his correspondents with tales of how Teresa's suspicions even extended to the appallingly ugly mistress of his devoted manservant Fletcher. However, the ludicrousness of his situation in no way mitigated his dissatisfaction at the subordinate role he now inhabited, reduced to a mere 'piece of female property'.[94] 'I feel & and feel it bitterly – that a man should not consume his life at the side and on the bosom – of a woman', he writes mournfully to Hobhouse, 'even the recompense and it is much – is not enough – and that this Cicisbean existence is to be condemned'.[95]

Although his letters start to linger on wistful thoughts of going home, Byron never did return to England. Instead, perhaps in response to his feelings of emasculation, he abandoned Italy (and Teresa) in 1823, travelling to Greece where he hoped to support in the Greek War of Independence against the Ottoman invaders.

'I Suspect I Know a Thing or Two About Italy'

Byron's vividly rendered letters from Italy might have been slyly satirical, mocking both his own hedonism and his readers' entrenched assumptions about foreign climes in general and those of Italy in particular, yet they reveal a unique appreciation of the country he had chosen to make his home. In this, they were drastically different in tone and topic from other contemporary travelogue accounts written by the British aristocratic elite. Both 'inside Italy and Italian life, and self-consciously outside', Byron's letters contain fascinating insights into the sociosexual customs surrounding Italian infidelity.[96] The self-exiled poet was proud of his uniquely privileged status as a quasi-naturalised Italian, and bragged of it on a number of occasions:

> I suspect I know a thing or two about Italy – more than Lady Morgan has picked up in her posting. What do Englishmen know of Italians beyond their museums and saloons [...]? Now I have lived in the heart of their houses, in parts of Italy freshest and least influenced by strangers, Italy – have seen and become [...] a portion of their hopes, and fears, and passions, and am almost inoculated into a family.[97]

After all, he admits with masculine pride, 'I am in the case to know more of them than most Englishmen', having 'lived among the natives' as both an 'amico di casa' and the '"Amica di cuore" of the Dama'.[98] It is therefore a shame that Byron did not create the 'volume of manners, &c. – on Italy' and the 'amicizia' which Murray requested.[99] It would undoubtedly have been a riotous and illuminating read. At least we have his lively letters, delightfully frank on the topic of 'honest liaisons' and 'fair fucking', and full of detailed descriptions of the differences between 'strictest adultery' and mere '*fuff-fuff*'.

Chapter 13

'I maintained my opinion – like a woman, and an obstinate one too': The Countess of Blessington, the Female Nude, and a Woman's Right to Gaze

Eleanor Reynolds

Marguerite, Countess of Blessington by Thomas Lawrence, 1822.

In her account of her time in Florence, the Countess of Blessington (1789–1849) shows her appreciation of a culture vastly different to her own, particularly in its artistic presentation of women, and shows how she navigated her experience in the presence of her male companions. She was a writer and salonnière. In 1822, she and her husband took a journey to the Continent and spent most of that decade in Italy and France. She kept a journal throughout this period and would publish it, years later, as *The Idler in Italy*.[1] Travelling to Italy broadened her mind, but it also highlighted differences in culture that made her aware of her restricted female gaze as determined by her upbringing. In writing about her time in Florence, the Countess of Blessington wove her knowledge of history and popular culture into her descriptions of architecture, painting and sculpture. Her account is of particular interest as it is a British woman's response to the various depictions of Venus, which Florence was famous for, and sheds light on eighteenth-century female narrative, women's interest and the female gaze.

The Countess of Blessington was born Margaret 'Sally' Power in 1788 in County Tipperary, Ireland. Her father was a corn merchant and local magistrate, famous for his violent temper and overly ruffled shirts.[2] He would later appear satirised in his daughter's novel *The Governess*, published in 1839, as the Irish baron at the Williamson's dinner table 'whose pedigree was longer than his rental and better filled than his purse.'[3] Margaret was quiet and bookish, and entertained her more boisterous siblings with stories, a skill that she would earn her living from later in life. After a nightmarish first marriage to the abusive Captain Maurice St. Leger Farmer, she married the Earl of Blessington, an Irish landowner, in 1818 when she became a widow and changed her name to Marguerite.[4] After visiting the Earl's estates in Dublin, the newly married couple rented a house in St James Square, London, and the Countess began her career as a renowned salonnière. Salons were places where women of rank could hold court, inviting writers, politicians and artists to discuss their work. A woman could establish herself in thinking society by acting as a hostess to these famous men, and the Countess of Blessington formed close friendships during this time that would help further her literary career twenty years on. Early biographers paint her as a woman of loose morals, taking gossip columns and the opinions of people who did not like her as their sources.[5] Richard Robert Madden published his biography in 1855, six years after the Countess of Blessington's death, assuring his readers of his credentials as biographer thanks to 'an intimate acquaintance and uninterrupted friendship' of twenty-seven years.[6] Even so, he could not resist writing with disapproval of the Earl's extravagant spending and patronising 'poor Lady Blessington' for being childish, pleased with the new furnishing her husband arranged in their Paris apartment in 1828.[7] Susan Matoff's recent biography paints the Countess of Blessington in a different and truer light and examines her writing – her letters, journals and the novels she published – to paint a picture of a well-read woman who was not afraid to form her own opinions. In her novels – the first being *The Repealers*, published in 1833, and the last *Country Quarters*, published six months after her death in 1849 – the Countess of Blessington gave readers what they wanted: a satirical view of high society couched in dramatic stories of love and scandal, set in grand houses and bursting with descriptions of fine clothes and expensive jewels. Her eye for detail and sharp humour made her travel journals equally entertaining.

In August 1822, the Countess of Blessington, her husband, the Earl of Blessington and her sister, Mary Ann Power, set off on a tour of Italy and France, a journey that would take them much of that decade. They took the ferry from Dover on 27 August 1822 during a rough crossing which, she noted in her journal, was full of 'sundry waves, so judiciously applied, as to drench several of the pale voyagers, who in revenge returned the visits far more offensively.'[8]

After a twelve-day stay in Paris where their preparations for departure caused a passing Frenchman to comment that they had enough baggage for a regiment,[9] they travelled through Geneva, Zurich, Lyons and Vienna, visited Lord Byron in Genoa, and arrived in Florence in June 1823. The Countess of Blessington recounted her days, the places she visited and the people she saw in simple, straightforward language. She rarely digressed into description and apologised to the reader when she did, writing:

> I had made a vow never to attempt a description of scenery, however it might have charmed me; for all descriptions that I ever read, however accurate they may have been, have generally produced only a vague, indistinct mass of images on my brain, rather fatiguing than gratifying.[10]

At the Benedictine Abbey in Rouen, which they visited 28 August 1822, she was shown a manuscript which a monk had spent thirty years decorating and observed later in her journal, 'What a waste of time!'[11] This straightforward, honest way of writing is surprising, making it all the more entertaining because it, no doubt, shocked readers who might have expected countesses to have more lofty opinions. It also makes her journal invaluable as a tool for obtaining greater insight into the unchecked opinions of women at the time.

In her writing on art, bodies and nudity, the Countess of Blessington showed an appreciation of the skill of painters and sculptures to capture the human form. Her wide reading, both historical and literary, gave her an introductory knowledge to the art she would see on her travels through the Continent so that, in her journal, she was able both to consider works of art within the period in which they were created and to analyse her own reaction to them in light of contemporary culture. Her account of a day passed in the sculpture galleries at the Louvre during her stay in Paris, 8 September 1822,[12] is an early example of the insightful writing that permeates *The Idler in Italy*. She compares the 'conscious bashfulness' of Venus with the 'cold, haughty, fearless' statue of Diana, ending, 'One hardly knows to which to yield the palm.'[13] The statue of Diana, she goes on to say, is 'not masculine; with all of woman's beauty, and none of its effeminacy' and concludes that both these forms show 'a nature far superior to that which we behold, because unspoilt by tight-lacing or compression.'[14] Her writing frequently shows that she had a clear idea of how she thought women should be: ambassadors of their sex without being insipid. In her novels, too, she created superior female protagonists, such as Clara in *The Governess* whose patience and good breeding wins over both her unruly students and the servants who are determined to dislike her. She concluded her account of her visit to the Louvre:

> It has frequently occurred to me that the sculptors of antiquity had an advantage in practising their art, denied to, or, at least, rarely possessed by, those of our own time. I refer to the physiognomies of that epoch; the expressions o [sic] which were more simple and concentrated than at present. Enough civilization then existed to admit of all the graceful adjuncts of decoration in the costumes, and in the care of the persons of their subjects, which is required to form a fine work; yet originality of expression, or peculiarity of tournure, was not impaired by the mannerism of fashion, or the insipidity of imitation, which in our days render so many people alike. The passions, too, were then more powerful, and consequently more strikingly developed in the countenances, than now; when affectation, engendered by extreme civilization, and nurtured by a false refinement, has much deteriorated natural expression. Women dared to frown or smile then, without remembering the effect of either movement of the muscles on their beauty. Now they seldom exceed a simper, and even this only when they have good teeth.[15]

The comic effect of this passage encourages the reader to forgive the criticism at the heart of it. Her journal gives an indication of the importance of beauty in the 1820s and how it had changed over time. There is no doubt that she was an exceptional woman who, frequently in her diary, expounded on the merit of intelligence over beauty. As shall be discussed later in this chapter, she often disparaged the less well-read women that she met and displayed an impatience with her own sex.

The Countess of Blessington kept her journal throughout the period in which she and her husband travelled on the Continent, which began with their departure from Dover in August 1822 and ended in Paris in November 1830 following the Earl of Blessington's death from apoplexy on 25 May 1829.[16] Widowed for the second time, and left an allowance of only £2,000 a year, she returned to London and began to earn money through her writing. *The Idler in Italy* was published in 1839, and notes of her time in France followed in 1840 as *The Idler in France*. Women travellers wrote more in their letters and journals about clean beds and well-cooked food than their male companions[17] and the Countess of Blessington's journal was no exception. In France, she praised the cuisine and the comfortable beds, adding, 'But defend me from the slamming of French doors, and the shaking of French windows.'[18] In Florence, she was grateful for the good weather, to be able to sit out of doors in the evening without a shawl when, 'In England a catarrh or rheumatism would be the inevitable result of such an imprudence.'[19] She blended accounts of her visits to places of interest with descriptions of the famous people she met. During the two months she and her husband spent in Genoa, they frequently rode and dined with Lord Byron. On recounting her first meeting with Byron on 1 April 1823, she wrote, 'I have seen Lord Byron and am disappointed!'[20] going on, wittily, to explain, 'the sublime passages in "Childe Harold" and "Manfred" cannot be associated in my mind with the lively, brilliant conversationist that I this day saw…he does not look like my preconceived notion of the melancholy poet.'[21] The diary entry for this day typifies her superb writing, her eye for detail and an understanding of what her readers wanted: an intimate account of Lord Byron's appearance and personality. She even knew how to poke fun at herself for the entertainment of the reader, concluding: 'I never will again allow myself to form an ideal of any person I desire to see, for disappointment never fails to ensue.'[22] Yet beyond capturing the superficial excitement of this first encounter with a celebrity, it is clear that she was acutely perceptive in her assessment of the people she met. On hearing Byron talk disparagingly of England, she wrote in her journal, 'Why talk so much and so continually of his country, if he felt that indifference, nay, hatred, to it, which he professes?'[23] She would go on to publish her *Conversations of Lord Byron* in 1834, which documents the two months she spent in the poet's society. They left Genoa on 2 June 1823, Byron bidding them such a tearful goodbye that she noted: 'the very idea that I shall not see him again overpowers me with sadness, and makes me forget many defects which had often disenchanted me with him'[24]. After breaking their journey in Lucca, they arrived in Florence on 8 June 1823.

With the exception of the time the family lived in Naples, where they stayed for two and a half years, Florence was the city they spent the longest period of time in; they stayed for the month of June in 1823, then returned, after their time in Naples, from March until December in 1826, and again in 1827 from June to November. The Countess of Blessington particularly enjoyed the city out of season when, in June, '[a]ll the world, that is to say the fashionable world' left for the surrounding villas and baths and she had the galleries to herself.[25] In her account of Florence, she visited all the places of interest listed in the contemporary guidebooks: the Laurentian Library, the Church of Santa Croce, Florence's Cathedral, the Church of Santa Maria Novella and the Palazzo Pitti.[26] Writing in her journal almost every day, she composed detailed descriptions of objects of beauty and decadence that other writers might have thought too trivial or time-consuming to mention. She had a discerning eye, noting with wry humour, 'the admiration of my sex for such gems' when she described some fifteenth-century jewelled vases by Cellini which she 'more than once wished that they were safely lodged in a certain antique cabinet, in a certain boudoir, in a certain mansion, in St. James' Square.'[27] British people were especially fond of Florence because the streets were clean and the Florentines reminded them of British people.[28] While in Genoa, she had complained of the 'pale and squalid mendicants' who sat outside the palaces and other places of interest to tourists,[29] yet she commented with delight that Florentine men 'are only to be distinguished from my countrymen by a greater display of politeness than the latter generally exhibit'.[30] They dressed *à l'Anglaise* and, much to her admiration, held their hats off their heads during conversation. Unlike most travellers, who went straight to the galleries to view the treasures listed in their guidebooks,[31] the Countess of Blessington delayed her visit to the Uffizi until her second week, preferring to walk through the streets 'until the effect of the first novelty of this place has subsided.'[32] She expounded the merits of travel to broadening the mind and showed a real love for Florence, the surrounding countryside,[33] and its people.[34] Even when she went to see galleries, she liked to think of herself as above the general rabble of tourists, those other women who talked loudly about art 'with all the gusto of amateurs',[35] and was pleased when, in June, they all left the city for the cooler surrounding countryside so that she could enjoy the art galleries in peace.

Florence had long been associated with the goddess Venus, and the statue of the Venus de' Medici and Titian's painting Venus of Urbino were at the top of all visitors' sight-seeing lists.[36] The Countess of Blessington saw both the

Venus of Urbino, Titian, 1538, Uffizi Gallery.

Venus de' Medici and Titian's painting Venus of Urbino at the Uffizi on 14 June 1823 and wrote in her journal:

> Much as I have been accustomed to see good casts from the statue, the Medicean Venus surprised as well as charmed me. There is a purity, a modesty in this inimitable work, that precludes the feelings of embarrassment with which women contemplate a nude statue in the presence of men. It is the personification of ideal loveliness, refined and spiritualized from every indication of human passion, coldly, chastely beautiful. Not so is the celebrated picture of the Venus by Titian, which is placed immediately behind it, forming a violent contrast to its celestial-looking neighbour. This glowing picture is all of earth, its beauty being wholly voluptuous, unredeemed by any expression of intellectual refinement.[37]

Such instances noted in her journal encapsulate the female gaze within the confines of early nineteenth-century discourse. In mentioning her male companions, the countess articulated her sense of unease when viewing sexualised representations of women in the presence of the opposite sex, as if their presence removed her right to gaze. Her categorisation of nudes as modest or voluptuous seems to have been informed by her varying emotional responses when looking at paintings and statues of naked women and, in particular, the embarrassment she experienced when she viewed more sexualised forms of women in the presence of men. She concluded her diary entry for the day most insightfully: 'The Venus de' Medici must always charm women; the Venus of Titian, men.'[38]

This feeling of a restricted right to gaze in the presence of men forms one of the Countess of Blessington's key complaints during her visit to the *Gabinetto Fisico*, the Museum of Physics and Natural History, nicknamed 'La Specola', on 21 June 1823. The Anatomical Venuses were built by the wax modeller Clemente Susini from 1780 up until his death in 1814. By the time of the Countess of Blessington's visit in 1823, the workshop had ceased production of new models and the anatomical collection on display was the same as it is today.[39] Lying on pink silk cushions in rosewood cases, the Anatomical Venuses displayed various bodily organs through their open torsos while the rest of the body – their arms, legs and faces – remained intact. False eyes and hair were added, these models assuming the appearance of life-like women. Their morbid beauty fascinated and bewildered viewers. In a town already replete with famous paintings and statues of the goddess, Rebecca Messbarger posits that the first female anatomical model made at La Specola was called the Medici Venus as a way of drawing a crowd, putting the museum on the list of places for people to see by linking this model in their minds with the others that they saw at the

Uffizi.[40] The Countess of Blessington, herself, visited with a female companion and was shocked to see men and women contemplating the exhibits together.

> 21st. I entered the Gabinetto Fisico to-day, and though I only remained a few minutes in it, I carried away a sense of loathing that has not yet left me. Surely some restriction should exist to preclude women and men from examining these models together! I entered with a female companion only, but retreated when I observed men and women, some of them, too, young ones, contemplating objects which, although highly useful for scientific purposes, are certainly of a character unfit for this promiscuous exhibition. It is meet that we should know that we are fearfully and wonderfully created; but not that we should witness the disgusting details of the animal economy in all its hideous and appalling nakedness and truth. What a lesson for personal vanity does this exhibition convey! Yet probably few view it in this light. For me, I fear that its fearful images will recur to my memory when I behold some creature, in the zenith of youth and beauty, who almost believes she is not formed of the perilous stuff so shockingly delineated in the Gabinetto Fisico.[41]

Her response to the anatomical exhibition is honest and far less pretentious than Louise Elisabeth Vigée Le Brun's who, in 1792, wrote, 'It is not possible to contemplate the structure of the human body without feeling convinced of some divine power. Despite what a few miserable philosophers have dared to say, in M. Fontana's laboratory one kneels and believes.'[42] As official portraitist to Queen Marie Antoinette, Le Brun's recorded response to the exhibition conveys her desire, as an artist, to show that she understood the importance of the collection and was not overcome by disgust. The Countess of Blessington, by her own admission, was not an expert in art or anatomy. In fact, she expressed her impatience with other visitors to the galleries who criticised the objects on view in order to show off their own knowledge.[43] Writing in the 1820s, the Countess of Blessington was very aware of her gaze and the extent to which she could make use of it within the bounds of her knowledge. When considering the sculpture of The Wrestlers in the Uffizi, she wrote, 'as I am neither an amateur of wrestling nor a connoisseur of anatomy, this group afforded me little pleasure, although willing to admit its acknowledged merit.'[44] Writing in 1827, just a few years after the Countess of Blessington's visit, the barrister Thomas Jefferson Hogg had this to say about the anatomical exhibition:

> The true wonder of Florence is the collection of anatomical models in wax, at the Specola; their number, beauty and perfection are astonishing. All the

> various systems of the animal economy are exhibited with perfect accuracy, as large as life, are shown as well by the most careful dissection. Nothing shocks the senses; on the contrary, a certain beauty of imitation and gracefulness in displaying and disposing the part and limbs, is even pleasing.[45]

It is clear that Hogg did not feel the need to move through the exhibition quickly, nor was his gaze restricted in any way. While the Countess of Blessington's account is not the only negative review of the period, it is exceptional because it was written by a woman and, thus, is one of the few accounts of the exhibition from the female perspective. As with her account of seeing the Venus de' Medici and Venus of Urbino at the Uffizi, her description of the Anatomical Venuses was, at least in part, influenced by her discomfort at viewing the exhibition in the presence of men. In contrast, Hogg can be imagined peering closely through the glass to take in all the 'perfect accuracy' of the models, giving no thought to how others might have viewed his interest in the exhibition. The Countess of Blessington may have felt embarrassed to be seen at the exhibition, but she did not feel the need to check her written opinion of it. Her account of her visit to La Specola, seeing the anatomical waxes' 'hideous and appalling nakedness and truth', is devoid of the pretentions of other visitors, like le Brun and Hogg. Since she was neither an artist nor an anatomist, she could write without censure, unconcerned about what her peers would think of her opinion. At the time of her journal-keeping, she may not even have been writing with the view to publication and, perhaps, wrote more simply than those, like le Brun and Hogg, who knew that their work was going to be read by others. But this makes it all the more valuable to historians looking to understand responses to the Anatomical Venuses contemporary to, or closely following, their production. At the time, the Countess was keeping a journal for herself, without a view to publication (though she would publish subsequently), whereas the other available sources were written with the view to be shared with peers. Her response is therefore a candid one, an account far less censored than those of other artists, scientists and writers of the time. Despite the 'sense of loathing' which she carried away from her experience at La Specola, the exhibition altered her gaze. It changed the way she looked at people, women in particular, recognising the 'perilous stuff' with which all human bodies are made with her newly acquired anatomical knowledge. The exhibition then, for the Countess of Blessington, had been a success.

When considered in the light of the Countess of Blessington's female and British gaze, the Anatomical Venuses must have seemed a puzzle when compared to the other examples of the naked female form which she saw in the galleries in Florence. While, as scientific representations of female anatomy, a viewer might expect to look on these models as 'naked', the artistic presentation of the Medici Venus – the head tilted back, one leg suggestively crossed over the other, a hand toying with a lock of hair or grasping the silken cover beneath it – aligns this object and her sister Anatomical Venuses with the statues and painting of 'nudes' that were on display at the Uffizi. When visiting Michelangelo's monuments Night, Day, Dawn and Twilight at the Sacristia Nuova 30 June 1823, she was captivated by the sculpture Night. She wrote:

> Nothing can exceed the solemn beauty of the figure of Night, which is placed at one side of the sarcophagus, while one of Day confronts it on the other. This last statue, though unfinished, possesses all the vigour for which the works of the great sculptor are remarkable; but Night breathes the very soul of melancholy contemplation, and fixes the attention by its depth of repose. One turns again and again to gaze on this exquisite statue, which addresses itself most powerfully to the imagination. The other monument has two figures, representing Dawn and Twilight, both worthy the chisel of Buonarotti; but Night fascinated me so much, that I could not give these figures the portion of attention which was their due.[46]

Both statues of naked women, Night and Dawn strike very different poses: while Dawn leans back, displaying her torso in a similar way to the Anatomical Venuses, Night bends forward, her forehead resting on her arm in the manner of classical thinkers. Night's pose is in stark contrast, also, to Titian's painting of Venus in the Uffizi which the Countess of Blessington had lamented on 14 June 1823 'is unredeemed by any expression of intellectual refinement'.[47] The presentation of women as bodies only, then, was clearly anathema to a woman who was already an established salonnière and would go on to earn a living from her writing.

A witty and entertaining journal, *The Idler in Italy* is unpretentious and tells the reader much about its writer. When considering paintings and sculptures of female nudes which she found unappealing, the Countess of Blessington was apt to consider the loose morals of models who posed for the tableaux, assigning at least some portion of the blame to them whenever a painting seemed indecent to her sensibility. When, during her visit to the Pitti Palace on 28 June 1823, she noted, 'Canova's Venus does not please me',[48] suspecting that he employed models from the Opera House, she seems to be blaming the outcome of the work more on the personality of the woman who posed for it rather than the artist who rendered the work, betraying a naïve belief that artists capture only what they see and not what they want to convey. She was aware of the male-female power dynamic, not only in the viewing of art but in its very composition. Even so, despite her sensitivity to the presence of male viewers, including male friends and acquaintances of her own party, the Countess of Blessington maintained her own opinions, and would have the self-confidence to publish an account of her own thoughts, choosing not to alter her writing to suit the opinions of others. Walking through the Uffizi on 16 June 1823, 'making acquaintance with the faces of the Heroes of Antiquity, and comparing the expression of their countenances with the notion I had formed of them from a perusal of their histories', she entertained her companions with her thoughts and recounted later in her journal, 'Yet, notwithstanding their *plaisanteries*, I maintained my opinion – like a woman, and an obstinate one too; and not the less pertinaciously because my argument was based only on fancy.'[49] A well-read woman, confident in her own ideas, she could play up to the stereotypes of the female sex for the amusement of her male friends.

British travellers in Italy saw many naked forms wrought in detail very different to that employed by artists at home. Back in London, the Royal Academy was exhibiting subtler, almost prudish paintings of nudes, when it exhibited them at all. William Hilton's 'Venus in search of Cupid surprises Diana in the bath', on display in 1820,[50] shows a group of bathers. The naked forms are soft, vague,

Venus in Search of Cupid Surprises Diana by William Hilton, 1820.

ethereal with no obvious anatomy. The Countess of Blessington had experienced a similar culture shock during a visit to a public bath, when the family had been in Baden the previous September (1822), and was disgusted to see bathers of both sexes 'promiscuously bathing…and apparently enjoying their ablution.'[51] Such entries in her journal show that there were certain practices that she could not accept as being appropriate in a different country, no matter how many times she expounded on the joys of travel for broadening the mind. Her gaze was, once again, directed by her upbringing and it was, perhaps, embarrassment at viewing such scenes in the presence of her male companions that caused her to complain about them later in her journal. These entries convey the sexual morality and restrictions of decorum imposed on women at the time. Although an Irish Catholic, the Countess of Blessington refers to herself and her family as English and Protestant many times throughout *The Idler in Italy*. She may have done this at the time of publication to align herself better, as an author, with her readers, the majority of whom, in Britain, would have been Protestant at the time. In addition, this self-identification shows that, in spite of her Catholic upbringing, the religious undercurrents found in the art that she saw in Italy were vastly different to the religious context that she had grown up in both in Ireland and when she moved to London. A journal entry from May 1824 illustrates her family's discomfort in a foreign church, suggesting that the use of the terms Roman Catholic and Protestant may have been used by the Countess of Blessington to distinguish between the passionate sensibility of stereotypical Italians and the more reserved manners of the English:

> As we sauntered through the town of Beneventum, we observed several persons entering a church, into which we also bent our steps, and witnessed one of those exhibitions so common in Italy; where the enthusiasm and passionate warmth of the preachers so frequently lead them to overstep the propriety of their calling. The matter of the sermon and manner of this expounder of the Roman Catholic Faith were truly surprising, and, to say the truth, not a little shocking to our feelings, although the rest of the congregation evinced great admiration, for what to us appeared so outré and indecorous.[52]

She would hear, a few days later, 'the melancholy intelligence' that Lord Byron had died in Greece.[53]

The satirical artwork of the Georgian period exposed British people to exaggerated and unromantic images of bodies. Women's preoccupation with beauty was ridiculed in cartoons, and stays, wigs and make-up were lambasted for their deceptive powers.[54] The Countess of Blessington was an admirer of beauty in other women, but it is clear from her writing that she scorned those who lacked intelligence. She took time in her journal to describe most of the women she met, commented on their social status and even, at times, transcribed snippets of conversation. The following two descriptions have been chosen for their detail. As always, her writing is witty and entertaining, and she did not spare those who she thought could improve themselves through reading as she, herself, had done. Of a duchess she met in Naples, she wrote condescendingly,

> The Duchesse is lively, good-natured, and good-looking: she is a descendant of the ancient and noble Roman family of Colonna, of whom, however, I discovered in a conversation with her, she knows much less than I do. She seemed surprised when I talked of the intimacy of Petrarch with her ancestor Stephen; and still more so, when I named her charming relative Vittoria Colonna, the wife of the celebrated Due del Vasto, and the friend of Michael Angelo; nor had she ever heard of her beautiful sonnets, until I spoke of them. She smiled at hearing that she had a poetess among her ancestors; when the Duc explained that the early marriage of the Duchesse, the care of her large family, and her love of music, prevented her knowing as much of past times as could be wished, to which assertion she assented with a charming naivete.[55]

In contrast, she wrote with greater warmth of the Duchesse de Guiche, with whom she socialised during her return visit to Pisa between December 1826 and June 1827:

> The Duchesse is one of the most striking-looking women I ever beheld; and though in very delicate health, her beauty is unimpaired. Tall and slight, her figure is finely proportioned, and her air is remarkably noble and graceful. Her features are regular, her complexion dazzlingly fair, her countenance full of intelligence, softened by a feminine sweetness, that gives it a peculiar attraction; and her limbs are so small and symmetrical, as to furnish an illustration of Byron's favourite hypothesis, that delicately formed hands and feet were infallible indications of noble birth. But had the Duchesse de Guiche no other charm than her hair, that would constitute an irresistible one. Never did I see such a profusion, nor of so beautiful a colour and texture. When to these exterior attractions are added manners graceful and dignified, conversation witty and full of intelligence, joined to extreme gentleness, it cannot be wondered at that the Duchesse de Guiche is considered one of the most lovely and fascinating women of her day.[56]

Both these accounts demonstrate the Countess of Blessington's love of conversation and her desire to discuss the varied body of knowledge she had gained from her wide reading. The duchess from Naples, a woman who smiled but seemed to have no opinions of her own, held much less fascination for her when compared with the Duchesse de Guiche's intelligent conversation. In the same way, her journal entries of the works of art she encountered that took women as their subject, detailed in this chapter, show that she appreciated beauty, but she valued intelligence and artistic execution far more. Thus, she preferred the refined statues of Venus in the Louvre and the Venus de' Medici in the Uffizi over the voluptuous paintings of Venus by Titian and Canova, and Night's contemplative pose over Day's reclining posture both executed by Michelangelo in the Sacristia Nuova. Her account of her visit to La Specola is lamentably short, but her diary entry is invaluable because she expresses her ambivalence towards looking at such objects in the presence of men, therefore giving the reader an understanding of the restricted female gaze in relation to art and nudity in the early nineteenth century.

As with all her writing, *The Idler in Italy* conveys the Countess of Blessington's sense of humour, her unusual insight and a true articulation of the female gaze. On her last day in Florence, the Countess of Blessington visited Bartolini's sculpture studio where:

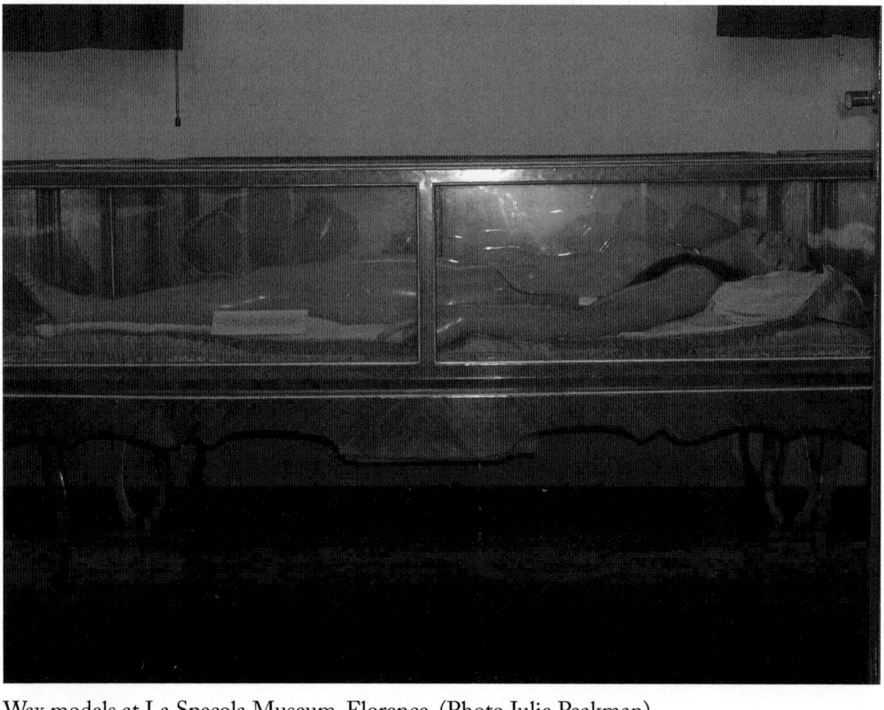

Wax models at La Specola Museum, Florence. (Photo Julie Peakman)

> Every lord and commoner, who has passed through Florence during the last few years, has left here a memorial of his visit; and every lady who had ever heard that she had a good profile (and Heaven knows how seldom the assertion was true), has left a model of it on the dusty shelves of Bartolini. The great love of the English for portraits, is by foreigners attributed to a more than ordinary degree of vanity; while its source might with greater truth be traced to a more amiable motive, to that of family affection. Many are the busts at Bartolini's that might serve to illustrate my hypothesis; for nothing but the desire of gratifying some beloved object could have induced the originals of them to bequeath to posterity such countenances as affection alone could contemplate with pleasure. Elderly gentlemen with double chins, resembling the breast of the pelican, and protuberant stomachs, requiring a double portion of marble in their representation; with wigs concealing half the organs by the development of which phrenologists judge of the intellectual powers; and coats that seem to have been invented to human beings, meet the eye in this studio. And portly matrons, too, are ranged in rows, with busts exuberant as those which Rubens loved to lavish on his canvas; and tresses so luxuriant, as to convey the impression that they belonged to the original, only because she had bought them. Young ladies, with compressed waists, and drooping ringlets, looking all like sisters; and young gentlemen, with formal faces, and straight hair, confront one at every step. But among them are busts, with features so delicately moulded, and heads so classically shaped, that they maintain the pre-eminence for beauty accorded to England over all other countries. Bartolini is a very clever sculptor, and some of his works justify the high reputation he has acquired.[57]

Once again, she exercises her incisive wit, which would become biting when she used it to describe the secondary characters in her novels, vain and idiotic females who harangue and persecute the protagonists at every turn. Lady Blessington not only provides us with a comprehensive account of a British woman traveller and her voices on places and the people she met, but leaves us with her own distinctive voice on her perceptions of art and beauty influenced by her own understandings about sexuality and morality.

Notes

Introduction

1. Susan Lamb, *Bringing Travel Home to England. Tourism, Gender, and Imaginative Literature in the Eighteenth Century*, (Newark, University of Delaware Press, 2009)
2. Chloe Chard, *Pleasure and Guilt on the Grand Tour. Travel Writing and Imaginative Geography 1600-1830* (Manchester, Manchester University Press, 1999)
3. Katherine Turner, *British Travel Writers in Europe 1750-1800 Authorship, Gender, and National Identity* (London, Routledge, 2001), p. 5; Cloe Chard, *Pleasure and Guilt on the Grand Tour: Travel Writing and Imaginative Geography*, 1600–1830 (Manchester, Manchester University Press, 1999), p.46
4. J. Black, 'Italy and the Grand Tour: The British Experience in the Eighteenth Century', *Annali d'Italianistica*, Vol. 14 (1996), pp. 532–41, p. 540
5. Jane Stabler, *Artistry of Exile,* (Oxford, Oxford University Press, 2013), p. 17; Rosemary Sweet, *Cities and the Grand Tour* (Cambridge, Cambridge University Press), p. 233
6. Quoted in Chloe Chard, *Pleasure and Guilt on the Grand Tour*, pp. 157–8
7. Raymond Bentman 'Thomas Gray and the Poetry of "Hopeless Love",' *Journal of the History of Sexuality* , Oct., 1992, Vol. 3, No. 2 (Oct., 1992), pp. 203–222
8. Elizabeth A. Bohls, *Women Travel Writers and the Language of Aesthetics 1716–1818* (Cambridge, Cambridge University Press, 1995), pp. 108–139

Chapter 1

1. Erotic utopias and landscape ideals are examined in Julie Peakman, *Mighty Lewd Books, The Development of Pornography in Eighteenth-Century England*, (London, Palgrave, 2003), pp. 93–125.
2. Eighteenth-century writer and publisher of pornography Edmund Curll published *Merryland Display'd* (1741) as a mock critique of *A New Description of Merryland*, and was an attempt to cash in on further sales and publicity. It came out in at least two editions in 1741, and by the same date, seven editions of *New Description of Merryland* had appeared. *Merryland Display'd* states that *New Description of Merryland* was published October last (1740) and in three months went through seven editions it was so popular 'besides some Thousands of pirated Copies that were sold in the Town and Country'. See Peakman, as above.
3. Cited in Jeremy Black, *The British Abroad, The Grand Tour in the Eighteenth Century* (New York, St. Martin's Press, 1992), p. 200.
4. İrvin Cemil Schick, 'Representation of Gender and Sexuality in Ottoman and Turkish Erotic Literature', *The Turkish Studies Association Journal*, 2004, Vol. 28, No. 1/2 (2004), pp. 81–103. Richard Burton's translation of this would only come out much later.
5. Letter written from Edinburgh to William Johnson Temple in Berwick upon Tweed, 22 September 1767. See C. B. Tinker, ed., *Letters of James Boswell*, Vol. 1 (Oxford, Clarendon Press, 1924), pp. 130–31. Quoted by Grierson below.
6. Ralph Walker (ed.), *Correspondence of James Boswell* (London, Heinemann, 1966), p. 174; Roderick Grierson 'The Bashaw of Merryland': The Sixth Baron Baltimore and the Dervises of Pera', *Mawlana Rumi Review*, 2015, Vol. 6, Special Issue on Rumi and the Mevlevi Sufi Tradition (2015), pp. 83–103.

7. 'Sophia Watson', *Memoirs of the Seraglio of the Bashaw of Merryland by a Discarded Sultana* (London, S. Bladon, 2nd ed, 1768).
8. F. A. Pottle, *Boswell on the Grand Tour*, (London, Heimann, 1953), p. 48.
9. For more on Dashwood and the Dilettani and Divan clubs, see Peakman, *Mighty Lewd Books*, pp. 32–3 and *Lascivious Bodies, A History of the Eighteenth Century* (London, Atlantic, 2004), pp. 103–128.
10. Minute Books, 4 May 1755, Volume I of Minute Books (2 May 1736–6 January 1745), on deposit at the Society of Antiquaries, London), quoted on p. 9.
11. Minute Books, 1 March 1761, as above.
12. Lewis, W. S., et al (eds.), *Horace Walpole's Correspondence*. 48 vols. (New Haven. Yale University Press, 1937–83), Vol. 18, p. 211 (to Horace Mann, 14 April 1743
13. Quoted in Bruce Redford, *Dilettanti. The Antic and The Antique in Eighteenth-Century England* (J. Paul Getty Museum, 2008), p. 34.
14. Jeremy Black, *The Grand Tour* (London, Croom Helm, 1985), p. 243.
15. Daniel P Mannix, *The Hell-Fire Club* (London, The New English Library, 1959), pp. 11–13. According to Mannix, his tutor wrote about the incident.
16. See Julie Peakman, *Mighty Lewd Books* for an assessment of anti-Catholic erotica, pp. 128–132.
17. See chapter on Byron in this book.
18. Susan Lamb, *Bringing Travel Home to England. Tourism, Gender, and Imaginative Literature in the Eighteenth Century*, (Newark, University of Delaware Press, 2009), p. 66.
19. Tamara Griggs, 'The Local Antiquary in Eighteenth-Century Rome', *The Princeton University Library Chronicle*, Vol. 69, No. 2 (Winter 2008), pp. 280–314, p. 299.
20. Charlotte Roberts, 'Living with the Ancient Romans: Past and Present in Eighteenth-Century Encounters with Herculaneum and Pompeii', *Huntington Library Quarterly*, Vol. 78, No. 1 (Spring 2015), pp. 61–85.
21. David D. Nolta, 'The Body of the Collector and the Collected Body in William Hamilton's Naples', *Eighteenth-Century Studies*, Vol. 31, No. 1, (Fall, 1997), pp. 108–114.
22. Letter dated 17 July 1781 to Joseph Banks in London from William Hamilton from Naples. British Library, MS. 34048, ff. 12–14.
23. See Julie Peakman, *Licentious Worlds. Sex and Exploitation in Global Empires* (London, Reaktion, 2019), pp. 62–70.
24. Giancarlo Carabelli, *In the Image of Priapus* (London, 1996).
25. Ibid, p. 20.
26. Ibid, p. 18.
27. Ibid, p. 22.
28. Ibid, p. 23.
29. Hamilton's Account *On The Worship Of Priapus In The Kingdom Of Naples* (London, privately printed,1786–7) p. 13.
30. Thomas J Mathias, *The Pursuits of Literature* (8th edition, Dublin, J. Milliken, 1798), p. 27.
31. Ibid, 2nd part, p. 77
32. *On The Worship Of Priapus In The Kingdom Of Naples* (London, privately printed,1786–7), p. 53.
33. G.S. Rousseau, 'The Sorrows of Priapus, anticlerical, homosocial desire and Richard Payne Knight' in G.S. Rousseau and Roy Porter, *Sexual Underworlds of the Enlightenment* Manchester University Press, 1987), pp. 101–153. The two volumes of erotica he published under false imprints (and possibly false dates) were *Monumens de la vie privée des XII Césars d'apres une suite de pierres et médailles gravées sous leur règne* (Capree, chez Sabellus, 1780); and *Monumens du culte secret des dames romaines* (Rome, De l'Imprimerie du Vatican, 1787).
34. Morrison MS 137 5 May 1784.
35. See Julie Peakman, *Emma Hamilton*. A biography (London, Haus, 2004).
36. J. W. Goethe,(translation WH Auden and Elizabeth Mayer), *Italian Journey* [1787] (London, Penguin, 1970), p. 208.

Chapter 2

1. British Library, Egerton Manuscripts, 2234.
2. Isobel Grundy, *Lady Mary Wortley Montagu, Comet of the Enlightenment,* (Oxford, Oxford University Press, 1999) p. 137.
3. Billie Melman, *Women's Orients: English Women and the Middle East, 1718–1918,* (University of Michigan Press, 1992) p. 14.
4. Walpole, Horace, *Letters*, 5. 258. To Mann, 3 October 1762.
5. *Monthly Review,*(1763) 28.385.
6. Robert Halsband, ed., *The Complete Letters of Lady Mary Wortley Montagu,* (Oxford, Clarendon Press 1965).1. pp. 466–468.: Abbrevaited CL below.
7. Teresa Heffernan, 'Feminism against the East/West Divide: Lady Mary's *Turkish Embassy Letters, Eighteenth-Century Studies,* Winter, 2000, Vol. 33, No. 2, (Winter, 2000), pp. 201–215.
8. To Lady -, 17 June 1717 in Halsband, *The Complete Letters,* Vol. I, p. 368.
9. Jean Dumont, *A New Voyage to the Levant* (London, 1696), p.167.
10. Dumont, *A New Voyage to the Levant,* p.261.
11. Anna Secor 'Orientalism, Gender and Class in Lady Msary Wortley Montagu's *Turkish Embassy Letters*: to persons of distinction, men of letters & c.'" *Ecumene,* October 1999, Vol. 6, No. 4 (October 1999), pp. 375–398.
12. CL. 1. p.326.
13. CL.1. p.305.
14. CL.1. p.307.
15. Ibid.
16. Ibid.
17. Ibid.
18. CL.1. p.317.
19. Ibid.
20. CL.1. p.318.
21. Ibid.
22. CL.1. p.308.
23. Ibid.
24. CL.1. p.312.
25. Montagu cites Sandys in her letter to Abbé Conti, Tunis, 31st July 1718, and seems to approve of him, 'One of my country men, Mr Sandys, whose book, I do not doubt you have read as one of the best of its kind…' cited in Anita Desai (ed.), *The Turkish Embassy Letters* (Virago, 1994), p. 145.
26. G. Sandys, *Sandys Travels: containing an history of the original and present state of the Turkish empire … the Mahometan religion and ceremonies. A description of Constantinople … also, of Greece … Of Ægypt … A description of the Holy-Land … Lastly, Italy described, and the islands adjoining. Illustrated with fifty graven maps and figures* (London, 1652).
27. Ibid.
28. Ibid.
29. CL. 1. p.313.
30. CL. 1. p.314.
31. Ibid.
32. Ibid.
33. Ibid.
34. CL. 1. p.314.
35. Elizabeth Craven, *A Journey through the Crimea to Constantinople* (London, 1789) p. 264.
36. Tyers, Thomas, *A Historical Rhapsody on Mr Pope,* (London, 1782) p. 42.
37. CL. 1. p.253.
38. Jeremy Black, *The Grand Tour:The British Abroad in the Eighteenth Century.* p. 1.

39. CL.1. p.331.
40. CL. 1. p.406.
41. *Annals of Stair,* (23 June 1716), 2. 36.
42. CL.1. p.311.
43. CL.1. p.366.
44. Ibid.
45. CL.1. p.368.
46. Dumont, *A New Voyage to the Levant*, (London, 1696), pp. 273–7.
47. *The Turkish Embassy Letters* (Virago, 1994), p. 81.
48. Malcom Jack (ed, *The Turkish Embassy Letters* (London, Virago, 1966), p. 81.
49. Paul Rycaut, *Present State of the Ottoman Empire*, (London, 1668), p. 39.
50. CL.1. p.383.
51. CL. 1. p.345.
52. CL. 1. p.329.
53. CL. 1. p.328.
54. Ibid.
55. CL. 1. p.329.
56. To Lady Mar, 1 Apr. 1717, in R. Halsband (ed.), *M. W. Montagu, The Complete Letters of Lady Mary Wortley Montagu I*: 1708–1720,) (Oxford, Clarendon Press, 1965), p. 3.
57. To Lady Bute, 23 Jan. 1755, in R. Halsband (ed.), *M. W. Montagu, The Complete Letters of Lady Mary Wortley Montagu III: 1752–1762*, (Oxford, Clarendon Press, 1965).
58. To Lady Bristol, 10 Apr. 1718, *The Complete Letters, op cit*, p. 401.
59. CL. 1. p.408.
60. CL. 3. p.21.

Chapter 3

1. J. Guillory, *Cultural Capital. The Problem of Literary Canon Formation* (London, University of Chicago Press, 1993), pp. 86–88.
2. R. L. Mack, *Thomas Gray. A Life* (New Haven, Yale University Press, 2000), pp. 96–97.
3. W. Mason, *The Poems of Mr Gray, to which are prefixed Memoirs of His Life and Writings* (London, 1775) Vol. 1, p. 40.
4. S. Johnson, *Life of Gray* in S. Johnson, , Ed. Lonsdale, R. *The Lives of the Most Eminent English Poets,* Vol. IV. (Oxford, Oxford University Press, [1781] reprint 2006), p. 176.
5. Ibid, p. 179.
6. One of the first being Nicolson, M., H. *Mountain Gloom and Mountain Glory: The Development of the Aesthetics of the Infinite* [1959] (Seattle, University of Washington Press, reprint 1997).
7. W. B. Ruddick, 'Thomas Gray's Travel Writing' in W. B. Hutchings, W. Ruddick (eds)., *Thomas Gray: Contemporary Essays* (Liverpool, Liverpool University Press, 1993), pp. 126–145. He highlights Gray's visual descriptions in which you can perceive the traveller's reactions to the landscape.
8. G. M. Dongu, *Thomas Gray Ludens: Frammenti dal Grand Tour*, (Transl. Title: *Playful Thomas Gray: Fragments from the Grand Tour* (Milan, FrancoAngeli, 2014).
9. Eighteenth-century studies did not distinguish between the two. J. Lamb, *The Evolution of Sympathy in the Long Eighteenth Century* (London, Pickering & Chatto, 2009), p. 42.
10. A.A Kerherve, 'Theory of British Epistolary Sociability?' in V. Capdeville and A. Kerhervé (eds), *British Sociability in the Long Eighteenth Century* (Woodbridge, The Boydell Press, 2019), pp. 145–162.
11. See L. J. Davis, *Factual Fictions: The Origins of the English Novel*, (Philadelphia, University of Pennsylvania Press, 1996); M. McKeon, *The Origins of the English Novel: 1600–1740* (Baltimore, Johns Hopkins University Press, 1987); J.P. Hunter, *Before Novels: The Cultural Contexts of Eighteenth-Century Fiction* (New York, Norton, 1990).

12. P. Bullard, Eighteenth-Century Minds: From Associationism to Cognitive Psychology in *Oxford Handbooks Online* (Oxford, Oxford University Press, 2016) doi: 10.1093/oxfordhb/9780199935338.013.95.
13. W. Mason, *The Poems of Mr Gray, to which are prefixed Memoirs of His Life and Writings* (London, 1775) Vol. 1, p. 40.
14. W. S. Lewis (ed.), *The Yale Edition of Horace Walpole's Correspondence*, Vol. 28, p. 68. (New Haven, Yale University Press, 1955), pp. 68–69.
15. This hypothesis has been put forward by Mack. He quotes a letter from Horace Mann, who hints at the oddness of Gray's behaviour with Suarez. R. L. Mack, *Thomas Gray. A Life.* (London, Yale University Press, 2000) pp. 260–262.
16. See R. F. Gleckner, *Gray Agonistes: Thomas Gray and Masculine Friendship* (Baltimore, John Hopkins University Press, 1997). Gray's modern biographer, Robert Mack, writes that it is necessary to include 'a more comprehensive and far less prudish discussion of Gray's romantic attachments to childhood friends', but admits that Mason's pruning of Gray's letters deprived us of first-hand testimonies, unless we think that his poems exposed his secret in a coded language. R. L. Mack, *Thomas Gray. A Life.* (New Haven, Yale University Press, London, 2000), pp. 33–34.
17. Norton says that Walpole must have 'suppressed his homosexuality'. R. Norton, *Horace Walpole and Homosexuality.* http://rictornorton.co.uk/thought2.htm.
18. William, second Earl of Fitzwilliam, Fitzwilliam MSS, cited in H. Belsey, (2004) Sir Horatio Mann, first baronet. 1706–1786. https://doi.org/10.1093/ref:odnb/17945. [last accessed 29/10/2020].
19. H. Belsey, (2004) Sir Horatio Mann, first baronet. 1706–1786. https://doi.org/10.1093/ref:odnb/17945. [last accessed 29/10/2020].
20. G. S. Rosseau, *Perilous Enlightenment.* (Manchester, Manchester University Press, 1991), p. 30. R. F. Gleckner, *Gray Agonistes: Thomas Gray and Masculine Friendship*, (Baltimore, Johns Hopkins University Press, 1997), p. 53. The Old Bailey gave evidence of many trials held in England against homosexuals in the eighteenth century. Notwithstanding it, there was a lively gay and molly subculture in London. Norton, R. 'Recovering Gay History from the Old Bailey', *The London Journal*, Vol. 30, No. 1, (2005), pp. 39–54.
21. G. S. Rosseau, 'The Pursuit of Homosexuality in the Eighteenth Century: 'Utterly Confused Category' and/or Rich Repository? in Maccubin, R. P. (ed.) *'Tis Nature's Fault: Unauthorized Sexual Behavior during the Enlightenment,* (Cambridge, Cambridge University Press, 1987), pp. 132–168, 143.
22. R. Bentman, 'Thomas Gray and the Poetry of "Hopeless Love"', *Journal of the History of Sexuality*, Vol. 3, No. 2, (1992), pp. 203–222, 204–205, 206–210.
23. R. Stephenson, 'Epicoene friendship: Understanding Male Friendship in the Early Eighteenth Century, with Some Speculations about Pope', *The Eighteenth Century*, Vol. 38, No. 2, (1997), pp. 151–170, 159.
24. R. W. Ketton Kreamer, *Thomas Gray: A Biography. (*Cambridge, Cambridge University Press, 1955), pp. 27–28.
25. R. F. Gleckner, *Gray Agonistes: Thomas Gray and Masculine Friendship.* (Baltimore, John Hopkins University Press, 1997), pp. 77–78.
26. S. Morrison, (2004) Smith, Joseph: 1673/4–1770. https://doi.org/10.1093/ref:odnb/25871, 2004. [accessed 30/10/2020].
27. R. L. Mack, *Thomas Gray. A Life,* (London, Yale University Press, 2000), p. 204.
28. J. Black, *The British and the Grand Tour* (London, Croom Helm, 1985), pp. 5–41.
29. Ketton-Cremer, R. W. *Thomas Gray: A Biography* (Cambridge, Cambridge University Press, (1955), p. 39.
30. Gray T., Eds. P. Toynbee, L. Whibley, *Correspondence of Thomas Gray* (Oxford, Clarendon Press, 1935), Vol. I, Letter 91, pp. 167–169.

31. A. Ilano, 'From Gray's Elegy to Foscolo's Carme: Highlighting the Mediation and Sublimation of the 'Sepulchral''. *Symposium: A Quarterly Journal in Modern Literatures*, (1993) Vol. 47 No, 2, pp. 117–131, 128.
32. E. Leeds, *The Mind of the Traveller: From Gilgamesh to Global Tourism* (New York, Basic Books, 1991), pp. 195–196.
33. Gray T., Eds. P. Toynbee, L. Whibley, *Correspondence of Thomas Gray* (Oxford, Clarendon Press, 1935) Vol. I, Letter 17, pp. 129–133.
34. Ibid, Vol. I, Letter 17, p. 379.
35. W. Powell-Jones, Thomas Gray's Library. *Modern Philology*, (1938) Vol. 35, No. 3, pp. 257–278. See also Powell-Jones, W. *Thomas Gray, Scholar: The True Tragedy of an Eighteenth Century Gentleman* (Cambridge, Mass., Harvard University Press, 1937) 13, which details Gray's interest in two branches of knowledge: classic literature and travel writings.
36. This was only published in its entirety in 2011. T. Grey, Ed. Roberts, W. G. *Notes on a Tour through France and Italy (1739–1741)* (Penrith, Northern Academic Press, 2011).
37. Gray T., Eds. P. Toynbee, L. Whibley, *Correspondence of Thomas Gray*, Vol. III, Letter 430, 944.
38. Gray T., Eds. Toynbee, P., Whibley, L *Correspondence of Thomas Gray*. Vol. III, Letter 471, 1019–1020.
39. Gray T., Eds. P. Toynbee, L. Whibley, *Correspondence of Thomas Gray*., Vol. II, Letter 311, 670.
40. Gray T., Eds. P. Toynbee, L. Whibley, *Correspondence of Thomas Gray*. Vol. III, Letter 474, 1027.
41. H. Thomson, 'The Poet and the Publisher' in Thomas Gray's Correspondence, *The Yearbook of English Studies*, 1998), pp. 28, 163–180.
42. K. Stewart, Towards Defining an Aesthetic for the Familiar Letter in Eighteenth-Century England. *Prose Studies*, 5, (1982), pp. 179–192, 186–187.
43. S. Johnson, *Life of Gray*. In: Ed. Lonsdale, R. *The Lives of the Most Eminent English Poets,* [1781] Vol. IV. (Oxford, Oxford University Press, 2006), p. 178.
44. '[H]is mind had a large grasp; that his curiosity was unlimited, and his judgement cultivated' S. Johnson, ([1781] *Life of Gray* in S. Johnson, , Ed. Lonsdale, R. *The Lives of the Most Eminent English Poets,* Vol. IV (Oxford, Oxford University Press, 2006), p. 178.
45. S. Johnson, *Life of Gray*, p. 180.
46. J. Brewer, *Pleasures of Imagination.* (Abingdon, New York, Routledge, 1997), 168 and ff.
47. Gray T., Eds. P. Toynbee, L. Whibley, *Correspondence of Thomas Gray*. Vol. I, Letter 61, p. 104.
48. Ibid, Vol. 1, Letter 79, pp. 138–143.
49. Ibid, p. 138.
50. Ibid, p. 142.
51. Ibid, p. 138.
52. Ibid, p. 138.
53. Ibid, 139.
54. Ibid, p. 140.
55. Ibid, p. 140.
56. Ibid, p. 141.
57. Ibid, p. 138.
58. Ibid, p. 139.
59. Ibid, p. 140.
60. ' … how it is to be devoured by a wolf' he scrupulously annotated, Ibid, p. 140.
61. Ibid, p. 138.
62. Ibid, p. 141.
63. Ibid, p. 138.
64. Ibid, p. 139.

65. Gray T., Eds. P. Toynbee, L. Whibley, *Correspondence of Thomas Gray*, Vol. I, Letter 65, p. 114.
66. Ibid, p. 115.
67. H. Sklar, *The Art of Sympathy in Fiction: Forms of Ethical and Emotional Persuasion* (Amsterdam / Philadelphia John Benjamins Publishing Company, 2013), pp. 26–27.
68. S. L. Feagin, *Reading with Feeling: The Aesthetics of Appreciation* (Ithaca NY, Cornell University Press, 1996), p. 116.
69. A. Lilti, *The World of the Salons: Sociability and Worldliness in Eighteenth-Century Paris*, transl. by L. G. Cochrane (Oxford, Oxford University Press, 2005), p. 8.
70. E. J. Clery, Women, Publicity and the Coffee-House Myth. *Women: A Cultural Review*, (1991). Vol. 2. No. 2, pp. 168–177, 172.
71. T. Eagleton, *The Function of Criticism*, (London, Verso, 2005), pp. 26–27.
72. B. Cowan, *Restoration' England and the history of sociability* in V. Capdeville, A. Kerhervé (eds), *British Sociability*, pp. 7–24, 11.
73. W. Mason, *The Poems of Mr Gray, to which are prefixed Memoirs of His Life and Writings* (London, 1775) Vol. 1, 2.
74. T. Grey, Eds. P. Toynbee, L. Whibley, *Correspondence of Thomas Gray*, Vol. I, p. 113.
75. Cowan, B. *Restoration England and the history of sociability*, pp. 7–24, 24.
76. Gray T., Eds. P. Toynbee, L. Whibley, *Correspondence of Thomas Gray*, Vol. I, Letter 65, p. 114.
77. '"Poi nacque un grazioso ballo", where the world danced, and I sat in a corner regaling myself with iced fruits and other pleasant rinfrescatives'. Gray T., Eds. P. Toynbee, L. Whibley, (1935) *Correspondence of Thomas Gray*, Vol. I, Letter 86, p. 158.
78. T. Grey, Eds. P. Toynbee, L. Whibley, *Correspondence of Thomas Gray*, Vol. I, Letter 79, p. 140.
79. Ibid, Vol. I, Letter 74, p. 128.
80. Ibid, Vol. I, Vol. 1, Letter 87, pp. 158–162.
81. Lines from Caesar's *De bello Gallico*, for instance, are quoted in Ibid, Vol. I, Letter 68, p. 118.
82. Ibid, Vol. I, Letter 92, pp. 172–173.
83. Ibid, Vol. I, Letter 97, pp. 181–182.
84. Ibid, Vol. I, Letter 59, p. 100.
85. Walpole mentions Salvator Rosa in a Grand Tour letter. Gray, Walpole, Ashton, West, Ed. P. Toynbee, *Correspondence* (Oxford, Clarendon Press, 1915), p. 244.
86. T. Grey, Eds. P. Toynbee, L. Whibley, (1935) *Correspondence of Thomas Gray*, Letter 87, p. 160.
87. Psychic mobility is a term used by the sociologist Lerner, and then by Greenblatt, S. *Self-Fashioning* (Chicago, University of Chicago Press, 1980), 224 ff.
88. E. B. McCarthy, *Thomas Gray: The Progress of a Poet*. (London, Associated University Presses, 1997), p. 19 and ff.
89. Walpole, Ashton, Gray, West called themselves the Quadruple Alliance during their Eton Years. R. L. Mack, *Thomas Gray. A Life* (London, Yale University Press, 2000), p. 148.
90. T. Grey, Eds. P. Toynbee, L. Whibley, *Correspondence of Thomas Gray*. (Clarendon Press, Oxford, 1935), Vol. I, Letter 87, pp. 159–160.
91. W. Mason, *The Poems of Mr Gray*, Vol. 1, p. 93.
92. T. Grey, Eds. P. Toynbee, L. Whibley, *Correspondence of Thomas Gray* (Oxford, Clarendon Press, 1935), Vol. I, Letter 80, p. 143.
93. Clare Brant, *Eighteenth-Century Letters and British Culture* (London, Palgrave MacMillan, 2006), p. 332.
94. T. Grey, Eds. P. Toynbee, L. Whibley, *Correspondence of Thomas Gray*. (Oxford, Clarendon Press, 1935) Vol. I, Letter 59, p. 100.

95. E. Leeds *The Mind of the Traveller: From Gilgamesh to Global Tourism.* (New York, Basic Books, 1991), p. 88.
96. T. Gray, Eds. P. Toynbee, L. Whibley, *Correspondence of Thomas Gray.* (Oxford, Clarendon Press, 1935), Vol. I, Letter 59, p. 100.
97. T. Gray, Eds. P. Toynbee, L. Whibley, *Correspondence of Thomas Gray.* (Oxford, Clarendon Press, 1935) Vol. I, Letter 75, p. 130.
98. Ibid, Vol. I, Letter 82, p. 147.
99. Ibid, Vol. I, Letter 82, p. 147.
100. Ibid, Vol. I, Letter 82, p. 147.
101. Ibid, Vol. I, Letter 96, p. 180.
102. Ibid, Vol. I, Letter 88, p. 162.

Chapter 4

1. John MacDonald, *Travels, in various parts of Europe, Asia, and Africa, during a series of thirty years and upwards* (London, J. Forbes, 1790). All biographical information on MacDonald is taken from these memoirs, unless otherwise stated.
2. Cf. Sophie Dunn, ''No objection to go abroad': Servants' Travel Advertisements in The Morning Post, London, 1815', *Journal of Eighteenth-Century Studies* Vol. 45, No. 4 (2022), pp. 487–506; Kathryn Walchester, *Travelling Servants, Mobility and Employment in British Fiction and Travel Writing 1750–1850* (London, New York, Routledge, 2020). On the lack of travel accounts by servants, cf. Stephen Conway, *Britain, Ireland, and Continental Europe in the Eighteenth Century: Similarities, Connections, Identities* (Oxford, Oxford University Press, 2011), p. 189.
3. Nigel Leask, 'Eighteenth-Century Travel Writing' in Nandini Das and Tim Youngs (eds.), *The Cambridge History of Travel Writing* (Cambridge, Cambridge University Press, 2019), pp. 93–107, p. 96.
4. Arturo Tosi, *Language and the Grand Tour: Linguistic Experiences of Travelling in Early Modern Europe* (Cambridge, Cambridge University Press, 2020), p. 107.
5. Tosi, *Language and the Grand Tour*, p. 108.
6. Tosi, *Language and the Grand Tour*, pp. 108–115.
7. On travelling servants' language skills, cf. Dunn, 'No objection to go abroad', p. 496. Kathryn Walchester acknowledges that travel 'afforded servants opportunities to learn foreign languages.' *Travelling Servants*, p. 147.
8. *Travels*, p. 281.
9. *Travels*, p. 281.
10. *Travels*, p. 144.
11. *Travels*, pp. 298–99.
12. *Travels*, p. 309.
13. *Travels*, pp. 309–10.
14. *Travels*, p. 310.
15. On French in gentlemanly education, cf. Richard Ansell, *Complete Gentlemen: Educational Travel and Family Strategy, 1650–1750* (Oxford, British Academy/Oxford University Press, 2022), pp. 111–116. Much has been written about the complex French-English relations with regard to the Grand Tour, and especially the decline of French as a significant element of elite education towards the end of the eighteenth century. Michele Cohen's account is still one of the most concise: Cohen, *Fashioning Masculinity: National Identity and Language in the Eighteenth Century* (London, New York, Routledge, 1996), pp. 55–56.
16. *Travels*, p. 313.
17. Cf. Sarah Goldsmith, *Masculinity and Danger on the Eighteenth-Century Grand Tour* (London, University of London Press, 2020), pp. 185–208; Brian Dolan, *Ladies on the Grand Tour* (London, Flamingo, 2002), pp. 138–141.

18. *Travels*, p. 313.
19. *Travels*, p. 341.
20. *Travels*, p. 334.
21. *Travels*, p. 335.
22. Cf. Leask, 'Eighteenth-Century Travel Writing', p. 96, 102; Rosemary Sweet, *Cities and the Grand Tour: the British in Italy, c.1690–1820* (Cambridge, Cambridge University Press, 2012). For a discussion of eighteenth-century aesthetics, Elizabeth A. Bohls, *Women Travel Writers and the Language of Aesthetics, 1716–1818* (Cambridge, Cambridge University Press, 1995), pp. 5–10.
23. *Travels*, p. 375.
24. *Travels*, pp. 375–376.
25. *Travels*, pp. 308–9.
26. *Travels*, p. 309.
27. *Travels*, p. 348.
28. *Travels*, p. 392.
29. *Travels*, p. 334.
30. *Travels*, p. 392.
31. *Travels*, pp. 79–80.
32. *Travels*, p. 94.
33. Cf. *Travels*, p. 154.
34. *Travels*, p. 291.
35. *Travels*, p. 369.
36. *Travels*, p. 139.
37. *Travels*, p. 139.
38. *Travels*, p. 139.
39. *Travels*, p. 145.
40. *Travels*, p. 314.
41. Ansell, *Complete Gentlemen*, p. 173.
42. *Travels*, pp. 382–83.
43. Cohen, *Fashioning Masculinity*, pp. 59–60.
44. For instance, the Society of Dilettanti, cf. Jason Kelly, 'Riots, Revelries, and Rumor: Libertinism and Masculine Association in Enlightenment London', *Journal of British Studies* Vol. 45, No.4 (2006), pp. 759–795.
45. *Travels*, p. 323.
46. *Travels*, p. 370.
47. Cf. Goldsmith, *Masculinity and Danger*, p. 187.
48. *Travels*, p. 321.
49. On the eighteenth-century town and its population, Anne Wohlcke, *The 'perpetual fair': Gender, Disorder, and Urban Amusement in Eighteenth-Century London* (Manchester, Manchester University Press, 2014); Peter Borsay (ed.), *The Eighteenth-Century Town: a reader in English urban history, 1688–1820* (London, New York, Longman, 1990).
50. *Travels*, pp. 314–15.
51. *Travels*, pp. 317–18.
52. *Travels*, p. 318.
53. Cf. Ansell, *Complete Gentlemen*, p. 173; Richard Bates, 'The Petit Tour to Spa, 1763–87' in Rosemary Sweet, Gerrit Verhoeven, and Sarah Goldsmith (eds.), *Beyond the Grand Tour: Northern Metropolises and Early Modern Travel Behaviour* (London, New York, Routledge, 2017), pp. 127–146, here p. 139.
54. Cf. Colin Haydon, '"I love my King and my Country, but a Roman Catholic I hate": anti-Catholicism, xenophobia and national identity in eighteenth-century England' in Tony

Claydon, Ian McBride (eds.), *Protestantism and National Identity: Britain and Ireland, c.1650–c.1850* (Cambridge, Cambridge University Press, 2009), pp. 33–52.

55. *Travels*, p. 351.
56. *Travels*, p. 351.
57. Cf. *Travels*, pp. 328–30.
58. *Travels*, p. 368.
59. *Travels*, p. 368.
60. On the home tour for young men, Ansell, *Complete Gentlemen*, pp. 44–52. See also, Jon Stobart (ed.), *Travel and the British Country House Cultures: Critiques and Consumption in the Long Eighteenth Century* (Manchester, Manchester University Press, 2017); Benjamin Colbert (ed.), *Travel Writing and Tourism in Britain and Ireland* (Basingstoke, Palgrave Macmillan, 2012); Zoë Kinsley, *Women Writing the Home Tour, 1682–1812* (Aldershot, Ashgate, 2008); Barbara Korte, *English Travel Writing from Pilgrimages to Postcolonial Explorations* (Basingstoke, Palgrave, 2000), pp. 66–81.
61. Cf. Henry French and Mark Rothery, *Man's Estate: Landed Gentry Masculinities, 1660–1900* (Oxford, Oxford University Press, 2012), pp. 139–142.
62. *Travels*, p. 143.
63. Cf. Rosemary Sweet, *Antiquaries: The Discovery of the Past in Eighteenth-Century Britain* (London, Hambledon and London, 2004).
64. On travel as life writing, cf. Simon Cooke, 'Travel Writing as Life Writing' in Carl Thompson (ed.), *The Routledge Companion to Travel Writing* (New York, Routledge, 2016), pp. 15–24.

Chapter 5

1. *London Chronicle*, 5–7 October 1769, p. 344.
2. Donald J. Newman, ed., *Boswell and the Press: Essays on the Ephemeral Writing of James Boswell* (Lewisburg, Bucknell University Press, 2021), p. 1.
3. See Moray McLaren, *Corsica Boswell: Paoli, Johnson and Freedom* (London, Secker and Warburg, 1966).
4. Note that I will be following Boswell's spelling of 'Pascal' in *An Account of Corsica*, rather than 'Pasquale,' from this point onward.
5. Brian Evenson, 'Boswell's Grand Tour of Selves' in Donald J. Newman, ed., *James Boswell: Psychological Interpretations*, (New York, St. Martin's Press, 1995), pp. 71–85, p. 157.
6. See Shirley F. Tung, '"An Isthmus which Joins Two Great Continents": Johnson, Boswell, and the Character of the Travel Writer' in *An Account of Corsica*,' *The Age of Johnson: A Scholarly Annual* Vol. 23 (December 2015), pp. 21–31.
7. James Boswell, *The Life of Samuel Johnson, LL.D.*, ed. G. B. Hill, rev. L. F. Powell, 6 Vols. (Oxford, Clarendon Press, 1934–64), 2:86: 'I had greatly wished that two men, for whom I had the highest esteem, should meet. They met with a manly ease, mutually conscious of their own abilities, and of the abilities of each other. The General spoke Italian, and Dr Johnson English, and understood one another very well, with a little aid of interpretation from me, in which I compared myself to an isthmus which joins two great continents.'
8. *Cf.* Timothy McLoughlin, 'Boswell and Corsica: The Art of Puffing,' *Bulletin de la Societe d'etudes anglo-americaines des XVIIe et XVIIe siecles* Vol. 55 (November 2002): p. 165. See Tung, 'An Isthmus which Joins Two Great Continents,' p. 22.
9. This account is taken from Dorothy Carrington, 'Boswell's Corsica,' *Essays by divers hands: being the transactions of the Royal Society of Literature of the United Kingdom* Vol. 44 (1986), p. 59.
10. Evan Gottlieb, *Feeling British: Sympathy and National Identity in Scottish and English Writing, 1707–1832* (Lewisburg, PA, Bucknell Univ. Press, 2007), p. 100.
11. Boswell, *An Account of Corsica, the Journal of a Tour to That Island, and Memoirs of Pascal Paoli*, eds. James T. Boulton and Timothy McLoughlin (Oxford, Oxford University Press, 2006), p. 60.

12. This is from Boswell's Preface to *An Account of Corsica*: 'I acknowledge my obligations to my esteemed friend Sir John Dick, Bart. his Britannick Majesty's Consul at Leghorn, to Signor Gian Quilico Casa Bianca, to the learned Greek physician Signor Stefanopoli, to Colonel Buttafoco, and to the Abbé Rostini. These gentlemen have all contributed their aid in erecting my *little monument to liberty*' (Italics mine), pp. 11–12.
13. Boswell, *An Account of Corsica*, p. 10.
14. Joseph Addison, 'Preface,' *Remarks on several parts of Italy, &c. in the years 1701, 1702, 1703* (London, 1705), n.p.
15. Boswell, *An Account of Corsica*, p. 10.
16. Boswell, *Life of Johnson*, 2:11.
17. Boulton and McLoughlin, Introduction to Boswell's *An Account of Corsica*, p.xxxv.
18. Thomas M. Curley, 'Boswell's Liberty-Loving Account of Corsica and the Art of Travel Literature' in *New Light on Boswell: Critical and Historical Essays on the Occasion of the Bicentenary of The Life of Johnson*, ed. Greg Clingham, pp. 89–103 (Cambridge, Cambridge University Press, 1999), p. 89. As Boswell reveals much later in *An Account of Corsica*, Rousseau uses Corsica as an example of a nation that deserves self-governance: 'M. Rousseau in his Political Treatise, entitled *Du Contract Social*, has the following observation: "…There is yet one country in Europe, capable of legislation; and that is the island of Corsica. The valour and the constancy with which that brave people hath recovered and defended its liberty, would well deserve that some wise man should teach them how to preserve it. I have some presentiment that one day that little island will astonish Europe"' (p. 209).
19. Boswell, *Life of Johnson*, 2:15.
20. Boswell, *An Account of Corsica*, p. 21. This echoes Boswell's letter to Johnson dated 26 April 1768: 'Empty my head of Corsica! Empty it of honour, empty it of humanity, empty it of friendship, empty it of piety. No!' (Boswell, *Life of Johnson*, 2:59).
21. Boswell, *An Account of Corsica*, p. 25.
22. Curley, 'Boswell's Liberty-Loving Account,' p. 89: 'There was a conscious artistic shaping of his experiences abroad around the theme of liberty in the life of the narrator, the nation, and its leader, Paoli, for the propagandistic purpose of uniting England to Corsica's struggle for freedom.'
23. Evenson, 'Boswell's Grand Tour of Selves,' p. 77.
24. Boswell, *An Account of Corsica*, p. 19.
25. Boswell, *An Account of Corsica*, p. 35.
26. Boswell, *An Account of Corsica*, pp. 35–6.
27. Boswell, *An Account of Corsica*, p. 36.
28. Boswell, *An Account of Corsica*, p. 49.
29. Boswell, *An Account of Corsica*, p. 50.
30. Boswell, *An Account of Corsica*, p. 51.
31. Boswell, *An Account of Corsica*, p. 52.
32. Boswell, *An Account of Corsica*, p. 56.
33. Boswell, *An Account of Corsica*, p. 59.
34. Boswell, *An Account of Corsica*, p. 60.
35. Ibid.
36. Ibid.
37. Ibid.
38. Boswell, *An Account of Corsica*, p. 132.
39. Boswell, *An Account of Corsica*, p. 97.
40. Boswell, *An Account of Corsica*, pp. 132–3.
41. Boswell, *An Account of Corsica*, pp. 132, 136.
42. Boswell, *An Account of Corsica*, p. 135.
43. Boswell, *Life of Johnson*, 2:11, 70.

44. Boswell, *An Account of Corsica*, p. 168.
45. Boswell, *An Account of Corsica*, p. 177.
46. Boulton and McLoughlin, Introduction to Boswell's *An Account of Corsica*, p.xlviii.
47. Boswell, *An Account of Corsica*, p. 171.
48. Boswell, *An Account of Corsica*, pp. 168, 179.
49. Quoted in Boswell, *An Account of Corsica*, p. 209.
50. Boswell, *An Account of Corsica*, p. 161.
51. Ibid.
52. Boswell, *An Account of Corsica*, pp. 42, 136. Jean Vivies, 'James Boswell and Scotland in *An Account of Corsica*,' *Studies on Voltaire and the Eighteenth Century* Vol. 305 (1992): p. 1651.
53. Boswell, *An Account of Corsica*, p. 24. Vivies, 'Boswell and Scotland,' pp. 1652–53.
54. Vivies, 'Boswell and Scotland,' p. 1651.
55. See Boswell, *An Account of Corsica*, pp. 162, 171, 157, 186.
56. Mcloughlin, 'Boswell and Corsica,' p. 161.
57. Boswell, *An Account of Corsica*, p. 169.
58. Ibid.
59. Boswell, *An Account of Corsica*, p. 188.
60. Ibid.
61. Stanley Brodwin, '"Old Plutarch at Auchinleck": Boswell's Muse of Corsica,' *Philological Quarterly* Vol. 62, No. 1 (Winter 1983): p. 75.
62. Boswell, *An Account of Corsica*, p. 174.
63. Boswell, *An Account of Corsica*, p. 175.
64. Boswell, *An Account of Corsica*, p. 179.
65. Boswell, *An Account of Corsica*, pp. 199–200.
66. Morgan W. Strawn argues that the filial model of Paoli's leadership facilitates a 'species of despotism.' See '"A Species of Despotism": Catholicism and Benevolent Authoritarianism in Boswell's *Account of Corsica*,' *The Age of Johnson: A Scholarly Annual* Vol. 22 (2012): p. 111. Boswell, *An Account of Corsica*, p. 200.
67. Boswell, *An Account of Corsica*, pp. 200, 179.
68. Boswell, *An Account of Corsica*, pp. 179, 174.
69. Boswell, *An Account of Corsica*, p. 193.
70. Boswell, *An Account of Corsica*, pp. 182, 192, 182, 178.
71. Boswell, *An Account of Corsica*, p. 175.
72. Boswell, *An Account of Corsica*, p. 176. Paul J. Korshin, '"Extensive View": Johnson and Boswell as Travelers and Observers' in *All Before Them: Attitudes to Abroad in English Literature, 1660–1780*, ed. John McVeagh, pp. 233–45 (Atlantic Highlands, NJ, Ashfield Press, 1990), p. 244.
73. Boswell, *An Account of Corsica*, p. 218.
74. Ibid.
75. Felicity Nussbaum argues that Boswell attempts to fashion a 'consistent public character' from two selves: 'the *retenu* or constrained, and a more disoriented interior being, the *etourdi*, or uncontrolled.' See *The Autobiographical Subject: Gender and Ideology in Eighteenth-Century England* (Baltimore, Johns Hopkins University Press, 1989), pp. 110–11.
76. Boulton and McLoughlin, Introduction to Boswell's *An Account of Corsica*, p.xxx.
77. Boswell, *An Account of Corsica*, p. 193. Samuel Johnson, *A Dictionary of the English Language*, 2 Vols. (London, 1755), s.v. *gallant* (adj.), *gallant* (n.s.).
78. Richard De Ritter, '"This Changeableness in Character": Exploring Masculinity and Nationhood on James Boswell's Grand Tour,' *Scottish Literary Review* Vol. 2, No. 1 (Spring/Summer 2010): p. 31. Boswell, *The Journal of a Tour to the Hebrides with Samuel Johnson, LL.D.* in *Life of Johnson*, 5:14. The Literary Club was a London dining club founded in

January 1764 by Samuel Johnson and Joshua Reynolds that regularly met at the Turk's Head Tavern located on Gerrard Street in Soho.

79. Boswell, *An Account of Corsica*, p. 163. Gordon Turnbull, 'James Boswell: Biography and the Union' in *The History of Scottish Literature: Volume II, 1660–1800*, ed. Andrew Hook, pp. 157–174 (Aberdeen Univ. Press, 1987), pp. 163–4.
80. See Boswell, '*An Account of the Armed Corsican Chief at the Masquerade, at* Shakespeare's *Jubilee, at* Stratford-upon-Avon, September 1769.' *London Magazine, or, Gentleman's Monthly Intelligencer, 1747–1783* (September 1769), p.455.
81. See Boswell, *An Account of Corsica*, p. 159.
82. See Boswell, *An Account of Corsica*, p. 159, n.1.
83. Boulton and McLoughlin, Introduction to Boswell's *An Account of Corsica*, p.xxxviii.
84. Boswell, '*An Account of the Armed Corsican Chief at the Masquerade*,' p. 455.
85. Martha Winburn England, *Garrick's Jubilee.* (Ohio State Univ. Press, 1964), p. 3. Paul Tankyard notes that 'What are now called heritage values were so little regarded that the mulberry tree that Shakespeare himself was supposed to have planted in the garden of his own house was chopped down by its owner in 1756, and the house itself demolished in 1759. In 1764 the bicentenary of Shakespeare's birth had passed by without any commemoration.' See James Boswell, *Facts and Inventions: Selections from the Journalism of James Boswell*, edited by Paul Tankard (Yale University Press, 2014), p. 18.
86. Robert Sawyer, 'From Jubilee to Gala: Remembrance and Ritual Commemoration,' *Critical Survey* Vol. 22, No. 2 (2010), p. 29.
87. Boswell, *An Account of Corsica*, p. 186.
88. This is from the broadside 'Verses in the Character of a *Corsican at Shakespeare's Jubilee*,' which Boswell reproduces in his *London Magazine* article, '*An Account of the Armed Corsican Chief at the Masquerade*,' p. 455.
89. Boswell, 'Verses in the Character of a *Corsican at Shakespeare's Jubilee*,' p. 455. Emphasis mine.
90. McLaren, *Corsica Boswell*, pp. 159–60.
91. McLaren, *Corsica Boswell*, p. 162.
92. McLoughlin, 'Boswell and Corsica,' p. 169.
93. Boswell, *Life of Johnson*, 2:70.
94. Ibid.
95. Brodwin, 'Boswell's Muse of Corsica,' p. 78.
96. 'An Account of the Stratford Jubilee,' *Public Advertiser*, 16 September 1769, pp. 1–2 (this letter also appears in *The Scots Magazine* [September 1769] pp. 453–6); 'An Account of the Armed Corsican Chief at the Masquerade,' *The London Magazine* (September 1769); 'Verses in the Character of a Corsican at Shakespeare's Jubilee' (Broadside [folio half-sheet], printed Stratford, 7 September 1769 and reproduced in 'An Account of the Armed Corsican Chief at the Masquerade'); 'Verses on Seeing the Print of James Boswell, Esq; in the Corsican Dress,' *The London Chronicle*, 5–7 October 1769, p. 344; *The Rampager* No. 1: 'Recent Discord in the "Political Orchestra,"' *Public Advertiser* (14 April 1770), p. 2; *The Rampager* No. 14: 'John the Painter and John the Peer' (21 August 1777), p. 1; 'An Authentick Account of General Paoli's Tour to Scotland, Autumn 1771,' *The London Magazine* (September 1771), pp. 433–34.

Chapter 6

1. Michael Burden, 'Mrs Billington's embonpoint; scandal, hysteria, and Mozart', Paper presented at British Society for 18th-Century Studies Annual Conference, St Hugh's College, Oxford, 4 January 2008. https://ora.ouls.ox.ac.uk/objects/uuid:db1f0ebf-6791-4949-a127-a210909d21a0.
2. Michael Kelly, *The Reminiscences of Michael Kelly*, Vol. 1 (London, Henry Colburn, 1826).

3. Susan Rutherford "Vocal pedagogy and Italian musical migration in London, 1664–1914." *Journal of Modern Italian Studies* Vol. 26 No. 1 (2021): 12. DOI: 10.1080/1354571X.2020.185580.
4. Venanzio Rauzzini (7 May 1782), Miscellanea, PRIS10; Piece 051 *King's (Queen's) Bench, Fleet, Marshalsea and Queen's Prisons,* The National Archives of the United Kingdom, Kew, Surrey.
5. Brianna E. Robertson-Kirkland, *Venanzio Rauzzini and the Birth of a New Style in English Singing: Scandalous Lessons,* (Abingdon, Routledge, 2022), pp. 190–1.
6. *Universal Magazine of Knowledge and Pleasure,* Vol. 106 (London, M. Brown, 1800), p. 413.
7. Domenico Corri (26 February 1807), Miscellanea, PRIS10; Piece 053 *King's (Queen's) Bench, Fleet, Marshalsea and Queen's Prisons,* The National Archives of the United Kingdom, Kew, Surrey.; Domenico Corri (11 January 1815), Miscellanea, PRIS10; Piece 053 *King's (Queen's) Bench, Fleet, Marshalsea and Queen's Prisons,* The National Archives of the United Kingdom, Kew, Surrey.
8. Daniel Nalbach, *The King's Theatre 1704–1867: London's First Italian Opera House,* (London, The Society for Theatre Research, 1972), p. xi.
9. Judith Milhous, and Robert D. Hume. "Opera Salaries in Eighteenth-Century London." *Journal of the American Musicological Society* 46, No. 1 (1993): 26–83. https://doi.org/10.2307/831805.
10. John Payne, *An Epitome of History,* (London, J. Johnson, 1795), p. 276.
11. Robertson-Kirkland, *Venanzio Rauzzini and the Birth of a New Style in English Singing,* pp. 120–1.
12. Ibid. 2.
13. James Buzard, 'The Grand Tour and After (1660–1840)', in Peter Hulme and Tim Youngs (eds) *The Cambridge Companion to Travel Writing,* (Cambridge, Cambridge University Press, 2002), p. 38.
14. Philip Olleson, *The Journals and Letters of Susan Burney Music and Society in Late Eighteenth-Century England,* (Abingdon, Routledge, 2016), p. 12.
15. Charles Burney, *The Present State of Music in France and Italy,* [second edition] (London, T. Becket and Company, 1773), pp. 336–7.
16. Ibid.
17. *Gazetteer and New Daily Advertiser*, 23 February 1778.
18. 'Currency converter: 1270–2017', *The National Archives,* Accessed 27 September 2022. https://www.nationalarchives.gov.uk/currency-converter/.
19. Isabelle Putnam Emerson, *Five Centuries of Women Singers*, (London, Praeger, 2005), p. 108.
20. 'improvement', n.s. *A Dictionary of the English Language, by Samuel Johnson*. 1755. Accessed 27 September 2022. https://johnsonsdictionaryonline.com/1755/improvement_ns.
21. Dorothea Link provides a detailed discussion on the singers at Emperor Joseph II's court. See Link, *The Italian Opera Singers in Mozart's Vienna*, (Champaign, Illinois, University of Illinois Press, 2022).
22. Kelly, *The Reminiscences of Michael Kelly*, Vol. 1, 12.
23. Bertil H. Van Boer has also placed some doubt that Venanzio Rauzzini even instructed Kelly, instead suggesting that it was Matteo Rauzzini (1754–1791), Venanzio's brother who lived in Dublin, who was his singing master. However, *The Reminiscences* make it very clear that the Rauzzini giving such advice was Venanzio, making sure to highlight his illustrious singing career and even that he composed 'Fuggiam dove sicura', the tune of which was used by Thomas Linley in the popular English opera *The Duenna,* which premiered at the Theatre Royal, Covent Garden in 1775. See Van Boer, *Historical Dictionary of Music of the Classical Period,* (Lanham, Maryland: Scarecrow Press, 2012), p. 460.
24. Kelly, *The Reminiscences of Michael Kelly*, Vol. 1, p. 31.
25. Ibid., p. 43.
26. Ibid., p. 80.

27. Possibly Genaro Manini (fl.1733-fl.1780), a dramatic composer who composed for one of the theatres in Rome. See John S. Sainsbury, *A Dictionary of Musicians From the Earliest Ages to the Present Time,* (London, Sainsbury and Company, 1824), p. 103.
28. The musical events at the festival were directed by Aprile. Kelly, *The Reminiscences of Michael Kelly*, Vol. 1, 88, T. Mortimer, 'The Adventures of Michael Kelly.' *Dublin Historical Record* vol,53, No. 2 (2000), 126. http://www.jstor.org/stable/30101256.
29. Kelly, *The Reminiscences of Michael Kelly*, Vol. 1, p. 88.
30. Ibid., p. 95.
31. Ibid., p. 96.
32. Ibid., p. 105 and p. 108.
33. Ibid., p. 114.
34. Ibid.
35. Ibid., p. 96 and p. 98.
36. *Public Advertiser,* 13 February 1786.
37. *Public Advertiser,* 17 February 1786.
38. *Morning Chronicle and London Advertiser,* 26 April 1786.
39. *Public Ledger,* 10 October 1786.
40. *Public Advertiser*, 21 July 1792.
41. The Italian reads: 'Voi sapete le mie pretese per cantare a Genova il carnevale sono due milla zecchini e alloggio. Sono sorpresa che voi raccomandate sempre i [prezzi] [...]'. I am grateful to Luca Guariento for assisting with the translation of this letter.
42. [Elizabeth Billington] Letter from Venice, to Emanuele Niecco, 1798, LWL Mss File 105, Lewis Walpole Library, Yale University, New Haven, Connecticut.
43. Rachel Cowgill, 'Billington [née Weichsel], Elizabeth (1765–1818), singer.' *Oxford Dictionary of National Biography*, (2004). Accessed 18 September 2022. https://www.oxforddnb.com/view/10.1093/ref:odnb/9780198614128.001.0001/odnb-9780198614128-e-2397.
44. *The Quarterly Musical Magazine and Review*, Vol. 1 (London: Baldwin, Cradock, and Joy, 1818), 176.; Richard Edgecumbe, *Musical Reminiscences, Chiefly Respecting the Italian Opera in England from the Year 1773 to the Present Time*, (London, George Clarke, 1828), p. 89.
45. *Morning Chronicle*, 14 August 1801.
46. *The Morning Chronicle,* 2 June 1787.
47. Kelly, *The Reminiscences of Michael Kelly*, Vol. 1, p. 296.
48. *The London Chronicle,* 19–21 April 1787.
49. *Morning Chronicle*, 11 May 1787.
50. *Morning Herald*, 20 March 1787; *General Advertiser*, 7 April 1787.
51. Joel Collver, 'Musical Sketches', *The English Lyceum,* (Hamburg, Mr. Bohnp, 1787), p. 188; Charles Morris, *Hilaria, the Festive Board,* (London, Printed for the Author, 1798), 26; *World and Fashionable Advertiser*, 11 May 1787.
52. Collver, 'Musical Sketches', *The English Lyceum*, p. 186.
53. Ibid., p. 187.
54. *Argus,* 18 November 1789.
55. *General Advertiser*, 8 March 1786.
56. *British Theatre,* Vol. 9, (London, John Bell, 1791), np.
57. *World*, 25 October 1788.
58. *Jackson's Oxford Journal*, 10 October 1801.
59. *Morning Chronicle*, 5 October 1801.
60. *Derby Mercury*, 7 April 1803.
61. I discuss this shift in detail in *Venanzio Rauzzini and the birth of a new style in English singing,* pp. 81–98.
62. Annoucements that Mrs. Billington was returning to the English stage emphasised that audiences should remember her voice from when she performed previously. See *Morning*

Post, 15 July 1801; *Morning Chronicle*, 30 September 1801; *Jackson's Oxford Journal*, 10 October 1801.

Chapter 7

1. A.J.W. Morrison (ed.), *Goethe's Travels in Italy: together with his Second residence in Rome and fragments on Italy*, Ch. Nisbet, Translated from the German (London, G. Bell and Sons, 1885), pp. 347–348.
2. D. Sobczyńska, *Między sztuką a nauką. Dwugłos artysty i uczonego o barwie*, 'Przegląd Filozoficzny – Nowa Seria' Vol. 16, No 3 (63), 2007, pp. 230–232.
3. H. Chmal, *Johann Wolfgang Goethe (1749–1832) – przyrodnik*, 'Czasopismo Geograficzne', No 81 (3), pp. 173–185.
4. Cf. R. Friedenthal, *Goethe. Jego życie i czasy*. Przeł. M. Rotter. (Warszawa, Czytelnik, 1969).
5. See ibid, p. 98: J.W. Goethe, *Faust. A tragedy by Johann Wolfgang von Goethe.* Translated, in the original metres, by B. Taylor. Two volumes in one, Vol. 2 (Boston and New York, Houghton, Mifflin and Co, 1913), p. 106.
6. *Goethes Italienishe Reise* (Leipzig, Insel-Verlag, 1914).
7. A.J.W. Morrison (ed.), *Goethe's Travels in Italy,* [Palermo, April 13, 1787], (London, G. Bell and Sons, 1885), p. 239.
8. K. Syta, *Skład osobowy sztabu regimentu pieszego buławy wielkiej koronnej w latach 1751–1771*, in: *Schriftlichkeit Beschreibung und Interpretation von Quellen. Festschrift zum 70. Geburstag von Professor Janusz Tandecki*, hrsg. v. R. Skowrońska, K. Kopiński, H. Flachenecker (Toruń, Wydawnictwo Naukowe Uniwersytetu Mikołaja Kopernika, Polska Misja Historyczna przy Uniwersytecie Juliusza Maksymiliana, 2020), p. 251.
9. K. Klavins, *Michael Johann Borch's meeting with Voltaire: a page from Latvia's European cultural history*. 'Humanities and Social Sciences: Latvia', Vol. 21, Issue 1 (Spring-Summer 2013), pp. 31–40.
10. A. Abramowicz, *Starożytności antyczne i Stanisław August*, in: idem: *Dzieje zainteresowań starożytniczych w Polsce, pt. 2: Czasy stanisławowskie i ich pokłosie* (Wrocław, Zakład Narodowy im. Ossolińskich, 1987), pp. 15–32.
11. Jolanta Polanowska claims that M.J. Borch won the favour of the King as an infantry captain of the guard and a member of the king's entourage during the Bar Confederation coup (3 November 1771). See. J. Polanowska, *Ogród w Warklanach – dzieło właściciela Michała Jana Borcha i architekta Vincenza de Mazottiego, „Biuletyn Historii Sztuki" 2012 nr 3-4*, p. 557.
12. See also R. Sweet, *Experiencing the Grand Tour*, in: eadem: *Cities and the Grand Tour* (Cambridge University Press, 2021), pp. 23–64.
13. J. Orzeł, A. Pacevičius, S. Roszak (eds.), *Dziennik podróży Józefa Jerzego Hylzena z lat 1752–1754* (Vilnius, Vilniaus universiteto leidykla, 2013).
14. See Letter from Jan Jędrzej Borch to Remigian (Remigiusz) Kossakowski from Warsaw, 6 March 1776, Stefanyk National Science Library, F. 13, No. 96 [Letters of Count Jan Borch to his son Michał from the time of his journey abroad], Fol. 89v.
15. *Polacy członkami Akademii w Lyonie w XVIII wieku*, in *Losy Polaków w XIX-XX w. Studia ofiarowane Profesorowi Stefanowi Kieniewiczowi w osiemdziesiątą rocznicę Jego urodzi*n (Warszawa, Państwowe Wydawnictwo Naukowe, 1987), p. 371.
16. P.A. Jeziorski, *Podróże edukacyjne zamożnej szlachty z województwa inflanckiego w XVIII wieku. Przykład Borchów i Hylzenów*, 'Miscellanea Historico-Archivistica', Vol. 24, (2017), pp. 13–14.
17. J. Stradins, *Michał Jan Borch – polski przyrodnik XVIII w.*, 'Kwartalnik Historii Nauki i Techniki', No. 25/3, (1980), p. 486.
18. A. Roćko (ed.), *Polski Grand Tour w XVIII i początkach XIX wieku* (Warszawa, Muzeum Pałacu Króla Jana III w Wilanowie, 2014).

19. M. Zawartko-Laskowska, *Mecenat naukowy Stanisława Augusta i jego przyrodnicze pasje.* 'Kronika Zamkowa', No. 1/2, (2008), p. 70.
20. See also. J. Stradins, *Michał Jan Borch – polski przyrodnik XVIII w.*, p. 485.
21. Ibid, pp. 486–487.
22. A. Gaweł, *Memoriał Borcha z roku 1780 jako pierwsza w Polsce próba geobiochemicznych poszukiwań kruszcowych*, 'Prace Muzeum Ziemi' No. 8, (1966), pp. 31–46.
23. The idea of M.J. Borch was rejected by the royal chemist, mineralogist, and the curator of the natural collection Stanisław Okraszewski. (1744–1824). See. Z. Libiszowska, *Polacy członkami Akademii w Lyonie w XVIII wieku*, in: *Losy Polaków w XIX-XX w. Studia ofiarowane Profesorowi Stefanowi Kieniewiczowi w osiemdziesiątą rocznicę jego urodzin* (Warszawa, Państwowe Wydawnictwo Naukowe, 1987) p. 373.
24. Ibid, p. 370.
25. E. Chapron, *L'Europe à Nîmes – les carnets de Jean-François Séguier (1732–1783)*, (Avignon, 2008), p. 38.
26. A French botanist and Jesuit published one of the scientific letters of Michał Jan Borch. See *Lettre de M. le comte Borch, de plusieurs Académies, à l'Auteur de ce recueil, Sur la manière de teindre les cuirs en vert*, in M. l'Abbé Rozier, M.J.A. Mongez, *Observations sur la physique, sur l'histoire naturelle et les arts*, 1779, p. 114.
27. A. Stroev, À la recherche de la correspondance savante du comte Michał Jan Borch, in: *Correspondances d'érudits au XVIIIe et XIXe siècles – France, Pologne, Lituanie*, ed. Marie-France de Palacio (Rennes 2014), pp. 171–198.
28. L. Hass, *Sekta farmazonii warszawskiej. Pierwsze stulecie wolnomularstwa w Warszawie (1721–1821)*, (Warszawa, Państwowy Instytut Wydawniczy, 1980), pp. 190–191.
29. K. Klavins, *Michael Johann Borch's meeting with Voltaire*, p. 33.
30. Ibid, p. 35.
31. P.A. Jeziorski, *Podróże edukacyjne zamożnej szlachty z województwa inflanckiego w XVIII wieku*, p. 18.
32. Ibid.
33. Государственная Третьяковская галерея: каталог собрания. Серия живопись *XVIII-XX* веков, ed. Я. В. Брук, Л. И. Иовлева (Москва, Красная площадь, 1997), p. 115.
34. See Sir William Hamilton by Sir Joshua Reynolds oil on canvas 1777, National Portrait Gallery, London. https://www.npg.org.uk/collections/search/portrait/mw02866/Sir-William-Hamilton.
35. See also J. Polanowska, *Ogród w Warklanach – dzieło właściciela Michała Jana Borcha i architekta Vincenza de Mazottiego.* 'Biuletyn Historii Sztuki' Vol. 74, No. 3–4 (2012), p. 555.
36. A. Lazzaro Spalanzzani, *Travels in the Two Sicilies and some parts of the Apennines*, in: *A general collection of the best and most interesting voyages and travels in all parts of the world; many of which are now first translated into English. Digest on a new plan by John Pinkerton*, Vol. 5 (London, Longman, Hurst, Rees, and Orme [etc.], 1809), pp. 78–83. Ruth Noyes Sagent notices that M.J. Borch probably had visited Hamilton's villa in Naples during his travels to Italy. See R. Sargent Noyes, *Count Michał Jan Borch as patron and collector: art between Italy and Inflanty in the Age of Partition*, 'Baltic Journal of Art History' (2021), p. 22.
37. T. Rączka-Jeziorska, *Romantyzm polsko-inflancki. Sylwetki, teksty, archiwa*, (Warszawa, Wydawnictwo: Instytut Badań Literackich PAN, 2016), pp. 53–80.
38. See the letter from M.J. Borch to his father Jan Jędrzej from Rome, 28 May 1778, Stefanyk National Science Library, F. 13, No. 90 [Correspondence of Jan and Ludwika Borch, mainly letters from Michał Jan Borch from his travels in Western Europe 1773–1780], fol. 325–326.
39. Michał Jan Borch mentions it in a letter to his father from Florence, 6 August 1779: 'The Parma Infant accepted the dedication of my Mineralogy, which, having printed it, I shall send. The Academy della Crusca, that is, the Academy of the Italian language, on seeing my

Italian memorial allowed me among its members. Same as scientarum of Siena.' Stefanyk National Science Library, F. 13, No. 90, fol. 437–437v.

40. J. Stradins, *Michał Jan Borch – polski przyrodnik XVIII w.*, pp. 490–92.
41. Ibid.
42. *Goethes Bibliothek Katalog*. Bearbeiter der Ausgabe H. Ruppert (Weimar, Arion Verlag, 1958), pp. 580, 633.
43. J. Drzymała, M. Mikołajczyk, D. Piwowar, B. Polak, H. Drzymała, J. Ragiel, M. Drzymała-Tronina, *Johann Wolfgang Goethe oraz jego wkład w rozwój górnictwa i geologii*, 'Prace Naukowe Instytutu Górnictwa Politechniki Wrocławskiej' No. 131 (2010), pp. 40–41.
44. A.J.W. Morrison (ed.), *Goethe's Travels in Italy*, p. 239.
45. J. Drzymała, M. Mikołajczyk, D. Piwowar, B. Polak, H. Drzymała, J. Ragiel, M. Drzymała-Tronina, *Johann Wolfgang Goethe oraz jego wkład w rozwój górnictwa i geologii*, p. 37.
46. See. A.J.W. Morrison (ed.), *Goethe's Travels in Italy*, pp. 239, 283.
47. Ibid, p. 239.
48. Michał Jan Borch commissioned the publication of 'Collection Complet' of his works to the Typographic Society of Neuchâtel, which is mentioned in the correspondence with King Stanisław August in 1787; it is kept at the Czartoryski Library in Kraków. Z. Libiszowska, *Polacy członkami Akademii w Lyonie w XVIII wieku*, p. 374.
49. A. Rottermund, *Polski grand tour, czyli problem królewskiej podróży po Italii*. 'Wiek Oświecenia', Vol. 15, (1999), pp. 135–147.
50. P.A. Jeziorski, *Podróże edukacyjne zamożnej szlachty z województwa inflanckiego w XVIII wieku*, p. 13.
51. He visited this city for the second time from February to April 1779. According to A. Stroev, he also borrowed microscopes for researching truffles from Giovanni Battista Beccaria (1716–1781), a famous Italian physicist and monk. See A. Stroev, À la recherche de la correspondance savante du comte Michał Jan Borch.
52. Ibid.
53. See M.E. Kowalczyk, *Drogi Polaków do Włoch, w tejże: Obraz Włoch w polskim piśmiennictwie geograficznym i podróżniczym XVIII wieku* (Toruń, Wydawnictwo Adam Marszałek, 2005), pp. 91–152.
54. See M.J. Borch's letter to his father Jan Jędrzej from Turin, 17 May 1780. Stefanyk National Science Library, F. 13, No. 90, Fol. 461v.
55. I.Z. Siemion, A. Szastyńska-Siemion, *O eksperymentach Michała Jana Borcha (1753–1811) dotyczących chemiluminescencji*, 'Wiadomości chemiczne' No. 67, Issue 3–4 (2013), pp. 362–374.
56. I.Z. Siemion, B. Latko, *Michała Jana Borcha rozprawa o truflach piemonckich*, „Annalecta: studia i materiały z dziejów nauki", Vol. 22, No. 1–2, pp. 7–16.
57. Michel-Jean de Borch, *Briefe ueber Sicilien und Maltha mir Charten vom Etna, von den alten und neuen Sicilien, nebst Kupferstichen, von dem Grafen Borch* (Bern, Neue typographische Gesellschaft, 1783) Michel-Jean de Borch, *Reise durch Sicilien und Maltha und von der Revolutionem so dieses Land erlitten hat.*, Th. 1–2 (Bern, Typographische Societat, 1796).
58. J. Stradins, *Michał Jan Borch – polski przyrodnik XVIII w.*, p. 492.
59. See *Comte de Borch's Letters on Sicily and Maltha*, 'The English Review, or an abstract of English and foreign literature", Vol. 2 (London, 1783), pp. 7–18.
60. The Polish translation of this work by J. Adamczewski (1763–1812) appeared in 1805. Its source was the German translation by Joachim Heinrich Campe. See. E. Walendziak-Genco, A. Sztuk, *Sulla traduzione Polacca di A Tour through Sicily and Malta: in a series of letters to William Beckford, ESQ. of Somerly in Suffolk di Patrick Brydone*, 'Kwartalnik Neofilologiczny', LXII, 2/2015, pp. 193–201.
61. A. Tylusińska-Kowalska, *Il conte Michał Jan Borch in Sicilia: il viaggio culturale di uno scienziato*, F. d'Angelo (ed.), *The Scientific Dialogue Linking America, Asia and Europe between*

the 12th and the 20th Century. Theories and Techniques travelling in Space and Time, (Naples, Viaggiatori, 2018), p. 277.

62. Hackert, a German court painter to King Ferdinand of Naples, and Wutky, an Austrian painter, also worked closely with Hamilton. Their geological studies of volcanoes in action often showed realistic groups of observers starkly outlined against an awesome natural spectacle. See Sarah Goldsmith, 'Fire and Ice: Mountains, Glaciers and Volcanoes' in her book *Masculinity and Danger on The Eightennth-Century Grand Tour* (London, University of London Press, 2020), p. 159.
63. M. Królikowska-Dziubecka, *Podróże artystyczne Jana Chrystiana Kamsetzera (1776–1777; 1780–1782)* (Warszawa, Wydawnictwo Neriton, 2003), p. 43.
64. The ban on their publication did not apply to Pietro Fabris (1740–1792), who cooperated with William Hamilton. See A. Sołtys, *Podróże Polaków do Italii w drugiej połowie XVIII wieku: kontekst neapolitański* in *Polski Grand Tour w XVIII i początkach XIX wieku*, p. 85.
65. J. Polanowska, *Ogród w Warklanach...*, p. 555.
66. 'The English Review, 1783, p. 18.
67. T. Freller, *Persons of reference: Maltese and Sicilian scholars and their importance for the Grand Tour* in A. Bonanno, P. Militello (eds.), *Interconnections in the Central Mediterranaean: The Maltese Islands and Sicily in History* (Palermo, Officina di Studi Medievali, 2008), pp. 81–98.
68. M.E. Kowalczyk, *'Na papierze z Etny'. Wizerunek Sycylii w listach z podróży Michała Jana Borcha* in M. Wrześniak, A. Bender (eds.), *Polak we Włoszech, Włoch w Polsce. Sztuka i historia* (Warszawa, Uniwersytet Kardynała Stefana Wyszyńskiego, 2015), p. 123. T. Mikocki, *A la recherche de l'art antique. Les voyageurs polonais en Italie dans les annés 1750–1830*, (Wrocław, 1988), pp. 108–111.
69. A. Stroev, À la recherche de la correspondance savante du comte Michał Jan Borch.
70. M.E. Kowalczyk, *'Na papierze z Etny"*, p. 122.
71. From the correspondence of M.J. Borch to his father we know that, while travelling around Sicily, he struggled with "two diseases", which, as he explained to him, kept him there longer than he originally planned. See The Letter from M.J. Borch to his father Jan Jędrzej from Naples, 22 July 1777. Stefanyk National Science Library, F. 13, No. 90, Fol. 280v.
72. Due to the lack of an English edition excerpts from *The Letters about Sicily and Malta* by Michał Jan Borch are cited in translation by Maciej Kapałczyński based on the Polish edition. See M.J. Borch, *Listy o Sycylii i Malcie*, transll. A. Szatyńska-Siemion i I.Z. Siemion (Warszawa, Aspra, 2015).
73. Ibid, pp. 67–68.
74. Ibid, p. 122.
75. Ibid, pp. 298–299.
76. Including Goethe himself, who, as L. Wolff notes, in 1790 went on a week-long trip to Poland, reaching Kraków, and in a letter to Herder, he did not speak very favourably about his impressions from this trip. See L. Wolff, *Inventing Eastern Europe. The Map of Civilization on the Mind of the Enlightenment* (Stanford, Stanford University Press, 1994), p. 530.
77. Ibid, pp. 59–95.
78. M.J. Borch, *Listy o Sycylii i Malcie*, p. 64.
79. A. Abramowicz, *Michał Borch i starożytności antyczne*, pt. 2*: Czasy stanisławowskie i ich pokłosie* (Wrocław, Polska Akademia Nauk, Instytut Historii Kultury Materialnej, 1987), p. 52.
80. A. Roćko, *Podróże oświeconych śladami antyku* in *Antyk oświeconych. Studia i rozprawy o miejscu starożytności w kulturze polskiej XVIII wieku*, ed. T. Chachulski (Warszawa, Wydawnictwo: Instytut Badań Literackich PAN, 2012), pp. 225–230.
81. A. Abramowicz, *Zainteresowania numizmatyczne Michała Jana Borcha w czasie podróży na Sycylię i Maltę w 1776/7 roku* in 'Wiadomości numizmatyczne', Vol. 28, Issue 1–2, pp. 106–110.

82. See Planches des Lettres sur la Sicile, et sur l'île de Malthe... graué par Dell Aqua i.a. *Danse des Paysanesse Siciliennes*, Vol. 1, p. XVII; *Jeune fille Lipparotte en habit de Nôces*, Vol. 2, p. 112.
83. M.J. Borch, *Listy o Sycylii i Malcie*, p. 248.
84. Ibid, p. 268.
85. See 'Count Borch leaves his readers in uncertainty; but, in fact, even he ascended only to a certain height: and the same may be said of many others.' A.J.W. Morrison (ed.), *Goethe's Travels in Italy,* [Catania, Friday, May 4, 1787], p. 283.
86. The final words attributed to Goethe.
87. Ibid.
88. A. Stroev, À la recherche de la correspondance savante du comte Michał Jan Borch.
89. R. Sargent Noyes et al., *'Baltic catacombs.' Translating corpisanti* catacomb relic-sculptures between Rome, Polish Livonia, and the Lithuanian Grand Duchy circa 1750–1800. Open Research Europe 2021, 1:18 (https://doi.org/10.12688/openreseurope.13259.1).
90. T. Rączka, *Księgozbiory Polskich Inflantczyków w świetle nieznanych archiwaliów (koniec XVIII-początek XIX w.)* in *Stan badań nad wielokulturowym dziedzictwem dawnej Rzeczypospolitej*, Vol. 6 (Białystok, Instytut Badań nad Dziedzictwem Kulturowym Europy, 2013), pp. 531–558; R. Sargent Noyes, *Count Michał Jan Borch as Patron and Collector: Art between Italy and Inflanty in the Age of Partition.*
91. I. Māra Janelis, *Manor Gardens and Parks of Latvia* (Rīga, 2010), pp. 118–122.; J. Polanowska, *Michał Jan Borch and his residence in Varklani: genesis and ideological programme*, in: 'Mākslas Vēsture un Teorija' Vol. 16, (2013), pp. 18–32; T. Rączka-Jeziorska, *Romantyczne mapowanie przestrzeni ogrodu według Polskiego Inflantczyka Michała Jana Borcha z Warklan (1753–1810),* in *Przestrzeń – literatura – doświadczenie. Z inspiracji geopoetyki* (Katowice, Wydawnictwo Uniwersytetu Śląskiego, 2016), pp. 111–123; O. Spārītis, *Three sources of Michael Johann von der Borch's poem «The sentimental park of Varakļāni palace»*, 'Baltic Journal of Art History', Vol. 20 (2020), pp. 109–144.
92. A.J.W. Morrison (ed.), *Goethe's Travels in Italy,* [Palermo, April 13, 1787], p. 239.

Chapter 8

1. Helen Maria Williams, *Souvenirs de la révolution française* (Paris, Dondey-Dupré, 1827), p. 199. Translation from original French by Deborah Kennedy, *Helen Maria Williams and the Age of Revolution* (Lewisburg, Bucknell University Press, 2002), p. 214.
2. Wole Soyinka, 'Exile', in Els van der Plas, Malu Halasa and Marlous Willemsen (eds), *Creating Spaces of Freedom: Culture in Defiance* (London, Saqi, 2002), p. 29.
3. I am particularly indebted to the writer and filmmaker Elsa Gomis (www.elsagomis.com), whose important work on modern-day migration first made me think about Helen Maria Williams in this light.
4. For an excellent critical biography of Williams, see Deborah Kennedy, *Helen Maria Williams and the Age of Revolution* above.
5. Helen Maria Williams was born in London in 1759, the youngest daughter of Welsh army officer Charles Williams and his second wife Helen. Charles Williams died in 1762.
6. Anonymous review of 'Miss Helen Williams' *Poems*' in the *European Magazine*, August 1786, pp. 89–93.
7. Wordsworth published 'Sonnet on Seeing Miss Helen Maria Williams Weep at a Tale of Distress' under the pseudonym 'Axiologus' in the *European Magazine*, March 1787, p. 202.
8. James Boswell recounts this story in *The Life of Samuel Johnson*, 3 Vols, (Dublin, R. Cross et al., 1792), Vol. 3, pp. 428–29.
9. Natasha Duquette describes how Williams's writing reflects her identity as a Presbyterian Dissenter in 'Dissenting Cosmopolitanism and Helen Maria Williams's Prison Verse', *Women's Writing*, 27:1 (2020), pp. 80–96.

10. Williams's first published poem *Edwin and Eltruda* (1782) is an anti-war tale about the War of the Roses; *An Ode on the Peace* (1783) celebrates the end of the war with America; and she contributed to the abolition campaign with *A Poem on the Bill Lately Passed for Regulating the Slave-Trade* (1788).
11. The seventy-eight-page subscription list for *Poems* (1786) includes royalty, nobility, actresses, writers, churchmen, and politicians.
12. Helen Maria Williams, *Letters Written in France*, (eds) Neil Fraistat and Susan S. Lanser, (Ontario, Broadview Press, 2001). For a discussion of Williams's revolutionary writing, see Elizabeth A. Bohls, *Women Travel Writers and the Language of Aesthetics, 1716–1818* (Cambridge, Cambridge University Press, 1995); and Adriana Craciun, *British Women Writers and the French Revolution: Citizens of the World*, (Basingstoke, Palgrave Macmillan, 2005).
13. For a discussion of Williams's vilification and marginalization, see Louise Duckling, 'From Liberty to Lechery: Performance, Reputation and the "Marvellous Story" of Helen Maria Williams', *Women's Writing*, 17:1 (2010), pp. 74–92.
14. Helen Maria Williams, *Letters Written in France*, p. 149.
15. As Deborah Kennedy describes, 'many of the people she was closest to in Paris were guillotined', including Madame Roland (Marie-Jeanne Roland) who was executed on 8 November 1793. See Deborah Kennedy, *Helen Maria Williams and the Age of Revolution*, p. 107.
16. Helen Maria Williams, *A Tour in Switzerland; or, A View of the Present State of the Governments and Manners of those Cantons: With Comparative Sketches of the Present State of Paris*, 2 Vols. (London, Printed for G.G. and J. Robinson, 1798), Vol. 1, p. 2. *A Tour in Switzerland* is freely available to read on Google Books.
17. Williams constructs a personal narrative of exile without naming her travelling companions, but external sources confirm that she was travelling with Stone. Critics have speculated on his involvement in an alleged 'mission' in Switzerland (with conflicting theories, one positioning him as a French agent and another as a British agent). The evidence is inconclusive. The mystery is fuelled by the fact that they were joined for part of the tour by the liberal MP Benjamin Vaughan (recently implicated in a treason trial in London) and Louis-Marc Rivals, a diplomat and French agent. For discussion, see Patrick Vincent, 'Introduction' to Helen Maria Williams, *A Tour in Switzerland*, (eds) Patrick Vincent and Florence Widmer-Schnyder, (Geneva, Slatkine, 2011), pp. 1–59.
18. Helen Maria Williams, *A Tour in Switzerland*, Vol. 1, pp. 57–58.
19. For political analysis of *A Tour in Switzerland*, see Paula Yurss Lasanta, 'The Writing of Politics and the Politics of Writing in Helen Maria Williams' *A Tour in Switzerland* (1798)', *The Grove – Working Papers on English Studies*, 23 (2016), pp. 199–212; and Nigel Leask, 'Salons, Alps and Cordilleras: Helen Maria Williams, Alex von Humboldt and the discourse of Romantic travel', in Elizabeth Eger et al. (eds), *Women, Writing and the Public Sphere, 1700–1830* (Cambridge, Cambridge University Press, 2001), pp. 217–235. Angela Keane describes Williams's 'sublime exile' but focuses primarily on her political motivations for writing. See Angela Keane, 'Sublime Exile: A Tour in Switzerland' in *Revolutionary Women Writers: Charlotte Smith and Helen Maria Williams*, (Liverpool, Liverpool University Press, 2013), pp. 119–130.
20. Helen Maria Williams, *A Tour in Switzerland*, Vol. 2, p. 111.
21. Ibid, Vol. 1, pp. 2–3.
22. Ibid, Vol. 1, p. 36.
23. Ibid, Vol. 1, p. 90.
24. Ibid, Vol. 1, pp. 40–2.
25. Ibid, Vol. 1, p. 4.
26. Chris Jones highlights Williams's optimism in her discussion of *Letters Written in France*. See Chris Jones, 'Travelling Hopefully: Helen Maria Williams and the Feminine Discourse

of Sensibility' in Amanda Gilroy (ed), *Romantic Geographies: Discourses of Travel 1775–1844*, (Manchester, Manchester University Press, 2000), pp. 93–108.
27. Helen Maria Williams, *A Tour in Switzerland*, Vol. 2, pp. 181, 197.
28. Ibid, Vol. 1, p. 94.
29. Ibid, Vol. 2, pp. 138–39.
30. Ibid, Vol. 1, p. 212.
31. Ibid, Vol. 1, pp. 254, 350. To build empathy, Williams quotes from 'Ovid to his Wife', a poem by her contemporary Anna Laetitia Barbauld on the theme of Ovid's exile: 'Forced from my native seats, and sacred home, / Friendless, alone, through Scythian wilds to roam'.
32. Helen Maria Williams, *A Tour in Switzerland*, Vol. 1, p. 351.
33. Ibid, Vol. 1, pp. 336–37.
34. Angela Keane, *Revolutionary Women Writers: Charlotte Smith and Helen Maria Williams*, p. 120.
35. Helen Maria Williams, *A Tour in Switzerland*, Vol. 1, p. 155.
36. Ibid, Vol. 1, p. 160.
37. Ibid, Vol. 1, p. 257.
38. Ibid, Vol. 1, p. 210.
39. Hamid Naficy, *The Making of Exile Cultures: Iranian Television in Los Angeles* (Minneapolis, University of Minnesota Press, 1993), p. 6.
40. Ibid, p. 9.
41. My discussion on liminality is informed by recent studies exploring the exilic condition in the twentieth and twenty-first centuries, including work on Latvian writers by Eva Eglāja-Kristone (2015), and Ingrīda Kupšāne and Sandra Meškova (2021).
42. Homi K. Bhabha, 'DissemiNation: Time, Narrative, and the Margins of the Modern Nation' in Homi K Bhabha (ed.), *Nation and Narration*, (London, Routledge, 1990), p. 300.
43. Helen Maria Williams, *A Tour in Switzerland*, Vol. 1, pp. 141–44.
44. The full poem – 'A HYMN written among the ALPS' – is included at the end of the first chapter in Volume 2 (pp. 16–19), and forms part of the rich generic tapestry of *A Tour in Switzerland*.
45. Helen Maria Williams, *A Tour in Switzerland*, Vol. 2, pp. 7–8.
46. Ibid, Vol. 1, p. 47.
47. Ibid, Vol. 1, pp. 58–60. As Deborah Kennedy has remarked, Williams's reaction 'bursts out of the bounds of the predictable.' See Deborah Kennedy, *Helen Maria Williams and the Age of Revolution*, p. 134.
48. Helen Maria Williams, *A Tour in Switzerland*, Vol. 1, p. 60.
49. Ibid, Vol. 1, p. 61.
50. Julia Kristeva, *Strangers to Ourselves*, Translated by Leon S. Roudiez (New York, Columbia University Press, 1991), pp. 187–88.
51. For a discussion of Williams's deconstruction and borrowing of key travel texts by William Coxe and M. Ramond, see Anthony Oxturk, 'Translating Helvetica: Travel Writing, Intertext, and Image' in Alison E. Martin and Susan Pickford (eds), *Travel Narratives in Translation, 1750–1830: Nationalism, Ideology, Gender* (New York and Abingdon, Routledge, 2012), pp. 56–73, p. 65. For a broader critical context, see Patrick Vincent, 'Introduction' to Helen Maria Williams, *A Tour in Switzerland*, pp. 1–59.
52. Helen Maria Williams, *A Tour in Switzerland*, Vol. 1, p. 6, p. 98.
53. Ibid, Vol. 1, p. 200.
54. Ibid, Vol. 2, p. 86.
55. Ibid, Vol. 1, p. 236.
56. Ibid, Vol. 2, p. 37.
57. Ibid, Vol. 2, p. 269.

58. Ibid, Vol. 1, p. 110.
59. Ibid, Vol. 1, p. 97.
60. Ibid, Vol. 1, pp. 103–4.
61. Ibid, Vol. 2, p. 87.
62. Glarus is cited as a notable exception of a canton where there is religious toleration (Ibid, Vol. 2, p. 80).
63. Ibid, Vol. 2, p. 175.
64. Ibid, Vol. 2, p. 41.
65. Ibid, Vol. 1, p. 5.
66. Ibid, Vol. 1, p. 117.
67. Ibid, Vol. 1, p. 13.
68. Ibid, Vol. 1, p. 238.
69. Ibid, Vol. 1, p. 268.
70. Ibid, Vol. 1, pp. 270, 271.
71. Ibid, Vol. 1, p. 175.
72. Ibid, Vol. 2, p. 191.
73. Ibid, Vol. 2, p. 13.
74. Ibid, Vol. 1, p. 195.
75. Ibid, Vol. 1, p. 250.
76. Ibid, Vol. 1, p. 52.
77. Ibid, Vol. 2, pp. 125–126.
78. Ibid, Vol. 2, p. 121.
79. Ibid, Vol. 2, p. 122.
80. Ibid, Vol. 2, p. 91.
81. Ibid, Vol. 2, p. 101.
82. Ibid, Vol. 1, p. 38.
83. Ibid, Vol. 1, pp. 74–75.
84. Ibid, Vol. 1, p. 276.
85. Ibid, Vol. 1, p. 283.
86. Ibid, Vol. 1, p. 291.
87. Ibid, Vol. 1, p. 298.
88. Ibid, Vol. 1, p. 313.
89. Ibid, Vol. 1, p. 305–6.
90. Ibid, Vol. 2, p. 230.
91. Ibid, Vol. 2, p. 256.
92. Ibid, Vol. 2, p. 271.
93. Ibid, Vol. 2, p. 277.

Chapter 9

1. Mary Wollstonecraft, 'Analytical Review, August 1790' in Jane Todd and Marilyn Butler (eds.), *The Works of Mary Wollstonecraft*, Vol 7 of 7 (London, Pickering, 1989), p. 277.
2. Mary Wollstonecraft, *A Vindication of the Rights of Woman* (1792) in Deidre Shauna Lynch (ed.), *A Vindication of the Rights of Woman: An Authoritative Text Backgrounds and Contexts Criticism* (3rd ed. New York, London, W. W. Norton, 2009), p. 9.
3. Mary Wollstonecraft, *Letters Written During a Short Residence in Sweden, Norway, and Denmark* (1796) in Richard Holmes (ed.), *A Short Residence in Sweden, Norway and Denmark, and Memoirs of the Author of the Rights of Woman* (London, Penguin, 1987), p. 62.
4. William Godwin, *Memoirs of the Author of a Vindication of the Rights of Woman* (1798) in Richard Holmes (ed.), *A Short Residence in Sweden, Norway and Denmark, and Memoirs of the Author of the Rights of Woman* (London, Penguin, 1987), p. 242.

5. Jeremy Black, *The British Abroad: The G rand Tour in the Eighteenth Century* (Stroud, Sutton, 2003), pp. 7–13; John Lough, *France on the Eve of Revolution: British Travellers' Observations 1763–1788* (London, Croom Helm, 1987), pp. 1–4; John Towner, *The European Grand Tour, circa 1550–1840: A Study of its Role in the History of Tourism* (Ph.D. Thesis, University of Birmingham, 1984), figure 1.
6. Linda Colley, *Britons: Forging the Nation, 1707–1837* (2nd ed. New Haven, Yale University Press, 2005), pp. 5–9, 52–54, 101.
7. Michael Rapport, *Nationality and Citizenship in Revolutionary France: The Treatment of Foreigners 1789–1799* (Oxford, Clarendon, 2000), pp. 200–201.
8. Helen Maria Williams, *Letters Containing a Sketch of the Politics of France, from the Thirty-first of May 1793, till the Twenty-eighth of July 1794, and of the Scenes which have Passed in the Prisons of Paris*, Vol. 1 of 2 (London, G. G. J. and J. Robinson, 1795), p. 17; Charlette West, *A Ten Years' Residence in France, During the Severest Part of the Revolution, from the Year 1787 to 1797, Containing Various Anecdotes of Some of the Most Remarkable Personages of that Period* (London, 1821), pp. 68–69; Grace Dalrymple Elliott, *Journal of my Life during the French Revolution* (London, 1859), pp. 166–167.
9. Mary Wollstonecraft, *Collected Letters of Mary Wollstonecraft*. Edited by Ralph M. Wardle (Ithaca, Cornell University Press, 1979), note 1, p. 231.
10. Claire Tomalin, *The Life and Death of Mary Wollstonecraft* (2nd ed. London, New York, Penguin, 1992), pp. 207–208.
11. 'Wollstonecraft to Everina', 20 June 1792 in Wollstonecraft, *Collected Letters of Mary Wollstonecraft*, p. 213.
12. 'Wollstonecraft to Everina', 14 September 1792 in Wollstonecraft, *Collected Letters of Mary Wollstonecraft*, p. 214.
13. 'Wollstonecraft to William Roscoe', 12 November 1792 in Wollstonecraft, *Collected Letters of Mary Wollstonecraft*, p. 218.
14. 'Wollstonecraft to Joseph Johnson', 26 December 1792 in Wollstonecraft, *Collected Letters of Mary Wollstonecraft*, p. 227.
15. 'Wollstonecraft to Joseph Johnson', 26 December 1792 in Wollstonecraft, *Collected Letters of Mary Wollstonecraft*, p. 227.
16. *Archives Parlementaires de 1787* à *1860*, Première série (1787 à 1799), (Paris, 1862–1914), Vol. 60, pp. 51–65, 293–294, 492–496.
17. 'Wollstonecraft to Eliza', 13 June 1793, in Wollstonecraft, *Collected Letters of Mary Wollstonecraft*, p. 232.
18. 'Wollstonecraft to Eliza', 24 June 1793 in Wollstonecraft, *Collected Letters of Mary Wollstonecraft*, p. 233.
19. *Archives Parlementaires de 1787* à *1860*, Première série (1787 à 1799), Vol. 74, 'la loi des suspects', pp. 303–305. 'La loi des suspects': Law of Suspects.
20. *Archives Parlementaires de 1787* à *1860*, Première série (1787 à 1799), Vol. 76, pp. 639–645.
21. 'Wollstonecraft to Everina', 10 March 1794 in Wollstonecraft, *Collected Letters of Mary Wollstonecraft*, pp. 250–1.
22. 'Wollstonecraft to Ruth Barlow', 8 July 1794 in Wollstonecraft, *Collected Letters of Mary Wollstonecraft*, p. 257.
23. Mary Wollstonecraft, *A Vindication of the Rights of Men* (1790) in D.L. Macdonald and Kathleen Scherf (eds.), *A Vindication of the Rights of Men and A Vindication of the Rights of Woman* (Peterborough, Ontario, Broadview Press, 1997), pp. 165–166.
24. Mary Wollstonecraft, *An Historical and Moral View of the Origin and Progress of the French Revolution; and the Effect It Has Produced in Europe* (London, 1794), p. 252.
25. Wollstonecraft, *An Historical and Moral View of the Origin and Progress of the French Revolution*, p. 497.

26. Chris Jones, 'Mary Wollstonecraft's *Vindications* and their Political Tradition', in Claudia L. Johnson (ed.), *The Cambridge Companion to Mary Wollstonecraft* (Cambridge, Cambridge University Press, 2002), p. 54.
27. Edmund Burke, *Reflections on the Revolution in France* (1790), edited by L. G. Mitchell (Oxford, Oxford University Press, 1999), p. 72, 76.
28. Wollstonecraft, *A Vindication of the Rights of Men*, pp. 61–62.
29. Wollstonecraft, *An Historical and Moral View of the Origin and Progress of the French Revolution*, p. 26.
30. Wollstonecraft, *An Historical and Moral View of the Origin and Progress of the French Revolution*, p. 71.
31. Wollstonecraft, *An Historical and Moral View of the Origin and Progress of the French Revolution*, p. 72.
32. Wollstonecraft, *An Historical and Moral View of the Origin and Progress of the French Revolution*, p. 296.
33. Wollstonecraft, *Letters Written During a Short Residence in Sweden, Norway, and Denmark*, pp. 168-169, 193.
34. 'Wollstonecraft to Everina', 10March1794, pp. 150–251; 'Wollstonecraft to Ruth Barlow', 8 July 1794, p. 257, both in Wollstonecraft, *Collected Letters of Mary Wollstonecraft*.
35. Wollstonecraft, *An Historical and Moral View of the Origin and Progress of the French Revolution*, p. 344.
36. Wollstonecraft, *An Historical and Moral View of the Origin and Progress of the French Revolution*, p. vii.
37. Wollstonecraft, *An Historical and Moral View of the Origin and Progress of the French Revolution*, p. 16.
38. Wollstonecraft, *An Historical and Moral View of the Origin and Progress of the French Revolution*, p. 235.
39. Another example was the public entertainments such as beasts fighting and wrestling in European society. As Wollstonecraft indicated, this kind of brutal and uncivilized activities were regarded as bravery. Wollstonecraft, *An Historical and Moral View of the Origin and Progress of the French Revolution*, pp. 15–16, 89, 227.
40. Wollstonecraft, *An Historical and Moral View of the Origin and Progress of the French Revolution*, pp. 16–17.
41. Wollstonecraft, *An Historical and Moral View of the Origin and Progress of the French Revolution*, p. 19.
42. Wollstonecraft, *An Historical and Moral View of the Origin and Progress of the French Revolution*, p. 17.
43. Wollstonecraft, *An History and Moral View of the Origin and Progress of the French Revolution*, p. 22.
44. Daniel I. O'Neill, *The Burke-Wollstonecraft Debate: Savagery, Civilization, and Democracy* (University Park, Pennsylvania State University Press, 2007), p. 236; see also Jane Rendall, '"The Grand Causes which Combine to Carry Mankind Forward": Wollstonecraft, History and Revolution', *Women's Writing*, Vol. 2: No. 4 (1997).
45. Wollstonecraft, *A Vindication of the Rights of Men*, pp. 28, 41.
46. Moira Ferguson and Janet Todd, *Mary Wollstonecraft* (Boston, Twayne, 1984), p. 77.
47. Mary Wollstonecraft, 'Letter on the Present Character of the French Nation (1793)', in Jane Todd and Marilyn Butler (eds.), *The Works of Mary Wollstonecraft*, vol. 6 of 7 (London, Pickering, 1989), p. 445.
48. Wollstonecraft, *An History and Moral View of the Origin and Progress of the French Revolution*, p. 467.
49. Wollstonecraft, *An History and Moral View of the Origin and Progress of the French Revolution*, p. 467.

50. Wollstonecraft, *An History and Moral View of the Origin and Progress of the French Revolution*, pp. 485–486.
51. Wollstonecraft, *An History and Moral View of the Origin and Progress of the French Revolution*, p. 512.
52. Wollstonecraft, *Letters Written During a Short Residence in Sweden, Norway, and Denmark*, p. 78.
53. Wollstonecraft, *Letters Written During a Short Residence in Sweden, Norway, and Denmark*, pp. 101–102.
54. Wollstonecraft, *Letters Written During a Short Residence in Sweden, Norway, and Denmark*, p. 149.
55. Wollstonecraft stressed the importance of the cultivation of arts and sciences several times in *A Short Residence*. See Wollstonecraft, *Letters Written During a Short Residence in Sweden, Norway, and Denmark*, pp. 73, 93, 103, 121, 141.
56. Wollstonecraft, *Letters Written During a Short Residence in Sweden, Norway, and Denmark*, p. 198.
57. Wollstonecraft, *Letters Written During a Short Residence in Sweden, Norway, and Denmark*, p. 120.
58. Wollstonecraft, *Letters Written During a Short Residence in Sweden, Norway, and Denmark*, p. 120.
59. Chris Jones, 'Mary Wollstonecraft's *Vindications* and their Political Tradition', p. 53.
60. Wollstonecraft, *Letters Written During a Short Residence in Sweden, Norway, and Denmark*, p. 150. Wollstonecraft took the society of England and America as examples: 'England and America owe their liberty to commerce, which created a new species of power to undermine the feudal system. But let them beware of the consequence; the tyranny of wealth is still more galling and debasing than that of rank.' Wollstonecraft, *Letters Written During a Short Residence in Sweden, Norway, and Denmark*, p. 150.
61. Wollstonecraft, *Letters Written During a Short Residence in Sweden, Norway, and Denmark*, pp. 93, 172.
62. Wollstonecraft, *Letters Written During a Short Residence in Sweden, Norway, and Denmark*, p. 103. Footnote of Wollstonecraft.
63. Wollstonecraft, *Letters Written During a Short Residence in Sweden, Norway, and Denmark*, pp. 121–122, 150.
64. Wollstonecraft, *Letters Written During a Short Residence in Sweden, Norway, and Denmark*, p. 103.
65. 'England and America owe their liberty to commerce, which created a new species of power to undermine the feudal system.' Wollstonecraft, *Letters Written During a Short Residence in Sweden, Norway, and Denmark*, p. 150.
66. Wollstonecraft, *Letters Written During a Short Residence in Sweden, Norway, and Denmark*, pp. 148–149.
67. Wollstonecraft, *Letters Written During a Short Residence in Sweden, Norway, and Denmark*, p. 131.
68. Wollstonecraft, *Letters Written During a Short Residence in Sweden, Norway, and Denmark*, pp. 168–169.
69. Wollstonecraft, *An History and Moral View of the Origin and Progress of the French Revolution*, p. 468.
70. 'Wollstonecraft to Everina', 7 November 1787, in Wollstonecraft, *Collected Letters of Mary Wollstonecraft*, p. 164.
71. 'Wollstonecraft to Everina', 10 March 1794, in Wollstonecraft, *Collected Letters of Mary Wollstonecraft*, p. 251.
72. Many journals described this extraordinarily cold winter 1794–1795. During this time, the price of food, firewood and turf was very high. According to the record in 'Meteorology at

Bracknell – Historic Weather Events', 'The winter of 1794/95 was exceptionally severe, with the very cold conditions setting in on Christmas Eve 1794. ... The cold was most intense during January, which resulted in the coldest January in the instrumental era (as assessed by CET [the Central England Temperature] measure/series begins 1659). The February value of 0.8 degrees C was 3.0C below the long-term mean. ... On the 25th January, an extreme temperature of (minus) 21 degrees C was recorded at an unspecified location in England', in Wirksworth Parish Records 1600–1900, *Weather 1600–1900* [online], www.wirksworth.org.uk/A14WEATH.htm [accessed 10 Feb 2023].

73. 'Wollstonecraft to Imlay', 30 December 1794, in Wollstonecraft, *Collected Letters of Mary Wollstonecraft*, pp. 272–273.
74. 'Wollstonecraft to Imlay', 22 May 1795, in Wollstonecraft, *Collected Letters of Mary Wollstonecraft*, pp. 287–288. See also 'Wollstonecraft to Imlay', 27 May 1795, pp. 288–289; 'Wollstonecraft to Imlay', 10 June 1795, pp. 289–290.
75. 'Wollstonecraft to Imlay', 10 June 1795, in Wollstonecraft, *Collected Letters of Mary Wollstonecraft*, p. 289.
76. 'Wollstonecraft to Imlay', 14 June 1795, in Wollstonecraft, *Collected Letters of Mary Wollstonecraft*, p. 293.
77. Mary A. Favret, '*Letters Written During a Short Resident in Sweden, Norway and Denmark*: Travelling with Mary Wollstonecraft' in Johnson (ed.), *The Cambridge Companion to Mary Wollstonecraft*, pp. 209–227.
78. Wollstonecraft, *A Vindication of the Rights of Woman*, p. 39.
79. Wollstonecraft, *Letters Written During a Short Residence in Sweden, Norway, and Denmark*, p. 62.
80. Wollstonecraft, *Letters Written During a Short Residence in Sweden, Norway, and Denmark*, p. 62.
81. For example, Wollstonecraft wrote, 'I forgot the horrors I had witnessed in France, which had cast a gloom over all nature, and suffering the enthusiasm of my character, damped by the tears of disappointed affection, to be lighted up afresh, care took wing while simple fellow feeling expanded my heart', Wollstonecraft, *Letters Written During a Short Residence in Sweden, Norway, and Denmark*, p. 68.
82. Wollstonecraft, *Letters Written During a Short Residence in Sweden, Norway, and Denmark*, pp. 152–153.
83. Wollstonecraft, *Letters Written During a Short Residence in Sweden, Norway, and Denmark*, p. 111.
84. As Wollstonecraft wrote: 'How fallacious! yet, without hope, what is to sustain life, but the fear of annihilation – the only thing of which I have ever felt a dread – I cannot bear to think of being no more – of losing myself – though existence is often but a painful consciousness of misery; nay, it appears to me impossible that I should cease to exist', Wollstonecraft, *Letters Written During a Short Residence in Sweden, Norway, and Denmark*, p. 112.
85. Wollstonecraft, *Letters Written During a Short Residence in Sweden, Norway, and Denmark*, p. 135.
86. 'Wollstonecraft to Joseph Johnson', late 1792, in Wollstonecraft, *Collected Letters of Mary Wollstonecraft*, p. 221.
87. Godwin, *Memoirs of the Author of a Vindication of the Rights of Woman*, p. 242.
88. William Godwin, *Things as They Are; or, the Adventures of Caleb Williams*. London: B. Crosby, 1794.
89. 'Wollstonecraft to Mary Hays', summer 1797, in Wollstonecraft, *Collected Letters of Mary Wollstonecraft*, p. 413.

Chapter 10

1. Regina Akel, *María Graham: Una Biografía Literaria.* Translated by Marlene Hyslop Becker and María Elena Donoso González (Santiago, Editorial Universitaria, 2012), p. 77.
2. Akel, 2012, pp. 78–79.
3. Akel, 2012, pp. 81–82.
4. Rosemary Sweet, *Cities and the Grand Tour: The British in Italy, c. 1690–1820,* (Cambridge, Cambridge University Press, 2012), p. 22.
5. Sweet, 2012, p. 26.
6. Akel, 2012, p. 30.
7. Sweet, 2012, p. 27.
8. Claudia, Georgi, 'Maria Graham, Travel Writing on India, Italy, Brazil, and Chile (1812–1824)' in Barbara Schaff (ed.), *Handbook of British Travel Writing* Berlin, Boston: De Gruyter, 2020), p. 315.
9. Georgi, 2020, p. 322.
10. Sweet, 2012, p. 39.
11. Sweet, 2012, p. 39.
12. Sweet, 2012, p. 34.
13. Maria Graham, *Three Months Passed in the Mountains East of Rome during the Year 1819*, London, Longman, Hurst, Rees, Orme and Brown, 1820), p. iv.
14. Sweet, 2012, p. 133.
15. Sweet, 2012, pp. 44–45.
16. Graham, 1820, p. iv.
17. Graham, 1820, p. iv.
18. Sweet, 2012, p. 133.
19. Thimothy Webb, '"City of the soul": English Romantic Travellers in Rome' in Michael Liversidge and Catherine Edwards, *Imagining Rome: British Artists and Rome in the Nineteenth Century* (London,: Merrell Holberton, 1996), p. 24.
20. Graham, 1820, p. v.
21. Johannes Fabian, *Time & the Other: How Anthropology Makes its Object* (New York, Columbia University Press, 2014), p. 31.
22. Joseph-Marie Degérando, *The Observation of Savage Peoples*, (London, Routledge, (1800) reprint 2004), p. 63.
23. Graham, 1820, p. 17.
24. Graham, 1820, p. 21.
25. Graham, 1820, p. 142.
26. Graham, 1820, p. 18.
27. Graham, 1820, p. 131.
28. Graham, 1820, p. 33, pp. 64–65.
29. Graham, 1820, p. 74.
30. Graham, 1820, p. 149.
31. Graham, 1820, p. 97.
32. Graham, 1820, p. 180.
33. Graham, 1820, p. 180.
34. Graham, 1820, p. iv.
35. Sweet, 2012, p. 47.
36. Graham, 1820, p. 105.
37. Graham, 1820, p. 24.
38. Polly, Thanailaki, '*Hera*, the Greek Goddess of Marriage: A Comparison Between Greek and Italian Peasant Women' in *Gender Inequalities in Rural European Communities During 19th and Early 20th Century* (Cham: Springer, 2018), p. 65.
39. Thanailaki, 2018, p. 57.

40. Thanailaki, 2018, pp. 64–65.
41. Nicola Verdon, *Rural Women Workers in Nineteenth-Century England: Gender, Work and Wages* (Suffolk, Boydell & Brewer, 2012), p. 10.
42. Graham, 1820, pp. 53–54.
43. Simonetta Ortaggi Cammarosano, 'Labouring Women in Northern and Central Italy in the Nineteenth Century' in *Society and Politics in the Age of the Risorgimento: Essays in Honour of Denis Mack Smith* (Cambridge, Cambridge University Press, 1991), pp. 152–183, p. 168.
44. Cammarosano, 1991, p. 165.
45. Cammarosano, 1991, p. 152.
46. Cammarosano, 1991, pp. 157–160.
47. Cammarosano, 1991, p. 156.
48. Cammarosano, 1991, pp. 153–154.
49. Thanailaki, 2018, p. 66.
50. Cammarosano, 1991, p. 161.
51. Graham, 1820, p. 24.
52. Graham, 1820, p. 54.
53. Cammarosano, 1991, p. 155.
54. Cammarosano, 1991, p. 167.
55. Cammarosano, 1991, p. 158.
56. Graham, 1820, p. 29.
57. Graham, 1820, p. 31.
58. Verdon, 2012, p. 8.
59. Georgi, 2020, p. 317.
60. Graham, 1820, p. 21.
61. Graham, 1820, p. 39.
62. Graham, 1820, pp. 59–60.
63. Graham, 1820, p. 60.
64. Graham, 1820, p. 60.
65. Jean-Jacques Rousseau, *Discourse on Inequality*, (Oxford, Oxford University Press, 1755, reprint 2009), p. 35.
66. Indira Ghose, *Women Travellers in Colonial India: The Power of the Female Gaze,* (Delhi, Oxford University Press, 1998), p. 27.
67. Saree Makdisi, *Making England Western: Occidentalism, Race, and Imperial Culture* (Chicago IL, University of Chicago Press, 2014), p. 18.
68. Makdisi, 2014, p. 4.
69. Makdisi, 2014, p. 15.
70. Makdisi, 2014, p. 16.
71. Makdisi, 2014, p. 2.
72. Maria Todorova, *Imagining the Balkans* (Oxford, Oxford University Press, 2009), p. 11.
73. Todorova, 2009, pp. 11–12.

Chapter 11

1. British Library, ADD MS 62945 A & B: bought Phillips, 16th Feb 1984, lot 350.
2. University of Wolverhampton, *Women's Travel Writing, 1780–1840 database:* http://www4.wlv.ac.uk/btw/ [accessed 20 November 2020].
3. *The European Magazine and Monthly Review,* Vol. 14 (July–December 1788), November, p. 487.
4. Walter Money, *Collections from the History of the Parish of Speen in the County of Berkshire* (Newbury: W.J. Blacket, 1892). p. 79.

5. National Archives, Kew, The Rev. Charles Henry Parry, Probate 11/1177/240, proved 21st March 1789, p. 157; Berks. Records Office, Reading, *Speen Parish Records,* Registers, DP116/1/20, Burials, 1st March, 1793, 'Charles Henry Parry'.
6. The Hon. Society of the Middle Temple Archive, MT/3/STL/4: Students' ledger 'H', 1797–1820; MT/3/BAL/6: *Barristers' ledger*, 1834–1852: For example, Francis Charles Parry; Hackney Archives, Dalston CLR James Library, M666: Assignment of the goods of Charles Harris, Bankrupt, 18th November 1811.
7. Marian, wife, died 1865, age 84; Frances Rachel Marianne, daughter, died 1877, age 58. See records collated at https://www.ancestry.co.uk/ [accessed 20 November 2020]; National Archives, Francis Charles Parry, son, Probate 2039/252, proved 17 July 1746.
8. Francis Charles Parry, *The Dissenters and the Universities; or, The Civil Rights of the Dissenters most effectually secured by the Erection of a new University* (London, 1835).
9. See detail from the area map; *Ordnance Survey*, first series, sheet 12, 1817. 1:63360.
10. *The Edinburgh Review, or Critical Journal,* Vol. 31 (March 1819), p. 518.
11. Parry, *An Account*, Appendix, p. 208; By 1837, the population had only marginally increased, to 2,392, Berks Records Office, *Speen Parish Records*, DP/116/1/8; John Nelson, curate from 1815, *Speen Parish records*, Banns of Marriage, Vol. 2, 1812–1823, DP 116/1/5.
12. Berks. Records Office, *Speen Parish Records,* Registers, DP116; Money, *Collections for the History of the Parish of Speen,* p. 90.
13. See Jenny Uglow, *In These Times: Living in Britain Through Napoleon's Wars, 1793–1815* (London, Faber & Faber, 2014), ch. 24.
14. Barbara Burman and Ariane Fennetaux, *The Pocket: A Hidden History of Women's Lives, 1660–1900* (New Haven, Yale University Press, 2019), pp. 92–98; for a fuller discussion of the journal and container as objects of material culture, see my chapter in Naomi Segal, Anna Jamieson and James Brown (eds.), *The Cultural Construction of Hidden Spaces: Essays on Pockets, Pouches and Secret Drawers*, ed. by James Brown, Anna Jamieson & Naomi Segal (Brill, forthcoming 2024).
15. See Harriet Guest., 'Travel writing', *The Cambridge Companion to Women's Writing in Britain, 1660–1789*, ed. by Catherine Ingrassia (Cambridge, Cambridge University Press, 2015), ch. 12, pp. 196–209, 197.
16. Abigail Williams, *The Social Life of Books* (New Haven, Yale University Press, 2017), pp. 53–58.
17. See Katrina O'Loughlin, *Women, Travel and Writing in the Eighteenth Century* (Cambridge, Cambridge University Press, 2018), p. 8.
18. Emma Gleadhill, *Taking Travel Home: The Souvenir Culture of British Women Tourists 1750–1830* (Manchester, Manchester University Press, 2022), p. 77.
19. Reichard, Heinrich August Ottokar, *An Itinerary of France and Belgium, or, An Account of the Post and Cross Roads, Rivers, Canals*...etc., translated from the French (London, Samuel Leigh, 1816), p. x.
20. Jennie Batchelor, 'Fashion and Frugality: Eighteenth-Century Pocket Books for Women', *Studies in Eighteenth-Century Culture*, No.32, (2003), 1–18; Rebecca E. Connor, *Women. Accounting and Narrative: Keeping Books in Eighteenth-Century England* (London, Routledge, 2004); Linda M. Kirkham and Anne Loft, 'The Lady and the Accounts; Missing from Accounting History?', *The Accounting Historians Journal*, Vol. 28, No.1 (June 2001). pp. 67–90; Sandro Jung,'The Illustrated Pocket Diary: Generic Continuity and Innovation, 1820–40', *Victorian Periodicals Review,* Vol. 45, No. 1 (Spring 2012), pp. 23–48; Amanda Vickery, *The Gentleman's Daughter: Women's Lives in Georgian England* (London, Yale University Press, 1998), p. 133.
21. Colclough, 'Pocket Books and Portable Writing', p. 169.
22. See Serena Dyer, 'Barbara Johnson's Album: Material Literacy and Consumer Practice, 1746–1823', *Journal for Eighteenth-Century Studies*, Vol. 42, No.3 (September 2019),

pp. 263–282; Serena Dyer, *Material Lives: Women Makers and Consumer Culture in the Eighteenth Century* (London, Bloomsbury Publishing, 2021).
23. William Playfair, *France as it is, not Lady Morgan's France*, Vol. 1 (London, 1819), p. 95.
24. Anon., review of 'Howell's Instructions for Forreine Travell' (London, 1642) in *The Retrospective Review,* Vol. 13, pt.2, 1826, pp. 18–29. 19.
25. Pieter François, '"The Best Way to See Waterloo is with Your Eyes Shut": British 'Historism', Authenticity and Commercialisation in the Mid-Nineteenth Century', *Anthropological Journal of European Culture*, Vol. 22, No.1 (2013), pp. 26–41, 30; see also Charles L. Batten, Jr., Pleasurable Instruction: Form and convention in Eighteenth-Century Travel Literature (Berkeley, University of California Press, 1978), p. 2.
26. Eugene N. White, 'Making the French Pay: The Costs and Consequences of the Napoleonic Reparations', *European Review of Economic History*, Vol. 5, No.3 (December 2001), pp. 337–365, 347; Luke Reynolds, 'There John Bull might be seen in all his Glory: Cross-Channel tourism and the British Army of Occupation in France, 1815–1818', *Journal of Tourism History*, Vol. 12, No.2 (2020), pp. 139–155.
27. White, 'Making the French Pay', p. 361.
28. Mariana Starke, *Travels on the Continent: Written for the Use and Particular Information of Travellers* (London, John Murray, 1820), p. 43.
29. Playfair, *France as it is,* pp.viii–xlix.
30. Playfair, *France as it is*, pp. 293–294.
31. For detailed discussion, see Sudhir Hazareesingh, *The Legend of Napoleon* (London, Granta, 2004), ch.1, pp. 15–39.
32. Anon [Richard Whately], *Historic Doubts Relative to Napoleon Buonaparte (*London, J. Hatchard, 1819), p. 31; see also Simon Bainbridge, *Napoleon and English Romanticism* (Cambridge, Cambridge University Press, 1995), ch.1, pp. 1–16.
33. See discussion in Emma Gleadhill, *Taking Travel Home,* p. 493.
34. Hazareesingh, *The Legend of Napoleon*, p. 75.
35. Hazareesingh, *The Legend of Napoleon,* p. 80.
36. Hazareesingh, *The Legend of Napoleon*. p. 150.
37. Stuart Semmel, 'British Uses for Napoleon', *Modern language Notes*, Vol. 120, No.4 (September 2005), French Issue, pp. 733–746, 745; see also Stuart Semmel, 'Reading the Tangible past: British Tourism, Collecting, and Memory After Waterloo', *Representations*, No.69 (Winter, 2000), pp. 9–37, 11.
38. Katherine Turner, 'Women's Travel Writing 1750–1830', *The History of British Women's Writing 1750–1830*, ed. by J.M. Labbe (Basingstoke, Palgrave Macmillan, 2010), ch.2. pp. 47–60, 48.
39. Starke, *Travels on the Continent*, pp. 4–5.
40. Playfair, *France as it is*, p. 6, fn.; see also Marianne Colston, *Journal of a Tour in France, Switzerland and Italy during the Years 1819, 20, and 21,'* 2 vols. (Paris, A. & W. Galignani, 1822) pp. 15–16.
41. Playfair, *France as it is*, p. 67.
42. See A.Hilliard Atteridge, *Marshal Ney: The Bravest of the Brave* (London, Methuen & Co. Ltd. [1912]).
43. For example, François Bouchot (1822–1896) and Gaetano Ferri (1800–1842), *Napoleon signs his Abdication at Fontainebleu, 11 April, 1814,* (1843, Château de Fontainebleu); see other examples by Jules Vernet (1792–1843); Étienne Prosper Bern-Bellecour (1838–1910); J.B.Allen, engraver (1802–1876).
44. Clayton and O'Connell, *Bonaparte and the British*, p. 234; Emma Gleadhill, *Taking Travel Home*, p. 500.
45. Linda Kelly, *Holland House: A History of London's Most Celebrated Salon* (London, I.B. Tauris, 2013). p. 87.

46. Leslie Mitchell, *Holland House* (London, Duckworth, 1980), p. 252, 260; Emma Gleadhill, 'Improving upon birth, marriage and divorce: the cultural capital of three late eighteenth-century female Grand Tourists', *Journal of Tourism History,* Vol. 10:1 (2018), pp. 21–36; '"Lady, reject the gift, 'tis ting'd with gore!": Lady Elizabeth Holland and Napoleon's snuff-box', *Dark Enlightenments,* DNS XVII 2020, conference paper, 13 November–11 December, 2020.
47. William Coxe speculates on the Roman remains in the area but describes the castle as 'an old episcopal castle', *Travels in Switzerland, in a series of letters to William Melmoth Esq.,* (London, Cadell, 1789), 3 vols., Vol. 1, letter 34, p. 391.
48. Lucy Morrison, ed. *Women's Travel Writings in Post-Napoleonic France*, Vol. 1, Marianne Baillie, *First Impressions on a Tour upon the Continent*, 1819 (London, Pickering and Chatto, 2011), p.xii.
49. Turner, *'Women's Travel Writing 1750–1830'*, p. 48; see for example William Wordsworth, *The Prelude: The four texts,* ed. by Jonathan Wordsworth (London: Penguin Books, 1995), Book VI, pp. 206–249.
50. Glirastes' (Percy Bysshe Shelley), 'Ozymandias', London: *The Examiner,* No.524, Sunday, 11 January 1818, p. 24.
51. John Goodman, ed., *Diderot on Art* (New Haven, Yale University Press, 1995), p. 217; see also Susan Stewart, *The Ruins Lesson: Meaning and Material in Western Culture* (Chicago, The University of Chicago Press, 2020).
52. Starke, *Travels in Europe, for the use of travellers on the continent, including the Island of Sicily where the author had never been till the year 1834,* 9th edition (London, John Murray, 1837), ch.2, p. 43.
53. W.S. Rose, *Letters from the North of Italy, Addressed to Henry Hallan, esq.* (London: John Murray, 1819), 2 Vols., Vol. 1, p. 6–7; see also Samuel Miller Waring, *The Traveller's Fire-side: A Series of Papers on Switzerland, The Alps, &c.* (London, Baldwin, Cradock and Joy, 1819), note, p. 33.
54. See, for example, the Arena Napoleonica, the 'ampitheatre' described by Harriet: https://web.archive.org/web/20070106154512/http://stadesmythiques.free.fr/arenacivica.htm [accessed 6 December 2020].
55. Major W.E. Frye, *After Waterloo: Reminiscences of European Travel, 1815–1819*, ed. By Salomon Reinach (London: William Heinemann, 1908), Preface. http://www.gutenberg.org/cache/epub/10939/pg10939-images.html [accessed 10 November 2020].
56. Lady Morgan, *France* (London, Henry Colburn, 1817), 2 Vols., Vol. 2, pp. 175–176.
57. M. Eugène Scribe, *Les Comices d'Athènes*, (Paris: Chez Mad. Ladvocat, 1817).
58. For discussion, see Edith Hall and Amanda Wrigley, eds., *Aristophanes in Performance, 421BC- 2007AD: Peace, Birds and Frogs* (London, MHRA & Maney Publishing, 2007), 1–30.
59. René-Charles Guilbert de Pixerécour, *La Fille de l'Exilé, ou Huit Mois en Deux Heures* (Paris: Chez J.-N. Barba, Libraire,1819).
60. The play may have been Jean-Nicolas Bouilly and Emmanuel Dupaty, *'L'Intrigue aux fenêtre', Opéra Bouffon en un acte* (1805).
61. Lady Morgan, France, pp. 229–231.
62. See Franklin Mesa, *Opera: An Encyclopedia of World Premieres and Significant Performances, Singers, Composers. Librettists, Arias and Conductors, 1597–2000* (Jefferson, North Carolina: McFarland, 2007), No.50, p. 14.
63. See Alessandro Roccatagliati, 'Romani (Giuseppe) Felice', *Grove Music Online,* 2001, https://doi.org/10.1093/gmo/9781561592630.article.23733 [accessed 23 November 2020].
64. See print, Anon., *'Milan, La Scala Interior, 1819'*, Image ID K2Y DAA, www.alamy.com [accessed 23 November 2020].
65. Anon, 'View of the Gallery & Bridge of the Ganther', 1818, coloured aquatint, 14.5 x 23.5cm., *R. Ackermann's Repository of Art*, Vol. VI, plate 7, August 1818.

66. Colston, *Journal of a Tour in France*, Vol. 1, p. 1; see also Cotman's experiences in H. Isherwood Kay, 'John Sell Cotman's Letters from Normandy 1817–1820: Part II, the Letters of 1820', *The Volume of the Walpole Society,* Vol. 15 (1926–1927), pp. 105–130, p. 105.
67. John Cary, engraver, map of Berkshire, *Cary's Traveller's Companion,* (London, 1814). http://freepages.rootsweb.com/~genmaps/genealogy/genfiles/COU_files/ENG/BRK/cary_brk_1814.html [accessed 20 November 2020]; see strip map showing a London to Portsmouth, etc. route in *The Gentleman's Magazine,* Vol. 35, July 1765, p. 301. http://www.geog.port.ac.uk/webmap/hantsmap/hantsmap/gentmag/gnt2larg.html [accessed 20 November 2020]; see also Daniel Maudlin, 'The Natural World through Early Modern Strip Maps: A Narrow View of Nature', essay from *Transforming Topography* conference, The British Library, 6 May 2016. https://www.bl.uk/picturing-places/articles/the-natural-world-through-early-modern-strip-maps [accessed 20 November 2020].
68. National Archives, Mary Parry, Probate 11/1879/1, proved 19th May 1837; Catherine Louisa Parry, Probate 11/1812/100, proved 23rd January 1833: see also Obituary, 27th Sep. 1832, *The Gentleman's Magazine,* Vol. 102, pt.2, (September 1832), p. 483.
69. Berks Records, *The Register of Marriages Solemnized in the Parish of Speen, Berks.*, DP/116/1/8, p. 129, 12th January 1832.
70. See Biographical Directory of the United States Congress: https://bioguideretro.congress.gov/Home/MemberDetails?memIndex=A000113, Allen, Andrew (1740–1825), [accessed 19 November 2020].
71. See University of Pennsylvania Archives & Records Center, Penn People: https://archives.upenn.edu/exhibits/penn-people/biography/william-allen, William Allen (1776–1850), [accessed 19 November 2020]. (I am indebted to genealogist Sandie Hunt for her research on these family connections.)
72. Bristol Archives, Bristol: EP/A/22/StAC/2c; EP/A/22/StAC/2d; EP/A/22/StAC/2e; St. Andrew's Church, Clifton, 43207/29/6/2; National Archives, Andrew Allen, Probate 11/2123/152, proved 21st December 1850.
73. Money, *Collections for the History of the Parish of Speen,* p. 36.

Chapter 12

1. Leslie A Marchand (ed.), *Byron's Letters and Journals*, Vols 1–13 (London: John Murray, 1973–1994). 5.259.
2. W. Wordsworth, *The Letters of William and Dorothy Wordswsorth: The Later Years*, ed. Alan Hill, (Oxford, Clarendon Press, 1978), 4.210.
3. M. Oliphant and G. Porter *William Blackwood and His Sons: Annals of a Publishing House* (Edinburgh, William Blackwood, 1883), III.227.
4. J. Black, 'Italy and the Grand Tour: The British Experience in the Eighteenth Century', *Annali d'Italianistica*, 14 1996 pp. 532–41, p. 540.
5. Ibid., p. 538.
6. *BLJ* 6.44.
7. *Beppo*, l.351.
8. *BLJ* 6.149.
9. K. Churchill, *Italy and English Literature 1764–1930*, p. 42.
10. S. Morgan, *Italy: by Lady Morgan* (London, Henry Colburn, 1821), 2.475.
11. *BLJ* 5.259.
12. *BLJ* 6.92.
13. 'Sexuality and Politics: Lady Morgan and the Morality of the Italians' in V. Babini, C. Beccalossi and L. Riall eds. *Italian Sexualities Uncovered, 1789–1914*, (London, Palgrave Macmillan, 2015), pp. 15–36.
14. *BLJ* 5.134.
15. *BLJ* 7.21.

16. *BLJ* 7.22, 112.
17. *BLJ* 6.186, 226.
18. *BLJ* 7.42.
19. *BLJ* 7.12, 6.23.
20. *A Lady's Man*, p. 1.
21. R. Bizzocci, *A Lady's Man: The Cicisbei, Private Morals, and National Identity in Italy*, translated by Noor Giovanni Mazhar (Basingstoke: Palgrave Macmillan, 2014) p. 1.
22. *BLJ* 7.52.
23. S. Morgan,. 1821. *Italy: by Lady Morgan*, 2.39.
24. J. Polidori *The Diary of John Polidori*, ed. W. M. Rosetti (London, Elkin Mathew, 1911), p. 33.
25. *Italy*, I.252.
26. *BLJ* 5.148.
27. *BLJ* 6.44.
28. *BLJ* 5.155.
29. *BLJ* 5.156.
30. *BLJ* 5.189.
31. *BLJ* 7.28.
32. *BLJ* 8.134.
33. *BLJ* 5.136.
34. *BLJ* 6.168.
35. *BLJ* 7.43.
36. *BLJ* 6.130, 107.
37. *BLJ* 5.129.
38. *BLJ* 5.148.
39. *BLJ* 5.129.
40. *BLJ* 5.133.
41. *BLJ* 5.134.
42. *BLJ* 5.155.
43. *BLJ* 5.134.
44. *BLJ* 7.28.
45. *BLJ* 5.189.
46. *BLJ* 5.166.
47. *BLJ* 5.166.
48. *BLJ* 5.166.
49. *BLJ* 5.167.
50. *BLJ* 5.167.
51. *BLJ* 6.23.
52. *BLJ* 5.167.
53. *BLJ* 6.194.
54. *BLJ* 6.192.
55. *BLJ* 6.70.
56. *BLJ* 6.193.
57. *BLJ* 6.208.
58. 6.208.
59. *BLJ* 6.193.
60. *BLJ* 6.197.
61. *BLJ* 6.196.
62. *BLJ* 6.181.
63. *BLJ* 6.181.
64. *BLJ* 6.69–70.

65. *BLJ* 6.193.
66. *BLJ* 6.194.
67. *BLJ* 6.197.
68. *BLJ* 6.196–197.
69. *BLJ* 6.107.
70. *BLJ* 6.185.
71. *BLJ* 6.130.
72. *BLJ* 6.185.
73. *BLJ* 6.124.
74. *BLJ* 7.18.
75. *BLJ* 6.262.
76. *BLJ* 6.231.
77. *BLJ* 6.154.
78. *BLJ* 6.181.
79. *BLJ* 7.43.
80. *BLJ* 6.107.
81. *BLJ* 7.49.
82. *BLJ* 7.51.
83. *BLJ* 7.105.
84. *BLJ* 7.103.
85. *BLJ* 6.226.
86. *BLJ* 7.28.
87. *BLJ* 7.51.
88. *BLJ* 6.226.
89. *BLJ* 7.186.
90. *BLJ* 6.189.
91. *BLJ* 6.186.
92. *BLJ* 5.147.
93. *BLJ* 7.43.
94. *BLJ* 7.28.
95. *BLJ* 6.214.
96. A. Rawes and D. Saglia, 'Introduction', in A. Rawes and D. Saglia eds. *Byron and Italy* (2018), p. 9.
97. *BLJ* 7.170.
98. *BLJ* 7.42.
99. *BLJ* 7.42.

Chapter 13

1. The Countess of Blessington, *The Idler in Italy*. In two volumes. 2nd edn. (London, Henry Colburn, 1839).
2. Matoff, Susan. *Marguerite, Countess of Blessington: The Turbulent Life of a Salonnière and Author* (University of Delaware Press, 2015), p. 4.
3. The Countess of Blessington, *The Governess* (London, Longmans 1839), p. 45.
4. Matoff, Susan. *Marguerite, Countess of Blessington: The Turbulent Life of a Salonnière and Author* (University of Delaware Press, 2015), p. 11.
5. In her biography of the Countess of Blessington, Susan Matoff refutes many of the claims made by Madden and Sadleir, identifying gossip columns and malicious correspondence as their sources. Ibid., p. 100.
6. Madden, R. R., *The Literary Life and Correspondence of the Countess of Blessington* (New York, Harper and Brothers Publishers, 1855), p. 3.
7. Ibid., pp. 116–7.

8. *The Idler in Italy*. Vol I, p. 2.
9. Ibid., p. 32.
10. Ibid., p. 35.
11. Ibid., p. 6.
12. Ibid., pp. 27–9.
13. Ibid., p. 27.
14. Ibid.
15. Ibid., pp. 28–9.
16. Matoff, Susan, p. 80.
17. Sweet, R. *Cities and the Grand Tour: The British in Italy, C. 1690–1820* (Cambridge University Press, 2012), p. 75.
18. *The Idler in Italy*. Vol I, p. 5.
19. *The Idler in Italy*. Vol II, p. 7.
20. *The Idler in Italy*. Vol. I, p. 286.
21. Ibid., p. 287.
22. Ibid.
23. Ibid., p. 295.
24. Ibid., p. 358.
25. *The Idler in Italy*. Vol. II, p. 25.
26. Ibid., pp. 19–26.
27. Ibid., p. 17.
28. Sweet, R. *Cities and the Grand Tour,* p. 76.
29. *The Idler in Italy*. Vol. I, p. 306.
30. *The Idler in Italy*. Vol. II, p. 9.
31. Sweet, R. *Cities and the Grand Tour,* p. 81.
32. *The Idler in Italy*. Vol II, p. 4.
33. The Countess of Blessington rarely interrupted her accounts of how she passed her day with description but, when she did, she used it sparingly to paint a picture of, 'the blue Arno winding through the land, rich in the most luxuriant vegetation'. *The Idler in Italy*. Vol II, p. 8.
34. The Countess of Blessington describes Florentine men who carry guitars in the evening 'to serenade some humble beauty'. *The Idler in Italy*. Vol II, p. 8.
35. Ibid., p. 15.
36. Sweet, R. *Cities and the Grand Tour,* p. 68.
37. *The Idler in Italy*. Vol. II, p. 10.
38. Ibid.
39. Maerker, A., *Model Experts: Wax anatomies and enlightenment in Florence and Vienna, 1775–1815* (Manchester, Manchester University Press, 2015), p. 200.
40. Messbarger, R. 'The Re-Birth of Venus in Florence's Royal Museum of Physics and Natural History', *Journal of the History of Collections*, 25(2), (2013), pp. 195–215.
41. *The Idler in Italy*. Vol. II, p. 18.
42. *The Memoirs of Élisabeth Vigée-LeBrun*, trans. by Sian Evans (Bloomington, Indiana University Press, 1989), p. 123.
43. *The Idler in Italy*. Vol. II, pp. 11–12.
44. Ibid.
45. Thomas Jefferson Hogg (1827) quoted in Knoefel, P. K. (1984) *Felice Fontana Life and Works* (Trento, Tipografia, TEMI), p. 259.
46. *The Idler in Italy*. Vol. II, p. 35.
47. Ibid., p. 10.
48. Ibid., pp. 28–29.

49. Ibid., pp. 12–3.
50. Royal Academy catalogue for 1820 found at: https://www.royalacademy.org.uk/art-artists/exhibition-catalogue/ra-sec-vol52-1820.
51. *The Idler in Italy*. Vol. I, p. 55.
52. *The Idler in Italy*. Vol. II, p. 194.
53. Ibid., p. 207.
54. See the Wellcome Collection online for the deceptive power of stays, wigs and make-up by eighteenth- and early nineteenth-century cartoonists such as James Gillray and Thomas Rowlandson. https://wellcomecollection.org/collections.
55. *The Idler in Italy*. Vol. II, p. 240.
56. Ibid., p. 292.
57. Ibid., pp. 36–7.

Bibliography

Primary Sources

Ackerman, Rudolph, *The Repository of Arts, Literature, Commerce, Manufactures, Fashions, and Politics* (London, R. Ackerman, 1818)

Addison, Joseph. *Remarks on several parts of Italy, &c. in the years 1701, 1702, 1703* (London, 1705)

Anon, 'Sophia Watson', *Memoirs of the Seraglio of the Bashaw of Merryland by a Discarded Sultana* (London, S. Bladon, 2nd ed, 1768)

Anon, *A New Description of Merryland* (London, 1741)

Anon, *Merryland Display'd* (London, 1741)

Anon, 'Miss Helen Williams' *Poems*', (*European Magazine*, August 1786), pp. 89–93

Blessington, The Countess of, *The Governess* (London, Longmans 1839)

Blessington, The Countess of, *The Idler in Italy,* 2 Vols. (London, Henry Colburn, 1839)

Borch, Michał Jan, *Briefe ueber Sicilien und Maltha mir Charten vom Etna, von den alten und neuen Sicilien, nebst 24 Kupferstichen, von dem Grafen Borch,* (Bern, Neue typographische Gesellschaft, 1783)

Borch, Michał Jan, *Reise durch Sicilien und Maltha und von der Revolutionem so dieses Land erlitten hat.*, Th. 1–2 (Bern, Typographische Societat, 1796).

Boswell, James, *An Account of Corsica, the Journal of a Tour to That Island, and Memoirs of Pascal Paoli* (ed.), James T. Boulton and Timothy McLoughlin (eds.) (Oxford, Oxford University Press, 2006)

Boswell, James, *The Life of Samuel Johnson*, 3 Vols. (Dublin, R. Cross et al., 1792)

Boswell, James, *The Life of Samuel Johnson, LL.D.* 6 Vols., G. B. Hill, rev. L. F. Powell (eds.) (Oxford, Clarendon Press, 1934–64)

Burke, Edmund, *Reflections on the Revolution in France* (1790). Edited by L. G. Mitchell. (Oxford, Oxford University Press, 1999)

Burney, Charles. *The Present State of Music in France and Italy* (London, T. Becket and Company, 1773)

Byron's *Letters and Journals*, Leslie A Marchand,(ed.),Vols 1–13 (London: John Murray, 1973-1994

Cary, John, *Cary's Traveller's Companion,* (London, 1814)

Collver, Joel. 'Musical Sketches', *The English Lyceum,* (Hamburg, Mr. Bohn, 1787)

Colston, Marianne, *Journal of a Tour in France, Switzerland and Italy during the Years 1819, 20,and 21,'* 2 Vols. (Paris, A. & W. Galignani, 1822)

Coxe, William, *Travels in Switzerland, in a series of letters to William Melmoth Esq.,* 3 Vols. (London, Cadell, 1789)

Craven, Elizabeth, *A Journey through the Crimea to Constantinople* (London, 1789)

Dumont, Jean, *A New Voyage to the Levant* (London, 1696)

Elliott, Grace Dalrymple, *Journal of my Life during the French Revolution* (London, 1859)

Ferguson, Adam, *Essay on the History of Civil Society* (Edinburgh, T. Cadell, 1773)

Godwin, William, *Memoirs of the Author of a Vindication of the Rights of Woman* (London, J. Johnson,1798)

Godwin, William, *Things as They Are; or, the Adventures of Caleb Williams* (London, B. Crosby, 1794)

Graham, Maria, *Three Months Passed in the Mountains East of Rome during the Year 1819* (London, Longman, Hurst, Rees, Orme and Brown, 1820)

Halsband, Robert ed., *The Complete Letters of Lady Mary Wortley Montagu,* (Oxford, Clarendon Press, 1965)

Knight, Richard Payne, *The Worship Of Priapus In The Kingdom Of Naples* (London, Privately Printed, 1786–7)

Lazzaro Spalanzzani, Abbé, *Travels in the Two Sicilies and some parts of the Apennines*, in: *A general collection of the best and most interesting voyages and travels in all parts of the world; many of which are now first translated into English. Digest on a new plan by John Pinkerton*, Vol. 5 (London, 1809)

Libiszowska, Zofia, *Lettre de M. le comte Borch, de plusieurs Académies, à l'Auteur de ce recueil, Sur la manière de teindre les cuirs en vert*, in M. l'Abbé Rozier, M.J.A. Mongez, *Observations sur la physique, sur l'histoire naturelle et les arts* (Paris, 1779)

MacDonald, John, *Travels, in various parts of Europe, Asia, and Africa, during a series of thirty years and upwards* (London, J. Forbes, 1790)

Mason, W. *The Poems of Mr Gray, to which are prefixed Memoirs of His Life and Writings,* 3 Vols. (London, 1775)

Mathias, Thomas J, *The Pursuits of Literature* (8th edition, Dublin, J. Milliken, 1798)

Minute Books of Dilettanti Society, Society of Antiquaries, London

Morris, Charles, *Hilaria, the Festive Board* (London, Printed for the Author, 1798)

Morrison, Alexander James William, (ed.), *Goethe's Travels in Italy: together with his Second residence in Rome and fragments on Italy*, Ch. Nisbet, Translated from the German (London, 1885)

Parry, Francis Charles, *An Account of the Charitable Donations to Places within the County of Berks* (London, 1818)

Parry, Francis Charles, *The Dissenters and the Universities; or, The Civil Rights of the Dissenters most effectually secured by the erection of a new university* (London, 1835)

Playfair, William, *France as it is, not Lady Morgan's France*, 2 Vols. (London, 1819/20)

Priestley, Joseph, *Life and Correspondence of Joseph Priestley*, edited by J. T. Rutt. (London, R. Hunter, 1831)

Reichard, Heinrich August Ottokar, *An Itinerary of France and Belgium, or, An Account of the Post and Cross Roads, Rivers, Canals*...etc., translated from the French (London, Samuel Leigh, 1816)

Rose, W.S., *Letters from the North of Italy, Addressed to Henry Hallan, esq.* 2 Vols. (London, John Murray, 1819)

Rycaut, Paul, *Present State of the Ottoman Empire*, (London, 1668)

Sandys, G., *Sandys Travels: Containing an History of the Original and Present State of the Turkish Empire ... the Mahometan Religion and Ceremonies. A Description of Constantinople ... Also, of Greece ... Of Ægypt ... A Description of the Holy-Land ... Lastly, Italy* (London, 1652)

Starke, Mariana, *Travels in Europe, for the use of travellers on the continent, including the Island of Sicily where the author had never been till the year 1834,* 9th edition (London, John Murray, 1837)

Tertre, Jean-Baptiste, *Histoire Generale des Antilles Habitées par les François: Divisée en Deux Tomes, et Enrichie de Cartes & de Figures*, 4 Vols (Paris, Thomas Iolly, 1667–1671)

Tyers, Thomas, *A Historical Rhapsody on Mr Pope,* (London, 1782)

Vigée-LeBrun, Elizabeth, *Memoirs of Élisabeth Vigée-LeBrun*, trans. by Sian Evans (Bloomington, Indiana University Press, 1989)

Walpole, Horace, *Horace Walpole's Correspondence*. Lewis, W. S., et al (eds.), 48 Vols. (New Haven, 1937–83)

Waring, Samuel Miller, *The Traveller's Fire-side: A Series of Papers on Switzerland, The Alps, &c.* (London, Baldwin, Cradock and Joy, 1819)

West, Charlette, *A Ten Years' Residence in France, During the Severest Part of the Revolution, from the Year 1787 to 1797, Containing Various Anecdotes of Some of the Most Remarkable Personages of that Period* (London, 1821)

Whately, Richard, *Historic Doubts Relative to Napoleon Buonaparte (*London, J. Hatchard, 1819)

Williams, Helen Maria, *A Poem on the Bill Lately Passed for Regulating the Slave Trade*, (London, T. Cadell, 1788)

Williams, Helen Maria, *A Tour in Switzerland; or, A View of the Present State of the Governments and Manners of those Cantons: With Comparative Sketches of the Present State of Paris*, 2 vols, (London, Printed for G.G. and J. Robinson, 1798)

Williams, Helen Maria, *An Ode on the Peace*, (London, T. Cadell, 1783)

Williams, Helen Maria, *Edwin and Eltruda, A Legendary Tale* (London, T. Cadell, 1782)

Williams, Helen Maria, *Letters Containing a Sketch of the Politics of France, from the Thirty-first of May 1793, till the Twenty-eighth of July 1794, and of the Scenes which have Passed in the Prisons of Paris* (London, G. G. J. and J. Robinson, 1795)

Williams, Helen Maria, *Poems, in Two Volumes,* (London, Thomas Cadell, 1786)

Williams, Helen Maria, *Souvenirs de la Révolution Française*, Traduit de l'anglais par Charles Coquerel, (Paris, Dondey-Dupré, 1827)

Wollstonecraft, Mary *A Vindication of the Rights of Men* (1790) in D.L. Macdonald and Kathleen Scherf (eds.), *A Vindication of the Rights of Men and A Vindication of the Rights of Woman* (Peterborough, Ontario, Broadview Press, 1997)

Wollstonecraft, Mary, 'Analytical Review, August 1790' in Jane Todd and Marilyn Butler (eds.), *The Works of Mary Wollstonecraft* (London, Pickering, 1989), Vol 7 of 7

Wollstonecraft, Mary, 'Letter on the Present Character of the French Nation (1793)' in Jane Todd and Marilyn Butler (eds.), *The Works of Mary Wollstonecraft* (London, Pickering, 1989), Vol 6 of 7

Wollstonecraft, Mary, *A Short Residence in Sweden, Norway and Denmark, and Memoirs of the Author of the Rights of Woman* (London, Penguin, 1987)

Wollstonecraft, Mary, *A Vindication of the Rights of Woman* (1792) in Deidre Shauna Lynch (ed.), *A Vindication of the Rights of Woman: an Authoritative Text Backgrounds and Contexts Criticism* (3rd ed. New York and London, W. W. Norton, 2009)

Wollstonecraft, Mary, *An Historical and Moral View of the Origin and Progress of the French Revolution; and the Effect It Has Produced in Europe* (London, 1794)

Wollstonecraft, Mary, *Collected Letters of Mary Wollstonecraft* in Ralph M. Wardle (ed.) (Ithaca, Cornell University Press, 1979)

Wollstonecraft, Mary, *Letters Written During a Short Residence in Sweden, Norway, and Denmark* (1796)

Wordsworth, William, ['Axiologus'], 'Sonnet on Seeing Miss Helen Maria Williams Weep at a Tale of Distress', (*European Magazine*, March 1787)

Journals

Annals of Stair
Edinburgh Review, or Critical Journal, The
English Review, The
European Magazine and Monthly Review, The
Examiner, The
Gentleman's Magazine
London Chronicle, The
London Magazine, The
Monthly Review
Philological Quarterly
Public Advertiser
Quarterly Musical Magazine and Review
Rampager, The
Retrospective Review, The
Scots Magazine, The
Universal Magazine of Knowledge and Pleasure

Archives and Websites

Archives Parlementaires de 1787 a 1860, Première série (1787 à 1799). Paris, 1862–1914
Berkshire Records Office
Bristol Archives
British Library
Hackney Archives
National Archives, Kew
Stefanyk National Science Library
The Hon. Society of the Middle Temple Archive

www.ancestry.co.uk.

University of Pennsylvania Archives & Records Center: Penn People. https://archives.upenn.edu/exhibits/penn-people/biography/william-allen

Biographical Directory of the United States Congress https://bioguideretro.congress.gov

Belsey, H. (2004) Mann, Sir Horatio, first baronet. 1706–1786. https://doi.org/10.1093/ref:odnb/17945

Cary, John, engraver, map of Berkshire, *Cary's Traveller's Companion*, (London, 1814).

http://freepages.rootsweb.com/~genmaps/genealogy/genfiles/COU_files/ENG/BRK/cary_brk_1814.html

https://www.visionofbritain.org.uk

University of Wolverhampton, *Women's Travel Writing, 1780–1840 database:* http://www4.wlv.ac.uk/btw/

Wirksworth Parish Records 1600–1900. *Weather 1600- 1900* [online], www.wirksworth.org.uk/A14WEATH.htm

Maudlin, Daniel, 'The Natural World through Early Modern Strip Maps: A Narrow View of Nature', essay from *Transforming Topography* conference, The British Library, 6 May 2016. https://www.bl.uk/picturing-places/articles/the-natural-world-through-early-modern-strip-maps

Burden, Michael. 'Mrs Billington's embonpoint; scandal, hysteria, and Mozart', Paper presented at British Society for 18th-Century Studies Annual Conference, St Hugh's College, Oxford, 4 January (2008). https://ora.ouls.ox.ac.uk/objects/uuid:db1f0ebf-6791-4949-a127-a210909d21a0.

Cowgill, Rachel. 'Billington [née Weichsel], Elizabeth (1765–1818), singer.' *Oxford Dictionary of National Biography* (2004). https://doi.org/10.1093/ref:odnb/2397

Girdham, Jane. 'A Note on Stephen Storace and Michael Kelly.' *Music & Letters* Vol. 76, No. 1 (1995): 64–67. http://www.jstor.org/stable/737763

Morrison, S. (2004) Smith, Joseph: 1673/4–1770. https://doi.org/10.1093/ref:odnb/25871, 2004

Norton, R. *Horace Walpole and Homosexuality.* http://rictornorton.co.uk/thought2.htm

Secondary Sources

Abramowicz, Andrzej, *Starożytności antyczne i Stanisław August*, in: idem: *Dzieje zainteresowań starożytniczych w Polsce, pt. 2: Czasy stanisławowskie i ich pokłosie* (Wrocław, 1987)

Abramowicz, Andrzej, *Zainteresowania numizmatyczne Michała Jana Borcha w czasie podróży na Sycylię i Maltę w 1776/7 roku* in 'Wiadomości numizmatyczne', Vol. 28, Issue 1–2

Akel, Regina, *María Graham*: *Una Biografía Literaria*. Translated by Marlene Hyslop Becker and María Elena Donoso González (Santiago, Editorial Universitaria, 2012)

Al Jamil, Miriam, 'Pen and Pin: Two Travel Journals and a box, 6th January 1829' in *Pockets, Pouches and Secret Drawers,* ed. By Naomi Segal, Anna Jamieson and James Brown (Brill, forthcoming)

Ansell, Richard, *Complete Gentlemen: Educational Travel and Family Strategy, 1650–1750* (Oxford, British Academy/Oxford University Press, 2022)

Atteridge, A. Hilliard, *Marshal Ney: The Bravest of the Brave* (London, Methuen & Co. Ltd. 1912)

Bainbridge, Simon, *Napoleon and English Romanticism* (Cambridge, Cambridge University Press, 1995)

Batchelor, Jennie, Manushag N. Powell eds., *Women's Periodicals and Print Culture in Britain: 1690–1820s, the Long Eighteenth Century* (Edinburgh, Edinburgh University, 2018)

Batchelor, Jennie, 'Fashion and Frugality: Eighteenth-Century Pocket Books for Women', *Studies in Eighteenth-Century Culture*, no.32, (2003), pp. 1–18

Bates, Richard, 'The Petit Tour to Spa, 1763–87' in Rosemary Sweet, Gerrit Verhoeven, and Sarah Goldsmith (eds.), *Beyond the Grand Tour: Northern Metropolises and Early Modern Travel Behaviour* (London, New York, Routledge, 2017), pp. 127–146

Batten, C. L. *Pleasurable Instruction: Form and Convention in Eighteenth Century Travel Literature* (University of California Press, Berkeley, Los Angeles, London, 1978)

Belsey, H. (2004) Mann, Sir Horatio, first baronet. 1706–1786. https://doi.org/10.1093/ref:odnb/17945

Bentman, R., 'Thomas Gray and the Poetry of "Hopeless Love"', *Journal of the History of Sexuality*, Vol. 3, No. 2, (1992), pp. 203–222

Berg, Maxine, 'What Difference Did Women's Work Make to the Industrial Revolution?' *History Workshop*, (1993), No. 35, pp. 22–44

Bhabha, Homi K., 'DissemiNation: Time, Narrative, and the Margins of the Modern Nation' in Bhabha, Homi K., (ed), *Nation and Narration*, (London, Routledge, 1990), pp. 291–322

Black, Jeremy, 'Italy and the Grand Tour: The British Experience in the Eighteenth Century', *Annali d'Italianistica*, Vol. 14 (1996)

Black, Jeremy, *The British and the Grand Tour* (London, Croom Helm, 1985)

Black, Jeremy, *The British Abroad, The Grand Tour in the Eighteenth Century* (New York, St. Martin's Press, 1992)

Bohls, Elizabeth A., *Women Travel Writers and the Language of Aesthetics 1716–1818* (Cambridge, Cambridge University Press, 1995)

Borch, Michał Jan, *Listy o Sycylii i Malcie*, transll. A. Szatyńska-Siemion i I.Z. Siemion (Warszawa, 2015)

Borsay, Peter (ed.), *The Eighteenth-Century Town: a reader in English urban history, 1688–1820* (London, New York: Longman, 1990)

Brant, C. *Eighteenth-Century Letters and British Culture.* (London, Palgrave MacMillan, 2006)

Brewer J. *Pleasures of Imagination.* (New York, Routledge, 1997)

Bullard, P., 'Eighteenth-Century Minds: From Associationism to Cognitive Psychology' in *Oxford Handbooks Online.* (Oxford, Oxford University Press, 2016) doi: 10.1093/oxfordhb/9780199935338.013.95

Burman, Barbara and Ariane Fennetaux, *The Pocket: A Hidden History of Women's Lives, 1660–1900* (New Haven, Yale University Press, 2019)

Buzard, James. 'The Grand Tour and After (1660–1840)' in Peter Hulme and Tim Youngs (eds), *The Cambridge Companion to Travel Writing* (Cambridge, Cambridge University Press, 2002)

Cammarosano, Simonetta Ortaggi. 'Labouring Women in Northern and Central Italy in the Nineteenth Century' in *Society and Politics in the Age of the Risorgimento: Essays in Honour of Denis Mack Smith* (Cambridge, Cambridge University Press, 1991, pp. 152–183

Carabelli, Giancarlo, *In the Image of Priapus* (London, Duckworth, 1996)

Carrington, Dorothy, 'Boswell's Corsica.' *Essays by divers hands: being the transactions of the Royal Society of Literature of the United Kingdom* Vol. 44 (1986)

Chapron, Emmanuelle, *L'Europe à Nîmes – les carnets de Jean-François Séguier (1732–1783)*, (Avignon, 2008)

Chard, C. *Pleasure and Guilt on the Grand Tour. Travel Writing and Imaginative Geography* (Manchester University Press, Manchester, New York, 1999)

Chmal, Henryk, *Johann Wolfgang Goethe (1749–1832) – przyrodnik*, 'Czasopismo Geograficzne', No 81 (3)

Clayton, Tim, and Sheila O'Connell, *Bonaparte and the British* (London, The British Museum, 2015)

Clery, E. J., 'Women, Publicity and the Coffee-House Myth', *Women: A Cultural Review*. Vol. 2. No. 2 (1991), pp. 168–177

Clingham, Greg (ed.), *New Light on Boswell: Critical and Historical Essays on the Occasion of the Bicentenary of The Life of Johnson* (Cambridge, Cambridge University Press, 1999)

Cohen, Michele, *Fashioning Masculinity: National Identity and Language in the Eighteenth Century* (London & New York, Routledge, 1996)

Colbert, Benjamin (ed.), *Travel Writing and Tourism in Britain and Ireland* (Basingstoke, Palgrave Macmillan, 2012)

Colclough, Stephen, 'Pocket Books and Portable Writing: The Pocket Memorandum Book of Eighteenth-Century England and Wales', *The Year Book of English Studies,* Vol. 45 (2015). https://research.bangor.ac.uk/portal/files/7251285/PDB5366-00.pdf

Colley, Linda, *Britons: Forging the Nation, 1707–1837*. 2nd ed. (New Haven, Yale University Press, 2005)

Connor, Rebecca E., *Women. Accounting and Narrative: Keeping Books in Eighteenth-Century England* (London, Routledge, 2004)

Conway, Stephen, *Britain, Ireland, and Continental Europe in the Eighteenth Century: Similarities, Connections, Identities* (Oxford, Oxford University Press, 2011)

Cooke, Simon, 'Travel Writing as Life Writing' in Carl Thompson (ed.), *The Routledge Companion to Travel Writing* (New York, Routledge, 2016), pp. 15–24

Cowan, B. *'Restoration' England and the History of Sociability* in V. Capdeville, A. Kerhervé (eds), *British Sociability* (Woodbridge, Boydell Press, 2019), pp. 7–24

Craciun, Adriana, *British Women Writers and the French Revolution: Citizens of the World* (Basingstoke, Palgrave Macmillan, 2005)

Curley, Thomas M., 'Boswell's Liberty-Loving Account of Corsica and the Art of Travel Literature' in Greg Clingham (ed.), *New Light on Boswell: Critical and Historical Essays on the Occasion of the Bicentenary of The Life of Johnson*, pp. 89–103 (Cambridge, Cambridge University Press, 1999)

Daniel I., *The Burke-Wollstonecraft Debate: Savagery, Civilization, and Democracy* (University Park, Pennsylvania State University Press, 2007)

Das, Nandini & Tim Youngs, eds., *The Cambridge History of Travel Writing*, (Cambridge, CUP, 2019)

Davis, L. J. *Factual Fictions: The Origins of the English Novel* (Philadelphia, University of Pennsylvania Press, 1996)

De Ritter, Richard '"This Changeableness in Character": Exploring Masculinity and Nationhood on James Boswell's Grand Tour,' *Scottish Literary Review* Vol. 2, No. 1 (Spring/Summer 2010)

Degérando, Joseph-Marie. *The Observation of Savage Peoples* (1800) (reprint London, Routledge, 2004)

Dolan, Brian, *Ladies on the Grand Tour* (London, Flamingo, 2002)

Dongu, M. G. *Thomas Gray Ludens: Frammenti dal Grand Tour*, (Transl. Title: *Playful Thomas Gray: Fragments from the Grand Tour* (FrancoAngeli, Milan, 2014)

Drzymała, Jan, Mikołajczyk, Mirosława, Piwowar, Dorota, Polak, Bożena, Drzymała, Henryka, Ragiel, Józef, Drzymała-Tronina, Małgorzata *Johann Wolfgang Goethe oraz jego wkład w rozwój górnictwa i geologii*, 'Prace Naukowe Instytutu Górnictwa Politechniki Wrocławskiej' No. 131 (2010)

Duckling, Louise, 'From Liberty to Lechery: Performance, Reputation and the "Marvellous Story" of Helen Maria Williams', *Women's Writing*, 17:1 (2010), pp. 74–92

Dunn, Sophie, 'No objection to go abroad': Servants' Travel Advertisements in The Morning Post, London, 1815', *Journal of Eighteenth Century Studies* 45,4 (2022), pp. 487–506

Duquette, Natasha, 'Dissenting Cosmopolitanism and Helen Maria Williams's Prison Verse', *Women's Writing*, 27:1 (2020), pp. 80–96

Dyer, Serena, *Material Lives: Women Makers and Consumer Culture in the 18th Century* (London, Bloomsbury, 2021)

Eagleton, T, *The Function of Criticism* (London, Verso, 2005)

Edgecumbe, Richard, *Musical Reminiscences, Chiefly Respecting the Italian Opera in England from the Year 1773 to the Present Time* (London, George Clarke, 1828)

Eglāja-Kristsone, Eva, 'Exile and Liminality: Experience between Cultures and Identities', *Interlitteraria*, 20(1) (2015), pp. 146–155

Emerson, Isabelle Putnam, *Five Centuries of Women Singers* (Westport, CT. Praeger Publishers, 2005)

Evenson, Brian, 'Boswell's Grand Tour of Selves' in Donald J. Newman (ed.), *James Boswell: Psychological Interpretations* (New York, St Martin's Press, 1995)

Fabian, Johannes, *Time & the Other: How Anthropology Makes its Object*. (1983) (New York, Columbia University Press, 2014)

Favret, Mary A., '*Letters Written During a Short Resident in Sweden, Norway and Denmark*: Travelling with Mary Wollstonecraft' in Claudia L. Johnson (ed.), *The Cambridge Companion to Mary* Wollstonecraft (Cambridge, Cambridge University Press, 2002), pp. 209–227

Feagin, S. L. *Reading with Feeling: The Aesthetics of Appreciation* (Cornell University Press, Ithaca NY, 1996)

Fenner, Theodore, *Opera in London: Views of the Press, 1785–1830* (Illinois, Southern Illinois University Press, 1994)

Ferguson, Moira and Janet Todd, *Mary Wollstonecraft* (Boston, Twayne, 1984)

François, Pieter, '"The Best Way to See Waterloo is with Your Eyes Shut": British 'Histourism', Authenticity and Commercialisation in the Mid-Nineteenth Century', *Anthropological Journal of European Culture*, Vol. 22, No.1 (2013), pp. 26–41

Freller, Thomas, *Persons of reference: Maltese and Sicilian scholars and their importance for the Grand Tour* in A. Bonanno, P. Militello (eds.), *Interconnections in the Central Mediterranaean: The Maltese Islands and Sicily in History* (Palermo, 2008)

French, Henry and Mark Rothery, *Man's Estate: Landed Gentry Masculinities 1660–1900* (Oxford, Oxford University Press, 2012)

Friedenthal, Richard, *Goethe. Jego życie i czasy* (Warszawa, 1969)

Gaweł, Antoni, *Memoriał Borcha z roku 1780 jako pierwsza w Polsce próba geobiochemicznych poszukiwań kruszcowych*, 'Prace Muzeum Ziemi' No. 8, (1966)

Georgi, Claudia, 'Maria Graham, Travel Writing on India, Italy, Brazil, and Chile (1812–1824') in Barbara Schaff (ed.), *Handbook of British Travel Writing* (Berlin, Boston, De Gruyter, 2020)

Ghose, Indira, *Women Travellers in Colonial India: The Power of the Female Gaze* (Delhi, Oxford University Press, 1998)

Gleadhill, Emma, *Taking Travel Home: The Souvenir Culture of British Women Tourists 1750–1830* (Manchester, Manchester University Press, 2022)

Gleadhill, Emma, '"Lady, reject the gift, 'tis ting'd with gore!": Lady Elizabeth Holland and Napoleon's snuff-box,' *Enlightenments,* DNS XVII 2020, conference paper, 13 November-11 December 2020

Gleadhill, Emma, 'Improving upon Birth, Marriage and Divorce: The Cultural Capital of Three Eighteenth-Century Female Grand Tourists,' *Journal of Tourism History,* Vol. 10:1 (2018), pp. 21–36

Gleckner, R. F. *Gray Agonistes: Thomas Gray and Masculine Friendship* (Johns Hopkins University Press, Baltimore, 1997)

Goethe, J. W. (translation WH Auden and Elizabeth Mayer), *Italian Journey* [1787] (London, Penguin, 1970)

Goethe, Johann Wolfgang, *Faust. A tragedy by Johann Wolfgang von Goethe.* Translated, in the original metres, by B. Taylor. Two volumes in one, Vol. 2 (Boston and New York, 1913)

Goethe, Johann Wolfgang, *Italienishe Reise* (Leipzig, Kurt Jahn, 1914)

Goldsmith, Sarah, *Masculinity and Danger on the Eighteenth-Century Grand Tour* (London, University of London Press, 2020)

Goodman, John, ed., *Diderot on Art* (New Haven, Yale University Press, 1995)

Gottlieb, Evan, *Feeling British: Sympathy and National Identity in Scottish and English Writing, 1707–1832* (Lewisburg, PA, Bucknell University Press, 2007)

Gray, T., Ed. Roberts, W. G. *Notes on a Tour through France and Italy (1739–1741)* (Penrith, Northern Academic Press, 2011)

Gray, T., Eds. Toynbee, P., Whibley, L. *Correspondence of Thomas Gray* (Clarendon Press, Oxford, 1935) 3 Vols.

Gray, Walpole, Ashton, West, Ed. Toynbee, P. *Correspondences* (Clarendon Press, Oxford, 1915)

Greenblatt, S. *Self-Fashioning* (Chicago, University of Chicago Press, 1980)

Grierson, Roderick '"The Bashaw of Merryland": The Sixth Baron Baltimore and the Dervises of Pera', *Mawlana Rumi Review*, 2015, Vol. 6, Special Issue on Rumi and the Mevlevi Sufi Tradition (2015), pp. 83–103

Griggs, Tamara, 'The Local Antiquary in Eighteenth-Century Rome', *The Princeton University Library Chronicle*, Vol. 69, No. 2 (Winter 2008), pp. 280–314

Grochulska, B., J. Skowronek (eds.), *Losy Polaków w XIX-XX w. Studia ofiarowane Profesorowi Stefanowi Kieniewiczowi w osiemdziesiątą rocznicę Jego urodzin* (Warszawa, 1987)

Grundy, Isobel, *Lady Mary Wortley Montagu, Comet of the Enlightenment,* (Oxford, Oxford University Press, 1999)

Gubar, Susan, 'Feminist Misogyny: Mary Wollstonecraft and the Paradox of "It Takes One to Know One"', *Feminist Studies*, 20:3 (1994), pp. 453–473

Guest, Harriet, 'Travel writing', *The Cambridge Companion to Women's Writing in Britain,1660–1789*, ed. by Catherine Ingrassia (Cambridge, Cambridge University Press, 2015), pp. 196–209

Guillory, J. *Cultural Capital. The Problem of Literary Canon Formation* (University of Chicago Press, Chicago, London, 1993)

Hass, Ludwik, *Sekta farmazonii warszawskiej. Pierwsze stulecie wolnomularstwa w Warszawie (1721–1821)* (Warszawa, 1980)

Haydon, Colin, '"I love my King and my Country, but a Roman Catholic I hate": anti-Catholicism, xenophobia and national identity in eighteenth-century England' in Tony Claydon, Ian McBride (eds.), *Protestantism and National Identity: Britain and Ireland, c.1650–c.1850* (Cambridge, Cambridge University Press, 2009), pp. 33–52

Hazareesingh, Sudhir, *The Legend of Napoleon* (London, Granta, 2004)

Heffernan, Teresa, 'Feminism against the East/West Divide: Lady Mary's *Turkish Embassy Letters*, *Eighteenth-Century Studies*, Winter, 2000, Vol. 33, No. 2, (Winter, 2000), pp. 201–215

Honeyman, Katrina, *Women, Gender and Industrialisation in England, 1700–1870* (Basingstoke, Macmillan, 2000)

Hudson, Pat and William Robert Lee, *Women's Work and the Family Economy in Historical Perspective* (Manchester, Manchester University Press, 1990)

Hultquist, A. Emotion, Affect, and the Eighteenth Century. *The Eighteenth Century*, Fall 2017, Vol. 58, (2017) No. 3, pp. 273–280

Hume, D., Ed. Selby-Bigge, L. A. *A Treatise of Human Nature* (Oxford, Clarendon Press [1742] 1896)

Hunter, J. P. *Before Novels: The Cultural Contexts of Eighteenth-Century Fiction* (Norton, New York, 1990)

Hurl-Eamon, J., *Women's Roles in Eighteenth-Century Europe*. (California: Greenwood, ABC-CLIO, LLC. 2010)

Iliano, A. 'From Gray's Elegy to Foscolo's Carme: Highlighting the Mediation and Sublimation of the 'Sepulchral", *Symposium: A Quarterly Journal in Modern Literatures,* (1993) Vol. 47, No 2, pp. 117–131

İrvin Cemil Schick, 'Representation of Gender and Sexuality in Ottoman and Turkish Erotic Literature', *The Turkish Studies Association Journal*, 2004, Vol. 28, No. 1/2 (2004), pp. 81–103

Janelis, Ilze Māra, *Manor Gardens and Parks of Latvia* (Rīga, 2010)

Jeziorski, Paweł Artur, *Podróże edukacyjne zamożnej szlachty z województwa inflanckiego w XVIII wieku. Przykład Borchów i Hylzenów*, 'Miscellanea Historico-Archivistica', Vol. 24, (2017)

Johnson, S. *Life of Gray* in Johnson, S., Ed. Lonsdale, R. *The Lives of the Most Eminent English Poets,* Vol. IV (Oxford, Oxford University Press, [1781] reprint 2006)

Jones, Chris, 'Mary Wollstonecraft's *Vindications* and their Political Tradition'. In Claudia L. Johnson (ed.), *The Cambridge Companion to Mary Wollstonecraft* (Cambridge, Cambridge University Press, 2002), pp. 42–58

Jones, Chris, 'Travelling Hopefully: Helen Maria Williams and the Feminine Discourse of Sensibility' in Amanda Gilroy (ed), *Romantic Geographies: Discourses of Travel 1775–1844*, (Manchester, Manchester University Press, 2000), pp. 93–108

Jung, Sandro,'The Illustrated Pocket Diary: Generic Continuity and Innovation, 1820–40', *Victorian Periodicals Review*, Vol. 45, No. 1 (Spring 2012), pp. 23–48

Kay, H. Isherwood, 'John Sell Cotman's Letters from Normandy 1817–1820: Part II, the Letters of 1820', *The Volume of the Walpole Society,* Vol. 15 (1926–1927), pp. 105–130

Keane, Angela, *Revolutionary Women Writers: Charlotte Smith and Helen Maria Williams*, (Liverpool, Liverpool University Press, 2013)

Kelly, Jason, 'Riots, Revelries, and Rumor: Libertinism and Masculine Association in Enlightenment London', *Journal of British Studies* 45,4 (2006), pp. 759–795

Kelly, Linda, *Holland House: A History of London's Most Celebrated Salon* (London, I.B. Tauris, 2013)

Kelly, Michael, *Reminiscences of Michael Kelly of the King's Theatre, and Theatre Royal Drury Lane, including a period of nearly half a century with original anecdotes of many distinguished literary persons, political, literacy, and musical* (London, H. Colburn, 1826)

Kennedy, Deborah, *Helen Maria Williams and the Age of Revolution*, (Lewisburg, Bucknell University Press, 2002)

Kerhervé, A. A, 'Theory of British Epistolary Sociability?' in V. Capdeville and A. Kerhervé (eds), *British Sociability in the Long Eighteenth Century* (The Boydell Press, Woodbridge, 2019)

Ketton Kremer, R. W. *Thomas Gray: A Biography (*Cambridge, Cambridge University Press, 1955)

Kinsley, Zoë, *Women Writing the Home Tour, 1682–1812* (Aldershot, Ashgate, 2008)

Kirkham, Linda M. and Anne Loft, 'The Lady and the Accounts; Missing from Accounting History?', *The Accounting Historians Journal*, Vol. 28, No.1 (June 2001), pp. 67–90

Klavins, Kaspars, *Michael Johann Borch's meeting with Voltaire: a page from Latvia's European cultural history*. 'Humanities and Social Sciences: Latvia', Vol. 21, Issue 1 (Spring-Summer 2013)

Knoefel, P. K., *Felice Fontana Life and Works*. (Trento, Tipografia TEMI, 1984)

Korshin, Paul J., '"Extensive View": Johnson and Boswell as Travelers and Observers' in John McVeagh (ed.), *All Before Them: Attitudes to Abroad in English Literature, 1660–1780*, (Atlantic Highlands, NJ, Ashfield Press, 1990), pp. 233–45

Korte, Barbara, *English Travel Writing from Pilgrimages to Postcolonial Explorations* (Basingstoke, Palgrave, 2000)

Kowalczyk, Małgorzata Ewa, *'Na papierze z Etny". Wizerunek Sycylii w listach z podróży Michała Jana Borcha* in M. Wrześniak, A. Bender (eds.), *Polak we Włoszech, Włoch w Polsce. Sztuka i historia* (Warszawa, 2015)

Kowalczyk, Małgorzata Ewa, *Drogi Polaków do Włoch, w tejże: Obraz Włoch w polskim piśmiennictwie geograficznym i podróżniczym XVIII wieku* (Toruń, 2005)

Kristeva, Julia, *Strangers to Ourselves*, Translated by Leon S. Roudiez, (New York, Columbia University Press, 1991)

Królikowska-Dziubecka, Marzena, *Podróże artystyczne Jana Chrystiana Kamsetzera (1776–1777; 1780–1782)* (Warszawa, 2003)

Kupšāne, Ingrīda and Meškova, Sandra, 'Settling in a Foreign Land: Women's Experiences in Exile in Latvian Writer Irma Grebzde's Prose Fiction', *Journal of International Women's Studies*, 22(3) (2021), pp. 110–119

Labbe, J.M. ed., *The History of British Women's Writing 1750–1830*, (Basingstoke, Palgrave Macmillan, 2010)

Lamb, J., *The Evolution of Sympathy in the Long Eighteenth Century* (London, Pickering & Chatto, 2009)

Lamb, Susan, *Bringing Travel Home to England. Tourism, Gender, and Imaginative Literature in the Eighteenth Century* (Newark, University of Delaware Press, 2009)

Leask, Nigel, 'Eighteenth-Century Travel Writing' in Nandini Das and Tim Youngs (eds.), *The Cambridge History of Travel Writing* (Cambridge, Cambridge University Press, 2019), pp. 93–107

Leask, Nigel, 'Salons, Alps and Cordilleras: Helen Maria Williams, Alex von Humboldt and the discourse of Romantic travel' in Elizabeth Eger, Charlotte Grant, Clíona Ó Gallchoir and Penny Warburton (eds), *Women, Writing and the Public Sphere, 1700–1830*, (Cambridge, Cambridge University Press, 2001), pp. 217–235

Leed, E. *The Mind of the Traveller: From Gilgamesh to Global Tourism.* (Basic Books, New York, 1991)

Lilti, A. *The World of the Salons: Sociability and Worldliness in Eighteenth-Century Paris,* transl. by L. G. Cochrane (Oxford, Oxford University Press, 2005)

Link, Dorothea. *The Italian Opera Singers in Mozart's Vienna* (Champaign, Illinois, University of Illinois Press, 2022)

Lough, John, *France on the Eve of Revolution: British Travellers' Observations 1763–1788* (London, Croom Helm, 1987)

Maccubin, R. P. (ed.) *'Tis Nature's Fault: Unauthorized Sexual Behaviour during the Enlightenment,* (Cambridge, Cambridge University Press, 1987)

Mack, R. L. *Thomas Gray. A Life.* (New Haven, London Yale University Press, 2000)

Madden, R. R., *The Literary Life and Correspondence of the Countess of Blessington.* (New York, Harper and Brothers Publishers, 1855)

Maerker, A., *Model Experts: Wax anatomies and enlightenment in Florence and Vienna, 1775–1815* (Manchester, Manchester University Press, 2015)

Makdisi, Saree, *Making England Western: Occidentalism, Race, and Imperial Culture* (Chicago IL, The University of Chicago Press, 2014)

Mannix, Daniel P, *The Hell-Fire Club* (London, The New English Library, 1959)

Martin E., and Susan Pickford (eds), *Travel Narratives in Translation, 1750–1830: Nationalism, Ideology, Gender*, (New York and Abingdon, Routledge, 2012)

Matoff, Susan. *Marguerite, Countess of Blessington: The Turbulent Life of a Salonnière and Author* (University of Delaware Press, 2015)

McCarthy, E. B. *Thomas Gray: The Progress of a Poet* (London, Mississauga, Ontario, Associated University Presses, 1997)

McKeon, M. *The Origins of the English Novel: 1600–1740* (Baltimore, Johns Hopkins University Press, 1987)

McLaren, Moray, *Corsica Boswell: Paoli, Johnson and Freedom* (London, Secker and Warburg,1966)

McLoughlin, Timothy, 'Boswell and Corsica: The Art of Puffing.' *Bulletin de la Societe d'etudes anglo-americaines des XVIIe et XVIIe siecles* Vol. 55 (November 2002), pp. 157–69

McVeagh, John (ed.), *All Before Them: Attitudes to Abroad in English Literature 1660–1780* (Atlantic Highlands, NJ, Ashfield Press, 1990)

Melman, Billie, *Women's Orients: English Women and the Middle East, 1718–1918*,(University of Michigan Press, 1992)

Mesa, Franklin, *Opera: An Encyclopedia of World Premieres and Significant Performances, Singers, Composers. Librettists, Arias and Conductors, 1597–2000* (Jefferson, North Carolina, McFarland, 2007)

Messbarger, R. 'The Re-Birth of Venus in Florence's Royal Museum of Physics and Natural History', *Journal of the History of Collections*, 25(2), (2013), pp. 195–215

Mikocki, Tomasz, *A la recherche de l'art antique. Les voyageurs polonais en Italie dans les annés 1750–1830* (Wrocław, 1988)

Milhous, Judith, and Robert D. Hume. 'Opera Salaries in Eighteenth-Century London' *Journal of the American Musicological Society,* Vol. 46, No. 1 (1993): 26–83. doi:10.2307/831805

Mitchell, Leslie, *Holland House* (London, Duckworth, 1980)

Money, Walter, *Collections from the History of the Parish of Speen in the County of Berkshire* (Newbury, W.J. Blacket, 1892)

Montesquieu, Charles-Louis de Secondat, Baron de, *The Spirit of the Laws* (1748) (Cambridge, Cambridge University Press, reprint 1989)

Morrison, S., Smith, Joseph: 1673/4–1770. https://doi.org/10.1093/ref:odnb/25871, 2004

Morrison, Lucy, ed. *Women's Travel Writings in Post-Napoleonic France*, Vol. 1, Marianne Baillie, *First Impressions on a Tour upon the Continent*, 1819 (London, Pickering and Chatto, 2011)

Mortimer, T. 'The Adventures of Michael Kelly.' *Dublin Historical Record* 53, No. 2 (2000), 126. http://www.jstor.org/stable/30101256

Naficy, Hamid, *The Making of Exile Cultures: Iranian Television in Los Angeles*, (Minneapolis, University of Minnesota Press, 1993)

Nalbach, Daniel, *The King's Theatre 1704–1867: London's First Italian Opera House* (London, The Society for Theatre Research, 1972)

Newman, Donald J., (ed.), *Boswell and the Press: Essays on the Ephemeral Writing of James Boswell* (Lewisburg, Bucknell University Press, 2021)

Nicolson, H. M. *Mountain Gloom and Mountain Glory: The Development of the Aesthetics of the Infinite* ([1959] University of Washington Press, Seattle reprint 1997)

Nolta, David D. 'The Body of the Collector and the Collected Body in William Hamilton's Naples', *Eighteenth-Century Studies*, Vol. 31, No. 1, (Fall, 1997), pp. 108–114

Norton, R. *Horace Walpole and Homosexuality.* http://rictornorton.co.uk/thought2.htm

Norton, R. Recovering Gay History from the Old Bailey. *The London Journal*, (2005) Vol. 30, No. 1, pp. 39–54

Nussbaum, Felicity A., *The Autobiographical Subject: Gender and Ideology in Eighteenth-Century England* (Baltimore, John Hopkins University, 1995)

Olleson, Philip. *The Journals and Letters of Susan Burney Music and Society in Late Eighteenth-Century England* (Abingdon, Routledge, 2016)

Orzeł, Joanna, Pacevičius, Arvydas, Roszak Stanisław, *Dziennik podróży Józefa Jerzego Hylzena z lat 1752–1754* (Vilnius, 2013)

Oxturk, Anthony, 'Translating Helvetica: Travel Writing, Intertext, and Image', in Alison E. Martin and Susan Pickford (eds), *Travel Narratives in Translation, 1750–1830: Nationalism, Ideology, Gender,* (New York and Abingdon, Routledge, 2012), pp. 56–73

Payne, John, *An Epitome of History* (London, J. Johnson, 1795)

Peakman, Julie *Mighty Lewd Books, The Development of Pornography in Eighteenth-Century England* (London, Palgrave, 2003)

Peakman, Julie, *Lascivious Bodies, A History of the Eighteenth Century* (London, Atlantic, 2004)

Peakman, Julie, *Emma Hamilton. A Biography* (London, Haus, 2004)

Peakman, Julie, *Licentious Worlds. Sex and Exploitation in Global Empires* (London, Reaktion, 2019)

Pettitt, Clare, 'Topos, Taxonomy and Travel in Nineteenth-Century Women's Scrapbooks' in Mary Henes and Brian H. Murray, eds., *Travel Writing, Visual Culture and Form, 1760–1900* (Basingstoke, Palgrave Macmillan, 2016), pp. 21–41

Polanowska, Jolanta, *Michał Jan Borch and his residence in Varklani: genesis and ideological programme*, in: 'Mākslas Vēsture un Teorija' Vol. 16, (2013)

Polanowska, Jolanta, *Ogród w Warklanach – dzieło właściciela Michała Jana Borcha i architekta Vincenza de Mazottiego.* 'Biuletyn Historii Sztuki' Vol. 74, No. 3–4 (2012)

Pottle, F. A., *Boswell on the Grand Tour*, (London, Heimann, 1953)

Powell-Jones, W. *Thomas Gray, Scholar: The True Tragedy of an Eighteenth Century Gentleman.* (Cambridge, Mass., Harvard University Press, 1937)

Powell-Jones, W., Thomas Gray's Library. *Modern Philology*, Vol. 35, No. 3, (1938) pp. 257–278

Rączka, Teresa, *Księgozbiory Polskich Inflantczyków w świetle nieznanych archiwaliów (koniec XVIII-początek XIX w.)* in *Stan badań nad wielokulturowym dziedzictwem dawnej Rzeczypospolitej*, Vol. 6 (Białystok, 2013)

Rączka-Jeziorska, Teresa, *Romantyczne mapowanie przestrzeni ogrodu według Polskiego Inflantczyka Michała Jana Borcha z Warklan (1753–1810)*, in *Przestrzeń – literatura – doświadczenie. Z inspiracji geopoetyki* (Katowice, 2016)

Rączka-Jeziorska, Teresa, *Romantyzm polsko-inflancki. Sylwetki, teksty, archiwa*, (Warszawa, 2016)

Rapport, Michael, *Nationality and Citizenship in Revolutionary France: the Treatment of Foreigners 1789–1799* (Oxford, Clarendon, 2000)

Redford, Bruce, *Dilettanti. The Antic and The Antique in Eighteenth-Century England* (J. Paul Getty Museum, 2008)

Rendall, Jane, '"The Grand Causes which Combine to Carry Mankind Forward": Wollstonecraft, History and Revolution', *Women's Writing*, 2: 4 (1997), pp. 155–172

Reynolds, E., *Incorruptible: The Female Body and the Anatomical Waxes at La Specola*, Doctoral thesis (Cardiff Metropolitan University, UK, 2023)

Reynolds, Luke, 'There John Bull might be seen in all his Glory: Cross-Channel tourism and the British Army of Occupation in France, 1815–1818', *Journal of Tourism History*, Vol. 12, No.2 (2020), pp. 139–155

Roberts, Charlotte, ' Living with the Ancient Romans: Past and Present in Eighteenth-Century Encounters with Herculaneum and Pompeii', *Huntington Library Quarterly*, Vol. 78, No. 1 (Spring 2015), pp. 61–85

Robertson-Kirkland, Brianna E., *Venanzio Rauzzini and the Birth of a New Style in English Singing: Scandalous Lessons* (Abingdon, Routledge, 2022)

Roćko, Agata, (ed.), *Polski Grand Tour w XVIII i początkach XIX wieku* (Warszawa, 2014)

Roćko, Agata, *Podróże oświeconych śladami antyku*, w: *Antyk oświeconych. Studia i rozprawy o miejscu starożytności w kulturze polskiej XVIII wieku*, ed. T. Chachulski (Warszawa, 2012)

Rottermund, Andrzej, *Polski grand tour, czyli problem królewskiej podróży po Italii.* 'Wiek Oświecenia', Vol. 15, (1999)

Rousseau, G. S. 'Science Culture and the Imagination' in R. Porter (ed.), T*he Cambridge History of Science. The Eighteenth Century* (Cambridge University Press, Cambridge, 2003), Vol. 4

Rousseau, G. S. *Perilous Enlightenment* (Manchester, Manchester University Press, 1991)

Rousseau, G.S., 'The Sorrows of Priapus, anticlerical, homosocial desire and Richard Payne Knight' in G.S. Rousseau and Roy Porter, *Sexual Underworlds of the Enlightenment* (Manchester University Press, 1987)

Rousseau, Jean-Jacques, *Discourse on Inequality* (1755) (Oxford, Oxford University Press, 2009)

Royal Society of Literature of the United Kingdom, Vol. 44 (1986), pp. 46–62

Ruddick, W. B. 'Thomas Gray's Travel Writing' in W. B. Hutchings and W. Ruddick (eds)., *Thomas Gray: Contemporary Essays* (Liverpool University Press, Liverpool, 1993), pp. 126–145

Ruppert, H. (ed.), *Goethes Bibliothek Katalog* (Weimar, 1958)

Sainsbury, John S. *A Dictionary of Musicians From the Earliest Ages to the Present Time* (London, Sainsbury and Company, 1824)

Sargent Noyes, Ruth, *Count Michał Jan Borch as patron and collector: art between Italy and Inflanty in the Age of Partition*, 'Baltic Journal of Art History' (2021)

Sargent Noyes, Ruth, et al., '*Baltic catacombs.' Translating corpisanti catacomb relic-sculptures between Rome, Polish Livonia, and the Lithuanian Grand Duchy circa 1750–1800.* Open Research Europe 2021, 1:18 (https://doi.org/10.12688/openreseurope.13259.1)

Sawyer, Robert, 'From Jubilee to Gala: Remembrance and Ritual Commemoration', *Critical Scholarly Annual* Vol. 23 (December 2015), pp. 21–31

Secor, Anna, 'Orientalism, Gender and Class in Lady Mary Wortley Montagu's "*Turkish Embassy Letters*: to persons of distinction, men of letters & c."' *Ecumene*, October 1999, Vol. 6, No. 4 (October 1999), pp. 375–398

Semmel, Stuart, 'British Uses for Napoleon', *Modern language Notes*, Vol. 120, No.4 (September 2005), French Issue, pp. 733–746

Semmel, Stuart, 'Reading the Tangible past: British Tourism, Collecting, and Memory After Waterloo', *Representations*, No.69 (Winter, 2000), pp. 9–37

Siemion, Ignacy Z., Latko, Barbara, *Michała Jana Borcha rozprawa o truflach piemonckich*, "Annalecta: studia i materiały z dziejów nauki", Vol. 22, No. 1–2

Siemion, Ignacy Z., Szastyńska-Siemion, Alicja, *O eksperymentach Michała Jana Borcha (1753–1811) dotyczących chemiluminescencji*, 'Wiadomości chemiczne' No. 67, Issue 3–4 (2013)

Sklar, H. *The Art of Sympathy in Fiction: Forms of Ethical and Emotional Persuasion* (Amsterdam / Philadelphia, John Benjamin Publishing Company, 2013)

Sloan, Kim, *A Noble Art: Amateur Artists and Drawing Masters, c1600–1800* (London, British Museum Press, 2000)

Smith, Adam, *The Theory of Moral Sentiments* (1759), (London, Penguin, 2009)

Sobczyńska, Danuta, *Między sztuką a nauką. Dwugłos artysty i uczonego o barwie*, 'Przegląd Filozoficzny – Nowa Seria' Vol. 16, No 3 (63), 2007

Sołtys, Angela, *Podróże Polaków do Italii w drugiej połowie XVIII wieku: kontekst neapolitański*, in: *Polski Grand Tour w XVIII i początkach XIX wieku* (Warszawa, 2014)

Soyinka, Wole, 'Exile', in Els van der Plas, Malu Halasa and Marlous Willemsen (eds), *Creating Spaces of Freedom: Culture in Defiance*, (London, Saqi, 2002), pp. 25–36

Spārītis, Ojārs *Three sources of Michael Johann von der Borch's poem «The sentimental park of Varakļāni palace»*, 'Baltic Journal of Art History', Vol. 20 (2020)

Stabler, Anne, *Artistry of Exile* (Oxford, OUP, 2013)

Stephanson, R., 'Epicoene friendship: Understanding Male Friendship in the Early Eighteenth Century, with Some Speculations about Pope', *The Eighteenth Century*, Vol. 38, No. 2, (1997), pp. 151–170

Stewart, K. Towards Defining an Aesthetic for the Familiar Letter in Eighteenth-Century England. *Prose Studies*, 5, (1982), pp. 179–192, 186–187

Stewart, Susan, *The Ruins Lesson: Meaning and Material in Western Culture* (Chicago, The University of Chicago Press, 2020)

Stobart, Jon (ed.), *Travel and the British Country House Cultures: Critiques and Consumption in the Long Eighteenth Century* (Manchester, Manchester University Press, 2017)

Stradins, Jānis, *Michał Jan Borch – polski przyrodnik XVIII w.*, 'Kwartalnik Historii Nauki i Techniki', No. 25/3, (1980)

Strawn, Morgan W., "'A Species of Despotism': Catholicism and Benevolent Authoritarianism in Boswell's Account of Corsica." *Age of Johnson* 22 (2012), p. 107.

Stroev, Alexander, À la recherche de la correspondance savante du comte Michał Jan Borch, in: *Correspondances d'érudits au XVIIIe et XIXe siècles – France, Pologne, Lituanie*, ed. Marie-France de Palacio (Rennes 2014)

Sweet, R. *Cities and the Grand Tour: The British in Italy, C. 1690–1820* (Cambridge, Cambridge University Press, 2012)

Sweet, Rosemary, *Antiquaries: The Discovery of the Past in Eighteenth-Century Britain* (London, Hambledon and London, 2004)

Syta, Krzysztof, *Skład osobowy sztabu regimentu pieszego buławy wielkiej koronnej w latach 1751–1771*, in *Schriftlichkeit Beschreibung und Interpretation von Quellen. Festschrift zum 70. Geburstag von Professor Janusz Tandecki*, hrsg. v. R. Skowrońska, K. Kopiński, H. Flachenecker (Toruń, 2020)

Tankard, Paul (ed.), *Facts and Inventions: Selections from the Journalism of James Boswell* (Yale University Press, 2014)

Taylor, Barbara, 'Feminism and the Enlightenment 1650–1850', *History of Workshop Journal*, 47:1 (1999), pp. 261–272

Thanailaki, Polly '*Hera*, the Greek Goddess of Marriage: A Comparison Between Greek and Italian Peasant Women' in *Gender Inequalities in Rural European Communities During 19th and Early 20th Century* (Cham, Springer, 2018), pp. 49–71

Thomson, H. 'The Poet and the Publisher' in Thomas Gray's Correspondence', *The Yearbook of English Studies*, 1998), pp. 163–180

Tinker, C. B. ed., *Letters of James Boswell*, Vol. 1 (Oxford, Clarendon Press, 1924)

Todorova, Maria, *Imagining the Balkans (*Oxford, Oxford University Press, 2009)

Tomalin, Claire, *The Life and Death of Mary Wollstonecraft*. 2nd ed. (London, New York, Penguin, 1992)

Tosi, Arturo, *Language and the Grand Tour: Linguistic Experiences of Travelling in Early Modern Europe* (Cambridge, Cambridge University Press, 2020)

Towner, John, *The European Grand Tour, circa 1550–1840: A Study of its Role in the History of Tourism*. Ph.D. Thesis, University of Birmingham, 1984

Tuite, Clara, *Lord Byron and Scandalous Celebrity* (Cambridge, Cambridge University Press, 2014)

Tung, Shirley F., '"An Isthmus which Joins Two Great Continents": Johnson, Boswell, and the Character of the Travel Writer in *An Account of Corsica*,' *The Age of Johnson: A Scholarly Annual* Vol. 23 (December 2015), pp. 21–31

Turnbull, Gordon, 'James Boswell: Biography and the Union' in Andrew Hook (ed.), *The History of Scottish Literature Volume II 1660–1800* (Aberdeen University Press, 1987)

Turner, Katherine, 'Women's Travel Writing 1750–1830', *The History of British Women's Writing 1750–1830*, ed. by J.M. Labbe (Basingstoke: Palgrave Macmillan, 2010)

Tylusińska-Kowalska, Anna, *Il conte Michał Jan Borch in Sicilia: il viaggio culturale di uno scienziato*, F. d'Angelo (ed.), *The Scientific Dialogue Linking America, Asia and Europe between the 12th and the 20th Century. Theories and Techniques travelling in Space and Time*, (Naples, 2018)

Uglow, Jenny, *In These Times: Living in Britain Through Napoleon's Wars, 1793–1815* (London, Faber & Faber, 2014)

Van Boer, Bertil H. *Historical Dictionary of Music of the Classical Period* (Lanham, Maryland, Scarecrow Press, 2012)

Van der Plas, Els, Malu Halasa and Marlous Willemsen (eds), *Creating Spaces of Freedom: Culture in Defiance*, (London, Saqi, 2002)

Verdon, Nicola, *Rural Women Workers in Nineteenth-Century England: Gender, Work and Wages* (Suffolk, Boydell & Brewer, 2012)

Vickery, Amanda, *The Gentleman's Daughter: Women's Lives in Georgian England* (London, Yale University Press, 1998)

Vincent, Patrick, 'Introduction' to Helen Maria Williams, *A Tour in Switzerland*, (eds) Patrick Vincent and Florence Widmer-Schnyder, (Geneva, Slatkine, 2011), pp. 1–59

Vivies, Jean, 'James Boswell and Scotland in *An Account of Corsica*,' *Studies on Voltaire and the Eighteenth Century*, Vol. 305 (1992), p. 1651

Wagner, C. 'Replicating Venus: Art, Anatomy, Wax Models, and Automata', *Interdisciplinary Studies in the Long Nineteenth Century*, 19: 24. (2017)

Walchester, Kathryn, *Travelling Servants: Mobility and Employment in British Fiction and Travel Writing 1750–1850* (London, Routledge, 2020)

Walendziak-Genco, Ewelina, Sztuk, Alicja, *Sulla traduzione Polacca di A Tour through Sicily and Malta: in a series of letters to William Beckford, ESQ. of Somerly in Suffolk di Patrick Brydone*, 'Kwartalnik Neofilologiczny', LXII, 2/2015

Webb, Timothy. '"City of the soul": English Romantic Travellers in Rome' in Michael Liversidge and Catherine Edwards (eds.) *Imagining Rome: British Artists and Rome in the Nineteenth Century* (London, Merrell Holberton, 1996). pp. 20–37

White, Eugene N., 'Making the French Pay: The Costs and Consequences of the Napoleonic Reparations', *European Review of Economic History*, Vol. 5, No.3 (December 2001), pp. 337–365

Williams, Abigail, *The Social Life of Books* (New Haven, Yale University Press, 2017)

Williams, Helen Maria, *Letters Written in France in the Summer 1790*, (eds) Neil Fraistat and Susan S. Lanser, (Ontario, Broadview Press, 2001)

Winburn, Martha, *Garrick's Jubilee* (Columbus, OH, Ohio State University Press, 1964)

Wohlcke, Anne, *The 'perpetual fair': Gender, Disorder, and Urban Amusement in Eighteenth-Century London* (Manchester, Manchester University Press, 2014)

Wolff, Larry, *Inventing Eastern Europe. The Map of Civilization on the Mind of the Enlightenment* (Stanford, 1994)

Wordsworth, William, *The Prelude: The four texts,* Jonathan Wordsworth (ed.) (London, Penguin, 1996)

Yurss Lasanta, Paula, 'The Writing of Politics and the Politics of Writing in Helen Maria Williams' *A Tour in Switzerland* (1798)', *The Grove – Working Papers on English Studies*, 23 (2016), pp. 199–212.

Zawartko-Laskowska, Maria, *Mecenat naukowy Stanisława Augusta i jego przyrodnicze pasje.* 'Kronika Zamkowa', No. 1/2, (2008)

Брук, Я. В., Л. И. Иовлева (ed.), Государственная Третьяковская галерея: каталог собрания. Серия живопись *XVIII-XX* веков, (Москва, 1997)

Index